Securing the Nation's Critical Infrastructures

Securing the Nation's Critical Infrastructures: A Guide for the 2021–2025 Administration is intended to help the United States Executive administration, legislators, and critical infrastructure decision-makers prioritize cybersecurity, combat emerging threats, craft meaningful policy, embrace modernization, and critically evaluate nascent technologies.

The book is divided into 18 chapters that are focused on the critical infrastructure sectors identified in the 2013 National Infrastructure Protection Plan (NIPP), election security, and the security of local and state government. Each chapter features viewpoints from an assortment of former government leaders, C-level executives, academics, and other cybersecurity thought leaders. Major cybersecurity incidents involving public sector systems occur with jarringly frequency; however, instead of rising in vigilant alarm against the threats posed to our vital systems, the nation has become desensitized and demoralized. This publication was developed to deconstruct the normalization of cybersecurity inadequacies in our critical infrastructures and to make the challenge of improving our national security posture less daunting and more manageable. To capture a holistic and comprehensive outlook on each critical infrastructure, each chapter includes a foreword that introduces the sector and perspective essays from one or more reputable thought-leaders in that space, on topics such as:

- The State of the Sector (challenges, threats, etc.)
- Emerging Areas for Innovation
- Recommendations for the Future (2021–2025) Cybersecurity Landscape

ABOUT ICIT

The Institute for Critical Infrastructure Technology (ICIT) is the nation's leading 501(c)3 cybersecurity think tank providing objective, nonpartisan research, advisory, and education to legislative, commercial, and public-sector stakeholders. Its mission is to cultivate a cybersecurity renaissance that will improve the resiliency of our Nation's 16 critical infrastructure sectors, defend our democratic institutions, and empower generations of cybersecurity leaders. ICIT programs, research, and initiatives support cybersecurity leaders and practitioners across all 16 critical infrastructure sectors and can be leveraged by anyone seeking to better understand cyber risk including policymakers, academia, and businesses of all sizes that are impacted by digital threats.

ABOUT THE EDITOR

As the Lead Researcher at the Institute for Critical Infrastructure Technology (ICIT), Drew Spaniel is an expert in information security and technology across the US critical infrastructure sectors. He serves the Institute as a technical expert in cybersecurity, technology, and data science, as well as emerging adversarial trends, threat actor profiling, and legislation and agency initiatives related to information security and privacy. Spaniel earned a Master of Science in Information Security, Policy, and Management from Carnegie Mellon University's Heinz College and a Bachelor of Science in Applied Physics from Allegheny College.

Securing the Nation's Critical Infrastructures

A Guide for the 2021–2025 Administration

Edited by
Drew Spaniel

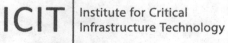

ICIT
Institute for Critical
Infrastructure Technology

The Cybersecurity Think Tank

CRC Press
Taylor & Francis Group
Boca Raton London New York

CRC Press is an imprint of the
Taylor & Francis Group, an **Informa** business

First edition published 2023
by CRC Press
6000 Broken Sound Parkway NW, Suite 300, Boca Raton, FL 33487-2742

and by CRC Press
4 Park Square, Milton Park, Abingdon, Oxon, OX14 4RN

CRC Press is an imprint of Taylor & Francis Group, LLC

© 2023 The Institute for Critical Infrastructure Technology (ICIT)

Library of Congress Cataloging-in-Publication Data

Names: Spaniel, Drew, editor.
Title: Securing the nation's critical infrastructures : a guide for the
2021-2025 Administration / edited by Drew Spaniel.
Description: First edition. | Boca Raton : CRC Press, 2022. | Includes
bibliographical references and index.
Identifiers: LCCN 2022010097 (print) | LCCN 2022010098 (ebook) |
ISBN 9781032152080 (hardback) | ISBN 9781032152103 (paperback) |
ISBN 9781003243021 (ebook)
Subjects: LCSH: Cyberterrorism--United States--Prevention. | Infrastructure
(Economics)--Security measures--United States. | Public works--Security measures--
United States. | National security--United States.
Classification: LCC HV6773.2 .S43 2022 (print) | LCC HV6773.2 (ebook) |
DDC 364.16/8--dc23/eng/20220615
LC record available at https://lccn.loc.gov/2022010097
LC ebook record available at https://lccn.loc.gov/2022010098

ISBN: 9781032152080 (hbk)
ISBN: 9781032152103 (pbk)
ISBN: 9781003243021 (ebk)

DOI: 10.1201/9781003243021

Typeset in Times
by KnowledgeWorks Global Ltd.

Contents

Foreword

By Glenn S. Gerstell
Former General Counsel, United States National Security Agency

> *Our society is becoming increasingly dependent on information technologies, which are changing at an amazing rate. This...offers both opportunities and challenges... [among them] vulnerabilities which represent severe security flaws and risks to our nation's security, public safety, and personal privacy.*[1]

The quotation is hardly remarkable today, except perhaps for its obviousness. But it was noteworthy when it was said by a United States Senator more than 20 years ago—well before the invention of the iPhone or YouTube, and just at the dawn of email—during the first Congressional hearing on cybersecurity. The 1998 hearing generated a clear and simple message: our computers, networks, and software are dangerously insecure. Despite this, it would take decades for our nation to appreciate the cyber threat, during which time we would see a steady accretion of malicious cyber activity.

Novel and indeed even dire warnings often go unnoticed. In retrospect, it's not that surprising that we didn't appreciate this warning for the serious threat that prompted it, let alone that our society was willing to act upon it. There are many reasons for this, but in any case, it has led to cyber insecurity pervading our public and private sectors, reaching every aspect of our personal and commercial lives.

The ever-increasing cyber vulnerability has alarmingly collided with the slower but equally significant deterioration in our nation's physical infrastructure, yielding risks on a scale we are only now fully apprehending. Given the interdependence of our varied infrastructure systems, the level of reliance we place on them for our personal and commercial activities, and the malicious targeting of those systems by Russia, North Korea, Iran, China, and others, the vulnerabilities of our infrastructure are not simply domestic policy issues—but a national security threat. This book makes clear just how acute the risks are and what steps we can now take to manage, if not solve, this important national security problem.

WE'RE SLOW TO DEAL WITH A KNOWN PROBLEM

We've had at least two, and arguably several, decades' worth of serious analysis of our infrastructure problems, replete with direful illustrations of how we have systematically underinvested in almost all infrastructure sectors: across the nation, we see dams and bridges needing repairs to the extent that some are unsafe, factories and farms using outmoded and inefficient technology and systems, electric grids straining to meet peak demands, manufacturers and generating plants polluting the environment due to lack of proper technology—and throughout it all, a susceptibility to cyber mischief that seems to increase with each day's headlines.

Despite the manifest nature of the deficiencies in our physical infrastructure, we have failed to address them, partly because there is only so much money to go around, but mostly because, like adapting to climate change, there's no one day that the problem must be tackled. The 2021 report card[2] from the American Society of Civil Engineers on the nation's infrastructure graded it a C-minus; but that's still a passing grade—and of course, the overwhelming amount of our infrastructure works just fine, even if some elements present safety concerns or are less efficient. Start a search on Google for "infrastructure," and you'll see "crumbling" automatically pop up. As with so many things, from opioid abuse to polluted waters, we wait until a crisis or disaster before we get serious about fixing the problem. It took the collapse of the I-35W Mississippi River Bridge in

2007, killing 13 people and injuring hundreds of others to make us give more attention to bridge safety – and the replacement bridge was up a year later. The polluted drinking water crisis in Flint, Michigan, first identified in 2014, led to the replacement of lead pipes and elevated drinking water safety in the public's consciousness throughout the nation. More recently, the deadly collapse of the Surfside apartment has triggered an inspection of oceanside cement structures throughout Florida.

To be fair, the ASCE report card for 2021 was the best grade the country has received in years, and, considering the extraordinary scale and sophistication of American infrastructure, even with its flaws, we arguably have among the best overall infrastructure in the world. Surely that is one of the reasons we are slow or hesitant to address the deficiencies. It works—most of the time. Unless something has captured the nation's attention to produce a consensus for action, competition over scarce resources in a democracy tends toward paralysis and inertia. The difficulty is exacerbated by the dispersal of infrastructure in the hands of federal, state, and local government, as well mostly in the private sector, impeding a coordinated approach with an optimal allocation of society's resources.

All these factors work against taking the steps our nation knows it needs to address deficiencies in physical infrastructure; the problem is not that we don't know what to do or that it's beyond our technical capabilities. But these factors pale in comparison to the array of circumstances that undermine our ability to address the cyber aspects of infrastructure deficiencies.

Undoubtedly the foremost reason we have yet to solve the cybersecurity problem is simply that the technology is complicated and relatively new—and tackling complex and novel problems takes time. Because it has become so pervasive and useful that it seems a natural aspect of our everyday personal and commercial worlds, we forget just how recent—in terms of the historical trends for technology— the digital revolution really is. We need to be reminded that the iPhone is merely 14 years old, that Facebook (founded as a college student app in 2004) didn't become a factor in daily lives until roughly 10 years ago, about the time YouTube (2005) and Twitter (2006) really took off. So, what's astonishing about the "fourth industrial revolution" is that it proved ubiquitously transformational in under a generation—not that it has taken us this long to figure out how to regulate the risks and misuses of cyber-enabled technology. (By contrast, technologies ranging from railroads to aviation to the automobile to electricity took decades between the time of invention and the time the technology became commonplace, and in every case, it took a rolling series of disasters or crises to summon the societal will to impose significant regulation to address risks of the technology.[3])

Moreover, fascinated by the manifestations of the digital revolution, we are hesitant to impede its evolution and crimp further innovation. And when problems arise, from buggy apps to massive cyber hacks, we tend to view the problems as isolated, peculiarly reluctant to recognize them as systemic. Instead, we view them as simply the price we must pay for the benefits of our online lives. Of course, there are many other factors at play, including the sheer complexity and expense of improving cyber defenses (such as moving to "zero trust architecture" as opposed to simply relying on firewalls and anti-virus programs), as well as the serious dearth of cybersecurity technical expertise in both the private and public sectors.

BUT WE NOW HAVE AN OPPORTUNITY

The confluence of all these reasons curtailing or precluding our addressing both traditional physical infrastructure and the cyber aspects of that infrastructure has led us to an inflection point. It's no longer possible to escape the need to address these accumulated deficiencies and to ward off future problems. Three principal reasons have brought us to the point—which represents both an opportunity to seize a moment of national consensus as well as a risk of falling perhaps irretrievably behind if we fail to act.

The reasons are apparent from the daily headlines. The first is the overwhelming and seemingly inexorably increasing spate of cyber hacks and attacks. Whether it is a ransomware attack on Colonial Pipelines that prompted lines of panicked gasoline buyers in the eastern states, an unprecedented "supply chain" attack using Solar Winds software updates to potentially infect tens of thousands of private networks and those of nine federal agencies, or a deluge of ransomware attacks on hospitals and municipalities, the public's attention is now focused on the ominous aspects of our almost total reliance on the internet.

Four countries in particular—Russia, China, North Korea, and Iran—use cyber maliciousness as part of their statecraft. I saw this firsthand at the National Security Agency in 2016, when Russia tried to subvert our democratic process by seeking to nefariously influence our national elections. Since then, Russia has engaged in wide-ranging pernicious disinformation campaigns seeking to sow distrust in our institutions and to exacerbate social discord. China continues to steal our patents and trade secrets in an organized and massive way, while Iran and North Korea engage in financial cybercrime and general mischief, including damaging our physical infrastructure. In addition to the cyber wrongdoing of other nations, foreign criminal gangs (often sheltered by those countries) engage in ransomware attacks and fraud, and ordinary domestic criminals exploit their cyber victims. In short, we are in a constant low-intensity cyber conflict. So, finally, we realize we are in the midst of a cyber crisis and recognize that it is likely to get worse.

The second reason is that, in the most dramatic and horrible way, we've seen what happens when a society ignores warnings for years. The examples of warnings of a pandemic are legion, but to pick one that has special meaning for me, the National Infrastructure Advisory Council *in 2007* said, "To avoid an economic and social catastrophe, pandemic preparedness demands full public- and private-sector participation." We were unprepared for a completely foreseeable crisis, and yet most of the tools that we would need to fight a pandemic were well known.

The parallel to our current state of cyber insecurity is unnervingly close; do we have to wait until a cyber-attack disables the electric grid, producing deaths and chaos? When I joined the NIAC a few years later, the proposed study item on the agenda of my first meeting was about the cyber security of infrastructure, and even after several years of NIAC (and many other) reports of the vulnerability of our nation's infrastructure, comparatively little was done. But as cyber vulnerabilities increasingly affect our personal and commercial lives—and cannot be dismissed as one-off phishing attempts to steal a credit card or social security number, but instead affect the privacy of our health records and the ability of our schools, hospitals, and municipal governments to function—we now start to appreciate the costs of being unprepared.

Finally, a more diffuse—but politically potent—reason is the fear of a rising China. With its wealth, size, and central authoritarian government, China is able to invest almost double the amount the United States spends annually on infrastructure in developing sectors ranging from ports and logistics to advanced manufacturing to biotech. Many in Congress, business, and academia are concerned that, much in the way other countries were able to leapfrog over England as the pioneer in the industrial revolution, so too might China, with its coordinated governmental and private effort, steal the lead from us in critical technologies such as artificial intelligence and quantum computing, as well as in potential warfare domains of space and cyber. The lack of our domestic investment coupled with a drive for offshore manufacturing for the sake of economic efficiency has been recently revealed in an unprecedented electronic chip shortage (affecting everything from laptop production to automobile manufacturing) and the paucity of domestic alternatives in 5G telecom equipment when our government decided for security reasons to ban Huawei equipment.

The combination of these three factors—a sharpened sense of cyber vulnerability, a recognition of what it's like to be unprepared for foreseeable crises, and a political fear that China may surpass us—have brought us to a national consensus in favor of substantial infrastructure investment. The adoption of a massive infrastructure spending bill by the Biden administration and Congress is, of course, one clear illustration of this consensus. On the cyber front, the Administration has made cybersecurity a priority, mandating enhanced security for the federal government's networks and working more closely with the private sector to fend off ransomware and foreign nation-state cyber-attacks. The bipartisan approval—after years of debate and inaction—by Congress of mandatory notification of cyber incidents affecting critical infrastructure augurs well for further legislation in this area. But much remains to be done: our nation must not only execute the programs envisioned by the new infrastructure law but also take the next and more difficult, step toward a wholesale upgrading of cybersecurity in our physical infrastructure throughout the nation, as contemplated by the excellent essays that follow in this book.

Although there may now be a stronger national consensus about remedying our infrastructure deficiencies, various inertial forces remain powerful. Beyond the unceasing demands for money to be spent elsewhere, our deep political divisions, the lack of a sense of immediacy (notwithstanding the crises mentioned above), and the sheer complexity of the problems all could cause us to miss this opportunity. At other times in our history, whether it was our lack of readiness in the late 1930s for a world war or in 1957 for the launch of Sputnik, we arguably were caught unprepared. In those cases, a redoubled effort enabled us to not merely catch up but also win (although no one can say what would have happened had we been better prepared in the first case). But this time, the sheer scope of the problem and, in particular, the trajectory China is on, creates concerns that if we don't act definitively now, perhaps we might fall so far behind that we won't be able to catch up. American indomitability cannot be taken for granted.

How We Can Start to Fix the Problem

To seize this opportunity, we need a coherent policy and coordinated execution between and within the public and private sectors—spread across all components of our economy from agriculture to aviation and from energy to emergency services. This book makes a unique contribution to that effort by outlining in specific sectors precisely what we can and should do now. Each essay is focused on one of the 16 "critical infrastructure sectors" designated by the Department of Homeland Security and presidential executive order and on election security (which is viewed by DHS as a subsector of the governmental sector). While there are many tailored recommendations, four key realizations are apparent from the following essays:

1. *The private sector plays a critical role in infrastructure development and investment.* The private sector, of course, owns and operates far more of the nation's infrastructure than do governments; the private sector will supply the overwhelming amount of the expertise, products, and services needed to repair and improve our infrastructure; and the private sector will supply much of the needed capital, even with extraordinary federal government expenditures.
2. Equally, *government at all levels has a crucial role to play*, both in the stewardship of public sector infrastructure and in the regulation of private-sector infrastructure. The latter responsibilities involve more than mere safety and economic regulation, but also the government's role as a catalyst in private sector development and investment, whether through direct expenditures, tax policy, or other legislative and regulatory endeavors. It will be critically important that the public and private sectors work together as we seize this opportunity to address infrastructure deficiencies.
3. There is *no aspect of infrastructure that can be divorced from cyber capabilities and vulnerabilities.* With the inevitable progression to artificial intelligence and machine learning, robotics, "smart cities," and the like, our cyber risk is only going to increase. Although this represents increased vulnerabilities, one benefit is that a common cyber element means that both defensive solutions and resilience efforts may become more efficient as entire sectors seek standard approaches.
4. Finally, from the wide and detailed array of recommendations offered, it's clear that *we have in hand solutions to managing the chronic condition of cyber insecurity.* Technology, both in the cyber element and physical element, is not itself the problem. A combination of steps will incrementally help reduce our vulnerability to cyber mischief.

We know how to fix this. And we will.

ABOUT THE AUTHOR

Glenn S. Gerstell served as the General Counsel of the National Security Agency from 2015 to 2020, and is now a Senior Adviser at the Center for Strategic & International Studies. He speaks and is quoted by the news media frequently on the intersection of national security and technology, and his writings have appeared in *The New York Times, Barron's, The Washington Post, The New Yorker*, and *Newsweek*. Previously an attorney focusing on international finance and technology, he is an elected member of The American Academy of Diplomacy and the recipient of various awards from the Department of Defense.

NOTES

1. *Weak Computer Security in Government: Is the Public at Risk?,* Hearing Before the S. Comm. on Gov't Affairs (1998) (statement of Sen. Fred Thompson, Chairman, S. Comm. on Gov't Affairs) available at https://fas.org/irp/congress/1998_hr/51998chairman1.htm.
2. *2021 Report Card for America's Infrastructure*, available at https://infrastructurereportcard.org
3. For some anecdotal illustrations of how we react belatedly to technological risks and misuse, consider how the Great Train Crash of 1856 led to the end of one-track, two-way traffic on railroads; how the 1906 Iroquois Theater Fire, killing 600 women and children, led to electricity standards and the formation of Underwriters Laboratory; how the 1934 airplane crash killing football coach Knute Rockne captured the public attention and led to aviation safety and the forerunner of the National Transportation Safety Board; how the virulent anti-Semitic and racist speeches by Father Coughlin in the 1930s, reaching almost one in five Americans at the time, triggered a backlash leading to regulation of radio content and the formation of the Federal Communications Commission; or how decades after the invention of the automobile, their prevalence and the associated deadly accident rate generated a demand for mandatory seat belts in 1968.

Acknowledgments

For generations, military strategists have heeded the guidance of Sun Tzu, who declared: "in the midst of chaos, there is opportunity." With every aspect of modern life digitally transforming due to the rapid adoption of technological innovation, the world's focus has rightfully turned to the risks associated with a computerized society. As awareness and incidents grow, it is the responsibility of organizations like the Institute for Critical Infrastructure Technology, a non-partisan 501(c)3 cybersecurity think tank, to create forward-looking education that helps public and private sector leaders develop informed policies and make business decisions with security as a priority. This guide is intended to be a tool for readers and we hope that it will ultimately result in the creation of actionable and impactful cybersecurity policies that will lead to a stronger economy, technological innovation, and improved national security.

Securing the Nation's Critical Infrastructures: A Guide for the 2021–2025 Administration represents the best of our community, with dozens of thought leaders coming together to share best practices on how this administration and all stakeholders can best protect our most critical assets. Experts were selected to represent the diversity of thought and experience, and the publication was organized to offer perspectives on the critical infrastructure sectors defined by the United States Department of Homeland Security. The perspectives, level of technical detail, and recommendations featured in the guide vary and are attributed solely to the attributed author; however, all content included has been reviewed by ICIT and is non-partisan, vendor agnostic, and objective.

On behalf of ICIT, I want to extend my sincere appreciation to the experts who made this publication possible. Thank you to BluVector, Capitol Technology University, Digital Lantern, Digital Ocean, DLT, GryphonX, Guidehouse, MFGS, Inc., Nozomi Networks, SafeBreach, Threat Warrior, US CyberDome, and Vectra AI, for representing the solution provider community who is critical to our fight against criminal threats. Thank you to all of the individual contributors whose content and essays provided a diverse tapestry of perspectives from the academic, public, and private sectors. A special thank you to the team at ICIT including Drew Spaniel, Joyce Hunter, Cathy Squeo, and Kathryn McKlver, whose commitment to this initiative and to the mission of ICIT has made an unquantifiable impact in our industry. We dedicate this guide to the current and next-generation of the critical infrastructure and cybersecurity community. We are grateful for everything you do to defend our national security and are honored to support you through our work.

With Gratitude,
Parham Eftekhari
Founder and Chairman
Institute for Critical Infrastructure Technology

ABOUT THE AUTHOR

With a lifelong passion for leadership and community building, Parham Eftekhari is a cybersecurity executive who has spent the past decade building trusted relationships with the nation's leading technology and national security leaders. Led by three core values—kindness, respect, and integrity—he regularly engages with policymakers, federal agency executives, and critical infrastructure leaders on initiatives that center around strengthening the resiliency of our nation against digital threats.

Parham served as ICIT's Executive Director until April 2020 and now serves as Chairman of the Board. During his time as Executive Director, he was responsible for building and executing the Institute's mission, including its content and education strategy, community engagement, and fundraising. Currently, Parham is SVP of the Cyber Risk Alliance and Executive Director of its

Cybersecurity Collaborative business, a membership community defined by CISO collaboration offering strategic and tactical guidance, CISO career development, and industry advocacy. Prior to ICIT, Parham co-founded the IT collaboration group GTRA and led the technology practice at a boutique competitive intelligence research firm. Over the course of his career, Parham has led the development of multiple research publications on a broad range of cybersecurity and national security issues, many of which he co-authored and has addressed forums ranging from Congress, the World Bank, RSA, and C-SPAN. He holds a BBA from the University of Wisconsin—Madison School of Business and spent two years at the Ecole Superieure de Commerce de Paris in Paris, France studying international business, and is fluent in French and Farsi.

1 Chemical

1.0 ABOUT THE CHEMICAL SECTOR

Drew Spaniel
Lead Researcher, Institute for Critical Infrastructure Technology (ICIT)

The Chemical Sector is an integral component of the US economy that manufactures, stores, uses, and transports potentially dangerous chemicals upon which a wide range of other critical infrastructure sectors rely. Securing these chemicals against growing and evolving threats requires vigilance from both the private and public sectors. According to the Cybersecurity and Infrastructures Security Agency (CISA) of the US Department of Homeland Security (DHS), the Chemical Sector is composed of several hundred thousand US chemical facilities in a complex, global supply chain that converts various raw materials into more than 70,000 diverse products that are essential to modern life. Based on the end product produced, the sector can be divided into five main segments, each of which has distinct characteristics, growth dynamics, markets, new developments, and issues:

1. Basic chemicals
2. Specialty chemicals
3. Agricultural chemicals
4. Pharmaceuticals
5. Consumer products

Following the September 11th attacks, the chemical industry immediately saw the need for increased security measures at chemical facilities and voluntarily began the process of reducing their physical and digital security risk. While historically there have been no Federal regulations mandating security standards for the entire sector, Congress passed the Maritime Transportation and Security Act (MTSA) of 2002 to reduce the security risk on navigable waterways including certain chemical port facilities. More recently, in 2007, Congress passed legislation giving the US DHS authority to regulate chemical facilities that present "high levels of security risk." The Chemical Facility Anti-Terrorism Standards (CFATS) established a risk-based approach to screening and securing chemical facilities, excluding those that MTSA and water/wastewater treatment facilities cover. As the National Infrastructure Protection Plan (NIPP) outlines, security issues in the sector are also addressed through a public–private partnership between industry and all levels of government as well as interested stakeholders.

Voluntary measures and new regulations mandating security measures at high-risk facilities are important in securing the sector. New threats to the continued reliability and integrity of all chemical infrastructure require all stakeholders and partners in the supply chain to remain vigilant. Due to its size and business characteristics, the Chemical Sector may be an attractive target for attack for cyber adversary ranging from script kiddies to digital terrorists to nation-state-sponsored advanced persistent threat actors. According to DHS, some reasons include:

- Inflicting a cyber-kinetic impact
- Compromising the integrity of products essential to the US economy and other critical infrastructure supply chains

DOI: 10.1201/9781003243021-1

- Inciting mass panic through prolific attacks that garner mass media attention
- Exfiltrating the data or physical materials necessary to launch targeted attacks on US critical infrastructure or the public
- Disrupting critical operations across essential supply chains

1.0.1   ABOUT THE AUTHOR

As the Lead Researcher at the Institute for Critical Infrastructure Technology, **Drew Spaniel** is an expert in information security and technology across the US critical infrastructure sectors. He serves the Institute as a technical expert in cybersecurity, technology, and data science, as well as emerging adversarial trends, threat actor profiling, and legislation and agency initiatives related to information security and privacy.

Drew earned a Master of Science in Information Security, Policy, and Management from Carnegie Mellon University's Heinz College and a Bachelor of Science in Applied Physics from Allegheny College.

1.0.2   ABOUT ICIT

The Institute for Critical Infrastructure Technology (ICIT) is a 501c(3) cybersecurity Think Tank with a mission to cultivate a cybersecurity renaissance that will improve the resiliency of our Nation's critical infrastructure sectors, defend our democratic institutions, and empower generations of cybersecurity leaders.

1.1 ICS SECURITY IN THE CHEMICAL SECTOR—BEYOND CFATS

Edward J. Liebig
Adjunct Professor, Webster University

1.1.1 INTRODUCTION

Since the "Final Rule" of the Chemical Facilities Anti-Terrorism Standard (CFATS) released in 2007, chemical manufacturers have been implementing controls and processes to comply and shore up their facilities' security. CFATS provided a good starting point to address the physical and (rudimentary) cybersecurity aspects of protecting our critical chemical production facilities. In 2014, Congress's Act to reauthorize and codify the CFATS program (6 USC §§ 621–29) was passed. This legislation laid the foundation for the continued maturation of the CFATS program. Even though extended through April 2020, these programs left considerable gaps to overcome, not addressed by the initial standards. This section will discuss some of the challenges that complicate the operational sustainability of cybersecurity programs of our critical chemical production facilities. Faced with Advanced Persistent Threats (APTs), comprised of nation-state actors, cybercriminal, and hacktivist organizations, a more sophisticated and coordinated attack capability has emerged, reaching beyond the original scope of CFATS. Quantifying and qualifying threats by location starts with the production or storage of "chemicals of interest," as outlined in CFATS, but transitions across all aspects of the business. Leveraging a consequence-based risk assessment process produces a "bottom-line impact" assessment to augment the financial element of implementing controls. The convergence of IT security tools and rigor with the operational technology (OT) environment unifies the visibility into Indicator of Compromise (IOC) and Indicator of Attack (IOA). Early February 2021, a would-be attacker(s) attempted to make parameter changes in a water treatment plant that would potentially poison the population by introducing deadly amounts of sodium hydroxide. This attack was not caught by automation or IOC or IOA monitoring, rather the astute observations of an operator intimately familiar with the water treatment process, watching the production control systems. This breach and configuration change attempt was a dangerously close call and lucky catch. This event highlights the need to be ultra-virulent in designing and maintaining an OT Security Operation Center (SOC) capability and locking down the data flow controls and micro-segmentation in the OT environment. These additional cybersecurity disciplines play an essential role in limiting the ability to establish Command and Control (C2). This essay's final topic is the challenge of budget allocation in the traditional business practice and setting expectations for cultural change to keep the cybersecurity programs prioritized.

1.1.2 CFATS AND THE CHANGING CYBERSECURITY LANDSCAPE

Following the attacks on our US soil in 2001, we collectively realized the rules of engagement had changed. Critical infrastructure was the new focus. As a result, the CFATS final rule, released in 2007, identified Chemicals of Interest (COI) which represented chemicals that played a significant role in American people's health, safety, and sustenance.

1.1.3 IN THE DAYS SINCE THE FINAL RULE

At the inception of CFATS, there was speculation that attacks would or could manifest against our critical infrastructure and the Chemical sector. The game has been ever-changing. Almost ten years later, we witnessed the rise of nation-state attackers, hacktivists, and cybercriminals becoming more brazen and sophisticated than in previous decades. These attacks are becoming more targeted and, at the same time, employing elusive and seemingly unrelated attack vectors. The water industry is a critical component of any chemical operation, and their IT/OT risks, challenges, and areas for improvement are very similar. Using the Oldsmar Water Treatment Facility Cyber Attack of February 5, 2021 that attempted to increase the amount of sodium hydroxide in the water from about 100 ppm to about 11,100 ppm (IndustrialCyber 1, 2021) as an example, it is clear that the kinetic attack objectives were planned to leverage a cyber intrusion. Theoretically, had the astute operator not thwarted the conditional change in the OT system, other downstream and safety systems may have caught the error. Typically, these critical parameters are monitored at multiple points throughout the treatment and transmission and distribution systems; however, even these safeguards are not adversary proof. Ben Miller (2021), an executive at cybersecurity company Dragos, in a blog post on February 8, 2021, stated, "It is entirely possible that this action could have resulted in people getting sick or potentially even dying." Industrial cybersecurity company Claroty revealed a 25 percent rise in the second half of 2020 in industrial control system (ICS) vulnerabilities compared to 2019, with over 70 percent of flaws remotely exploitable through network attack vectors. This observation reinforces that fully air-gapped OT networks that are fully isolated from cyber threats have become exceedingly uncommon, highlighting the critical importance of protecting Internet-facing ICS devices and remote access connections (IndustrialCyber 2, 2021). The challenge of integrating IT (Internet-connected business systems) and OT systems is compounded by the legacy systems and aging infrastructure that has had automation and technology "applied" ad hoc along the evolution of the overall plant. The incremental environmental changes in the technology landscape represent an "as-built" design and security strategy significantly askew from current reality and cyber resiliency. When assessing a plant, often the assessor will be handed an as-built drawing of the plant with annotations (sometimes in pencil) of upgrades and architectural changes.

1.1.4   THE RISE OF CYBERCRIME

The cybercriminal organizations have been targeting all critical infrastructure with the outward (perceived) intent to extort money through crypto-locking malware. The effects of these criminal activities have proven near-catastrophic in the case of the Colonial Pipeline, where the flow of fuel was disrupted, and a fuel shortage impacted entire regions. Healthcare has also suffered even though some of the cybercrime organizations publicly stated they would not target healthcare due to the global nature of the COVID-19 pandemic. This same kind of attack could trigger deadly consequences in the Chemical sector or other organizations that handle toxic or fatal material. Collusion between the cybercrime entities has compounded the challenge as the organization known as Graceful Spider has transitioned their targeted cybercrime operations into big game hunting (BGH) and has launched their own ransomware-as-a-service (RaaS) operation.

1.1.5   TO TRULY EFFECT "CHANGE," WE MUST ADDRESS THE SHORTCOMINGS

To summarize the ICS/OT infrastructure concerns, we must look at categoric situations and address these at an individual plant or facility level. For example, it is not uncommon to have different facilities producing the same end-product with a completely different infrastructure configuration, thereby operating under a completely different risk profile. In addition, mergers and acquisitions of manufacturing capabilities open the potential disparity between production facilities. Therefore, we must look critically at each facility as if unique.

1.1.6 TECHNICAL CONCERNS IN ICS/OT

A simplified overview of some specific categories of concern regarding the technical issues surrounding ICS/OT manufacturing environments follows. In addition, there may be other concerns noted while assessing individual facilities.

1.1.6.1 NETWORK SEGMENTATION

Through the nature of business evolution, the physical "air-gap" separation of IT and OT environments has become less and less sustainable. The need for remote monitoring and limited production influence has opened the environments to access that can become exploitable. Understanding just how the network architecture will thwart would-be attacks and attackers is key to isolating issues. Equally important is the need to segment the OT environment into isolated control loops so that an incident in one loop does not bring adjacent loops down.

Some techniques to consider for addressing the Network Segmentation challenges are (CISA, 2020):

- Compartmentalization and micro-segmentation (in a zero-trust fashion) give granular control of applications and infrastructure (respectfully). Additionally, understanding and limiting C2 dataflows throughout the C2 lifecycle allows for the limitation of malware's ability to impact systems in an "east/west" fashion across the network layers.
- Establish a perimeter around the ICS Control infrastructure. Configure firewalls to control traffic between the ICS network and corporate IT network.
- Defend against nation-state adversaries in "bulk" by utilizing IP geo-blocking as appropriate.
- Harden the remote access process to reduce risk to an acceptable level.
- When dealing with older and sometimes irreplicable technologies, use jump servers as a central authorization location between ICS network security zones.
- Do not allow persistent remote vendor or employee connections to the control network.
- Implement a network topology for ICS with multiple layers, with the most critical communications occurring in the most secure and reliable layer.
- Use one-way communication diodes to prevent external access whenever possible.
- Setup demilitarized zones (DMZs) to create a physical and logical subnetwork that acts as an intermediary for connected security devices to avoid exposure.
- Be sure to catalog and monitor all remote connections to the network.

1.1.6.2 SYSTEM HARDENING

System owners must ensure any vulnerabilities are systematically evaluated and remediated according to the risk and impact presented. This process also includes how assets are built and deployed into the network. Just because a vulnerability exists, it may not necessarily be an exploitable condition. When implementing a vulnerability management program, it is important to have a method to discover the relevance of the vulnerability to the environment for which the proposed patch or update will be applied, ensuring that vulnerability management is being maintained per an acceptable level of risk.

Start by promoting a culture of patching and vulnerability management. Be sure to test all patches in offline test environments before implementation. Utilize a formal and comprehensive change control method to minimize mistakes and irreversible errors in configurations. Where possible, implement application whitelisting on human–machine interfaces. Use "golden images" and harden field devices, including tablets and smartphones. Keep technical debt to a minimum and replace out-of-date software and hardware devices. To assist in hardening components, disable unused ports and services on ICS devices after testing to assure this will not impact ICS operation. Have a have a plan, implement it, and test system backups and recovery processes. Finally, configure encryption and security for ICS protocols.

1.1.6.3 ACCESS CONTROL

The majority of ICS systems use a Role-Based Access Control (RBAC) schema. According to the Center for Internet Security (CIS), used in non-federal environments, five controls are applicable to access control implementation. These controls are described below:

- **Controlled Use of Administrative Privileges:** One way potential hackers gain access to a system is by using phishing techniques to get a privileged user to open a malicious email and deliver the payload. Another is using the same method on a less-privileged user and exploiting password weaknesses to elevate their privileges and wreak havoc on the system. Therefore, strong password policies and separation of duty practices are vital in protecting an ICS environment. Some ways CIS states to implement this control include:
  - Implement multi-factor authentication
  - Enforce the use of a 14+ character password or password with capitals, special characters, and numbers
  - Remove all default admin accounts
  - Force admin users to only use admin accounts when necessary and use standard user accounts when performing non-administrative functions (if applicable)
  - Automate alerts for when new accounts are created

  There are exceptions to this practice that need to be recognized. For example, in a facility with a control room full of engineers watching over operations, there may not be the ability to log off and log onto systems individually. To address this, plants must employ techniques or technologies that allow the operators to remain diligent and in control while meeting the "spirit of the standard" for access control. For example, leveraging proximity badges, RFID, camera images, facial recognition, or other biometrics will control access level and accountability while satisfying the spirit of the standard for individual user ID entry.

- **Maintenance, Monitoring, and Analysis of Audit Logs:** Audit logs identify what is happening on a system. These can be things like whether new accounts are created or altered, who is logging in when they are logging in, and other access-related items of interest. Monitoring audit logs is an essential step in ensuring proper access habits are enforced. Embedded systems do not constantly audit security events at the same default level as traditional IT systems. It also may not be easy to have those logs sent to a centralized monitoring system. Using a Security Information and Event Management (SIEM) designed for industrial control system (ICSes) could prove beneficial. When implementing a SIEM, if you choose to do so, you may not have the ability to monitor the audit logs on the same level as a traditional IT system. Despite this, work to configure the SIEM to monitor and analyze the logs as detailed and extensively as you can.
- **Controlled Access Based on the Need to Know:** The protection of data, particularly sensitive data, is the heart of security objectives. Some ways to implement access-based need to know include:
  - Compartmentalize data into controlled segments. This compartmentalization includes creating both physical and logical separation of assets (the control loops mentioned above)
  - Creating Access Control Lists (ACLs) to ensure only authorized personnel access data they are supposed to

- **Wireless Access Control:** Ensure wireless traffic uses controlled, preferably private, networks. Wireless traffic should use, at a minimum, AES or ECC encryption to protect network traffic.
- **Account Monitoring and Control:** Some ways to implement account monitoring and control include:
  - Use shared accounts and passwords only when necessary
  - Create a process for changing shared account passwords and deleting accounts immediately upon termination of any workforce member
  - Remove applications leveraging cleartext authentication or basic security authentication. Where not possible, use unique credential sets and monitor their usage
  - Enforce complex passwords (where feasible, as noted above)
  - Automatically lock accounts after periods of inactivity (where feasible as stated above)

1.1.6.4 SUPPLY CHAIN, IDENTITY MANAGEMENT

Vetting the security posture of suppliers has proven to be a concern for operational sustainability. As a result, seeking validation of security and change control practices has become necessary (accentuated by the recent highly publicized supply chain security events). The cybersecurity maturity model certification (CMMC) process for the Department of Defense (DOD) is a good start, and it is feasible to be foreseen as a forerunner to set expectations across all critical infrastructure.

1.1.7 BUSINESS CONCERNS IN ICS/OT

Technical nuances between IT and OT are not the only thing driving security challenges. Some business practices compound the issue.

1.1.7.1 COLLABORATION, RISK, AND WEAK GOVERNANCE

Working between IT and OT, two owners of systems convolute the governance and establish holistic risk for an organization. The security practices are well defined in the IT area through standard frameworks such as NIST 800-53 and the ISO 2700x series. In the OT or ICS realm, there is the ISA 99/IEC 62443 Standard. The challenge in managing these two areas of risk is ownership. The IT security professionals oversee the IT systems, where the OT/ICS systems are owned and governed by process and area-specific engineers. Rightly so, the IT org knows the IT processes while the engineers know what the production requirements are. This bifurcated focus and knowledge are, in many cases, longing for cross-training and collaboration. Tightly coordinating prevention and response to security challenges requires both security professionals and engineers to own parts of the overall network and security activities. These two groups must act "as one" in governing and responding during and after an event. As part of the security awareness and education training, attention to include the OT/ICS nuances is a must for success in preventing or responding to events.

1.1.7.2 PLAYBOOK TESTING AND VALIDATION

It is imperative that the roles of IT and ICS/OT personnel are clearly defined when forming playbooks for IR and BCP/DR. Tools must interact and coordinate log results across the environments. Ideally, Artificial Intelligence (AI) and Machine Learning (ML) technologies will help accentuate anomalies.

1.1.7.3 THINKING DIFFERENTLY

For the Chemical sector and other similar critical infrastructure, we need to "think differently" regarding cybersecurity. Even the business process of allocating budget could hinder how cybersecurity risk and controls roll out. Some chemical companies issue an operational budget and leave it to the plant managers to invest in their interests. Establishment of a baseline for risk and cybersecurity across the whole of an organization requires there to be standard solutions. The effort to bring a plant up to modern standards may not fit into the operational budget necessary to keep up on production. Ultimately, the business process for funding may need to be adjusted. Some other areas where we must "think differently" are as follows.

1.1.7.3.1 Asset by Control Loop Identification

When we look at the ICS assets in a plant (and across various plants), it is common to discover "like assets" (same piece of gear, operating system, etc.) that perform different functions in their respective control loop. Identifying assets is the first step, but looking critically at the role as it applies to the control loop (and the loop's subsequent risk ranking) will give insight into vulnerabilities and identify consequences should the exposure become exploited.

1.1.7.3.2 Consequence-Based Risk Assessment

By understanding the impact of the loss of pieces of a facility (by asset and control loop), it is possible to comprehend a bottom-line effect on how the loss of an asset or loop will impact the organization.

1.1.7.3.3 Incident Response Team Performance Measurement

As stated earlier, and because IT and ICS/OT personnel must "act as one," tabletop exercises are crucial to look at the essential playbook and business continuity/disaster recovery planned activities. Successful tabletop exercises prove that a team knows "what to do." However, it is a much different exercise to prove that a team "can do" and "can do well" in the face of a live event. As a holistic incident response (IR) team (both IT and OT), we must measure the performance and look for avenues for improvement. Utilizing a live-fire cyber range is key to measuring how well the teams move through IR and remediation activities and offer opportunities to adjust the playbooks or supporting processes.

1.1.8 PLAYBOOK ALIGNMENT WITH EMERGING NATIONAL STANDARDS

In the wake of the Colonial Pipeline shut down, the current administration signed an Executive Order (EO) that calls for many things that will span across critical infrastructure as captured in Figure 1.1.1.

In Response

12 May 2021 Executive Order/Regulatory Reform

EO Section 1-4	EO Section 5-8	EO Section 9-11
Call for partnership Pub/Private	Cybersecurity safety review board	Adoption of minimum standards
Improved Threat Sharing	Standardized playbook	Definitions for understanding
Modernize – Leading Practices	Vulnerability and incident detect	NCD and Timelines
Software Supply Chain Security	Investigative and Remediation	

FIGURE 1.1.1 EO section breakdown.

Section 6 of the EO outlines a "Standardized Playbook" across critical infrastructure. However, alignment to a standard playbook is a particularly challenging task as each industry vertical, each organization, and those organization's plants will vary in the necessary playbook steps. Therefore, coordination and alignment to a national standardized playbook requirement need to be governed and tested.

1.1.9 FORGING INTO THE FUTURE

Spanning security monitoring and event correlation across IT and OT proves to be valuable and essential for incident containment and response. Identifying plant assets and assessing risk based on the use, topology, and impact to the overall production capabilities will better justify security spend by location. Striving to keep focused on the "real and present danger" for your organization will put a reliance upon threat feeds and threat sharing between would-be competitors. We need to collectively "think differently" and look at our business practices to support IT and OT to be successful. Leveraging newer technologies allows for real-time anonymized threat intel from "like" companies fighting the same battles. The critical infrastructure community will be pushing to strengthen our ability to defend against attack. The cyber battlefield is already full of cyber warriors. Our mission is to keep organizations ready and able to act.

1.1.9.1 ABOUT THE AUTHOR

Edward J. Liebig is a proven, recognized expert on IT/OT security management, cybersecurity, and policy and privacy rights. His focus is on business enablement and value, integrating technology, people, policy, and processes. With over four decades in IT, three of which are dedicated to cybersecurity, Mr. Liebig commands a comprehensive understanding of the end-to-end, national, and international cybersecurity challenges in enterprises and critical infrastructure. His experience as the Chief Information Security Officer (CISO) for several multinational corporations and the head of Managed Security Service Provider (MssP) professional services for critical infrastructure has demonstrated excellence, incorporating corporate IT/OT and cybersecurity, achieving business value, and strategic IT and OT roadmaps.

REFERENCES

CISA, 2020 https://www.cisa.gov/sites/default/files/publications/Cybersecurity_Best_Practices_for_Industrial_Control_Systems.pdf
CISA, 2021 https://www.cisa.gov/cfats-statutes
Dragos, 2021 https://www.dragos.com/neighborhood-keeper/
IndustrialCyber 1, 2021 https://industrialcyber.co/threats-attacks/industrial-cyber-attacks/hackers-attempt-to-poison-water-treatment-plant-in-florida/?utm_campaign=meetedgar&utm_medium=social&utm_source=meetedgar.com
IndustrialCyber 2, 2021 https://industrialcyber.co/article/claroty-finds-that-over-70-of-flaws-remotely-exploitable-through-network-attack-vectors/
Miller, B. "Recommendations Following the Oldsmar Water Treatment Facility Cyber Attack | Dragos", Dragos | Industrial (ICS/OT) Cyber Security, 2021. [Online]. Available: https://www.dragos.com/blog/industry-news/recommendations-following-the-oldsmar-water-treatment-facility-cyber-attack/. [Accessed: March 4, 2021].

2 Commercial Facilities

2.0 ABOUT THE COMMERCIAL FACILITIES SECTOR

Pete Slade
CTO and Chief Scientist, ThreatWarrior

The Commercial Sector is typically defined as any non-manufacturing business establishment, including all organizations not defined by other critical infrastructure sectors—making this sector particularly diverse and complex.

According to the Cybersecurity and Infrastructure Security Agency (CISA), the commercial sector consists of eight subsectors:

1. Entertainment and media (e.g., movie theaters, media studios)
2. Gaming (e.g., casinos)
3. Lodging (e.g., hotels, motels)
4. Outdoor events (e.g., amusement parks, campgrounds)
5. Public assembly (e.g., arenas, stadiums, museums, convention centers)
6. Real estate (e.g., apartment buildings, offices, mixed use facilities)
7. Retail (e.g., retail centers, shopping malls)
8. Sports leagues (e.g., professional sports leagues and federations)

Commercial facilities generally operate with open public access, which can exacerbate security concerns. Additionally, the majority of commercial facilities are privately owned and have limited interaction with the federal government or other regulatory agencies, making any sort of widespread regulatory action—whether cybersecurity-related or otherwise—across the entire commercial sector is difficult.

Because the commercial sector is so large and diverse, so too are the types of threats it faces. Commercial organizations must combat constantly evolving malware, zero-day exploits, digital supply chain attacks, and more. These attacks can be carried out by a variety of bad actors from malicious insiders and lone hackers to criminal ransomware gangs and nation-state actors.

Not only are the threats this sector faces increasing in volume and velocity, but they are also evolving at an alarming rate. Modern cyber threats are polymorphic and multidimensional. Just as organizations use advanced technology to defend against these threats, threat actors can leverage that same technology to bombard businesses with increasingly sophisticated threats. Because so many types of organizations exist within the commercial sector, they are often the victims of many of the cyberattacks you hear about in the news.

Perhaps the most diverse of the critical infrastructure sectors, it will take targeted, collaborative efforts to improve the resiliency of the commercial sector, which is absolutely critical given the massive economic impact of commercial facilities. Government entities, public and private organizations must come together to create innovative solutions to protect this sector and enhance the safety of our critical infrastructure nationwide.

2.0.1 ABOUT THREATWARRIOR

ThreatWarrior is a leader in cloud-native network threat intelligence, delivering true signals through the noise to eliminate alert fatigue and keep analysts focused on critical threats. The platform escalates the most serious threats to the people who need to see them, filters out low-value events from being a distraction, and helps cybersecurity professionals prioritize their work with far greater efficiency.

ThreatWarrior combines unsupervised neural networks, continuous deep packet inspection, behavior monitoring, and response capabilities in a single platform. Leading organizations use ThreatWarrior to stop known and unknown threats across cloud, on-premises, and hybrid networks and across the digital supply chain.

DOI: 10.1201/9781003243021-2

2.1   DIGITAL SUPPLY CHAIN SECURITY: WHAT HAPPENS WHEN AN ORGANIZATION'S TRUSTED SOLUTIONS CAN NO LONGER BE TRUSTED?

Pete Slade
CTO and Chief Scientist, ThreatWarrior

Dave Summitt
Former CISO, Moffitt Cancer Center

2.1.1   WHAT IS DIGITAL SUPPLY CHAIN SECURITY AND WHY DOES IT MATTER?

Traditionally, the supply chain refers to every component involved in the delivery of a product; from production to distribution and everything along the way that affects the end consumer from receiving it.

However, the world runs on software now. From the computers we use at work to our personal mobile devices, connected homes, and IoT—we're powered by code. The software supply chain is anything that touches that code from development to production and updates and enhancements. It includes version releases, known vulnerabilities, and security controls. It even includes other software running on the same infrastructure the applications are running on.

This means that digital supply chain risks are inherited from an organization's dependencies, which are pervasive. The digital supply chain runs the entire technology stack from code embedded in hardware all the way up to software packages used to develop a user interface. Any of these software dependencies can be used to leverage an attack, and bad actors will always attempt to compromise the weakest link in the security ecosystem. Because our global ecosystem is completely intertwined, exploiting a common connection is a dangerously effective (and economic, for the hackers) way to victimize a large group at once.

Adversaries can inject malicious code through auto-updates, poison a network with clandestine malware through a backdoor, or use any number of ways to breach an organization or plant logic bombs. If the infrastructure used to deliver the software or the software itself is breached, the damage is done. An organization has to deflect every attack, a bad actor only needs to succeed once.

Organizations today rely on hundreds if not thousands of software suppliers, and users are constantly consuming and updating that software. In the cloud era, everything is part of the supply chain, and security models must adapt to reflect that.

Past security thinking was primarily for the protection of organizational data. In today's world, security now means protecting from malicious events by threat actors that want to do harm for a variety of reasons. Breaching a network to disrupt operations has become more financially lucrative than stealing data and attempting to resell it. For this reason, the new century has brought in the requirement for organizations to "rethink" their security strategies.

2.1.2   EFFECTS OF SUPPLY CHAIN BREACHES IN THE COMMERCIAL SECTOR

Supply chain attacks in the commercial sector are not new.

In the now-infamous Target hack, the company admitted it was breached due to weak security at one of its HVAC vendors. The breach resulted in the theft of more than 40 million customer credit cards, 70 million addresses, phone numbers, and other personally identifiable information. The company saw a potential $1 billion in breach-related damages and hundreds of potential lawsuits.

In 2017, US credit reporting giant Equifax blamed its massive breach on an outside software it was using. It was later discovered that much of the executive team was aware of the incident, sitting on the news for months and mishandling its initial response to the breach, including not installing an available security patch for the known vulnerability. Equifax ended up paying an estimated $1.4 billion in remediation and cleanup costs.

Also, in 2017, hackers breached Ukrainian accounting software firm MeDocs and spread the NotPetya ransomware through malicious updates. The attack targeted the country's infrastructure but quickly spread across the globe, causing more than $10 billion in damages and bringing down organizations like US pharmaceutical giant Merck and prestigious multinational law firm DLA Piper.

A 2018 report from CrowdStrike found that supply chain attacks are increasingly common, with almost 90 percent of respondents believing they are at risk. The report also found that the average cost of a supply chain attack in the US is $1.27 million. That amount could be a death sentence for many smaller organizations.

However, monetary losses due to remediation, clean-up fees, potential legal fees, and more are not the only consequence of a security breach. In the immediate aftermath of the Equifax breach, the company's chief information officer and chief security officer "stepped down" from their positions. Just a week later, the CEO (who had run the company for 12 years) also "retired."

After the Target breach, the company saw a massive drop in holiday sales and the immediate loss of brand reputation and consumer trust. Shortly after, CEO Gregg Steinhafel resigned from his position after a "him or us" ultimatum was issued by the executive board.

For a commercial organization, consumer confidence is everything. Without it, there is no business. Disruption to a supply chain via security breach will always result in damage at the individual level, which in turn results in damage to the economy at large.

2.1.3 THE SOLARWINDS BREACH

In December 2020, it was discovered that cybersecurity company SolarWinds had been breached in a possibly months long attack. The breach was likely part of a larger cyberespionage campaign in which suspected Russian threat actors used SolarWinds' Orion product to attack potentially thousands of SolarWinds customers across multiple sectors, including the US Departments of Homeland Security, Commerce, and Treasury.

Hackers were able to infiltrate SolarWinds' infrastructure and compromise Orion's automatic update function. This allowed the bad actors to insert malicious updates, which were distributed to all Orion users.

The malware used was designed to lie dormant on victims' networks, activating only after observation from security tools to avoid being detected. Organizations need to utilize security tools that remain invisible on the network for this reason. If bad actors cannot see the solutions being used to monitor them, they may activate while being observed and be detected.

This attack highlighted a glaring issue with the digital supply chain. While all vendors in the chain pose a cybersecurity risk, organizations often overlook one player who should be equally scrutinized: the actual cybersecurity vendor. It's important that we take the same approach with security vendors that we do with everything else in the supply chain—with an "it's not if, but when a breach will occur" mentality.

SolarWinds is a cybersecurity provider. They are hired to protect organizations from the very activity they unwittingly helped spread. Many IT leaders have a "set it and forget it" mindset with what they believe are trusted products and vendors. However, this supply-chain attack is a grim reminder that organizations must scrutinize the security standards and practices of even their security vendors.

Because of its trusted status within these organizations and the sophistication of the attack, bad actors were able to go unnoticed within breached networks for months. The case is still unfolding as of this writing; however, victims potentially include a majority of the Fortune 500 companies, top US telecommunications and accounting firms, all five branches of the US military, and more.

Confirmed breaches occurred at big tech companies Cisco, Nvidia, Intel, Belkin, and hundreds of other organizations. Other cybersecurity vendors, including Malwarebytes, CrowdStrike, Mimecast, Palo Alto, Qualys, and Fidelis, also confirmed SolarWinds-related incidents.

In fact, because of our pervasive software dependencies and connected supply chains, this attack extended far beyond SolarWinds, becoming a study in global software supply chain exploitation rather than a cautionary tale of a single vendor.

In an interview reported by the *Wall Street Journal*, Brandon Wales, acting director of the Cybersecurity and Infrastructure Security Agency, said that approximately 30 percent of both the private-sector and government victims linked to the campaign had no direct connection to SolarWinds [1].

According to that same article, investigators said that "the incident demonstrated how sophisticated attackers could leapfrog from one cloud-computing account to another by taking advantage of little-known idiosyncrasies in the ways that software authenticates itself" [1].

This revelation means the extent of the exploit is massive, possibly extending to business software used daily by millions.

2.1.4   SUPPLY CHAIN SECURITY IMPLICATIONS ON NATIONAL SECURITY

The SolarWinds breach extended far beyond the commercial sector, compromising several US government agencies, including the US Departments of Homeland Security, Commerce, and Treasury.

This sophisticated attack is not the last software supply chain attack we will see. Threat actors use this tactic to conduct mass breaches via one weak point, and this attack was a warning: we must secure our supply chains, or this will happen again. This will require real incentives for US corporations and the government to take a holistic view of supply chain security and create an ecosystem that allows us to quickly expel attackers.

Cyberwarfare techniques advance daily, and defense must be at the forefront of our national security agenda.

2.1.5   REEXAMINING TRUST

The SolarWinds attack highlighted a critical problem in the software supply chain—a problem no one considered a problem until it was. The idea that is deploying solutions only from "trusted vendors" means your network is clean is a fallacy.

Trusted vendors, even cybersecurity vendors, can be used to leverage attacks against an organization. Just because a solution is already deployed inside an enterprise does not make it immune to compromise. Every vendor an organization uses must be vetted and continuously reevaluated within the user's environment. Organizations must have a way to monitor vendor risk even after their solutions are deployed and "trusted."

It is critical that consistent standards for software development and guidelines for how those technologies are deployed and maintained are followed, however, this should not come at the cost of agility and innovation. Additionally, we must have the ability to monitor and security test components of the software supply chain, even the security software itself. This is especially necessary in critical infrastructure sectors where the potential for damage is exceptionally high.

We must secure our critical technology and rethink the notion that some solutions deserve blind trust. Trust itself has become the attack surface and our most trusted solutions require the same level of scrutiny as our least.

2.1.6   PROBLEMS IN SOFTWARE DEVELOPMENT

There are a number of inherent problems with software development that have unfortunately become normalized as a result of time-to-market pressures, consumer convenience, etc. Of course, no matter how disciplined the process, there will always be some flaws that sneak through (hence the value of DevSecOps), but there needs to be a high degree of focus on securing deployment, distribution, and response.

The reality is it is easier and cheaper for manufacturers to create software this way. Because software development remains largely unregulated, a reduced price of production and maximum convenience for the end-user often comes at the expense of a loosened or no security policy. Without benchmarks and best-practice standards for every aspect of software development, these issues are bound to continue.

Perhaps an even more difficult challenge is that changing this will require a cultural shift. Manufacturers have traditionally cared more about profit, trading security for rapid development and deployment.

Additionally, organizations almost always leverage open source code to speed up development. These code "building blocks" now account for up to 70 percent of enterprise code, and every dependency creates additional security vulnerabilities that must be mapped and addressed.

Users are also traditionally willing to trade security, but for convenience and ease of use. Organizations with trusted vendors don't review their security because "they are already trusted."

Another problem with software development and delivery is patches. While patches are meant to fix vulnerabilities, they are often not discovered or deployed quickly, leaving organizations open to exploits for long periods of time. Many times, it's not until hackers have exploited the flaw that they are discovered. What's worse, patches themselves sometimes introduce exploitable vulnerabilities, and attackers can use software patches and auto-updates as an avenue to breach your organization.

Both of these scenarios were demonstrated in the SolarWinds attack. Malware was introduced through SolarWinds Orion software update and remained within organizations for possible months until being detected and remediated. Once inside, attackers were able to begin monitoring and stealing data including internal emails from their target organizations. More concerning is that bad actors, once successful, usually establish alternative avenues of access, which they can use to regain access in the future, should they be discovered.

2.1.7 COMPOUNDING ISSUES

Indirect attacks against one weak link in the supply chain are an easy attack vector—and they now account for 40 percent of security breaches, according to a report from Accenture.

Any breach in the infrastructure used to deliver software, or even the software itself, can be hugely damaging. Hackers don't have to bother singling out victims when they can breach one player, one software provider, or one security provider to victimize every organization that software touches. Its cyber compromise at scale.

Not only are threat actors becoming stealthier and more sophisticated, but their opportunities for attack are also greater than ever before. The hyper-connectivity of modern organizations makes supply-chain attacks notoriously difficult to detect and prevent. There are so many multidimensional dependencies that our supply chains are no longer linear. Instead, they are more of a tangled web. Customers become vendors to their customers. Vendors have vendors. These relationships are constantly expanding over our digital universe.

It's important to note that while this is fundamentally a software supply chain problem, it will also require a global mind shift to fix. Users have long believed that the third-party tools they've already invited into their "circle of trust" are safe, especially the tools designed to keep them safe.

Cybersecurity questionnaires given to vendors to fill out before their products are brought into a network can be deceivingly dangerous. These should only be used to initially screen the vendor and as a method to ask further questions and investigate less-than-good answers. Unfortunately, many organizations take the questionnaire and resulting report as confirmation to proceed, as long as it doesn't return anything serious. These organizations rely on their assessment of the answers provided to limited questions, then wonder what went wrong when something goes wrong.

2.1.8 UTILIZING ZERO-TRUST ARCHITECTURE TO PREVENT SUPPLY CHAIN BREACHES

Zero trust architecture (ZTA) can be beneficial, but it is not without limitations. It's become a buzzword for cybersecurity leaders, but many don't fully understand its true definition or how to actually implement it.

Zero trust seems like a simple enough concept when dealing with managed machines. However, unmanaged and IoT devices like smart TVs, medical devices, and industrial systems present a challenge. These devices do not support security agents, don't generate logs, and make a network more difficult to secure in general, which is the primary reason IoT is highly targeted.

Additionally, zero trust architecture is time and resource intensive to create. Organizations must consider their existing technology stack and strategic direction when implementing ZTA. How will they transform existing systems to support ZTA? *Can* they be transformed? It's important to remember that, in theory, ZTA is an approach used to create good cyber hygiene from the ground up, not something meant to be purchased and retrofit over an entire organization.

Financial constraints make it difficult to achieve a true zero-trust architecture. Organizations implementing ZTA often find themselves choosing between the security they're seeking and affordability due to the economies of scale pushing toward centralization.

The basic idea of zero-trust is sound, but it's not a cybersecurity catchall. It's more meaningful to say, "never trust, ever verify," or, "no product fits all," which is why it's absolutely critical that organizations practice defense in depth (DiD) to combat supply chain threats.

2.1.9 DEFENSE IN DEPTH

DiD creates intentionally redundant defense mechanisms to protect an organization. Because there is no silver bullet for cybersecurity and many different tools focus on different aspects of protection, applying DiD methodologies creates a stronger security posture that can defend against a wider range of attacks.

Using a series of different security measures together, such as firewalls, intrusion detection systems, data encryption, network monitoring, etc., bolsters security and closes gaps that might be left by a singular solution.

The increasing sophistication of cyberattacks, number of attack vectors, and volume of threats makes an effective DiD strategy essential.

2.1.10 TANGIBLE RECOMMENDATIONS

- *We must invest in solutions that remain invisible on the networks they are protecting.* This requires a more advanced approach to network threat detection and response and solutions with capabilities beyond first-generation cybersecurity and legacy technologies. As demonstrated in the SolarWinds attack, sophisticated threat actors can design their malware to lie dormant on a victim's network to avoid being observed by security analysis tools, with the goal of activating later when the threat of initial discovery has reduced.
- *We must remain focused on improving software development practices, reexamining our digital supply chains, and reevaluating the concept of "trust."* There is no silver bullet for cybersecurity; no one solution that can solve every problem. Organizations must utilize DiD to remain fully protected from cyber assaults.
- Organizations must constantly review their security posture and take every opportunity to enhance it. Every organization with sensitive information to protect must employ a proactive and dynamic approach to cybersecurity. *Traditional security programs are no longer*

effective and cannot rely on reactive approaches, they must be proactive and mature into active threat hunting and pre-emptive initiatives.

- Security by design is essential. This will take regulatory requirements and real incentives for organizations to participate. The bipartisan Cyberspace Solarium Commission leads many initiatives that will help drive changes in this area.
- *Constantly assess risk from all third parties and do not fall victim to the myth of trust. Even your security vendors must be continuously monitored and scrutinized.* Do not blindly trust any solution or vendor, pay close attention to auditing requirements, third-party assessments, and security awareness. *Make sure that vendors are held to a higher standard for the role they play within the supply chain.*

Now, more than ever, it is critical that we focus on securing the vulnerable digital supply chain. If vulnerabilities are exploited, they can have cascading impacts that affect buyers, suppliers, and users. Our country faces lost innovation, reduced economic advantage, threats to national security, and more when these attacks are successful.

In a statement recognizing April as National Supply Chain Integrity Month, Cybersecurity and Infrastructure Security Agency assistant director Bob Kolasky said, "As the number of sophisticated cyberattacks increase, we're reminded that supply chain security is not a nice to have, but an urgent necessity. Government and industry must work together to strengthen and enhance the security and safety of our critical infrastructure and the associated supply chains that support the resilience of our nation" [2].

Commercial organizations, cybersecurity vendors, critical infrastructure, government agencies, and everyone in-between must heed that warning and start working now to protect our digital supply chains.

2.1.10.1 ABOUT THE AUTHORS

Pete Slade is the Founder, CTO, and Chief Scientist at ThreatWarrior, and he is the visionary behind ThreatWarrior's groundbreaking cyber defense platform. Pete leads the company's threat intelligence team and drives the research and development of ThreatWarrior.

Pete is an expert in threat intelligence and network security with more than 30 years of experience in cybersecurity, information technology, and machine learning. He has designed and built systems for both commercial and intelligence communities and is a regular public speaker on cyber defense, national security, AI, and entrepreneurship. Pete is also a patented inventor, a Fellow at the Institute for Critical Infrastructure Technology, a member of Forbes Technology Council, and a congressional advisor on the topics of systems and infrastructure security.

Dave Summitt's experience includes nearly 40 years in information technology for both the federal and private sectors. He has concentrated predominantly in information systems, network, and engineering operations. He has experience in developing and implementing strong cyber security management programs and has held security roles within national healthcare organizations and the Department of Defense (DoD). After leaving a 21-year federal career with the DoD, he ventured into consulting and the healthcare sector. While with the DoD, he held various positions including the Naval Sea Systems Command's Technical Representative for a major missile defense program, security data custodian, Information Systems Security Officer, Data and Configuration Manager, and Change Control Chairman.

Dave earned his undergraduate degree in Information Systems Management from the University of South Florida and his master's degree in Information Assurance with a Digital Forensics concentration from Norwich University. He maintains the Computer Information Systems Security Professional (CISSP), Certified Chief Information Security Officer (C|CISO), HealthCare Information

Security and Privacy Practitioner (HCISPP), and is currently a member of the Florida FBI/InfraGard group and the Florida Electronic Crimes Task Force.

REFERENCES

1. R. McMilan and D. Volz, "Suspected Russian Hack Extends Far Beyond SolarWinds Software, Investigators Say", Wall Street Journal, 2021. [Online]. Available: https://www.wsj.com/articles/suspected-russian-hack-extends-far-beyond-solarwinds-software-investigators-say-11611921601?mod=djemCybersecruityPro&tpl=cy. [Accessed: 06- Sep- 2021].
2. "CISA and Partners Promote Call to Action During National Supply Chain Integrity Month | CISA", Cisa.gov, 2021. [Online]. Available: https://www.cisa.gov/news/2021/04/01/cisa-and-partners-promote-call-action-during-national-supply-chain-integrity-month. [Accessed: 6- Sept- 2021].

3 Communications

3.0 ABOUT THE COMMUNICATIONS SECTOR

Tyler Healy
Vice President and Head of Security, DigitalOcean

Communications and computing networks are the backbones of our modern economy. The evolution of this critical infrastructure sector over the past two decades has reshaped daily interactions globally. We've experienced an important reminder and affirmation of just how critical communications are during the COVID pandemic as our economy and society shifted to operate remotely. The communications infrastructure underlying our software-driven society runs on terrestrial, wireless, and satellite networks and continues to proliferate in coverage and interconnection. The blending of infrastructure and protocol defined late last century with continuously evolving and expanding layers of software riding these backbones creates a multi-faceted critical infrastructure environment. The physical layer of communications infrastructure is only now a small piece of what can be considered "critical," the services and software that leverage and optimize that physical layer are equally as important.

For all of the benefits of an interconnected economy and society, the mal-intended have found ways to abuse our communications critical infrastructure for harm. The resilience of our communications infrastructure is about availability, integrity, and our ability to respond to attacks leveraging our networks. Communications infrastructure is not built to identify harm at its most basic layer. Riding on the same protocols and traffic patterns as normal, healthy behaviors, malicious traffic ranging from grey market to nation-state backed attacks, embed themselves into our communications and computing technologies. This misuse of communications networks represents a significant risk to our socio-economic constructs and has residual impacts on every other critical infrastructure sector.

Our communications infrastructure is designed to operate with an open, unrestricted flow of information as a core principle. This open exchange underpins free and fair competition for the software and services built on top of our infrastructure. This core operating principle also comes with a set of unique risks and underscores a difficult truth about our communications infrastructure: we will never fully prevent the adversarial use of our networks. Instead, we must focus on deterrence, detection, and rapid mitigation of harmful use of communications infrastructure.

As we consider how our communications infrastructure will evolve over the next decade, our reliance on computing networks will continue to expand. The types of devices that create information flow around the world and the technologies that underpin them will advance faster than we will have the ability to protect them. This is not a bad thing. While we should still strive to protect each device and each protocol as they interconnect globally, acknowledging and accepting flawed implementations rather than assuming perfection will drive a more resilient communications infrastructure.

3.0.1 ABOUT DIGITALOCEAN

DigitalOcean simplifies cloud computing so developers and businesses can spend more time building software that changes the world. With its mission-critical infrastructure and fully managed offerings, DigitalOcean helps developers, startups, and small and medium-sized businesses (SMBs) rapidly build, deploy, and scale applications to accelerate innovation and increase productivity and agility. DigitalOcean combines the power of simplicity, community, open source, and customer support so customers can spend less time managing their infrastructure and more time building innovative applications that drive business growth.

DOI: 10.1201/9781003243021-3

3.1   ACCELERATING INTELLIGENCE TO ACTION

Tyler Healy
Vice President and Head of Security, DigitalOcean

3.1.1   INTRODUCTION

Communication networks hold a unique position in the critical infrastructure threat stack as the medium on which other infrastructures can be targeted by hostiles. Changes in how internet service and cloud computing companies counter threats have a multiplier effect, every other sector of critical infrastructure stands to benefit. The threats and impact are likewise multiplied as our economic dependency on the internet and cloud grows, particularly with shifts toward work from home, even in traditionally non-tech industries. Over the next half-decade, internet service providers and cloud computing can reshape the ecosystem to create a more expensive environment for those seeking to do harm. The basis for success in this approach requires three core components: (1) agreed definitions for hostile use and harm, (2) pace of observation to action, and (3) standards for accuracy and creating protections for inaccurate outcomes. Public-private coordination is a prerequisite in achieving the potential in this evolution for threat management. Sponsorship from and investment in the Cybersecurity and Infrastructure Security Agency (CISA) to create an industry coalition chartered with the three components above would help empower private industry to battle advanced threats.

3.1.2   HOSTILE USE OF COMMUNICATIONS NETWORKS

In recent months operations coordinated by global law enforcement partnerships, and supported by hosting companies, resulted in the takedown of botnet and malware infrastructure. A highlight of this growing trend is Operation Ladybird, during which international public-private collaboration led to the largest-ever botnet takedown. The outcomes are proof that a defend forward mindset (though not necessarily offensive security) has a larger role to play in how we protect critical infrastructure. The ferocity of distribution and illusive design behind these criminal operations leads to potential compromise in every sector from healthcare to banking, and the economic harm is staggering. And botnets continue to propagate and until recently, did so with impunity.

Even with the recent strides in coordinated takedowns, the cycle time is too slow to have a lasting impact. Playing whack-a-mole on large players provides one means of deterrence through legal ramifications but does not address the other primary means of deterrence: economics. The cost to build and operate malicious infrastructure must outweigh the economic reward, or at least come close, or criminal enterprises will continue to operate and evolve. Attack infrastructure-as-a-service has expanded in popularity, further improving the economics of bad actors. By creating multipurpose and multi-use malware and botnet delivery infrastructures, attackers have formed a supply chain. Building the case and coordinating global law enforcement to remove a large botnet is too slow to counter fraud economics. Speed to action is paramount, and therefore, timely and accurate intelligence becomes a prerequisite. But intelligence on what scope? Defining "hostile use" aligned to industry expectations is the first challenge.

Communications infrastructure companies cannot simply destroy user infrastructure or stop routing traffic from high-quality intelligence alone. Hostile infrastructure (compromised/stolen/paid for) is built for resiliency. Taking action in a vacuum results in further games of whack-a-mole and may adversely impact legitimate users/consumers. The risk of collateral damage is high when evaluating the appropriateness of infrastructure takedown. A core fact that must be considered for this equation is that not all fraudulent use of computing infrastructure is equal in its potential for harm. Spam and cryptomining on stolen infrastructure may be damaging and do have economic consequences, but the potential damage is quite a bit different than of a major botnet operation that opens the door to corporate espionage or costly recovery actions.

The most challenging element of a shared "harm scale" for hostile use is the timing relationship between the discovery of potentially harmful behavior and understanding the full extent of the damage across multiple communications providers and networks. Even with an established lexicon for every type of hostile use, the breadth and scale are difficult to evaluate across distributed communications networks. Coordination across multiple private companies and supported or coordinated by public organizations is a prerequisite for success. Rapid classification of attacker behavior, followed by confirmation in scope and potential harm, increases the possibility of a just-in-time response for certain hostile behaviors.

3.1.3 SPEED OF INTELLIGENCE TO ACTION

The pace of action is critical for flipping the economics of hostile use of communication networks. And the pace is a product of confidence in intelligence, compounded by the level of force proposed for action. Stopping all traffic from an entire service provider because some IP addresses in that range are causing an issue is a large overreaction that could result in massive collateral damage. Being able to stop a single IP to IP connection or even at a single port or protocol enables a much finer-grained response and calibrates a response commensurate with potential harm. Communications service providers with this level of granular control create a far faster feedback loop because the potential for collateral damage is greatly reduced.

In an ideal world where communications service providers have the ability to selectively and rapidly disable/enable individual IPs or ports on single pieces of infrastructure and do so safely, at scale, the second factor of speed to action is the quality and timeliness of threat intelligence made available to those who can act on it. The wealth of threat intelligence feeds collected with various degrees of focus for different types of hostile use creates a baseline from which to build confidence in takedown action. In addition to the automated collection and curation of threat intelligence, the importance of trusted sources of manually gathered intelligence cannot be underestimated. Collecting "internet-scale" threat intelligence serves an important function for a significant number of hostile use scenarios. For some of the most nefarious behaviors, digital forensics for the discovery and analysis of tactics, techniques, and protocols (TTPs) by highly skilled individuals is necessary to obtain actionable intelligence.

Timing the release of intelligence requires the balance between private entity interests, a gains/loss analysis, and actionability. Sharing intelligence among larger circles puts a timer on its potential action. But sharing intelligence too late means the propagation of a threat may enable it to cause significant levels of harm. Communications service providers should have a shared understanding of when and how to share this intelligence with private and public partnerships. Many of these avenues do exist today but could be put to better use when combined with appropriate actuators.

Peer validation of indicators in a reliable and repeatable method would provide another means for accelerating the intelligence to action timetable. Multiple communications providers are likely to see the same hostile behaviors on their networks. Creating confidence, leading to faster responses, can be built on the back of these shared intelligence sources. Knowing who and how to receive peer validation on indicators may allow individual communication providers to move to the coordinated action phase more quickly. Channeling threat intelligence through individuals with industry connections is a strong starting point but relies too heavily on the propagation of tribal knowledge. Formalizing an approach to peer validation, where a peer-accepted group of publishers can bless intelligence for approved subscribers, provides the starting point for broader coordinated action. As it is with embargoed vulnerabilities, the groups that are able to subscribe may vary depending on the type of intelligence and their potential to help deliver an outcome based on that intelligence.

Establishing these categories for communications providers to share insights will create the guardrails for participants. Beyond guardrails, a peer review of intelligence efficacy after action can create a "trusted reporter" mindset where certain groups can, and should, be relied upon for certain kinds of TTP analysis. By enabling trusted reporters to deliver intelligence faster, private communication entities (subscribers to that intelligence) can evaluate their options and react accordingly. Business risk, customer impact, and many other factors will contribute to a private entity's choice in how to act on intelligence, but that choice is only made possible by pre-established, trusted channels of peer-blessed intelligence.

3.1.4 GUARDRAILS AND STANDARDS

Governance of a threat intelligence sharing and hostile takedown framework will require a careful balance of private sector enablement with legal protections. A private company's actions must be that of the private company and not at the influence or request of a government entity. However, a private company must be empowered and therefore protected when taking that action in good faith. Selectively blessing certain kinds of threat intelligence and allowing private companies to act in accordance with guardrails will further speed up the cycle for bad actor removal.

Currently, this style of information sharing is a coalition of the trusted and willing and likely needs to remain that way to some extent. If a government entity were to force participation in a program of this kind, the rules would shift significantly in the attacker's favor. Communications and internet service providers have the ability to act swiftly and should benefit from private-public cooperation and coverage but not be beholden to any regulatory framework. Such a framework would stifle the flexibility required to combat in this space. With regulation comes audit, with audit comes a focus on documenting and tracing rather than a focus on outcomes.

Mistakes of both intelligence preparation and action against that intelligence are going to occur. The public sector role in a framework is protecting participants from one another or from other outside organizations (both public and private) who may be impacted by action resulting from TTPs blessed by a public-private partnership. For example, if threat intelligence about an ongoing intrusion at a major health system were assembled, but no harm was currently occurring, there's a window for remediation before harm propagates. Acting preemptively may create a degradation of service, or even force downtime for a compromised network, however, the harm from the preemptive action would be far less than allowing further propagation of hostile behavior. Isolation of the problem and preemptive eradication may be an uncomfortable scenario for some because of the collateral impact. This is the risk that must be weighed when blessing threat intelligence by both peers and with the public partnership.

Guardrails that accompany the publication of threat intelligence to approved subscribers will create the criteria on which future participation can be judged. How and when certain intelligence can be used is critical to achieving the desired action. Allowing partners to prepare for action is also important. Therefore, guardrails that allow preparation, investigation, and coordination while maintaining trust among communications and service providers are key. By staying within the guardrails and showing a good faith effort to further the cause of removing hostile use should be enough to indemnify a private organization should the result of a particular action be accompanied by some negative consequences. Without this protection, many of the organizations critical to operating against the intelligence will be bound not to act due to the legal risks involved.

Repeated actions outside of the guardrails or failure to show meaningful outcomes based on blessed intelligence would be grounds for a communication network to fall out of reputable standing. As providers decide how and who to peer with for routing traffic into and out of their networks, such a reputation standard could help define how those peering relationships are established. Operating a network with a poor reputation should come at a cost, which can largely be enforced by how peer service providers treat that network. However, the concepts of net neutrality must still lead the way. The concept of a trust-based scorecard for traffic coming from certain networks should not be used as a launchpad for traffic restrictions or cost models that allow communication providers to create a preferential treatment. Such anti-competitive behavior would erode participation in information sharing collectives, negating its core purpose, and create a massive barrier to entry for any new cloud or internet service provider.

3.1.5   THE ROLE OF CLOUD

Historically, consumer PCs on cable and fiber networks were the targets of cybercrime attacks. The pattern has shifted over the past ten years into cloud computing, where scalable and always-on computing infrastructure with publicly routable IP addresses have provided attackers with a much richer attack surface. The good news is that cloud providers either already have, or can develop, the right capabilities to manage persistent threats more effectively than ever before. Unlike traditional consumer PC compromises, where the communication provider has essentially zero influence over the devices themselves, cloud computing companies do have the power to take action against the infrastructure rented to their customers. That power cannot be treated lightly. Coordinated appropriately, with components of the framework outlined in the paragraphs above, action with the pace and accuracy to create deterrence may be achievable.

Even if a cloud computing company does have the ability to react to threat intelligence in a rapid manner, with great effect, this does not mean that company can preempt or prevent hostile behaviors. One of the great benefits of cloud computing is that anyone in the world (aside from specifically designated nations or persons) can rent computing power to bring their business or project to life. Removing the barriers of physically buying computers in a data center has unlocked innovation. Predicting whether a customer will fail to secure their cloud infrastructure or use their infrastructure for harm is impossible. Any expectation to do so would be misplaced. Enabling an intelligence to action lifecycle that encourages and protects good faith efforts against hostile behaviors may prove to be a strong deterrence for certain varieties of harm.

The implementation of an intelligence to action framework, powered by enhancements across the cloud and communications private sector, will not happen overnight. Incentives and feedback that encourage progress, not just membership, are imperative. The technical capabilities to gather, vet, and act on intelligence across cloud and communications may require a significant implementation roadmap across public-private teams. By creating the right incentives, we have an opportunity to reshape the landscape of cloud and communications to become less hospitable to attacker behaviors.

3.1.5.1   ABOUT THE AUTHOR

Tyler Healy is Vice President and Head of Security at DigitalOcean, a US-based cloud infrastructure and platform-as-a-service company with data center locations around the globe.

In his 12 years as an information security professional, Tyler has held roles driving technical and strategic transformation within public and private sector organizations. Alongside his full-time responsibilities, he has served as a tech startup advisor, helping new companies navigate the complexities of when and how to invest in security. Tyler has a passion for scaling security programs with highly automated functions to meet ever-evolving challenges.

Tyler joined DigitalOcean in 2018 as the Director of Security Engineer and, in 2019, elevated to lead the overall security organization. The security team at DigitalOcean provides engineering and operations that cover platform abuse, trust and safety, fraud, customer security, privacy, and the traditional corporate security landscape.

Tyler received a Bachelor of Science and Engineering in Computer Engineering from the University of Virginia.

3.2   ZERO TRUST FOR CRITICAL INFRASTRUCTURE REQUIRES A NEW FOCUS ON SECURE COMMUNICATIONS

Glen Gulyas
Founder and Chief Strategy Officer, Onclave Networks, Inc.

3.2.1   INTRODUCTION

It is time we revisit our approach to protecting communications for our most vulnerable assets to prevent nation state attacks from doing damage and costing lives. The source of cyber-attacks has shifted from random attackers to nation-state-sponsored advanced persistent threat groups (APTs), cybercriminals, and cyberterrorists. Our enemies are seeking intelligence and funding for their operations. It's time to accept the fact that the protection we have is no longer "enough" and set our sights on deploying the best solutions available in every public and private enterprise. The drive toward "Zero Trust" is really a push to get every enterprise and individual to adopt the same approach to cybersecurity that our Department of Defense and Intelligence Community have employed for decades. Making this transition will require that we all accept a foundational change in how we build our networks, systems, endpoints, and workforce. This will mean letting go of traditional technologies and approaches that we are comfortable with and rapidly adopt new paradigms that better fit our new reality.

Since the Internet launched, we have all prioritized connectivity over security in our pursuit of fast, easy access and exchange of data. Our enterprise architectures were designed around the premise that using the Internet was mandatory. Once installed, our networks were handed to teams of engineers who then had to spend countless hours trying to find and eradicate malware and strictly manage what and who gets in and out. While commercial companies continually developed and deployed new methods of finding malware and breaches, our enemies spent that same time creating new ways to break into our networks and devices to steal and gain advantages. This cycle continues today.

In 2020, COVID-19 changed the world. It also highlighted for us all how important and vulnerable our networks and communications are to our economy and our lives. Doctors scrambled to treat patients remotely, and technicians running the power and water systems were pushed to do more remotely. Zoom, Teams, and a variety of other online platforms were thrust upon us all as the lockdown began. Many of us, even those not in the business of technology, looked at one another screen-to-screen and began asking, "… are the communications we use every day really secure?"

It is indisputable that information technology (IT) and the communications we use for online conferencing and the exchange of data are important. But what about operational technologies (OT) and the communications they use to run our cities, power, water, transportation, and more? In this publication, ICIT has chosen to ask and, where possible, answer a very important question:

How can we protect OT and the communications used in our Critical Infrastructure?

Finding the answers to this question introduces a need for a different approach for OT due to its inability to utilize the standard IT-based solutions. Those devices are running more than 90,000 operating systems and can be 30 years old or more. The Office of the Secretary for the US Department of Defense has shared in multiple public presentations that they own and operate an estimated 2.6 billion OT devices—about 267 times the number of IT devices deployed [1]. This problem is big, complex, and seemingly impossible to address. The Cybersecurity and Infrastructure Security Agency (CISA) was formed to help protect our nation's critical infrastructure, and it is important to note that the 16 sectors they focus upon employ a massive inventory of legacy OT to run their operations.

This essay will not focus on those devices. Instead, we will explore the one capability all OT and IT devices share: *communications*. To find and address the vulnerabilities associated with OT communications, we must start by asking what OT needs to communicate and operate properly and whether or not it needs to remain in a converged infrastructure (or co-mingled network). Today's networks were all designed primarily for human communications, and as a result, we are now all struggling with how to handle OT and new "things."

3.2.2 NATION-STATE ATTACKS THAT MUST BE MET WITH NATION STATE-GRADE PROTECTION

The first step in improving the protection of our Critical Infrastructure is accepting that today's threats are sophisticated and insidious in nature. Our nation has the most talented and well-funded cybersecurity experts in the world, those working to protect our nation are challenged every day. When those experts open their laptops each day, they do so "under assumed breach" (i.e., they assume a bad actor has compromised their computer). If this group of very talented people assumes the worst, then it is wise for the rest of us to operate under the same premise, which is why our collective goal should include applying National Security-grade protection to all our IT and OT. Everyone and every enterprise need the best protection available—because we are all connected.

The latest, most comprehensive and widely accepted approach to reducing the risk of cyber-attacks is Zero Trust. It is defined and championed by the National Institute of Standards and Technology (NIST) in their Special Publication 800-207 Zero Trust Architecture [2]. Years of research and collaboration with public and private sector experts combined with hands-on testing have led to their advanced recommendations and best practices outlined in this publication. The basic premises of Zero Trust are already well established in the US Department of Defense and Intelligence Community, where they have been implemented for decades to prevent breaches related to national security.

While implementing a Zero Trust framework is a detailed process, the basic concepts are straightforward: Do not connect with any person or use any endpoint or system until it can be continuously verified as "trusted." The broad categories of risk are:

- People
- Devices (endpoints used by people or deployed at the edge)
- Systems and applications, and finally, the
- Communications used to connect all the above

These are the cornerstones of security and are addressed to some degree today. However, the enhanced focus on verifying *beforehand* that we can trust someone, some "thing" or a wire we plug into is where a Zero Trust approach can have a significant, positive impact.

Every enterprise should start with an in-depth security assessment. Then, using the above categories as a high-level guide, apply the premise that *nothing can be trusted until it is verified as trustworthy*—and incorporate processes and technologies that continuously verify that trust. That means:

- *People* may need initial and ongoing security training, background checks and be limited in what assets they could access digitally and physically. For those involved in supporting IT and OT, this process should be extensive and address insider threats.
- *Devices* (endpoints), both new and old, should undergo a thorough review of where their hardware and software were produced and procured, who installed them, and the security practices of all suppliers (i.e., their supply chain).

- *Systems* should undergo the same scrutiny as devices and include all users and administrators who access the system. Integrated or connected systems and devices will also need to be validated to ensure they undergo similar reviews and validation by their owners.
- *Communications* must be encrypted, managed, and monitored continuously. Suppliers and participants involved in delivering communications should have their supply chains reviewed. Our Government recently passed legislation ordering the removal of equipment deemed "untrustworthy" because of where it was built or who was involved in production.

3.2.3 THE FASTEST PATH TO ZERO TRUST MAY BE TO START THERE

After the SolarWinds breach, there were public comments from many experts suggesting extreme action. Some, to paraphrase, suggested that if we really wanted to address this problem, we needed to *"... burn our networks to the ground"* [3].

Why go that far? The SolarWinds attack demonstrated that our enemies, due to weaknesses in our supply chains, are deeper into our networks and devices than we previously thought or wanted to believe. If we use the analogy of a home infested with termites, tearing down the entire home and rebuilding from the ground up sounds extreme until you determine that the infestation is so great that no other options exist.

This breach was particularly troublesome because it was the SolarWinds development environment—and the systems used to build their network management and monitoring system—that was infected. So when SolarWinds distributed updates to their system, they were also unwittingly spreading the infection [4].

This type of breach is particularly disturbing when we think about OT because the number and diversity of devices and the risk they represent. The possibility that billions of OT devices with hard drives may be hiding malware is unnerving. The diversity and age of these devices make scanning or touching every one of them for malware an impossible task. This threat extends beyond systems running power, water, healthcare, and government facilities. Even more distressing is the thought that SolarWinds is not the only supply chain target to be compromised. We just have yet to uncover the others.

There is a parallel we can draw from the evolution of desktop anti-virus solutions. These solutions are being gradually replaced by "Next Generation Anti-Virus" (NGAV) solutions that use artificial intelligence and can address entire networks. Several years ago, the desktop version of this approach was declared by many to be obsolete. This happened because desktop AV failed to improve the lag between the introduction of new malware by bad actors and the mitigation of the threat by enterprises. Unfortunately, even NGAV has not eliminated the "lag." It still takes too long for enterprises to mitigate new malware and the losses from attacks like ransomware continue to grow. Detection is essential and will always need to be improved. So, what are we missing?

3.2.4 BETTER SECURED COMMUNICATIONS AND IMPROVED ISOLATION AND CONTAINMENT IS NEEDED

Isolation and containment capabilities must be tightly coupled to detection to prevent potential problems from spreading. In a converged infrastructure, this process is frequently governed by policies implemented by multiple systems and pieces of equipment. It is important to remember that those policies are created and updated by humans—the weakest link in the security chain. That means OT is running on networks designed for IT with policy management designed for IT. This mismatch combined with the potential for human error is not a path for us to continue taking. Adding to this with more IoT and 5G will add to the risks. If we continue to use networks and equipment designed for human communications instead of networks designed for OT, the breaches and damage incurred will escalate.

Managing, monitoring, and controlling communications for 1,000 employee endpoints like laptops is difficult. Now imagine hundreds of times that many OT endpoints using that are not standardized like laptops all running on the same network. The challenge faced by CIOs and CISOs to protect everything is daunting. Today's network teams are overwhelmed and doing all they can to fend off the already large volumes of attacks from the outside and threats from insiders and hidden malware that lay dormant, waiting to launch. Unlike in IT, the tools needed to scan, profile, manage, monitor, connect, and protect OT endpoints are limited. Recently there has been a flurry of emerging companies and technologies dedicated to OT Cybersecurity that have advanced into the mainstream—and we should expect to see more of them.

3.2.5 MAYBE THE IMPULSE TO "UNPLUG" IS NOT ENTIRELY WRONG

One way to protect a device from a cyberattack is to unplug it from the network and the Internet. Given our growing dependency on OT endpoints and systems used in power, water, and healthcare, applying that logic could result in a catastrophe. However, there are options emerging that can make unplugging from the Internet and the IT network possible.

CIOs and CISOs have conflicting demands when it comes to data and the infrastructure they use in their enterprise and across the Internet. There is a need to converge data and present it in one place to ensure that critical decision-making can happen quickly and accurately. At the same time, the need to segment and separate IT devices and systems from OT on the network is rising because of the risks posed by shared infrastructure. Running truly separate networks for IT and OT across the same wires is an option worth considering. It can improve protection simplify the management of networks and assets [5].

When we look closely at OT, we find that it is different in many ways from the IT that we use every day. That means we should be open to protecting OT differently. Shifting to an OT-centric approach to networking and cybersecurity through new more manageable, secure communications can avoid the pain of trying to protect both OT and IT with the same "IT approach."

While OT needs to connect and transfer data, it does not always need to use an IT network or the networking of the Internet to get the job done. It is possible to utilize the enterprise and Internet *wires* without relying on the IT network or Internet addressing system to build networks. Traditional network segmentation is certainly a place to start, but co-mingled environments and shared infrastructure are vulnerable to the sophisticated attacks employed by our enemies.

Hardened, secure private networking technologies are emerging and offer surprisingly affordable ways to build networks and improve protection. For example, imagine if we could move all the equipment in a manufacturing facility or a water treatment plant into a truly secure, clean, closed network that is separate from IT and the Internet—and still have everything operate as it should. There are an increasing number of options available that can extend this type of separation down to the devices themselves itself. These approaches improve the ability for administrators to contain infections or breaches at every endpoint and even help protect against physical attacks perpetrated by insiders [5].

Adopting a Zero Trust Framework is the first step. Having the willingness to drop the use of traditional IT-based networking that was designed for yesterday's networks is the next step. For example, legacy IT communications equipment and systems can fail "open" when they break or are compromised. This can allow breaches to spread rapidly. IT-centric infrastructures can also become overly complex and involve lots of policies managed by lots of humans leading to a lot of errors. Simple mistakes can be quickly exploited by nation-state bad actors.

Deploying newer, Zero Trust-based solutions that align with the NIST ZTA, DISA policies, and best practices by organizations like MITRE can offer enterprises a safer path forward.

For OT, Zero Trust offers an accelerated but safe adoption of new technologies like IoT and 5G across market sectors. By unplugging OT from IT networks and the Internet and moving it to networks designed to be Zero Trust, we can avoid disasters from attacks on our Critical Infrastructure.

Moving to Zero Trust will require serious commitment and, depending on your current enterprise architecture and needs, increase costs. However, reducing costs will also come from applying techniques and technologies that automate and simplify management.

3.2.6 IMPROVING OT CYBERSECURITY WILL REQUIRE IMMEDIATE ATTENTION AND INCREASED FUNDING

Working remotely during COVID-19 stressed our communications. The pressure from the pandemic has highlighted this already troubling problem and can no longer rely on "just enough" protection. It is time for everyone to understand the importance of maximizing our Critical Infrastructure protection. Federal, state, and local governments working hand in hand with commercial companies who provide OT and related services must evaluate new approaches, allocate adequate funding and work together to ensure the safety of our nation.

One thing is certain, we are fully engaged in this cyberwar, and it will escalate on both sides. If those seeking to do us harm want to use our money to fund their operations, ransomware is one of the most popular tools for them to employ [6]. Using the undisputed increase in the healthcare sector of ransomware attacks as an example, we can see by the data shows ransomware is a profitable cybercrime. To put the value of protecting OT into focus, maybe we should be asking a different question:

> If attackers can get a ransom of $200,000 to return the data they took hostage, how much will they ask for to return control a power plant or medical devices in an Intensive Care Unit?

Assessing the risk in your enterprise will determine the specific approach needed to protect lives and other assets. However, given the rise in cyberattacks and who is behind them now leaves us little if any choice on whether or not we make cyber protection our number one priority. Whether or not to adopt a Zero Trust framework and mindset is not just a technology decision—it is a business decision. As this cyberwar escalates, so will the cost of breaches. If enterprises fail to act and continue to treat security like an "option," the losses could be devastating to them and cost lives. DoD's recent commitment to Zero Trust provides hope and a good path for us all to follow.

3.2.6.1 ABOUT THE AUTHOR

Glen Gulyas has over 30 years of experience in pioneering innovative technology companies providing secure, enterprise solutions. He has served on the Board of multiple technology firms and on the Advisory Board to Microsoft for their Partner Program team. Glen's background includes being involved in or responsible for delivering IA and Cyber solutions to the US Intelligence Community, Department of Defense, and multiple commercial entities. Onclave, his current venture, is focused on the protection of our national critical infrastructure and offers unique ways for public and private sector enterprises to run, manage and protect Operational Technologies that we all depend upon.

REFERENCES

1. D.H. Haegley, "Overview of DoD Operational Technologies and Control Systems", The data cited has been presented at multiple public events by Daryl Haegley GICSP, OCP, Director, Mission Assurance & Cyber Deterrence for the Department of Defense and was provided with his permission from his handouts.
2. National Institute of Standards and Technology, Special Publication 800-207 Zero Trust Architecture. August 10, 2020 Copies can be downloaded at their site: https://www.nist.gov/publications/zero-trust-architecture.
3. "Hacked federal networks will need to be burned down to the ground." LA Times, December 18, 2020.
4. The Verge. M. Clark. January 7, 2021. Federal courts go low-tech for sensitive documents following SolarWinds hack. https://www.theverge.com/2021/1/7/22219275/federal-judiciary-system-further-securing-sealed-documents-solarwinds-hack
5. IBM Ponemon Study | Ponemon Institute Study. IBM, Armonk, NY, 2020.
6. Ransomware Demands continue to rise as Data Exfiltration becomes common, and Maze subdues. November 4, 2020. https://www.coveware.com/blog/q3-2020-ransomware-marketplace-report#

4 Critical Manufacturing

4.0 ABOUT THE CRITICAL MANUFACTURING SECTOR

Chris Grove

Product Evangelist, Nozomi Networks

The US Government defined 16 Sectors of Critical Infrastructure that are crucial to the continuity of the nation. Some sectors are clearly defined and labeled, making them easily understood by the masses, for example, Sectors such as Dams, Energy, and Government Facilities should be clear to the reader what they encompass. Contrarily, some organizations operate in more than one Sector due to having multiple products and services or multiple uses for a specific product, and resultantly, have a more complex alignment with the sectors descriptions. Additionally, some sectors have very specific or very broad applicability. On the "more specific" end of the scale might be the Defense Industrial Base, and on the broad end of the scale, the Critical Manufacturing Sector.

Using the nomenclature "Sector" could falsely imply that they are independent verticals that operate alongside each other. A better way to describe the Sectors would be "nodes" within an interconnected ecosystem. Each node has multiple inputs and outputs and multidimensional supply chain dependencies on each other. Node "A" relies on Node "B," which depends on Node "C," which depends on Node "A." A web of nodes is a better way to picture how the Sectors interoperate with each other. An example could be the Defense Industrial Base depends on the output from the Chemical Sector, which is reliant on the Transportation Systems Sector, which needs the Energy Sector, which depends on the Dam Sector, which is dependent on the Chemical, Communications, and other Sectors.

Each of the defined Critical Sectors has it's own supply chain and dependencies. Imagine the connections between the nodes as the inputs/outputs of the connected node. The Energy Sector takes the output of the Dam and Nuclear Sectors and supplies the input of the Chemical Sector, which outputs to the Food & Agriculture Sector, which then outputs to the Healthcare Sector, and so on. Ensuring continuity of these disparate industries that supply the Sector ecosystem is critical to maintaining and sustaining operations within each sector.

On any given day, the infrastructure within each Critical Sector needs maintenance, upgrades, repairs, retrofits, and other inputs to continue operating. These day-to-day needs create a heavy demand for raw and finished goods, which subsequently need to be transported to other critical sectors to sustain the infrastructure and the operations of it.

The creation of the Critical Manufacturing Sector in 2008 highlighted the importance of serving the underlying needs of the other critical sectors. An interruption in the Critical Manufacturing sector could quickly cascade into much larger issues, affecting national strategies and other critical infrastructure, preventing them from fully performing their functions. In a way, the Critical Manufacturing Sector is the fuel that helps feed the other sectors and keep them up and running.

The Critical Manufacturing Sector is responsible for the production, manufacturing, and processing huge amounts of raw goods that help make a wide array of other products. These include various types of primary metals, like iron, steel, ferroalloys, aluminum, nonferrous metals, and others. An interruption in this supply chain could cause other sectors to grind to a halt, as they may rely on the metals to produce their respective goods or used to maintain the factories that produce the goods.

In addition to raw goods, the Critical Manufacturing Sector is also responsible for securing the Machinery Manufacturing industries. These organizations manufacture the equipment used within other industries, including earth moving equipment, machinery for farms, mines, and construction, as well as power transmission equipment. Also included are engine and turbine manufacturing industries.

DOI: 10.1201/9781003243021-4

The Critical Manufacturing Sector also includes industries that produce large electrical components and devices, such as power transformers used in the power grid, household appliances, power generators, and electric motors. In order to ensure goods and materials can continue to be successfully transported throughout the supply ecosystem, the Critical Manufacturing Sector also includes industries that manufacture vehicles, trains, railway tracks, transit cars, aerospace products and parts, as well as commercial ships.

When viewed in it's totality, the Critical Manufacturing Sector can be seen as the fuel that binds the other critical sectors together. Additionally, during a time of a national emergency, such as a pandemic or war, many of these industries can be converted to other critical functions in support of those efforts. For example, consumer product factories converted to Defense Industrial Base manufacturing during war shortages or a vehicle manufacturer that produces ventilators in support of Healthcare and Public Health Sector initiatives during the pandemic.

Few other Critical Sectors have such a wide variety of industries included with their scope. In addition to the complexities of defining and securing a dissimilar group of industries, the fiscal enormity of the Sector is a major driver for addressing the risks to this crucial aspect of the national supply chain. In fact, on it's own, it would be the eighth largest economy in the world, represents 12.5% of our national GDP, and contributed $2.08 trillion to our economy (according to the figures totaled for 2013 by the National Association of Manufacturing in 2015).

It's clear that the Critical Manufacturing Sector is crucial to several of our national strategies, and the challenge to secure them is enormous. Equally as challenging is attempting to legislate solutions that will positively impact such a wide array of industries. Cybersecurity standards organizations and developers of best practices have wrangled with this for years, resulting in a myriad of industry and geography specific recommendations. Some of the most widely accepted standards organizations have multiple variants or flavors that provide more specific guidance for verticals where nuances exist, causing that industry to have requirements that differ from other recommended practices. That makes crafting regulations or legislating solutions particularly challenging for the Critical Manufacturing Sector, particularly compared to other, more narrowly defined Sectors like the Energy or Health Sectors.

Although the industries within the Critical Manufacturing Sector are different, they do (mostly) have one thing in common; they are profit-driven organizations. In many other CI Sectors, the infrastructure is in the hands of public entities, like Federal or municipal government, utility organizations, or heavily regulated private entities. To the contrary, most of the Critical Manufacturing Sector comprises of private enterprises where in many cases, availability and uptime are the primary strategic goals, driven by the business requirements to generate profit. This similarity could help guide the legislative decision-making process to ensure misguided or over-regulation is avoided, which could have a negative impact on the organizations' original business objectives.

Defenders are in need of resources at a time when resources are expensive, scarce, and in some cases, ineffective. Private enterprises within the Critical Manufacturing Sector are struggling to stay afloat in the midst of supply chain issues, pandemic-related problems, labor shortages, and shifting markets. Furthermore, problems such as ransomware, cybercrime, and manmade disasters will continue to evolve and grow. To further complicate matters, the technological footprint of the targeted organizations grow, providing more opportunity for risks to become a reality. As such, we will need to solve the national cybersecurity labor shortage to not only drive down costs but also sustain and manage the necessary defenses to safeguard the future.

4.0.1 ABOUT NOZOMI NETWORKS

Nozomi Networks accelerates digital transformation by unifying cybersecurity visibility for the largest critical infrastructure, energy, manufacturing, mining, transportation, building automation, and other OT sites around the world. Nozomi Networks is a leader in OT and IoT security and visibility and their innovation and research make it possible to tackle escalating cyber risks through exceptional network visibility, threat detection, and operational insight.

4.1 TRANSITIONING CRITICAL MANUFACTURING TO CYBER RESILIENCY

Chris Grove
Product Evangelist, Nozomi Networks

4.1.1 INTRODUCTION

The need to move from a state of cybersecurity resistance to one of cyber *resilience* is now more important than ever. Our nation's infrastructure has become increasingly complex—protective measures are no longer sufficient. With each new technology we introduce, our nation becomes more reliant on those technologies. It's not just those new technologies that need our focus, it is also all of the required supporting technologies.

Our reliance on using navigational maps on the phone is a good example for putting the spotlight on supporting technologies. To use the maps, we are dependent on a stack of technologies that need to be in operation before the mapping app can function. The mobile phone needs a cell signal, a TCP connection to the internet, a local GPS chip, the GPS satellites, a server for the mapping application with an OS, device drivers, security, applications for navigational abilities, and the cloud backend itself. Attempting to list the vast and complex amount of layers stacked upon each other, with interdependencies between them, is a huge undertaking. Every single technology and layer comes with its own supply chain ecosystem, resulting in layer upon layer of unknown (and thus unaddressed) risk.

There are several methodologies and frameworks in the field that attempt to identify and address the risks posed *to* the technology ecosystem. Very few address the risks of the technology ecosystem, in particular the risks of dependence on the technologies. When we discuss risk from this perspective, we begin a shift to a resilience mindset, away from a resistance mindset.

The Rand Corp. Measuring Cybersecurity and Cyber Resiliency Report underscore this point in terms of Red and Blue team drills:

> To measure how survivable and effective a mission or system can be in a cyber-contested environment, we must understand how well Red cyber operations are being countered. Therefore, the focus of cyber metrics must be on Red's estimated success or failure, not on the specific countermeasures that Blue might try. Blue countermeasures are important, of course, but their importance is as a means to an end—that of hindering or thwarting Red. Cyber metrics that concentrate on the compliance with lists of candidate Blue countermeasures fail to indicate whether those measures are effective, properly implemented, or sufficiently comprehensive to thwart Red. The compliance approach, therefore, is insufficient. In addition, a simple set of metrics in the form of a "dashboard" does not exist that satisfies these needs. [1]

4.1.2 RESISTANCE VS RESILIENCY

Another way to illustrate the contrast between resistance and resilience is in car technologies. In order to *resist* having car accidents, automobiles have headlights, windshield wipers, and brakes. To become *resilient* against car accidents, manufacturers added seatbelts, airbags. Neither seatbelts nor airbags prevent car accidents, both are born from the resilience mindset of preparing for failure in other areas, like the brakes or headlights. Planning on failures resulted directly in lives being saved.

A commonly heard theme among Security Operations Center (SOC) operators and analysts is that they're in a constant state of recovery. On any given day, a typical large enterprise SOC could see hundreds of thousands or millions of alerts and handle hundreds of cases and actual incidents per day. Advances in technology such as Bring Your Own Device (BYOD), the Cloud, and remote access have all but eviscerated the traditional IT perimeter.

Significant investment continued to be made in *resisting* cyber incidents using traditional methods and technologies such as firewalls, two-factor authentication, vulnerability management, and other tactics. However, aligning with the goal of being resilient to failure with the prevention technologies, a SOC is usually tooled for identifying the failures within the measures to resist.

The organization has hope and confidence in their vendors, but they are *resilient* to failure by planning for it. Organizations deploy intrusion detection systems, network segmentation, encryption, and a host of other layers of cybersecurity, and employ a team of people to monitor the network because the best practice is to anticipate that some attacks will penetrate the protections.

Being able to address risks and become resilient requires one to abandon the thought that we can always prevent an incident. One must move to the mindset that the incident wasn't prevented, we're in the midst of it, and now action is needed. In some cases, we would need a few basic forensic tools, in other cases, we would need to burn the network and re-credential the entire enterprise. Are we resilient to those events? If we can't continue operations without that aspect of our operations being available, finding ways to reduce the consequence of failure is the best strategy.

As planners begin to plan on failures as a result of considering resiliency, it quickly becomes apparent that identifying, tracking, and measuring the consequences is a huge undertaking. While some are well equipped in certain fields necessary to identify risk, such as experts in fire, cyber, or factory architecture, we run the risk of becoming too entrenched in the process by being forced to follow a specific set of measurements. This is sometimes referred to as "analysis paralysis." Often this happens when too much effort is put into one detail, resulting in stagnation, high costs, and an inability to move forward with progress. This is an enemy of resiliency and should be avoided as much as possible.

Taking into account the many layers of technology that exist in modern ecosystems, different layers will have different standards, ratings, measurements, best practices, and scope. In some realms, a standard or framework may have a very narrow focus on one protocol, like using OWASP to measure and improve the usage of applications using HTTP or have a wide scope and include a large part of the enterprise with many smaller subsets of processes and measurements, like NIST SP800-171, PCI, SOX, or others.

Furthermore, there are other frameworks that help organizations determine what resources to spend on reducing particular risks. Typically, this is accomplished by measuring the current state, the desired future state and prioritize expenditures to reduce the delta between the two. Although these frameworks weren't designed for cyber-resiliency, the measurement of the current state is beneficial information. Less practical, the future state requires the investment to bear the expected benefits after successful execution to happen beforehand. Therefore, in the spirit of planning on failures, it's safer to measure the current state because, in most instances, the threat of an adversary exists today, not only in the future.

4.1.3   MEASURING CAPABILITY GAPS BETWEEN THE ANTAGONISTS AND PROTAGONISTS

Imagine you come home from work to find a notice on your front door from a government agency. The notice warns of bad actors and has recommendations and tips on how you can increase your security to mitigate their methods. Based on this advice, we choose to either discard the information and assume the risks or spend time and money preventing the risk.

If the government entity that placed the notice was my local police station with a warning about car break-ins, I would probably lock my car doors, leave an outside light on, and maybe install a camera. If the government notice warned about a local scammer/identity theft ring, I might monitor my credit, secure my mailbox, and place "no soliciting" signs around the property. If the government notice was about hackers targeting our businesses or homes, we might get a better firewall, deploy higher grade end-point protection, and secure the Wi-Fi. If the government was warning local residents about street violence targeting families in their homes, we would probably invest in

TABLE 4.1.1
Example Threat Mitigations

Protagonist	Antagonist	Primary Mitigations
Family	Category 1 hurricane	Early warning radar, building codes, power generator, backup Wi-Fi, pumps, water filtration, home protection
Family	Category 5 hurricane	Early warning radar, mobile data, currency, homeowners insurance
Manufacturing company	Hacktivist	Standards, best practices, network segmentation, firewalls, intrusion detection, DDOS protection
Manufacturing company	Malicious insider	Law enforcement consequences, best practices, network segmentation, intrusion detection, anomaly detection
Manufacturing company	Cyber-criminal ring	Law enforcement consequences, firewalls, detection systems
Manufacturing company	Large Nation State APT	Diplomatic or military consequences, detection systems

stronger locks, steel bars on the windows, and install an alarm system. We would choose where to invest resources based on filling the gaps between the capabilities of the attacker and the defender. Depending on which government entity is offering the advice, the likelihood of an incident, and the consequences of an incident, we choose to accept or spend resources to mitigate the risks accordingly.

In order to determine how much to typically spend to mitigate typical risks, most people would look to the high-end of the available technologies and to the lower end, determine where the Antagonist exists, determine where they exist in that spectrum, and subsequently, what delta exists and how large the gap is. Table 4.1.1 captures some example protagonists and suggests mitigation strategies relative to the scale of the antagonist.

A *Protagonist* is the main character in the story, and an *Antagonist* is the villain or enemy of the main character. Regardless of the storyline, we can begin to assess the capabilities of our defenses versus the risks by taking inventory of the technologies, people, and processes we can leverage to "resist" an incident.

Some examples of mitigations used between Protagonists and Antagonists could be:

In a scenario favorable to the Protagonist (or defender), the diagram would show clear space between the capabilities of the Protagonist and those of the Antagonist, as depicted below in Figure 4.1.1.

In a scenario where the Antagonist could overcome the defenses of the Protagonist would be depicted as follows:

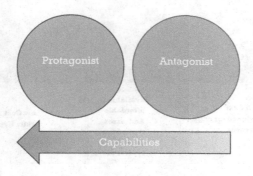

FIGURE 4.1.1 Relative defense effectiveness. *(Continued)*

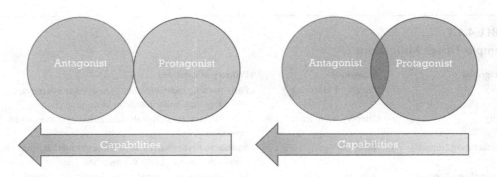

FIGURE 4.1.1   *(Continued)*

If we think of the high end on the left, low end on the right, we can put perspective on the capabilities.

4.1.4   THE DEFENSIVE TECHNOLOGY MARKET

Since the industrial revolution, the market for defensive technology has always offered varying products with varying degrees of technology available to high-end users with extreme use cases. Alongside that segment of the market exists the marketspace for common use cases, where typical defense technologies are affordable by the masses and mitigate the typical use cases facing the user. And on the bottom end of the spectrum, also in parallel, is the antiquated technologies sector, where the technology is cheap and only mitigates a few use cases.

Over time, high-tech, cutting edge technologies become more commonplace and in the hands of the masses. Eventually, after mass adoption, they become antiquated. At one point in time, using a simple emergency valve as a defense against a risk was cutting edge. Today, using a valve is commonplace. Cyber defense technologies appear to have the same lifecycle.

Similar to a typical product lifecycle, we can visualize and compare the capabilities of the Protagonist versus the Antagonist. Figure 4.1.2 estimates the degrees of effectiveness of a solution according to its position on the lifecycle relative to its resource cost and sophistication.

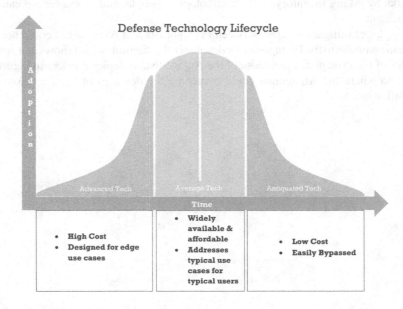

FIGURE 4.1.2   Defense technology lifecycle.

If we take a lock as an example of a defensive technology and apply it to the lifecycle above, we can see the various degrees of effectiveness according to its position on the lifecycle. On the far left, a very advanced lock would probably be in the hands of a museum, military installation, or classi- fied facility. This lock would be designed to prevent the most advanced attackers. Most of the public doesn't have access to, couldn't afford, or has no use for technology in this category.

In the middle of the lifecycle, at the average technology stage, most of the general public can afford to buy effective locks that work against the most common use cases. Keyed locks, combina- tion locks, and bike locks are all designed around affordable devices preventing access for the common use cases (such as a pedestrian without tools looking for opportunities to steal).

On the right of the lifecycle, antiquated locks are used in low-risk scenarios, like a desk drawer, jewelry box, or liquor cabinet lock. They are cheap, easily bypassed by most adversaries, and only address limited use cases, for example, detecting entry rather than preventing it.

When considering the capabilities of an adversary, they can also be portrayed in the lifecycle as seen in Figure 4.1.3.

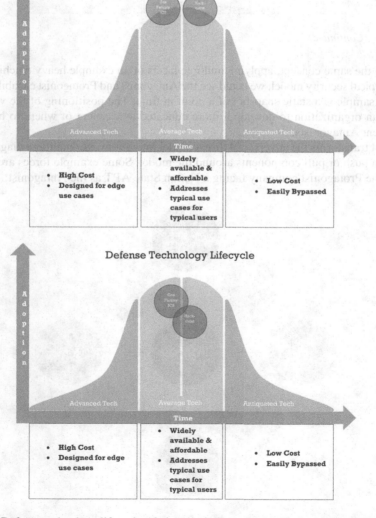

FIGURE 4.1.3   Defense technology lifecycle relative to adversary sophistication. *(Continued)*

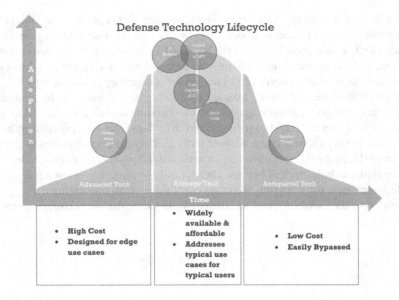

FIGURE 4.1.3 *(Continued)*

Leveraging the same concept, applying multiple facets of an example heavy machinery manufacturer, with a typical security model, we could see the Antagonist and Protagonist capabilities displayed:

The above sample is a static snapshot of a point in time. The positioning of the various components allows an organization to develop a more educated assessment of where to build resilience against different Antagonists.

Figure 4.1.4 transforms the adversarial threat model into a conventional force diagram. There are forces that can push or pull components around the model. Some example forces are displayed, for an example, the Protagonist company facing a Nation State APT as the Antagonist:

FIGURE 4.1.4   Potential threat forces.

4.1.5 CHANGING THE MINDSET

State-sponsored supply chain attacks on the technology ecosystem directly challenge the mindset that any of us have complete control over our technology today. Even more challenging is the notion that this technology will be fully under control in the future. While it simplifies the conversation and provides some sense of confidence to approach the problem as a single incident, or a single link in a supply chain, or a single supply chain in a process, it does very little to solve the issue. It's short-sighted, doesn't account for the intelligence of the adversary, and results in continuous cat-and-mouse games with the attackers. For example, early responders in the SolarWinds incident had to disinfect and remove the same APTs from victims on multiple occasions, over long periods of time, in different areas of the enterprise.

While it is important to continue efforts in resisting or preventing cyber incidents such as the SolarWinds attack, it's also important to keep in mind that the attack has already happened, and there are undiscovered breaches currently in process now. We must ask: What will we find tomorrow? What knowledge and tools do we need to be resilient to attacks? When an attack is successful, how can we reduce the consequences within the critical manufacturing sector? Each organization will have its own set of processes, capabilities, risks, and antagonists, thus its own set of resiliency plans.

4.1.6 RECOMMENDATIONS FOR CRITICAL MANUFACTURING SECTOR

1. Make the conscious decision to shift the culture. Cyber resiliency builds upon existing foundations and brings cybersecurity into the modern era, but it requires a cultural, top-down shift to agility and adaptability in the face of an incident.
2. Plan to fail or fail to plan. Of course, we must continue efforts to prevent an incident but also expend effort to understand the impact of failing to prevent the incident. Plan on the incident occurring in addition to trying to prevent it.
3. Have a deep level understanding of all assets in the environment, what they do, how they do it, and the impact on the industrial process should they become unavailable.
4. Invest in advanced technologies.
5. Invest in consequence reduction efforts. Tactics such as using layered technologies can help limit the impact of an attack by created barriers for attackers. Using various complementing OS's, protocols, manufacturers, and the like can limit the scope of ransomware or zero-day attacks. OT Safety Instrumented Systems frequently follow this methodology by using a different vendor for ICS than SIS.
6. Develop 360-degree situational awareness of all aspects of the operation. Monitor as much as possible, seek anomalies and look for known or unknown attacks at all possible layers in the technology stack. Be able to compare what you see today to what was there last week and last month. Know the details of every device in the enterprise. Plan for various types of failures, have resiliency plans to continue operations in the face of those failures.

4.1.7 HOW THE GOVERNMENT CAN ASSIST THE CRITICAL MANUFACTURING SECTOR OF TOMORROW

1. **Deter:** One of the strongest forces available to defenders is deterrence and consequence of actions. This typically requires law enforcement or other government cooperation because it's not in the hands of private organizations. Strong actions in the form of sanctions, offensive cyber operations, and other consequences are crucial to the success of the defenders.
2. **Lead:** Continue efforts leading the various CI Sectors in the form of information sharing, collaboration, partnerships, reports, and warnings. Rapidly expand upon the capabilities in place at CISA.

3. **Deny:** Push legislation that makes it easier for defenders to defend, such as denying attackers access to advanced technologies. For example, denying attackers access to US-based cloud technologies could have helped defenders in the SolarWinds breach by forcing the attackers into the international cyberspace, and under the purview of more advanced and equipped defenders, like the National Security Agency (NSA). Another historical example is denying access for strong encryption.

4. **Streamline:** The government itself has also been victim to the same attacks that have plagued private industry and also needs access to cutting edge, advanced technology from the marketplace. Streamlining the acquisition process would allow technology vendors to free up resources to build the necessary programs to accommodate federal regulations meant to protect federal systems. If the regulations are costly and burdensome for tech vendors, many will avoid compliance altogether or take shortcuts. By combining Secure Software Development Life Cycle (SSDLC) and other relevant frameworks (such as National Institute of Standards and Technology [NIST]) as up-front requirements with making acquisitions easier, vendors will be persuaded to make secure products.

5. **Innovate:** Promote innovation through grants and partnerships. Leading edge thought leadership will be key to powering critical technologies such as Artificial Intelligence.

6. **Inspire:** Fill the skills gap. Continue efforts to train the next generation of cyber operators that will innovate and defend the critical infrastructure of tomorrow.

4.1.7.1 ABOUT THE AUTHOR

Chris Grove, CISSP, NSA-IAM, serves as a Technology Evangelist at Nozomi Networks, where he brings more than 25 years of cybersecurity experience with deep knowledge of IT, OT, and IoT networks and mission-critical infrastructure. His prior experience includes managing large, critical and complex security projects around the world for customers of leading IT and OT security vendors. Security executives turn to Chris for his expertise in almost every sector including commercial, government, defense, law enforcement, and the intelligence community.

REFERENCE

1. D. SNYDER et al., "Measuring Cybersecurity and Cyber Resiliency", Rand.org, 2020. [Online]. Available: https://www.rand.org/content/dam/rand/pubs/research_reports/RR2700/RR2703/RAND_RR2703.pdf. [Accessed: 18- Sept- 2021].

5 Dams

5.0 ABOUT THE DAMS SECTOR

Laura Whitt-Winyard
CISO, Malwarebytes

The United States' critical infrastructure sector for Dams is not limited to the dams themselves but a vast variety of water-related services. The immense scale of this sector means that opportunities for cyber security events are plentiful and with sweeping consequences. Before moving into the cyber security aspect of this sector, one must first understand the sector itself. In the United States, there are more than 90,000 dams. Of those, 64% are privately owned or managed, 20% are owned or managed by local government, 7% are owned or managed by state government, 4% are owned or managed by public utility and just 4% are owned or managed by federal government. The average age of a dam is 57 years old. There are ten states with the most high hazard dams, which means a failure or mis-operation would likely cause the loss of human life. For example, between the great states of Missouri, Texas, and North Carolina, there are a combined total of 4,181 high hazard dams.

Moving on from the dams themselves, the water retention control services touch every aspect of human life in every single state. In the pacific northwest, 60% of electricity is generated by hydroelectric power and in New York State it is 23%. Municipal water supplies come from reservoirs created by dams and makes up a large percentage of the nation's drinking water. More than 87% of the US population relied on public water supplies, and approximately 148,000 publicly owned water systems provide piped water for human consumption in 2020, of which 78% of the population receives their water from only 9% of the community water systems. Sediment and flood control protect 43% of us population. Around 10% of the US croplands are supplied with agricultural irrigation stemming from dammed waterways. River navigation for inland bulk shipping is comprised of approximately 600 million tons of us cargo resulting in $229 billion per year. These 12,000 miles of inland marine networks rely on locks to move valuable products around the US such as 60% of farm exports for travel through inland waterways for export overseas as well as 20% of coal for US electricity. Not only do dams and waterways provide life sustaining services, but they also provide prime recreational facilities such as water skiing, canoeing, boating, fishing, and swimming. According to the US Bureau of Reclamation, recreation and tourism is the largest industry within the western US and the second-largest employer in the United States as a whole. Public waters make up a $40 billion dollar recreation industry. Water is essential for all living things and has a profound impact on the daily lives of the US population, its' economy and safety.

5.0.1 ABOUT MALWAREBYTES

Malwarebytes is a offers innovative, robust, and tech-effective cybersecurity and privacy solutions to consumers, large and small businesses, and the public sector. They are trusted by families, businesses, and critical infrastructures for their effective, intuitive, and inclusive security and privacy solutions.

DOI: 10.1201/9781003243021-5

5.1   UNDER-FUNDING DAM SECTOR CYBERSECURITY LEADS TO A FLOOD OF THREATS

Laura Whitt-Winyard
CISO, Malwarebytes

5.1.1   INTRODUCTION

In May 2020, industrial cybersecurity company Dragos stated that "Water has always been the one industry that is least resourced and the most capable of causing impact to life and safety." The facilities from dams to locks to water treatment plants more often than not are underfunded and have a limited number of technical staff responsible for the day-to-day operations as well as cybersecurity. They are typically generalists with a finite understanding of cybersecurity and even less time to dedicate to cybersecurity efforts, education, and training. Industrial control systems were designed to last many decades spanning 20–30 years to be amortized by public utilities. However, funding was not built in to maintain these systems for as long as they were designed to last. As they were originally designed, they were never intended to be connected to the internet. In today's modern age, everything, including these legacy industrial control systems, now has an internet protocol address and at some point, if not already, will be connected to the internet. In the past year, with the onslaught of the COVID-19 pandemic, exposing these systems to the internet has become a necessity as workers are mandated to work remotely to maintain CDC social distancing requirements and ensure continuous operation of facilities. That connection opens up a whole world of vulnerabilities and exploits, leaving this critical system exposed for bad actors to take advantage.

Case in point, on February 5, 2021, just two days before Super Bowl LV, a suburb of Tampa Bay, Florida, announced that a bad actor had gained access to the water treatment facility by using an employee's credentials acquired through a phishing campaign to authenticate to remote access software. This software was used by water treatment facility staff to operate and maintain the systems, as a result, the COVID-19 pandemic pushing many workers to work from home. Someone remotely accessed a computer, using this remote access software, for the city's water treatment system using compromised credentials and increased the amount of sodium hydroxide to 100 times the normal level. While safeguards were in place to prevent contaminated water from entering the Oldsmar, Florida, water supply, this incident should serve as a reminder that more needs to be done. Cybersecurity professionals have touted that many such types of attacks are precursors or "tests" for similar attacks on larger facilities. One could hypothesize that this particular attack could have been a test for an attack on the Tampa Bay water supply during Superbowl Sunday. Attacks on dams, hydroelectric power, locks, levees, water treatment facilities appear very low providing a false sense of security. It is suspected that these reports of attacks are low since there is no mandate to publicly report such attacks.

Despite recent prolific attacks, efforts are underway to secure the Dams sector. The Department of Homeland Security's CISA (Cybersecurity and Infrastructure Security Agency) Dams Sector-Specific Agency has drafted guides, plans, and training in order to aid the sector in its efforts to improve its cybersecurity preparedness and create a robust cybersecurity posture. There is a Suspicious Activity Reporting tool for sharing information among others in the Dams sector with a high focus on physical security and less so on cybersecurity. Because the vast majority of the sector's assets are privately owned and operated, Homeland Security Information Network—Critical Infrastructure (HSIN-CI) has created the Dams Portal, which is an information sharing network that provides situational awareness and allows sector partners to effectively access and disseminate sensitive but unclassified information among federal, state and local agencies and the private sector. America's Water Infrastructure Act (AWIA) of 2018 requires water systems serving more than 3,300 people "to develop or update risk assessments and emergency response plans," including assessing the security of any electronic, computer, or other automated systems that community water system uses and must self-certify to the Environmental Protection Agency (EPA) by specified dates. Unfortunately, much of what has been done or mandated to date offers little incentive to implement cybersecurity controls and best practices. The National Institute for Standards and Technology (NIST) Cybersecurity Framework (CSF), which was developed to help organizations to better understand and improve their management of cybersecurity risk, lists five pillars, Identify, Protect, Detect, Respond, and Recover. Only one of those pillars, Identify, is being addressed in the aforementioned.

From a technical perspective, the Dams Sector should prioritize their budget to do what can be done now by identifying quick wins and implementing them without delay. As an example, the SCADA Modbus protocol was published in 1979 for use over ethernet, and it is unauthenticated and unencrypted. It should no longer be used and be replaced by more secure options. Implementation of strong passwords is no longer enough, and therefore multi-factor, or two-factor authentication must be used, especially in remote access software. Similarly, no hardware should have hard coded passwords. All forms of communication should be encrypted and monitored including radio communications and cellphones should never be allowed to connect to head ends. Threat hunting should be routine by monitoring communication and network traffic patterns to identify suspicious activity and investigated for possible attack vectors and reconnaissance by nefarious actors. Any system in which the vendor is no longer in business should be replaced for ones with active support and updates and establish trusted relationships with those vendors. Design layers of trusted and protectable systems by protecting crown jewels from less protected systems with a minimum of 3-5 layers. Information Technology systems should be segregated from operations systems. A bi-annual review of firewall rules is recommended with a focus on the removal of temporary rules, access from the corporate network to ICS and vendor access rules. A review of access management to reduce the number of domain administrators, reduce or eliminate privilege on service accounts, remove any default credentials and ensure access is still appropriate.

There is much that can be done with a partnership between the Dams Sector and the cybersecurity community as a whole. For instance, bug bounty reward programs by which individuals can receive recognition and compensation, thus encouraging security researchers to identify and submit reports pertaining to security exploits and vulnerabilities. These programs allow the developers to discover and resolve bugs before the general public is aware of them, preventing incidents of widespread abuse. The United States Department of Defense (DOD) have been using bug bounty programs, notably their Hack the Pentagon events. The Pentagon's use of bug bounty programs is part of a posture shift that has seen several other US Government Agencies (Hack the Army, Hack the Air Force, etc.) to change course from the legal recourse avenue in which exposing a vulnerability or exploit related to the US Government warranted jail time to inviting the public to participate as part of a comprehensive vulnerability disclosure framework. A bug bounty program for Industrial Controls Systems would help offset the work needed by Dams Sector technologists. In January 2020, the first-ever Industrial Control Systems "Pwn2Own" or hacking contest was held in Miami, Florida. The three-day contest place ICS products at the mercy of hackers. This type of information and even participation by ICS vendors and users would prove beneficial. Another partnership to consider is with non-profit organizations such as the Institute for Critical Infrastructure Technology (ICIT), which can provide advisory and education. ICS Village, a not for profit established in 2018 that equips industry experts and policymakers with tools to better defend the nation's critical infrastructure. ICS village has partnered with Dragos to help provide community outreach and support for hands-on global ICS cybersecurity education through an interactive learning approach that invites people to get their hands on equipment to develop their skills bridging the gap between ICS systems and cybersecurity knowledge.

Since the majority of privately owned and managed Dams sector infrastructure companies have underfunded and understaffed information technology teams and tools, financially incentivizing cybersecurity seems the most logical option. Congressman Ted W. Lieu and Senator Edward J. Markey introduced the Cyber Shield Act to the 115th and 116th congress, which would establish an advisory committee of cybersecurity experts from academia, industry, consumer advocates, government, and the public to create cybersecurity benchmarks for Internet of Things (IoT) devices. During one of the Institute for Critical Infrastructure Technology discussions of the Cyber Shield Act, an idea was brought forth to actually issue a shield to be displayed on products that had proven superior cybersecurity (similar to the Energy Star rating program run by the US EPA and Department of Energy) allowing consumers to make the decision to buy more secure products. In the case of the Dams Sector, rate increases by Public Service Commissions (PSC) and Public Utility Commissions (PUC) for water, sewage, irrigation, lock fees, hydropower, etc., would only be permitted if a satisfactory cyber security rating were issued and made public. Similar to the AWIA act, grants could be issued for shoring up cybersecurity and removal of legacy systems and protocols. There must be a clear mandate to fix, not just assess the problem with clear guidelines on who is responsible for fixing them (vendors, utilities, regulatory agencies, etc.). Issuing new regulations, historically, has proven ineffective, as is evident by the sheer increase in cybersecurity attacks and data breaches. These regulations foster a "check the box" mentality and are merely a start to increasing cybersecurity posture.

5.1.1.1 About the Author

Laura Whitt-Winyard, CISM, CISA, CRISC, RSA-ACA, is the CISO of Malwarebytes. Prior to her time at Malwarebytes, Laura was the Global CISO at DLL Group, the Director of Security for Billtrust and has held senior leadership positions in security at Comcast and Bloomberg, LP. Laura has been a member of the cybersecurity community for nearly 20 years, is an ICIT Fellow, and was featured in the book *Women Know Cyber: 100 Fascinating Females Fighting Cyber Crime*. She and her teams have been nominated for and the recipients of many awards spanning multiple years such as ISE® North America & Northeast Project Nominee & Finalist, ISE® North America & Northeast Executive of the Year nominee, CSO 50/40 Awards winner, RSA Archer Innovation Awards & Excellence Awards.

6 Defense Industrial Base

6.0 ABOUT THE DEFENSE INDUSTRIAL BASE

Travis Rosiek
Chief Technology and Strategy Officer, BluVector

Robert F. Lentz
President and CEO, Cyber Security Strategies, LLC

The Defense Industrial Base (DIB) Sector is the worldwide industrial complex that *enables research and development, as well as design, production, delivery, and maintenance of military weapons systems, subsystems, and components or parts* to meet US military requirements. Thus, making the DIB data rich and prime targets for adversaries. As there are many threats facing the DIB, cyber threats have been of particular focus. Post 9-11, as we entered the early stages of persistent cyber threats against the US and especially the DIB, the Secretary of Defense authorized the establishment of the DIB cyber security (CS) program. Initially, the DIB CS Program was started with only our top industry partners who were under constant attack by adversaries to steal very valuable technology, some of that intellectual property now being used against US vital interests around the globe. The DIB is now open to all cleared defense contractors. The DIB CS program is built upon a strong, trusting relationship between DoD and Industry participants. DoD preserves the integrity of the program to protect sensitive non-public *information from unauthorized use and disclosure*.

After 15+ years, the DIB has facilitated increased awareness and cooperation but has not kept pace with the changing tactics, techniques, and operational speed of a growing array of cyber adversaries who not only desire advanced technology but can now disrupt operations anywhere and anytime. Plus, because the DIB comprises thousands of companies, it represents the most tangible example of supply chain risk management or, should we say, Mismanagement. The implementation of the Cyber Maturity Model Certification (CMMC) should help, but the bottom line is without expediting, higher levels of cyber security maturity will leave the DIB and US national security in a very perilous situation beyond today's dangerous posture. The good news is that commercial technology is now available to speed up the achievement of the highest order of cyber security maturity, especially proactive and predictive threat and vulnerability information sharing, faster threat detection, reduction in triage times with less time wasted on tracking down false positive alerts, advanced identity security and encryption. A more modern form of information sharing will go a long way in fostering more effective and longer lasting mitigations to threats. As cyber threat actors dynamically evolve their attack tools and techniques and leverage artificial intelligence to gain the upper hand, we too must evolve. Sharing signatures for malware that only detects a specific instance is like fighting the last war and must evolve such that what is shared to detect malware will be effective for more than seconds. We have already lost a treasure of IP and must immediately change our strategy and investment approach to stop the bleeding and turn the tide, so we as a nation begin to get the upper hand.

6.0.1 ABOUT BLUVECTOR

BluVector, a Comcast Company, is a leader in network security that empowers security teams to get answers about real threats and allows businesses and governments to operate with greater confidence that data and systems are protected.

DOI: 10.1201/9781003243021-6

6.1   ACCELERATING DIB CYBER SECURITY AND INFORMATION SHARING TRANSFORMATION

Travis Rosiek
Chief Technology and Strategy Officer, BluVector

Robert Lentz
President and CEO, Cyber Security Strategies, LLC

6.1.1   INTRODUCTION

As we have learned over the last couple of decades, the Cyber Domain levels the playing field and adds tremendous risk to the United States public and private sectors who have become dependent on the Internet. As there are no borders in the Cyber Domain, it is a global problem. To make matters worse, cyber adversarial capabilities are advanced, ever evolving, well-resourced and have already penetrated a significant portion of the Defense Industrial Base (DIB). Investing in the status quo or incremental advancements will not turn the tide. It is imperative to understand that doing more of the same will not adequately protect the DoD's supply chain or critical infrastructure. Information (signature) sharing must be reinvented, and the adoption of the Cyber Maturity Certification (CMMC) framework is insufficient and must be evolved to a more "dynamic protection" and "continuous performance" basis. As this paper focuses on the DIB Sector within the Department of Homeland Security (DHS) Critical Infrastructure (CI) sectors, the concepts can easily be applied to the other 15 CI sectors. Dynamic protection can include Artificial Intelligence/ Machine Learning (AI/ML)-based detection at different layers of the security stack to dramatically increase the effort and cost inflicted on cyber adversaries. This application, as an example of dynamic protections, does not rely on signatures and thus will require cyber adversaries to work much harder to attempt to overcome these types of defenses. A DIB-sponsored cyber security performance model *as a complement to the CMMC* warrants discussion. We also recommend organizations focus on outcome-based cybersecurity because there are limitations that come with check the box compliance. It's imperative for organizations to focus on outcomes and not the output of a checklist. More companies achieving levels 4 and 5 are imperative, and another possible solution may be to offer these companies preferred scoring in the acquisition process (e.g. SDVOB, SBA, 8(a), etc.).

Real cybersecurity maturity is not achieved by passing an audit (snapshot in time), it is achieved when an organization's people, processes, and technologies work well together 365 days a year and, most importantly, adapt when under stress by external factors. The CMMC framework is focused on assessments for hygiene and static compliance and, if unmodified, will increase risks to DIB/ supply chain and national security and, in fact, increase the likelihood of major compromise. The concept of CMMC is a great first step as it begins to hold organizations accountable for not investing in cybersecurity, however, the steps to achieve compliance must align with the desired effect and the reason why it is so critical.

There is a growing concern with the cybersecurity of supply chains given the most recent Solar Wind's breach. CMMC's initial focus and resources will be on accessing the DIB for cybersecurity maturity and how bad the problem is and will put less focus on aggressive action to mitigate cyber risks to the DIB and critical infrastructure. Therefore, it is imperative for national security to move beyond process intensive information (signature) sharing, basic implementation of cyber hygiene and static controls (such as required in CMMC Levels 1–3), reconsider those systems covered by CMMC Level 3, and most importantly accelerate the implementation of "dynamic protection" and "continuous performance" (such as those required in CMMC Levels 4 and 5) (CMMC 2021).

As nation-state threat actors have been, and continue to be, the biggest risk to the DoD's supply chain and intellectual property, the Defense Industrial Base (especially small and medium businesses) is still vulnerable to pervasive nation-state cyber threats as they continue to evade traditional signature and threat intelligence-based detection as well as other cyber defense tactics, techniques, and procedures.

6.1.2   UNDERSTANDING THE DEFENSE INDUSTRIAL BASE

It's important first to understand where the DIB has been to best determine where to go next. In 2008, US Deputy Secretary of Defense Gordon England recognized cyber threats to the Defense Industrial Base (DIB) represented an unacceptable risk of compromise to sensitive DoD information. To "Stop the Bleeding," he directed the DoD CIO to establish a multi-dimensional pilot program with the top 16 Defense Industrial contractors to operationalize a joint effort to combat escalating penetrations to steal critical intellectual property. In those early days of Cybersecurity, it was clear our most trusted and sophistical defense partners in the industrial base were woefully unprepared to mitigate adversarial Internet-based threats and that an effective public and private sector partnership was immediately necessary. While better government cooperation and coordination with key vendors were critical, it was simultaneously essential to deploy advanced commercial industry architectures and tools to support the very fragile and dispersed defense supply chain.

Over the last decade, since the DIB "voluntary" cybersecurity program was launched, key pillars of the original strategy have been implemented to increase awareness, raise the security bar, and initiate a more effective response. The DoD-DIB Collaborative Information Sharing Environment (DCISE) is a good example of having successfully grown to hundreds of mission critical vendors. In 2019, the DoD kicked off the Cybersecurity Maturity Certification (CMMC) program to expand adherence to the entire industrial base. The CMMC is an extension of Gordon England's original tasking from 2008, where he demanded the DoD leadership and critical partners focus on a unified cybersecurity vision and strategy. The good news is DIB membership has increased exponentially, threat awareness is much improved, and after fighting through many bureaucratic and legal hurdles, the Defense acquisition system is positioned to bring better accountability to the DIB. One of the big and costly differences between DIB voluntary and CMMC is not the regulatory and cybersecurity requirements but the 3rd Party certification. As we both heavily influenced and analyzed the DoD's internal cybersecurity assessments, inspections, and certification efforts, we know how resource intensive it is for organizations to surge to close vulnerabilities as to pass an audit on some multi-year schedule. The thinking was this is how success was measured versus investing to achieve the desired effects of withstanding sophisticated cyber adversaries.

6.1.3   FOUNDATIONS OF EFFECTIVE CYBERSECURITY

The Confidentiality-Integrity-Availability (CIA) Triad has been a foundation of cybersecurity over the years, where C stands for Confidentiality, I for Integrity, and A for Availability. However, during our time in the DoD, we measured Cyber readiness/maturity by using a triangle that revolved around people, process, and technology depicted in Figure 6.1.1. If an organization had a weakness in any of those three areas, the effectiveness of their cybersecurity program became diminished. All three build off of each other, and organizations that have weak processes and rely solely on legacy toolsets likely have trouble recruiting and retaining a strong technical talent.

For example, if an organization lacked in processes when a crisis or incident occurred, the time lost while they tried to create processes on the fly exasperated the impact. On the other hand, if they lacked skilled analysts, then attacks likely slipped by on their watch regardless of having sound processes or technologies that identified malicious actors. Lastly, if the organization had legacy tools that would not provide advanced analysis and views that kept pace with cyber adversaries, then their analysts would likely miss the attack as well.

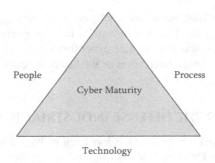

FIGURE 6.1.1   Cybersecurity maturity triangle.

The CMMC is a vital component for identifying the optimum path for businesses to mature their cybersecurity practices and policies while also creating a much-needed framework and sense of urgency to do so. Lack of rigor, transparency and control in cybersecurity processes introduces unacceptable risk into the DIB supply chain and our nation's capabilities. Static compliance requirements are necessary to set the minimum level of security and help build a strong foundation, but it is critical that checking the certification box should include security controls that are less rigid and actually are required to evolve rapidly to mitigate dynamic threats. One other key point is that audits don't always account for context and operational aspects of cyber risk to an organization and thus becomes counterproductive. A better balance is needed in some cases to achieve the desired effect of protecting the DoD, DIB, critical infrastructure from cyber adversaries. But in the face of systemic, nation-state threats to small and medium businesses, compliance alone will not ensure sufficient cybersecurity performance. This is only amplified by the fact the adversary has had a decade's head start and may already have infiltrated many organizations that are deemed trusted, which in turn can also be used to conduct attacks by leveraging technical and nontechnical trust relationships. Achieving compliance does not mean an organization is secure. That has far too often been the objective of many public and private organizations over the years, consuming a large portion of budget focusing on outputs, not outcomes.

The deliberate adversarial targeting of our contractor base continues apace. Sophisticated nation-state threats continue to wreak havoc with government programs and the companies (small, medium, and large) which support them. One of the motives is to steal as much intellectual property from as many companies as possible, and this has been incredibly successful. Another motive that garnered a lot of attention at the end of 2020 was the targeting of the vendor supply chain and distributing malicious backdoors via a vendor's legitimate software update process. The Identity Theft Resource Center's (ITRC) 2020 Data Breach Report noted that supply chain attacks are gaining in popularity as they are an easier way for attackers to gain access to larger organizations or to multiple organizations via a single attack.

The problem is particularly acute for small, innovative firms. In many cases, these firms have to break through a Lowest Price Technically Acceptable (LPTA) dominated procurement model to get noticed and often trade security for "time to market" and a "return on investment." Devoting additional resources and time to meet previously unmet compliance requirements is a heavy burden for many small businesses. The LPTA model all but ensures that security isn't baked in and companies know they can only win by cutting costs (overhead is the easiest place to cut). As we know, cybersecurity is a tough and expensive problem, bare minimum is all that the DoD should expect their supply chain will meet. Solving this problem must go above and beyond CMMC and also look at rethinking the favor of the LPTA model.

While the industrial base transitions its cybersecurity resources to a compliance/conformance model, it is our assertion that insufficient resources are being devoted to actual cybersecurity performance against the very threats driving the need for CMMC in the first place. Too much attention will be focused on achieving the check the box compliance requirements of CMMC and not enough on implementing effective cybersecurity technologies, processes, and training programs. We are very familiar with the limited cybersecurity workforce and that spending more is not a silver bullet. We believe that reprioritizing finite resources will go a long way, but some targeted budget increases will likely be necessary to fill gaps. The time has come for CMMC to drive complementary performance milestones and reinventing government information sharing programs to better ensure the DIB/critical infrastructure. This is not only to achieve compliance, but the ultimate goal of effective cybersecurity for their organization and is sustainable 24/7. CMMC and referenced NIST guidance (SP800-171b, SP800-172, et al.) drive continuous monitoring practices, but when 3rd Party Assessor Organizations (3PAOs) conduct audits, they are only a snapshot in time and are challenged to assess the continuous monitoring requirements (NIST 2021). It is not uncommon where compliance driven programs are gamed such that risky systems are turned off to meet a snapshot in time compliance effort for a few days or weeklong assessment. It is important to not have a *false sense of security* by believing that because organizations are compliant or because they are members of an information sharing program, that they are secure. Adversaries are opportunistic and target victims when they are most vulnerable (e.g. gaps in laws/process, change in CISO or security leadership, snowstorms, a pandemic, etc.).

A DIB-sponsored cybersecurity performance model *as a complement to the CMMC* warrants discussion. Performance metrics can be established across an agreed-upon cyber-attack profile (e.g. the MITRE ATT&CK Framework) (MITRE 2021). It is imperative that organizations leverage adequate detection technologies that don't rely solely on signature updates, have staff that are trained in cybersecurity, and have effective processes in place. Process maturity models which address post-breach circumstances should also consider practices and processes and technologies which prevent the breach in the first place. The dynamic protection model should equally account for pre-emption, then solely reaction.

6.1.4 FIGHTING THE LAST WAR

Fundamentally, many organizations and the DoD spend a very large amount of their security budgets on assessing and achieving compliance. The historical approach is very reactive in nature and thus contributes to the success of cyber adversaries. Reactive cybersecurity is by far the norm and is heavily influenced by stale compliance requirements. Reactive cybersecurity programs are like driving a car forward by only looking into the rear-view mirror (i.e. blocking attacks that have already been used/seen as well as trying to maintain patching on known vulnerabilities). This approach provides little protection for what lies ahead and in the cyber domain, which is occupied by very sophisticated and dynamic cyber threat actors. Measuring the root cause of cyber incidents or analyzing metrics from red, blue, and purple team events have identified time and time again that an area that adversaries like to target are gaps that reside in the grey area (i.e. gaps in people, process, or technologies). For years now, cyber adversaries routinely recompile their tools such that they have a new hash (signature), ensuring that the half-life for their tools in the wild is less than a minute. No approach to signature sharing, threat intelligence, or a commercial product that relies on these methods to detect will work and have not for this problem set. Sandboxing was next in line to help mitigate this challenge but is computationally expensive and doesn't scale well (sandboxing was originally intended for automated malware analysis and not detection). It is commonly known that there are gaps in organizations' IT teams and Security teams and adversaries will recompile tools, shifting tactics to attacks where security capabilities have blind spots (e.g. processing limitations, only analyze executable files or completely blind to fileless attacks that use PowerShell or other "living off the land attacks").

Cyber adversaries know very well the security controls necessary to achieve compliance and rapidly adapt their tools and techniques to do just enough to defeat those benchmarks and circumvent gaps in legal authority, skillsets, processes, and security tools, among others. Advertising you are about to add security is also a good motivation for them to target/attack urgently and get entrenched in DIB information systems. Again, cyber adversaries do not have rules or constraints and can even be successful with a very low batting average.

6.1.5   A SMALL DIB COMPANY'S PERSPECTIVE

Out of the approximately 300,000 companies in the US DoD Supply Chain, and more as this relates to Federal/State supply chains, many do not have dedicated cybersecurity teams as they be small consultancy-based firms. Even if they do, they likely do not have teams focused on analyzing cyber threats and applying proactive cybersecurity measures within their organizations. In most cases, these organizations are challenged by the lack of supply of cybersecurity professionals, the high cost to bring on a team, and are even more challenged by the shrinking margins in Defense contracting driven by Lowest Price Technically Acceptable (LPTA) shift in acquisition. Less margin on contracts leaves less discretionary funds to invest in cybersecurity, seen as corporate overhead. Given these constraints and many others, cyber adversaries are the invisible enemy to much of the DoD supply chain ecosystem. However, if dynamic protection becomes part of what must be required to do work with the government, then the security of the DIB/Critical Infrastructure's fate will not rely on discretionary funds from a company's overhead. DIB companies must have a healthy margin that enables them to invest in the future of national security (e.g. cybersecurity, research, education, etc.).

Many of the DIB companies have an unrealistic expectation to achieve high enough levels of cyber maturity, such that their goal is to be capable of thwarting a nation-state level cyber adversary. With a 500k+ shortfall in cybersecurity expertise in the United States alone, a lack of budget to invest in security programs, limited tools, and little or no processes make it a very difficult expectation to assume, let alone achieve success (Cyberseek, 2021). Some of this increased cybersecurity spend will be passed back to the DoD but will be expensive and thus must be very targeted to achieve the desired effects. It is imperative to realize that now is the time to get the solution right for this crisis and not spend a fortune to gain a false sense of security. We cannot afford to revisit this problem in five or ten years.

6.1.6   DIB CYBERSECURITY INFORMATION SHARING PROGRAM

The DIB program has fostered collaboration between the public and private security but only includes a small fraction of the DIB, who are the largest and best resourced in cybersecurity. This is problematic since we are only as secure as our weakest link and cyber adversaries routinely target the weak links in the supply chain and leverage trust relationships to access information from more sophisticated companies. As noted above, this program requires dedicated teams and access to classified systems to participate. Success in securing a supply chain at this scale requires the democratization of the capabilities and insights of the larger organizations such that it can be consumable and repeatable by the less capable. The gap in the haves and have-nots in cybersecurity is vast and is like drawing up plays for a basketball team that include alley-oops, but none of the players on the team stand more than four feet tall. Calling a play doesn't mean it can be executed well enough to be successful.

Fundamentally information sharing programs are also very reactive in nature (block what we know is bad) and do not enable or encourage their community to be more proactive. As noted earlier, the half-life of certain indicators of compromise is getting shorter, even less than a minute. Rethinking the approach of what is shared in these sharing programs and to whom is key to the DIB's ability to thwart nation-state cyber adversaries and protect precious DoD intellectual property.

6.1.7   LASTING EFFECT—EVOLVING INFORMATION SHARING PROGRAMS

Sharing something beyond signatures and indicators of compromise (IoCs), e.g. machine learning-based classifiers built for the DIB, provide detection and protection beyond seconds and could last months or even years. One area that should also be explored is whether building classifiers to detect malware in a classified setting makes the classifier itself unclassified and thus more easily deployable to unclassified settings. This could be a game changer for democratizing cybersecurity for the DIB. This approach is dynamic, more proactive, and supports the theme of dynamic protection. It transforms an organization's approach and complements the reactive aspects of cybersecurity. This approach isn't dependent on sharing what is known as bad for the short time window, which is relevant in the wild, rather, it is sharing a mechanism to detect malicious code/behavior without relying on constant updating of signatures. This will dramatically impede the ability of cyber adversaries to be effective and will be a strong first step in turning the tide for the years to come.

6.1.8   CONCLUSION

Now is the time to implement the right solution(s) to shore up the cybersecurity of the DIB, the supply chain, and Critical Infrastructure. While categorizing and knowing the level of maturity of the entire DIB is valuable, it will only confirm what is already known: A vast majority of these organizations are not prepared or equipped enough to mitigate national level cyber threats. As 99% of the 300k DIB partners will only need to achieve levels 1–3 of CMMC, achieving these basic levels of compliance is very reactive in nature and will not impede threat actors which are most likely targeting them. It is highly encouraged that re-investment (new where necessary) and focus on game changing and proactive measures will better ensure the 99% will be more secure against the determined and adaptive cyber threat actors. Revamping Information Sharing programs to share beyond an ever-growing list of signatures/IoCs and instead share (or potentially build) ML-based classifiers tailored to the threats that target the DIB or Critical Infrastructure. This could be done in a way that allows classified insights to be incorporated into unclassified defensive measures without the risk of exposing national security information in the process and reduce the overhead in getting approvals to share this information.

It has been shown that well-built ML-based classifiers can go months or years without the need for updates to detect ever-changing malware and attacker techniques. Incorporate dynamic compliance requirements that ensure dynamic protections are in place such that they can evolve with, and hopefully ahead of, threat actors automatically. These dynamic compliance requirements should also be incorporated into L1–L3 of the CMMC as they will have the biggest difficulty in adapting to cyber threat actors. Dynamic compliance requirements will also help ensure that 3PAO audits are not only checking static requirements but also assessing the existence of dynamic protections that are effective beyond that snapshot in time. In summary, while there are many foundational aspects to effective cybersecurity that were mentioned above, investing in these key areas for threat detection and response is imperative:

- **Expanding Levels 4 and 5 of CMMC to the masses:** Develop, operationalize and scale mitigations (CMMC Levels 4 and 5) for advanced threat actors, who are currently targeting companies only covered by CMMC Levels 1–3 and have no perceived path to mitigate.
- **Enhance Information Sharing with Machine Learning Classifiers:** Expand beyond signature and IoC sharing to include ML classifier sharing, which reduces the tremendous burden necessary to create, obtain approval to share, and enable their customers to deploy in their environments. Leveraging tools that enable the ability to tailor and deploy ML classifiers will reduce the tremendous burden on organizations and the government while improving their ability to detect new malware created by cyber threat actors.

- **Move to Dynamic Compliance and Protections:** Ensure that compliance requirements and protective measures are defined to dynamically evolve with the adaptive nature of cyber threat actors. For example, the requirement for the use of capabilities that detect file and fileless malware without reliance on signatures. Another example could be for continuous use of automated threat hunting solutions to identify threat actors who may have slipped through the cracks or have been embedded for many years.
- **Consolidated and Enhanced Collaboration:** Cyber adversaries will go after the path of least resistance, which in the cyber domain is the small DIB contractor or vendor in the supply chain. As we are all stakeholders and intertwined in a global economy, being able to effectively communicate and collaborate without fear of retribution (legal consequences of disclosing a breach or security mishap) will ensure a global/industry vertical view that enable all applicable parties to work together effectively and efficiently to minimize the impact. Prime contractors should also be incentivized to work with their subcontractors and enable them to raise their level of cybersecurity as you are only as strong as your weakest link.

6.1.8.1 ABOUT THE AUTHORS

Travis Rosiek is the Chief Technology and Strategy Officer at BluVector. With 20 years of experience in the security industry, Travis is a highly accomplished cyber defense leader, having led several commercial and US government programs. He is known for innovating and executing strategic plans to build the technical capacity across product development, quality assurance, technical marketing, professional services, and sales engineering.

Prior to his role at BluVector, Travis held several leadership roles including CTO at Tychon and Federal CTO at FireEye, as well as senior roles at McAfee and the Defense Information Systems Agency (DISA). Travis graduated with Honors from WVU with a BS in Computer Engineering, BS in Electrical Engineering, and MS in Electrical Engineering w/emphasis in Information Assurance and Biometrics. Travis was one of ten students receiving the US DoD's Information Assurance Scholarship Program (IASP) in 2001, intended to recruit cybersecurity experts into the US DoD.

He helped start and lead several pilots that became DoD enterprise cybersecurity capabilities that are still in use today. He also led the DoD's endpoint security program, red teams, incident teams, CND Tactics, and Analytics team creating playbooks for US Cyber Command, conducting cyber readiness assessments for the DoD and NTSB like investigations for breaches.

Travis is an ICIT Fellow, served as a contributing member to the President's NSTAC, contributing author to NICE Framework, and a public speaker. He also enjoys mentoring cybersecurity professionals and promoting the cybersecurity career field to prospective students.

Robert F. Lentz is the President and CEO of Cyber Security Strategies, LLC. He recently was on the Cyber Security Hall of Fame committee and Presidential Cyber Commission. Mr. Lentz was the first Deputy Assistant Secretary of Defense for cyber security. He wrote groundbreaking policies that set the pathway for operating in cyberspace, including the first offensive cyber security policy, a comprehensive risk management strategy used today as a baseline for NIST, transformative approaches to addressing supply chain vulnerabilities, to include CFIUS, operationalizing identity security with the issuance of the CAC hardware token, the first effort for endpoint security, insider threat mitigation and software security. He spent 26 years at the National Security Agency, where he served in the historic National Computer Security Center with many of the Internet pioneers and ultimately became NSA's Chief of Network Security. In November 2000, he was appointed CISO for the Secretary of Defense, culminating in 2009 assisting the President to approve the Comprehensive National Cyber Security Strategy and DOD Cyber Command. He stimulated unprecedented venture capital investment in cyber technology post 9-11, established numerous international Cyber Security agreements, organized the Defense Industrial Base Cyber Security Program, and launched the Dept of Defense Cyber Security Maturity Model. The maturity model is now the benchmark for certifying the entire defense supply chain and, ultimately, all Federal agencies. He is recognized for creating the centers of academic excellence with now over 200 certified colleges and universities championing Cyber Education and Training worldwide.

REFERENCES

CMMC, DoD Cybersecurity Maturity Model Certification (2021). Retrieved from: https://www.acq.osd.mil/cmmc/

CyberSeek, Supply/Demand Heat Map (2021). CyberSeek. Retrieved from: https://www.cyberseek.org/heatmap.html

MITRE, ATT&CK Framework (2021). Retrieved from: https://attack.mitre.org

NIST, SP 800-172: Protecting Controlled Unclassified Information in on federal Systems (2021). Retrieved from: https://csrc.nist.gov/publications/detail/sp/800-171/rev-2/final

6.2   WHAT IS CMMC AND WHY IS IT IMPORTANT

Dr. Darren Death
ICIT Fellow

6.2.1   INTRODUCTION

The Cybersecurity Maturity Model Certification (CMMC) is a cybersecurity framework and certification model that is designed to increase the security of the Defense Industrial Base (DIB) supply chain. This standard is needed because the DIB as a supplier to the Department of Defense (DoD), can be used as a vector for entrance into the DoD networks. An adversary can infect the DIB and other supplier systems with backdoors that can be used to compromise defense and other governmental systems. Via this vector, the adversary can then infect government networks through contaminated digital components installed on federal networks, exfiltrating critical government information. Additionally, from a contractor-supplied network, Controlled Unclassified Information (CUI) hosted by the contractor can be directly exfiltrated from the vendor bypassing any safeguard or security controls on government systems.

The SolarWinds attack that occurred in 2020 highlights how a government supplier (and supplier to suppliers) can adversely affect the government's cybersecurity posture. Emergency Directive 21-01, which the Cybersecurity and Infrastructure Security Agency released on December 13, 2020, was the beginning of the public disclosure of a cyber-attack that has drastically affected both the security of government and private sector enterprise networks. Requiring suppliers to adhere to fundamental cybersecurity practices is needed. The SolarWinds example clearly shows that the cybersecurity maturity of a supplier can directly affect a purchasing entity's security. A second example published in March 2021 pertains to the Microsoft Exchange messaging software. CISA issued Emergency Directive 21-02 to "Mitigate Microsoft Exchange On-Premises Product Vulnerabilities." This example yet again highlights how a trusted software product within an organization's infrastructure can be leveraged to allow a nation-state attacker to take control and exfiltrate sensitive data from the government and private sector. These examples highlight a need to change how suppliers are required to address cybersecurity within their organizations, as the cybersecurity posture of a supplier can directly impact the cybersecurity posture of the government and private sector.

Sensitive information may be stored, processed, and transported on supplier networks. An adversary can target these networks to exfiltrate this sensitive information without ever attempting to enter the DoD network. The DoD supplier network consists of "hundreds of thousands of independent and competing domestic and foreign companies" [1]. As part of CMMC 1.0, all vendors would require a third party CMMC audit as a condition of a DoD contract award. As we have seen CMMC evolve throughout 2021, changes were introduced to the framework that has relaxed requirements imposed on the DIB. Changes include a reduction in the total number of controls a vendor must implement based on the CMMC level and the requirements for all DIB vendors to receive a third party audit of their CMMC compliance. The development of the CMMC is associated with what is seen as a general lack of commitment from the DIB as it relates to implementing 800-171 security controls required under Defense Federal Acquisition Regulation Supplement (DFARS) 252.204-7012 and severe breaches of sensitive government information that resided on supplier networks.

An interview published with Major General Thomas Murphy in Breaking Defense in 2019 discussed that contractors unable to meet the DoD's cybersecurity requirements would be unable to compete for future contracts [2]. The interview described an environment created within the DoD where its mission could be compromised by its selected suppliers' inaction and their lack of cybersecurity controls. The DoD views it as unacceptable for security vulnerabilities introduced via its suppliers to affect the agency's critical national security mission. The mechanism that DoD will use to address this shortcoming is implementing the CMMC. Contractors that are unable to meet the certification level for a specific contract, General Murphy explained, would not be eligible to perform work for that contract.

At a March 2020 CMMC Conference hosted by DreamPort, a DoD representative described the CMMC's underlying requirements and the expectations that the DIB is expected to satisfy [3]. In an article published by Attila Security from the event, the representative informed the defense contractor community that the contractor community must implement the DoD's new cybersecurity compliance requirements to win new contracts and will be mandatory in all DoD contracts by 2025 [4]. Topics related to requirements and expected costs were discussed at the conference and their importance in securing the DoD supply chain. The above-mentioned DoD leaders' statements clearly show that the government expects its suppliers to comply with essential federal cybersecurity standards and take its suppliers' security seriously.

Before the introduction of CMMC, DIB contractors were responsible for developing, implementing, and monitoring their cybersecurity program. In 2017, the DoD released guidance as part of the DFARS 252.204-7012. This supplement required defense contractors to implement the security controls outlined in NIST SP 800-171, released in 2016. The DFAR rule required that DoD contractors implement and self-attest that their organization has successfully complied with the requirements defined in 800-171. Today, the DoD has determined that 800-171 has not been widely adopted and that action needs to be taken. A key component of CMMC is that the standard will require a third-party auditor certified by the CMMC-Accreditation Board to assess the DIB supplier for compliance with CMMC requirements. This is a significant departure from DFAR 252.204-7012, which allowed the vendor to self-certify themselves as compliant with NIST SP 800-171.

6.2.2 NIST 800-171, CMMC, AND DIB SUPPLIER SECURITY TODAY

The DoD released interim rule DFARS Case 2019-D041 on September 29, 2020, as part of the CMMC 1.0 implementation, reinforcing the vendor community's requirement to adhere to NIST SP 800-171 and establishing the mechanisms that allow CMMC to be added to DoD contracts. This interim rule set a clear strategy for the DoD related to supplier security. While CMMC 2.0 and its accompanying rulemaking are under development, DFARS 252.204-7020 "NIST SP 800-171 DoD Assessment Requirements" is the guidance utilized by vendors to ensure that they meet the requirements from DoD related to cybersecurity and CUI protection.

While CMMC 2.0 is being finalized, suppliers will be required to perform 800-171 assessments using the DoD's assessment methodology in the short term [5]. Once CMMC 2.0 is finalized, suppliers will be required to conduct CMMC third party audits to ensure supplier security. The final subset of DIB suppliers requiring a third party assessment is still being determined by the DoD and has changed to include a more extensive set of vendors since CMMC 2.0 was first introduced. DoD's current assessment methodology requires that suppliers submit a current NIST SP800-171 assessment to the DoD through their Supplier Performance Risk System (SPRS) [6]. Except for where commercial off-the-shelf (COTS) items are procured, all DoD solicitations will be required to perform these assessments. The rule allows the assessments to be conducted at three levels: Basic, Medium, and High. Basic assessments are self-assessments needed for a new contract and the exercise of contract options after November 30, 2020. Once a contract is awarded, the DoD may choose to conduct an audit of the contractor's attestation in the form of a medium and high assessment. The DoD will perform these audits as needed and based on the criticality of the program and data being handled by the supplier.

These assessments are characterized as follows:

- **Basic Assessment:** This assessment is conducted by the contractor through a self-assessment. A company that has wholly implemented all 110 NIST SP 800-171 controls would receive a score of 110. This is the number of CUI requirements that need to be implemented. A weighted score is also provided and is entered into the SPRS system. For vendors that do not have a score of 110, they are required to enter the date they will achieve full compliance.

- **Medium Assessment:** The government conducts this assessment based on the government program's criticality and the contractor's data. The assessment would include a review of the vendor's basic assessment, the artifacts that support the development of the assessment, and interviews with the vendor to understand the supplier's security posture.
- **High Assessment:** The government also conducts this assessment and includes all medium assessment aspects. This assessment will also conduct a thorough review of the contractor's System Security Plan to validate the supplier's implementation of NIST 800-171.

6.2.2.1   CMMC 2.0 AND ITS RELATIONSHIP WITH NIST SP 800-171/172

As CMMC has evolved into its second iteration, the overall framework has been trimmed from five maturity levels under CMMC 1.0 to three maturity levels under CMMC 2.0.

The DFAR interim rule lays the foundation for requiring CMMC as part of DoD contracts. The CMMC comprises three cumulative levels that a contractor must comply with to compete for a contract. An individual solicitation would define the CMMC level that the contractor would need to demonstrate compliance with as part of their qualifications to be awarded the contract opportunity.

- **Level 1 Foundational:** For companies with FCI only. The information managed by the vendor requires protection but is not critical to national security. This level comprises 17 security practices and requires that a company perform basic cyber hygiene practices to protect Federal Contract Information (FCI). FCI data is information generated or provided by the government as part of a contract that allows the vendor to deliver the specified work. The basic cyber hygiene practice encompasses activities such as implementing anti-malware tools and effective management of employee authentication information. This level will require annual self-assessments to be performed by the supplier.
- **Level 2 Advanced:** For companies with CUI. This level contains 110 security practices that align with NIST 800-171. The vendors that fall under the Level 2 requirement for CMMC 2.0 will be required to conduct triennial third-party assessments where critical national security information exists or an annual self-assessment on select programs. In the case of the triennial audit, companies will be responsible for obtaining a third-party audit through a CMMC Third-Party Assessor Organization (C3PAO) before the contract award. For companies that are required to perform annual self-assessments, the vendor will complete and report a CMMC Level 2 self-assessment and submit senior company official affirmations to the DoD SPRS system. It is important to note that the DoD is still determining which vendors fall into the two reporting requirements under this level. As of the writing of this article, it is unclear which vendors will fall under the third-party audit requirement and which vendors will be allowed to self-certify. The need for third-party assessment has grown since CMMC 2.0's first release. This was discussed during the DoD CISO special session Townhall on CMMC held on February 10, 2022 [7].
- **Level 3 Expert:** for the highest priority programs with CUI. This level contains the 110 security practices from NIST SP 800-171, with additional controls being sourced from NIST SP 800-172. Government officials will audit this level exclusively to ensure that proper oversight is given to suppliers entrusted with highly sensitive CUI [8].

CMMC matures the DoD supplier risk management approach by moving away from self-assessments and requiring a third-party auditor to conduct CMMC audits based on the criteria discussed above. With CMCM, all contractors must be assessed by a third-party organization or directly attest to their company's security level with a senior official's concurrence. The third-party assessor will help to ensure that a contractor can demonstrate maturity commensurate with the specific CUI data being managed and the CMMC level being sought related to the organization's security processes and practices.

6.2.3 TAKEAWAYS FOR LEGISLATORS, AGENCY OFFICIALS, AND THE ADMINISTRATION

6.2.3.1 FOCUS ON EDUCATING CORPORATE LEADERS (CEO, CFO, COO)

Securing senior leadership commitment is vital in that the changes required to implement an effective cybersecurity strategy within an organization require that the organization has the appropriate funding and approvals. Cybersecurity should be treated as a strategic investment by the government supplier. A robust cybersecurity focus ensures that an organization is resilient and can resist a cyberattack that could result in lost productivity, business disruption, intellectual property theft, or brand damage. Additionally, implementing these capabilities ensures that the government contracting organization remains competitive. An outreach program would be focused on providing tools and techniques to secure an organization and empower business executives with the information and knowledge to understand how this security focus is an investment in their organization and not just a sunk cost.

6.2.3.2 FOCUS ON SECURITY VS COMPLIANCE

Any standard like CMMC should be scrutinized to ensure that security is improved within organizations and that compliance is not the program's goal. It can be a simple activity to comply with a specific security requirement without improving the supplier's security. When assessing suppliers, care must be taken so that security controls are inspected for serviceability and robustness. An organization should be failed for each control implementation that does not lead to a secure outcome for the organization. Additionally, risk management processes within an organization can allow a supplier to "accept the risk" for practices that ultimately will cause harm to the suppliers' products and services. This acceptance of risk by the supplier ultimately has downstream effects on the government. Any standard must ensure that these types of dangerous risk management activities are discouraged. Organizations should be encouraged through third part audit requirements like CMMC and contract down-selection processes by agencies to make the appropriate security decisions.

6.2.3.3 CMMC SHOULD EXPAND ACROSS GOVERNMENT

Supply chain security is not only a concern for the DoD but also affects all of the government. The SolarWinds attack affected non-DoD agencies providing the requirements to consider implementing supplier cybersecurity requirements across the government. CUI is produced and managed throughout the government. This information can be impacted via insecurely developed contractor services. Additionally, sensitive information can be exfiltrated via improperly secured contractor networks. A whole-of-government approach to supplier security will help ensure that suppliers across the government are developing tools and services that can meet modern cyber warfare challenges. This approach will ensure that suppliers are resilient and provide a more secure operating environment for the government.

6.2.3.4 CMMC SHOULD CONTINUE TO MATURE

An initiative should also be made to ensure that the CMMC framework continues to mature. The SolarWinds vulnerability is an example of a sophisticated threat actor. The continued exploitation of vulnerabilities by the United States adversaries requires that standards and frameworks related to supplier security be reviewed and updated to address the ever-evolving threat. An example of a maturity approach to CMMC is reviewing the applicability and need for a Zero Trust architectural approach within the CMMC framework. A cybersecurity architecture such as Zero Trust should be reviewed and integrated into government and private sector information systems to ensure adequate protection for sensitive and proprietary information. The CMMC framework, as it matures, can include controls that will put into place Zero Trust capabilities that can provide for the security of CUI.

6.2.3.5 VENDOR/SUPPLIER SECURITY DIRECTLY AFFECTS AGENCY SECURITY

Focusing on supplier security will allow the government, over time, to build a more secure, resilient, and trustworthy vendor community. The SolarWinds hack brings into sharp focus how when supply chain security practices are not implemented effectively, government agency and private sector security are affected. Without a strong focus on ensuring that government suppliers are held accountable for their products, services, and networks, agencies will continue to be less secure. CMMC as a standard immediately allows the government to downselect less capable vendors from the bidding process. CMMC narrows down the pool of potential bidders to only the vendors willing to or capable of incorporating cybersecurity maturity into their technical and business processes. By imposing cybersecurity requirements on vendors, the government will have greater security from its supplier community while also strengthening the nation's security through a more resilient focus on corporate security.

6.2.4 TAKEAWAYS FOR THE SUPPLIER COMMUNITY

Contractors that fall under CMMC should ensure that they have a firm grasp of CMMC and how CMMC will affect their organizations, both from certifying to the framework and resiliency. As previously discussed, these requirements are not going away, and the DIB should only conclude that requirements like these will become more robust over time. Some essential takeaway items are mentioned below.

6.2.4.1 PREPARING FOR CMMC AND CYBERSECURITY LEADERSHIP

Cybersecurity leadership within a government suppliers organization must be elevated to ensure that business risks related to an organization's digital footprint are adequately assessed and managed. If an organization has not taken the time to address cybersecurity concerns, now is the time. From a resiliency perspective, cybersecurity must be addressed across a firm's digital ventures to ensure they can be defended against actors that would cause harm. From a competitiveness perspective, organizations in the DIB that are not preparing to meet CMMC set themselves up to be non-compliant with future contract requirements. More information on how to best integrate cybersecurity leadership into your organization can be found in the Doctoral Dissertation The CISO Role within US Federal Government Contracting Organizations: A Delphi Study [9].

6.2.4.2 PLAN OF ACTION AND MILESTONES

The current process related to the 800-171 self-assessment generated by the contractor and entered into the SPRS system allows for Plans of Action and Milestones (POAMs), where a contractor is deficient with a specific 800-171 control. However, the DoD asks for a date where the contractor expects to be fully compliant with 800-171 without any POAMs being in place. CMMC 2.0 does depart from the no POAM approach of CMMC 1.0. However, POAMs are currently expected to be time-boxed and closely reviewed by DoD officials. Ultimately to be compliant with the standard, the supplier must be fully compliant with all CMMC processes and practices at the CMMC level required for the contract.

6.2.4.3 GOVERNMENT AUDITS

The interim rule allows the government to audit the vendor based on a risk determination informed by the government program's criticality or the contractor's data handling as part of a contract. It is incumbent upon the supplier to ensure that they adequately meet the NIST SP 800-171 and have the necessary information and artifacts to support the contractor's self-attestation.

6.2.4.4 SUPPLY CHAIN MANAGEMENT RISKS

Organizations need to initiate a critical review of their suppliers across their digital portfolios to understand their suppliers' and partners' security. Ensure that you are only buying authentic technology from the vendor and that you are not inadvertently purchasing counterfeit/modified equipment/software that could result in organizational compromise. Also, ensure that your suppliers and partners meet the same standards as you are for the deals you have in place. CMMC must be flowed down to all members of a contract.

6.2.4.5 PREPARE TO ADAPT

Changes related to vendor supply chain risk management/contractor security requirements have changed dramatically over the past few years. This level of adaptation should be expected to continue to increase as standards solidify and as threats in the environment cause changes to the standards in response to adversary actions. The new interim DFAR rule change is an excellent example of a new requirement that requires immediate action by the vendor community.

As a prediction, over time, do not expect the levels within CMMC to remain static. In five years, expect to see Level 3 to be replaced with all or a portion of the levels above it. This change in the standard will be in response to needed maturity as we as a nation respond to becoming more secure, and the adversary will need to become more sophisticated as a response.

6.2.4.6 CIVILIAN AGENCY ADOPTION

Additionally, outside of DoD, on October 22, 2020, the Deputy Assistant Commissioner for Acquisitions with the General Services Administration (GSA), Keith Nakasone, stated that GSA would continue to embed cybersecurity requirements within government contracts and that these requirements would be aligned to CMMC [10]. Also, on October 22, 2020, the acting Chief Information Security Officer for the Department of Homeland Security (DHS) stated that the agency is looking at pilots that would include CMMC standards [11]. The key takeaway from the two above examples is to expect an expansion of the CMMC standard within the civilian community to require an additional level of adaptation from the contractor community.

6.2.5 CONCLUSION

While frameworks such as NIST SP800-171 and CMMC have been in place and continue to mature, the recent hacks highlighted by CISA Emergency Directive 21-01 and 21-02 have brought into sharp focus the need for increased scrutiny related to supplier security. The security of an organization's suppliers can directly impact both the government and private sectors' security. While the risk of interconnected supplier networks has been well understood, recent vulnerabilities related to SolarWinds and Microsoft Exchange highlight the impact of a vendor's security program for software purchased and placed onto an organization's enterprise network. The CMMC framework provides a unifying standard to ensure that government suppliers meet a baseline security level. The recommendations outlined in this article offer both government and private sector leaders areas to improve and expand CMMC adoption and mature the CMMC framework in response to the ever-evolving threats against the United States and its suppliers.

6.2.5.1 ABOUT THE AUTHOR

Dr. Darren Death is a proven technology leader with over 20 years of experience deploying enterprise systems for large private and public organizations. Death has led, designed, and implemented large-scale, organizational-wide enterprise IT systems with far-reaching impact.

Dr. Death currently serves on the EC-Council International Advisory Board for TVM (Threat and Vulnerability Management) and as the CISO and serves as the InfraGard Maryland—Cyber Threat Special Interest Group Chief and American Council for Technology/Industry Advisory Council (ACT-IAC)—Cyber Security Community of Interest Program Chair. He serves on the Board of Advisors and as faculty for the Cyber Intelligence Initiative at the Institute of World Politics. Death holds a master's degree in Cybersecurity and Information Assurance and a Doctorate in Information Technology—Information Assurance and Cybersecurity.

REFERENCES

1. "Defense Industrial Base Sector-Specific Plan An Annex to the National Infrastructure Protection Plan," Cisa.gov, 2010. [Online]. Available: https://www.cisa.gov/sites/default/files/publications/nipp-ssp-defense-industrial-base-2010-508.pdf. [Accessed: 12 April 2022].
2. S. Freedberg, "Protect Your Data Or Lose DoD Business: Maj. Gen. Murphy," Breaking Defense, 2019. [Online]. Available: https://breakingdefense.com/2019/12/protect-your-data-or-lose-dod-business-maj-gen-murphy-exclusive/. [Accessed: 12 April 2022].
3. "Defense Industrial Base Cybersecurity Maturity Model Conference," Dreamport.tech, 2020. [Online]. Available: https://dreamport.tech/events/event-defense-industrial-base-cybersecurity-maturity-model-conference.php. [Accessed: 12 April 2022].
4. "CMMC FAQs: Lessons From Katie Arrington's DreamPort 2020 Talk," Attilasec.com, 2020. [Online]. Available: https://www.attilasec.com/blog/cmmc-faqs-lessons-from-katie-arringtons-dreamport-2020-talk. [Accessed: 12 April 2022].
5. "NIST SP 800-171 DoD Assessment Requirements," DFARS, 2022. [Online]. Available: https://www.acquisition.gov/dfars/252.204-7020-nist-sp-800-171-dod-assessment-requirements.ssessment-requirements. [Accessed: 12 April 2022].
6. "SPRS 3.3 Overview Training," DISA, 2022. [Online]. Available: https://www.sprs.csd.disa.mil/. [Accessed: 12 April 2022].
7. "DoD CISO Special Session Town Hall," Youtube.com, 2022. [Online]. Available: https://www.youtube.com/watch?v=74E5V3pjB0s. [Accessed: 12 April 2022].
8. "Cybersecurity Maturity Model Certification Version 2.0," Acq.osd.mil, 2022. [Online]. Available: https://www.acq.osd.mil/cmmc/docs/CMMC-2.0-Overview-2021-12-03.pdf. [Accessed: 12 April 2022].
9. D. Death, "The CISO Role within US Federal Government Contracting Organizations: A Delphi Study—ProQuest," Proquest.com, 2022. [Online]. Available: https://www.proquest.com/openview/8bc490a6fe62c5cce354fc75ae78d902/1?pq-origsite=gscholar&cbl=51922&diss=y. [Accessed: 12 April 2022].
10. J. Edwards, "Keith Nakasone: GSA to Continue Adding Cyber Requirements Into GWACs," GovConWire, 2020. [Online]. Available: https://www.govconwire.com/2020/10/keith-nakasone-gsa-to-continue-adding-cyber-requirements-into-gwacs/. [Accessed: 12 April 2022].
11. D. Nyczepir, "DHS Considering CMMC Supply Chain Applications," FedScoop, 2020. [Online]. Available: https://www.fedscoop.com/dhs-cmmc-supply-chain-thresa-lang/. [Accessed: 12 April 2022].

7 Election

7.0 ABOUT ELECTION SECURITY: PERSPECTIVES ON PAST, PRESENT, AND FUTURE US POLITICAL CAMPAIGNS

Brigadier General (ret.) Francis X. Taylor
Executive Director, US CyberDome

Joseph Drissel and Matt Barrett
Founder and Director, US CyberDome

As we reflect on the recent 2020 US Presidential and Senatorial elections, it's important to focus on what we have accomplished and what still needs to be accomplished.

Cyber operations by those who seek to undermine the United States are not a new concept in the Defense and Intelligence Communities. However, the role of foreign powers in the 2016 compromise of the Hilary Clinton campaign brought cybersecurity and information operations thereof (like exposing internal-only e-mails) to a wide public awareness. This awareness compelled positive action in preparation for the 2020 campaign season such as the:

- designation of the Election Infrastructure (EI) subsector as a part of the Government Facilities critical infrastructure (CI) sector (January 6, 2017),
- official formation of the Department of Homeland Security Cybersecurity and Infrastructure Security (CISA; signed into law November 16, 2018),
- appropriation of federal funds to DHS CISA and other government agencies for EI, and
- publication of key Federal Election Commission (FEC) Advisory Opinions (AO) throughout 2018–2019 enabling conforming non-profit and for-profit organizations to support political campaigns with cybersecurity products and services.[1]

While these developments are positive for the community, there is still much work to be done. Foundationally, there continues to be much confusion by experts and lay people alike about the differences between election security, EI cybersecurity, and campaign cybersecurity, including whether federal funds can be applied to these communities.

While not well-defined,[2] often phrases like election security are used in an overarching way to include EI and campaign community security concerns. Election security includes cybersecurity, as well as other security concerns such as tamper proofing and auditing voting machines.

EI is a well-defined phrase meaning "storage facilities, polling places, and centralized vote tabulations locations used to support the election process, and information and communications technology to include voter registration databases, voting machines, and other systems to manage the election process and report and display results on behalf of state and local governments."[3] Since EI is a subsector within the Government Facilities critical infrastructure sector, EI can be supported by the Federal government as other critical infrastructure sectors are. Namely, EI receives ongoing and prioritized support from Sector-Specific Agencies (SSA), EI has a Sector Coordinating Council (SCC) as a formal coordination mechanism with the Federal government,

DOI: 10.1201/9781003243021-7

EI has an Information Sharing and Analysis Center (ISAC), and EI receives priority attention from DHS as requested. In other words, EI receives focus and funding from the Federal government, including cybersecurity support from organizations such as DHS CISA.

The campaign community is not formally defined. In the essays that follow, we take our lead from key FEC AOs and consider the campaign community a composite of individual political campaigns (e.g., federal campaign committees) and party committees, as well as the think tanks and vendors that service them. This broad view of the campaign community is separate[4] and similarly complex as the EI subsector. The campaign community's key feature is political campaigns that are necessarily short-lived and singularly focused on voters. These unique properties cause unique cybersecurity challenges, such as aligning the volume and timing of cybersecurity protections with the monumental cyber risks campaigns face.

The risk of not implementing appropriate cybersecurity for the EI subsector and the campaign community is far beyond momentary computer disfunction. The following things are at-stake:

- **Constitutional Rights:** The American People have the Constitutional Right to vote, and Constitutional amendments further our people cannot be prohibited from voting based upon race, color, sex, or age (once 18 years old). When our votes might be modified by an adversary of the United States, we lose our Constitutional Rights.
- **Confidence in Election Outcomes:** The American people are entitled to elections that are fair and free of manipulation. This means the confidence that votes are counted accurately and that votes are cast based upon the true and unadulterated stances of the candidates.
- **Long-Term National Security:** As candidates and their campaign staff become instilled in governmental roles, covert cyber breaches from past political campaigns may be re-activated to access sensitive information within US government agencies. Some of the most valuable information our adversaries seek are non-public political stances and decisions, trade information, and defense secrets. Our candidates and their campaign staff will likely have access to some of this information, and our adversaries are content to wait for those valuable moments.
- **Perception of the United States:** Technical weaknesses in election and campaign infrastructure can lead nations, nation-states, terrorist organizations, and others to believe the United States is weak in general. Beyond our global reputation, this may embolden both physical and cyberattacks on the United States domestically and overseas.

We encourage you to read these essays with the refined lenses of EI cybersecurity and campaign community cybersecurity. While we should not forget the great positive things that have already been accomplished, readers should also keep in mind what is at stake and reflect on their part in avoiding those dire outcomes.

7.0.1   ABOUT US CYBERDOME

US CyberDome (www.uscyberdome.com) is a non-profit dedicated to helping improve cybersecurity in political campaigns and party committees, as well as the think tanks and vendors that service them (collectively, the Campaign Community). US CyberDome provides cybersecurity services to the Campaign Community in adherence to Federal Election Commission guidelines. The objective of US CyberDome is to ensure confidence in election outcomes by protecting the Campaign Community. US CyberDome manages the Political Campaign Information Sharing and Analysis Organization (PC-ISAO), the first ISAO for the Campaign Community, and founded the US CyberDome Education Center, which is developing the next generation of cybersecurity professionals.

REFERENCES

1. Federal Election Commission Advisory Opinions 2018-11 6 September 2018, https://www.fec.gov/updates/ao-2018-11/; AO 2018-12 21 May 2019, https://www.fec.gov/updates/ao-2018-12/; AO 2019-12 11 July 2019, https://www.fec.gov/updates/ao-2019-12/
2. Congressional Research Service, *Campaign and Election Security Policy: Overview and Recent Developments for Congress*, p. 2, https://crsreports.congress.gov/product/pdf/R/R46146
3. https://www.dhs.gov/news/2017/01/06/statement-secretary-johnson-designation-election-infrastructure-critical
4. Congressional Research Service, *Federal Role in U.S. Campaigns and Elections: An Overview*, p. 21, https://crsreports.congress.gov/product/pdf/R/R45302

7.1   ACTION PLAN FOR MORE SECURE CAMPAIGNS— ADDRESSING THE GAPING HOLE IN OUR ELECTORAL PROCESS

Brigadier General (ret.) Francis X. Taylor
Executive Director, US CyberDome

Joseph Drissel
Founder and Director, US CyberDome

Matt Barrett
Founder and Director, US CyberDome

7.1.1   INTRODUCTION

While there was significant improvement in the security of the country's election infrastructure since the 2016 election, little attention has been paid to the primary target of the 2016 attack, the political campaign. That attack vector provided all that Russian intelligence needed to conduct a very successful mis/disinformation attack on our electoral process. That same vulnerability continues to exist in political campaigns. Add to that is the nature of how political campaigns form and operate. They are essentially start-ups with little infrastructure until the campaign gains traction and becomes a more viable contender.

7.1.2   WHAT'S AT-STAKE

The risk of not securing the campaign community from cyber risks is monumental and far beyond a momentary computer disfunction. The following things are at-stake:

- **Confidence in Election Outcomes:** When we lose confidence that votes are cast based upon the true and unadulterated stances of the candidates, we lose confidence in election outcomes. Campaign cyber-attacks can lead to weaponization of information or sensationalism to purposefully discredit a candidate or warp their messages to voters.
- **Long-Term National Security:** When adversaries access non-public political stances, pending decisions, trade information, and defense secrets, we lose our long-term national security. Campaign cyber-attacks allow our adversaries to leverage current and future government roles of candidates and campaign personnel to access this valuable and sensitive information.
- **Perception of the United States:** Technical weaknesses in campaign infrastructure can lead nations, nation-states, terrorist organizations, and others to believe the US is weak in general. This may embolden both physical and cyberattacks on the US domestically and overseas.

Given what is at-stake and typical cybersecurity challenges of political campaigns, it is essential that the government take action to set the stage for more secure elections in 2024 and beyond. Observations and lessons learned over the past 18 months providing support to think tanks, national party committees, and US Presidential candidates indicate the following four imperatives require immediate action.

7.1.2.1   ALIGN POLITICAL CAMPAIGN CYBERSECURITY RISK MANAGEMENT WITH CYBER RISK

There is reason to believe that adversaries are highly attentive to political campaigns from day 1. Cyber risk increases significantly as milestones such as primary wins and party nominations occur.

For instance, the 2016 Hilary Clinton campaign won their first primary (Iowa) on February 1, 2016. The e-mail phishing attack on Hilary Clinton's campaign occurred on March 19, 2016, 8 months before Election Day.

Campaign funding needed to address this cyber risk is typically not aligned with the timing of that cyber risk. Further, the magnitude of that funding is often less than required for the cyber risks campaigns face. Campaigns launch with minimal funding and operate through primary season without a major security budget. Campaign priorities are solely focused on driving turnout for the candidate through advertising and events. This singular focus is sometimes amplified by a lack of understanding of the cyber risks and how to adequately address those cyber risks.

Party committees are often assumed to be taking care of cybersecurity for candidates. Due to campaign competitive sensibilities, true collaborative efforts between campaigns and party committees often wait until a given candidate is formally nominated. This means there is a significant part of the cyber risk timeline where the party committee does not participate in cybersecurity.

We must apply cybersecurity risk management, and the investments thereof, earlier in the campaign lifecycle and commensurate with the actual cyber risk.

7.1.2.2   ADDRESS CYBER RISK OF VENDORS TO POLITICAL CAMPAIGNS

A significant threat to political campaigns is political campaign *vendors*. Campaign information technology exists for a short period of time. Vendor information technology is persistent and reaches across many campaigns and many campaign cycles. Cybersecurity needs to be a significant part of the buying decision in the campaign vendor marketplace. *We must reduce community risk by greatly reducing campaign vendors as a viable path for threat actors.*

7.1.2.3   UTILIZE NON-PARTISAN NON-PROFIT ORGANIZATIONS FOR LONG-TERM EFFORTS AND CAPABILITIES

Political campaigns, especially those of US Presidential, often operate with an unparalleled level of independence. Non-incumbent federal campaigns avoid the use of federal agency services due to competitive sensibilities. Alliances shift rapidly in a political setting, leading to a more conservative approach to partnerships. Even the relationship between political campaigns and their party committees is distant until that party committee makes its nomination. In a world where trust and loyalty is everything, the for-profit interests of private sector are sometimes viewed as competing interests, and for-profit organizations sometimes participate heavily in party politics. These circumstances and views narrow the scope of organizations that can serve as trusted cybersecurity intermediaries between government programs, private organizations, party committees, and political campaigns. *We must leverage non-partisan non-profits to be a trusted broker of cybersecurity in the campaign community.*

7.1.2.4   REFINE POLICY AND LAW TO BE CYBERSECURITY ENABLERS

The Federal Election Commission (FEC) Advisory Opinion (AO) 2018-12 enables conforming non-profit organizations to support political campaigns with cybersecurity products and services.[1] AO 2018-12 was an excellent way to test whether non-profit organizations can serve as trusted intermediaries to political campaigns. The model proved itself with organizations such as US CyberDome and Defending Digital Campaigns facilitating cybersecurity services and products to campaigns.

Other dimensions of this model are not sustainable. AO 2018-12 enables free or reduced cost cybersecurity using in-kind and financial donations. While the campaign community is well-practiced at donor-based funding, non-profits inadvertently ended up competing with political campaigns for donor Dollars. Further, donors were confused by the new and different request for Dollars to support campaign cybersecurity.

We must build on the successes of FEC AO-based efforts by implementing more sustainable funding models.

7.1.3   RECOMMENDATIONS AND ACTIONS

Congress, government agencies, private sector, and the campaign community must take transformative action to better protect the community. The following recommendations and actions are suggested.

7.1.3.1   ALIGN POLITICAL CAMPAIGN CYBERSECURITY RISK MANAGEMENT WITH CYBER RISK

- **Recommendation:** Political campaigns should allocate budget and resources for cybersecurity from their first day of operation.
- **Action item:** Congress should require that Presidential candidates list a qualified Chief Information Security Officer (CISO; or equivalent) as a pre-requisite for initiating a campaign (e.g., in their Statement of Organization). Many 2020 campaigns operated without a cybersecurity leader, and the campaigns that had a CISO hired them long after the campaign's cybersecurity risk had escalated. A qualified CISO should have at least five years of previous CISO experience including two years of expertise in adversarial cyber behavior.

7.1.3.2   ADDRESS CYBER RISK OF VENDORS TO POLITICAL CAMPAIGNS

- **Recommendation:** Both product and service vendors should meet certain standard cybersecurity practices, before being allowed to transact with political campaigns and party committees. The Political Campaign community should evolve buying decisions within the campaign vendor marketplace to use a "seal of approval" indicating vendor cybersecurity best practices and maturity. Campaigns and party committees can use this as a way to make smart buying decisions. Vendors can use this as a way to credential and differentiate themselves.
- **Action item:** Congress should require that service and product vendors to campaigns and party committees have their cybersecurity practices validated as adhering to published standards in cybersecurity best practices. The objective is for vendors to have a clear way to represent their cybersecurity status to campaigns and party committees, so those campaigns and party committees can make an informed buying decision.
- **Action item:** The National Party Committees should *publicly commit to* a community-wide timeline to ensure 100% of service and product vendors to campaigns and party committees have their cybersecurity practices validated. This community-wide timeline will allow for the gradual phase-in of vendor validations to allow both vendors and the campaign community to adjust to a validation-based marketplace. The National Party Committees should administer an exception process to ensure vendor validations do not prevent campaigns from forming or become a significant challenge for campaign operation.
- **Action item:** The National Party Committees should *convene design meeting(s)* with participants from qualified non-partisan non-profit organizations and the National Institute of Standards of Technology to:
  - discuss, document, and publish a fiscally-viable vendor validation model, and
  - identify candidate cybersecurity guidance for vendor best practices.
- **Action item:** The National Party Committees should *convene working group meetings* with participants from:
  - standards development organizations such as the National Institute of Standards of Technology, British Standards Institute or American National Standards Institute,

- accreditation organizations such as the Cybersecurity Maturity Model Certification Accreditation Body, and
- non-partisan non-profit organizations such as US CyberDome

to discuss, develop, and publish standards in cybersecurity best practices and maturity for the political campaign vendor community.

- **Action item:** The National Party Committees should formally *implement vendor validations* by publishing an implementation timeline describing:
  - percentage of validated vendors,
  - (if applicable) validation levels, and
  - by milestone dates.

7.1.3.3 UTILIZE NON-PARTISAN NON-PROFIT ORGANIZATIONS FOR LONG-TERM EFFORTS AND CAPABILITIES

- **Recommendation:** The neutrality of the Red Cross enables it to do things the militaries of the world cannot. Campaign sensibilities about receiving cybersecurity support from federal agencies, for-profit corporations, and party committees indicate a neutral cybersecurity provider is needed. While party committees offer central and persistent cyber capabilities for a given party, cybersecurity outcomes transcend political parties. Non-partisan non-profits are the best way to ensure cybersecurity outcomes are achieved across party lines.
- **Action item:** Congress should require campaigns and party committees, as well as the think tanks and vendors that service them, to participate in a non-partisan cyber threat information sharing community. Historic threats encountered by campaigns and committees do not get broadly communicated. This is a missed opportunity for the community to quickly identify threats and increase protections. To maximize the positive impact for participants, participation is defined as both receiving cyber threat intelligence and sharing cyber threat intelligence. The information-sharing community should not be affiliated with any one political party because cyber threats are non-partisan. Cyber threat intelligence should be anonymized by the non-partisan non-profit to protect the sensibilities of the contributing organization. Member-based models are recommended, such as the information sharing and analysis centers (ISAC) used in critical infrastructure and the information sharing and analysis organizations (ISAO) used in other communities.
- **Action item:** Congress should require campaigns and party committees, as well as the think tanks and vendors that service them, to field detection infrastructure that automatically applies the cyber threat information from the sharing community. This addresses a historic challenge with ISACs and ISAOs. It is common for valuable cyber threat intelligence to be exchanged, only to not have it applied, because a given member organization does not have a technology to apply it.

7.1.3.4 REFINE POLICY AND LAW TO BE CYBERSECURITY ENABLERS

- **Recommendation:** Congress and the Administration should leverage pre-existing and time-tested programs and models to enable cybersecurity protections for the political campaign community.
- **Action item:** The Administration should direct the FEC to evaluate the legality and feasibility of using the pre-established public funding program[2] as a means of providing cybersecurity budgets to political campaigns. Any legality issues should be referred to Congress

for consideration. Receipt of public funding should be free of campaign fundraising ceilings and should require campaigns to:
- implement security policy, plans, and procedures based on best practice and that satisfy all five functions of cybersecurity risk management—identify, protect, detect, respond, and recover (as described in the National Institute of Standards and Technology Cybersecurity Framework), and
- only use vendors that are validated as following cybersecurity best practices (as described above in *Address Cyber Risk of Vendors to Political Campaigns*).
- **Action item:** Congress should support qualifying non-profit organizations (as described above in *Utilize Non-Partisan Non-Profit Organizations for Long-Term Efforts and Capabilities*) to serve as trusted cybersecurity intermediaries between government programs, private organizations, party committees, and political campaigns by:
  - allowing non-profit organizations to provide free or reduced-cost cybersecurity products and services without those products and services being considered a campaign contribution,
  - enable distribution of federal grant monies to non-profits that provide free or reduced-cost cybersecurity products and services to campaigns and party committees,
  - appropriating grant funding to support the efforts of non-profit organizations in providing cybersecurity products and services to campaigns and party committees, and
  - enabling the use of public funding, such as taxpayer donations to presidential elections, as a source of funds for non-profits.
- These actions will implement a public-private funding model for campaign cybersecurity similar to the National Center for Missing and Exploited Children.
- **Action item:** Congress should appropriate grant funding to help small businesses address the expense of political campaign vendor validation (as described above in *Address Cyber Risk of Vendors to Political Campaigns*).

7.1.4   CONCLUSION

We can and must strengthen our capacity to protect the campaign community from cyber-attacks. Campaign cybersecurity is about more than momentary inconvenience when our computers do not work. Confidence in election outcomes and long-term national security is at-stake. The recommendations and actions above will greatly improve the cybersecurity of future campaigns.

7.1.4.1   ABOUT THE AUTHORS

Brigadier General (ret.) Francis X. Taylor is the Executive Director pro tempore for US CyberDome. Brig. Gen. Taylor brings perspective to US CyberDome based on his background as Under Secretary of Homeland Security for Intelligence and Analysis, Assistant Secretary of State for Diplomatic Security, Commander of Air Force Office of Special Investigations, and the US State Department Ambassador at Large and Coordinator for Counterterrorism.

Joseph Drissel is a Founder and Director of US CyberDome, where he helps protect the political campaign community from cybersecurity threats. Mr. Drissel previously had roles such as the Acting Chief of Intrusions for the Department of Defense Computer Forensics Laboratory, the world's largest accredited computer forensics laboratory.

Matt Barrett is a Founder and Director of US CyberDome, where he helps protect the political campaign community from cybersecurity threats. Mr. Barrett was formerly Program Manager of the National Institute of Standards and Technology Cybersecurity Framework, one of the most prevalent world-wide approaches to cybersecurity risk management.

REFERENCES

1. Federal Election Commission Advisory Opinions 2018-11 6 September 2018, https://www.fec.gov/updates/ao-2018-11/; AO 2018-12 21 May 2019, https://www.fec.gov/updates/ao-2018-12/; AO 2019-12 11 July 2019, https://www.fec.gov/updates/ao-2019-12/
2. "Public funding of presidential elections", FEC, 2020. [Online]. Available: https://www.fec.gov/introduction-campaign-finance/understanding-ways-support-federal-candidates/presidential-elections/public-funding-presidential-elections/. [Accessed: 18- Jul- 2022].

7.2   PREPARING FOR THE FUTURE OF ELECTION SECURITY—RECOMMENDATIONS FOR THE 46TH PRESIDENT

The Center for Internet Security

7.2.1   INTRODUCTION

In the wake of the 2016 General Election, two things became clear about election security:

1. Election infrastructure at state and local offices was under threat from nation-states, intent on attacking America's democratic institutions, whether directly or undermining our own confidence in those institutions.
2. Misinformation and disinformation, from sources foreign and domestic, threaten to divide Americans, inflame tensions between us, and further erode confidence in America's institutions.

In response to these growing threats, the Department of Homeland Security (DHS), the National Association of Secretaries of State (NASS), the National Association of State Election Directors (NASED), the Elections Assistance Commission (EAC), as well as local election organizations, and the independent, non-profit Center for Internet Security (CIS) discussed the possibility of creating an ISAC devoted solely to the Nation's elections infrastructure.

In 2018, the US DHS and the Election Infrastructure Subsector Government Coordinating Council tasked CIS to stand up the Elections Infrastructure ISAC (EI-ISAC). Leveraging the services offered and experience gained through 15 years running the Multi-State ISAC, the EI-ISAC is now fully operational with all 50 states and D.C. participating, and over 3,000 total members, including the election vendor community.[1] The EI-ISAC provides elections officials and their technical teams with regular updates on cyber threats, cyber event analysis, and cyber education materials.

Since 2018, and through the 2020 election, the EI-ISAC worked with the election community to establish a variety of programs to improve information sharing; incident response; misinformation reporting; the security of election infrastructure networks, endpoints, procurements, supply chains; and more. Other partners, including Harvard's Belfer Center for Science and International Affairs, the Brennan Center for Justice, have contributed valuable resources in the form of policy recommendations, playbooks, and toolkits for the community. CIS, in partnership with the Cybersecurity and Infrastructure Security Agency (CISA), has served as the leader for technical support, providing security best practice guidance to facilitate stronger cyber defense and suite of provisioned services to augment members' activities.

This cumulative effort resulted in the cybersecurity posture of US elections rapidly closing deficits of investment to protect voting. The 2020 election taught us that, with appropriate focus and resources, we can make progress; however, we also learned that threats are continuing to evolve, sophisticated cyberthreat actors remain determined to attack the United States, and misinformation of all types sow and exacerbate discord and division among Americans.

In short, we have much more work to do. This essay presents policy recommendations for the new Administration to strengthen relationships and collaboration, continue innovating, and mitigate the damage of mis- and disinformation. Many of these recommendations are about CIS and its work, while others are based on our experience with stakeholders across the election community and represent actions that we believe would benefit the community, even if they aren't activities that would have direct involvement from CIS.

7.2.2   CONTINUE THE COALITION

The 2020 election season owed much of its success in cybersecurity to the tireless efforts of election officials and the public-private partnership built over the course of 2016–2020.

The NASS, the NASED, the Election Center, the International Association of Government Officials, and their respective members remain central in running American elections. Collectively, they continue to provide the deep expertise in the complex functioning of administering elections, and how new processes and technology can best be used in each jurisdiction. Other state and local associations like the National Governors Association, the National Conference of State Legislatures, the National Association of State Chief Information Officers, the National Association of Counties, the National League of Cities, the National Emergency Management Association, and others have stepped up and collaborated to identify and facilitate the best approaches to improving the security of election infrastructure.

The election technology providers, public and private universities, think tanks and foundations, and non-profit organizations like CIS have come together to help address the technical, process, and educational challenges facing the US election community. The result is that the protection capabilities of our election infrastructure have been enormously improved from 2016.

Maintaining that momentum is not a given. These partnerships require continued investment to sustain and, hopefully, accelerate the progress we have seen since 2016. The EI-ISAC, through CISA, operates the most comprehensive partnership of election officials and election stakeholders in the United States.

We recommend continued support for CISA's election security efforts and the EI-ISAC.

7.2.3   DEPLOY DEFENSE-IN-DEPTH

CIS implemented a defense-in-depth strategy with a multi-layered set of tools and processes that enable the entire elections community to successfully protect the elections. Leading up to the 2020 election cycle CIS developed a suite of cybersecurity best practice guides for the election community to implement to improve their cybersecurity defense posture. The guidance and tools are based on the globally recognized CIS Controls.

As a part of this defense-in-depth strategy, cybersecurity tools such as Albert Network Intrusion Detection System (IDS), Malicious Domain Blocking and Reporting (MDBR), and Endpoint Detection and Response (EDR), were deployed on election offices systems to provide network security alerts, detection of anomalous behavior and malicious patterns, and blocking of outgoing network traffic to known malicious web domains. We have also begun working with the election community on a coordinated vulnerability disclosure (CVD) program.

These programs, along with the host of services funded by Congress and offered to election officials by CIS in coordination through CISA, provide a powerful set of defensive tools that election officials can employ to protect against the myriad threats facing America's elections.

We recommend continued and expanded focus on this multi-faceted approach to tools and processes that make up the election defense-in-depth suite.

7.2.4   INVEST IN INNOVATION

Our adversaries are constantly innovating. While the progress made in deploying additional technical measures and in education and training since 2016 is impressive, there are opportunities to improve. A danger when addressing the sensitive area of elections is to be overly cautious in assessing and piloting new methods and technical solutions.

CIS has been working to develop and deploy innovative technologies for state, local, tribal, and territorial governments, including election offices, for many years. Expanding on these efforts,

CIS has several innovative projects it expects to conduct over the next few years to advance cyber-security in elections.

We recommend continued efforts to drive innovation and advance technology in elections and encour-age continued support for experimentation and innovation, including each of the efforts below.

7.2.5 RAPID ARCHITECTURE BASED ELECTION TECHNOLOGY VERIFICATION (RABET-V)

Technology innovation is often underpinned by processes innovation. Traditional voting systems are verified against large monolithic standards using lengthy and expensive certification campaigns. The election community has long recognized inefficiencies with this and related processes. It creates disincentives for innovation by making technology updates more expensive and lead times longer.

The RABET-V process focuses initially on the need for non-voting election technology to be responsive and adapt quickly to changes in the threat landscape. In 2020, CIS piloted a much quicker and less costly process for verifying elections systems. The RABET-V process model pro-vides assurances of security, reliability, and functionality in a risk-based, flexible, change-tolerant process. This effort is in partnership with several election technology vendors and a steering com-mittee consisting of the EAC, CISA, the Federal Voting Assistance Program, and the States of Wisconsin, Ohio, Maryland, Texas, Pennsylvania, and Indiana.

Process innovation can lead to technology innovation, resulting in greater assurances of security, reliability, and functionality in a risk-based, flexible, change-tolerant process.

We recommend support for programs such as RABET-V to accelerate the adoption of innovative tech-nologies in election infrastructure.

7.2.6 IMPROVED COLLABORATIVE TOOLS FOR SITUATIONAL AWARENESS

On election days, real-time collaboration is the heartbeat of information sharing. CIS has worked with CISA to deliver a virtual situational awareness room to report on and monitor ongoing cyber-security threats during these critical periods. However, election officials would derive a great deal of value from a more regular real-time collaboration platform that provides expanded features and allows the community to gather and communicate information during non-election periods.

Such a platform would help address threats more comprehensively across the community and augment existing technologies, such as machine-to-machine sharing of threat indicators. The lat-ter allows for rapid distribution of actionable information but can leave analysis of that informa-tion siloed within individual organizations. A collaborative platform could allow election offices to share that analysis and correlate across organizations more broadly.

This type of sharing has sufficiently proven itself in day-of setting and would be a boon to threat mitigation every day of the year.

We recommend additional dedication to developing innovative platforms for information sharing and real-time collaboration.

7.2.7 MANAGING MISINFORMATION

Misinformation reached new heights in 2020. This escalating threat presents a severe risk to the United States in any number of domains, to include elections.

We recommend addressing this issue through a multi-faceted approach by addressing in each of the recommendations below.

7.2.8 INTERRUPT FOREIGN INFLUENCE

Over the last several years, intelligence agencies, social media platforms, and analytics companies increased efforts to stop foreign information operations. These campaigns continue and have expanded well beyond elections.

> We recommend redoubling efforts to disrupt and dismantle foreign information operation campaigns, to include additional analysis and remediation efforts through intelligence agencies and independent organizations.

7.2.9 SERVING ELECTION OFFICIALS

With the support of Democracy Fund, NASS, NASED, CISA, and the Election Integrity Partnership at Stanford University, CIS implemented a misinformation reporting system for the 2020 General Election to assist election officials in reporting a case of election infrastructure misinformation to a single source regardless of the platform(s) on which it appeared.

These efforts to support election officials in 2020 were successful, and we are proud of the work accomplished on their behalf and with their help. As the problem of misinformation grows, we need to scale our solutions to meet the threat by expanding misinformation reporting capabilities for election officials.

> We recommend a strategic focus on meeting the needs of election officials to report misinformation in an efficient, streamlined manner.

7.2.10 PUBLIC EDUCATION ON MISINFORMATION

In 2020, CISA successfully ran multiple campaigns to educate the public on misinformation. The War on Pineapple social media awareness campaign and the Rumor Control website were both highly regarded for bringing attention to the problem of misinformation.

Yet, clearly, more education is needed. Misinformation continues to plague discourse in America and reporting and analysis, while important, must be augmented by education efforts.

> We recommend additional focus and partnership on education and awareness of misinformation through CISA, the EAC, the EI-ISAC, and other stakeholders.

7.2.11 SUPPORT SMALL JURISDICTIONS

The increased efforts in election security have had an uneven impact on local election jurisdictions. Generally, larger, better-resourced jurisdictions can implement the cybersecurity guidance and tools, while smaller, less-resourced jurisdictions struggle to take advantage of even the free resources available to them.

> We recommend additional support for smaller, less resourced election jurisdictions, to include each of the recommendations below.

7.2.12 EXPERTISE AT THE LOCAL LEVEL

Some states have successfully implemented "cyber navigator" programs to support technology deployment and infrastructure development at the local level. When properly implemented, these programs can provide much-needed expertise and a boots-on-the-ground capability that many local jurisdictions would be unable to find elsewhere.

Where possible, local skilled talent can serve in these roles, improving outcomes in smaller communities and providing election officials with individuals they may be more readily included to trust with locally administered elections. This role can also be supported by the National Guard, and in some cases, the Guard has provided this type of expertise to elections offices.

We recommend strong support for the hiring and development of local talent to serve as cybersecurity expertise.

7.2.13   EASIER TO DEPLOY TECHNOLOGY TOOLS FOR SMALLER ELECTIONS OFFICES

The breadth, diversity, and complexity of information technology systems in elections can overwhelm even the best election officials. In smaller jurisdictions, there is often less talent to manage the multitude of systems required to administer an election. In turn, this makes it difficult to manage risks posed by nation-state threat actors.

Developing tools for these jurisdictions requires additional investment as many commercial off-the-shelf cybersecurity tools require too much technical knowledge for an election office with no technologists.

We recommend implementation of appropriate incentives to stimulate focus on developing basic tools and services that can be deployed by highly under-resourced election jurisdictions.

7.2.14   GETTING GOVERNMENTS ON THE .GOV

Far too many election offices don't have .gov addresses. While this was a major push in 2019 and 2020, insufficient progress was made. Moreover, even if given a .gov address, there is still a question of the ability of election officials in some jurisdictions to maintain a site, properly host and secure it, and design it to serve the needs of constituents.

We recommend the federal government

1. *assist smaller local election offices in obtaining. gov services,*
2. *develop a set of simple template website for these offices to use and populate with their own content,*
3. *offer hosting services for these websites and assist states in hosting these sites on behalf of their locals.*

7.2.15   CONFIDENCE THROUGH COMMUNICATION

Despite the impressive security outcomes of the 2020 General Election, confidence in the democratic process continues to erode. A lack of public understanding about election administration and the security of election processes risks undermining the gains that have been made in security.

We recommend an aggressive effort to increase understanding of election administration and increase transparency.

7.2.16   ELECTION ADMINISTRATION: THE STORY OF MODERN DEMOCRACY

Giving the public a better understanding of how election administration works will require a comprehensive state-by-state effort to clearly describe the processes, redundancies, and safeguards built into the system. This must be done through storytelling in a clear, simple, illustrative manner that gives individuals the opportunity to learn the high-level activities down to the details of each process.

We recommend a campaign to develop storybook-style educational material that carefully walks individuals through the details of election administration.

7.2.16.1 About the Center for Internet Security

The independent, non-profit Center for Internet Security is the home of the Multi-State Information Sharing & Analysis Center, the Elections Infrastructure ISAC, and the CIS Critical Security Controls.

NOTE

1. Find out more information about the EI-ISAC here: https://www.cisecurity.org/ei-isac/. For a list of EI-ISAC services see https://www.cisecurity.org/ei-isac/ei-isac-services/

7.3   THE RACE WITH NO FINISH LINE: SECURING THE NEXT ELECTION IN THE WAKE OF 2020

Matthew Travis
Former Deputy Director, CISA

7.3.1   INTRODUCTION

When it comes to election security, there is no rest for the weary. The 2020 elections were successfully conducted, canvassed, and certified just a few months ago, and the protracted contestation of its results and the associated assertions of widespread fraud and rigging were certainly more exhausting and draining on the election community than any election since at least 2000. But there is no time to waste in continuing—and proactively building upon—the existing momentum from the full range of election security measures that have been taken at the local, state, tribal, territorial, and federal levels in recent years, all of which were all instrumental in ensuring that the November 3rd national elections were "the most secure in American history."[1]

Understandably, the new Biden Administration will have to invest most of their time, attention, and resources into the top tier of critical challenges confronting the nation: namely, the ongoing coronavirus pandemic and national economic recovery. *But President Biden and his team must properly prioritize election security, broadly defined for our purposes here, as a national imperative worthy of both Federal investment and his personal involvement. And unlike most of the historical efforts to date, the challenge ahead in election security may be less about modernizing physical election infrastructure and more about fighting election disinformation and reinforcing the understanding of, and transparency in, election systems, processes, and laws among the American electorate.*

Election security is not a once-every-four (or two)-years project. That might be the general impression among many Americans, but it has never been the case within the election community itself.[2] The thousands of earnest, honorable, and dedicated election officials at the state and local levels work tirelessly between each election to ensure that the integrity and security of the next election are better than the previous one. But they will need continued help from the Federal Government, especially in light of the discord, disinformation, and sizeable dissatisfaction associated with the 2020 presidential contest. Election security is a race with no finish line.

This attack on our elections (including unconscionable threats to election officials themselves), incurred from shameless domestic sources, coupled with the still very real and very present nation-state menace from the likes of Russia, China, and Iran, present a threat landscape to our election system that compels meaningful and tangible support—right now—from both the Biden Administration and Congress.

7.3.2   STATE OF THE SUBSECTOR

The state of America's election infrastructure is more secure, better monitored, and more effectively coordinated than ever. This health represents a dramatic change in the state of the elections subsector in just four years.[3]

Coming out of the 2016 elections and our subsequent understanding of Russia's attempts at meddling in them, there was universal agreement among Federal security agencies that such foreign election interference could not be allowed to continue. The existence of the interference itself, doubted by some, was clearly established and confirmed by both the US Intelligence Community and congressional investigations.[1,2] As a result, the mission of defending our most democratic of institutions was clear, and the Federal Government commenced an unprecedented campaign of partnership with state and local election officials beginning in 2017.

My former agency, the Cybersecurity and Infrastructure Security Agency, or CISA, was at the forefront of this effort. And with the 2018 midterm elections less than two years away, we got to work immediately. The election security team at CISA had primary responsibility for working with state and local election officials and the private sector to secure their election infrastructure—including the machines, networks, and data systems supporting elections—from electronic and physical attacks. Other agencies, like the FBI and its law enforcement partners, handled fraud and other criminal election-related activity.

The United States Constitution charges the States (and, accordingly, territories, tribes, and districts) with conducting the nation's elections. At CISA, our job was to help them do it securely. Our first task was to establish partner relationships with State and local election officials and build trust with the Federal Government where heretofore there had been none. We also worked closely with industry, the companies that design and manufacture election infrastructure equipment. One key initiative was the establishment of the Elections Infrastructure Information Sharing and Analysis Center (EI-ISAC) to share election-related security information with others who could act on it for defensive purposes. By the 2018 midterm elections, all 50 states and thousands of election jurisdictions had joined the center and were actively sharing information.

CISA also offered a range of cybersecurity services to the elections community, such as intrusion detection monitoring, vulnerability scanning, network penetration testing, and cyber hygiene information and training. Election officials themselves, with critical funding appropriated by the Congress and delivered through the Election Assistance Commission (EAC), improved their cybersecurity baseline by upgrading to more modern systems, hardening user accounts through additional log-on measures, conducting election security tabletop exercises, and hiring dedicated security staff.

The most critical weak spot confronting our election ecosystem was (and remains so) the absence of paper-based or paper-backup voting equipment. Voting machines known as direct-recording electronic machines, or DREs, do not generate paper records for individual votes. And paper ballots are essential pieces of evidence for conducting a post-election audit or checking a count's accuracy. With DREs, the vote is recorded on the individual voting machine and then combined with voting data from other machines during the tabulation process with no "safety net" of a paper record.

In 2016, five states used DREs statewide, including Georgia and Pennsylvania, with a handful of others using DREs in multiple jurisdictions. Congress provided grant funding to the States in 2018 and 2020 to help them retire the paperless machines and procure auditable systems. As the 2020 election season began, Delaware, Georgia, Pennsylvania, and South Carolina all transitioned over to paper-based voting systems. Whereas it was estimated that, in 2016, approximately 82% of election jurisdictions operated voting systems with a paper record, heading into 2020, our collective efforts with the States raised that figure up to nearly 95%, including those in critical battleground states.

7.3.3   THE COVID-19 ELECTION

The year 2020 soon showed itself to be not only an election year but a pandemic year of historic consequence as well. The rampant spread of COVID-19 throughout every State and its acute communicability prompted, understandably, a nationwide surge toward the use of voting by mail. COVID-19 was the unanticipated curveball that fundamentally changed the national conversation regarding the security of the November elections, even though the security of the November elections was not jeopardized by the pandemic.

COVID-19 and its resultant mail-in voting did not have to be, nor should it have become, the catalyst for election security scapegoating. The advent of large-scale voting-by-mail options did not introduce more risk to the election security landscape, rather it *transferred* risk that was already resident to different elements within the election infrastructure ecosystem. Instead of the voting machines themselves that would have been a prime focus of any adversarial attack campaign, statewide vote-by-mail initiatives shifted nearly the entirety of that risk to the voter registration databases, *i.e.*, the actual voter rolls. Voter registration data was a target for the Russians in 2016, and the 2020 election under pandemic conditions would make those electronic rolls even more attractive to attack. If voter registration data were compromised, then the accurate and proper allocation and distribution of valid ballots were at risk, not the actual vote itself as cast. Additionally, the increased production of paper ballots necessitated by a state-wide vote-by-mail option obviously placed greater weight to the security measures (*e.g.,* barcodes, watermarks, etc.) that are used to control the manufacture and storage of official ballots.

Nonetheless, many people wondered if this increased volume of mail-in voting meant the presidential contest would be compromised. A rational examination of the difficulty in trying to "rig" or "fix" and election through massive paper-ballot fraud—at scale—is evident upon even a cursory examination. Absentee or mail-in ballots are controlled documents. They feature individual barcodes and/or watermarks. Most contain "timing marks" along the edge of the ballot that enable the tabulators to read them and that are hard to reproduce. In some cases, even the weight and stock of the ballot paper are controlling characteristics. And these are just but a few of the security measures surrounding paper ballots. But much of the popular media and punditry failed to exert even a basic level of analysis on this matter, and the result was a national-level of misunderstanding that diverged from the truth and was amplified in an echo chamber of social media and cable networks. And herein is where the seeds of the greatest threat to election security in 2020 were sown.

7.3.4 DOMESTIC DISINFORMATION

When CISA began in earnest its election security campaign in 2017, it established three general "lanes" of activity: (1) secure the physical election infrastructure (i.e., voting machines, tabulators, etc.) from hacking; (2) raise the cybersecurity baseline of candidate campaigns and national parties; and (3) counter Russian or other foreign election disinformation to the American public and the deleterious influence those activities could have on the electorate.

Those first two lines of effort are where CISA invested the majority of its time and attention. The Intelligence Community Assessment of interference in the 2016 election clearly established the existence of Russian attempts to penetrate election-related data networks as well as its successful compromise of both Democratic National Committee (DNC) and Clinton campaign employee email accounts.[1] Arguably, this is where the greatest damage had been done. The foreign influence and disinformation aspect of the 2016 election was an area where CISA played a limited and supporting role to the FBI and the social media platforms.

But as we look at the story of the 2020 elections, it was clearly the disinformation campaign—undoubtedly the *domestic* disinformation campaign—that had the greatest impact in undermining American's confidence in the election. Disinformation emerged as the greatest threat to the actual election results themselves.

Simply stated, a determined disinformation campaign unchecked by truth and facts creates disinformed citizens. And disinformed citizens, predisposed to believe that future national elections are rigged or stolen, constitute a greater challenge to the election security community's efforts than any cybersecurity breach coming from foreign threat actors.

7.3.5 CALL TO ACTION: RECOMMENDATIONS FOR THE BIDEN ADMINISTRATION

Even without the demoralizing disinformation aftermath of the 2020 elections, the election infrastructure agenda for the Biden Administration would be considerable. Taking into account the current state of election confidence throughout the country, combined with the existing foreign nation-state threats, make further investment in election security an absolute imperative to our democracy.

President Biden and his Cabinet can continue the momentum that has been established in election infrastructure security over the past four years, and commence new effort in key priority areas that have come to light in the wake of the 2020 elections, by actively working with the Congress to achieve positive security outcomes through the following initiatives:

- **Institutionalize Election Assistance Grants:** Through the 2002 Help America Vote Act (HAVA) and the 2020 Coronavirus Aid, Relief, and Economic Security (CARES) Act, Congress has appropriated over $1.2 billion for election-related security measures since 2018. These funds were absolutely instrumental in elevating the election security baseline across the entire country. States and election jurisdictions used these resources to upgrade equipment, solicit cybersecurity technical assistance, and hire full-time election security staff. But these grants, as considerable as they were, remain episodic and unpredictable for their recipients. Strategic plans for election infrastructure modernization cannot be fully executed and security staff positions cannot be made permanent when the future status of these resources cannot be ascertained for the out-years. Most any national security program of consequence within DoD, DHS, or other departments enjoy dependable status within the President's budget where managers and recipients can plan for the future, find efficiencies, and predict lifecycle cost estimates. FEMA has been awarding post-September 11th and post-Katrina preparedness and resilience grants to States and localities for nearly twenty years. Protecting our elections should be at least be as important as paying for more police officers and mitigating our flood plains. And while there is a legitimate debate as to whether permanent grant programs for the States create an unhealthy dependency dynamic within our federalist system, especially when funds are not optimally aligned to risk, having some reliability for election security investment for the near future is important to continue to address existing security gaps in election systems.
- **Attain 100% Conformance for Paper-Based/Paper-Backup Voting Systems:** Paper ballots and post-election checks ensure the accuracy of any election count. Presently there are eight (8) remaining states where voting infrastructure is still utilized that does not produce an auditable, paper-based record:
  - Indiana,
  - Kansas,
  - Kentucky,
  - Louisiana,
  - Mississippi,
  - Tennessee,
  - Texas, and
  - New Jersey.

The Biden Administration, and President Biden himself, should directly appeal to these governors and secretaries of state to effect the necessary investments and modernization needed to achieve paper-based record keeping of their voting systems. If necessary, HAVA grants should be prioritized to meet the needs of these states first before the merits of other investments are determined. The most powerful way to address disinformation about voting fraud is having the ability to produce an auditable trail of non-electronic voting records. According to news accounts in several of the key 2020 states, the November results showed no significant discrepancies attributed to manipulation in the post-election canvassing, audit, and recount processes. The secretaries of state in Georgia, Michigan, Arizona, Nevada, and Pennsylvania, as well officials in Wisconsin, all worked very hard in preparing their states for the November elections to ensure there was a paper trail that could be audited or recounted by hand, independent of any allegedly hacked software or hardware.

Georgia conducted multiple recounts of the presidential election and the outcome of the manual recount was consistent with the computer-based count.

- **Discourage Any Efforts to Migrate to Internet Voting or Voting via Blockchain:** This is a bad idea and will remain so. For any doubters, the SolarWinds compromise reminds us just how vulnerable all Internet-connected data networks are, especially to supply-chain-based intrusions. Internet-based voting introduces unacceptable risk into the election equation, by possibly compromising the anonymity of the cast ballot, the integrity of the results, and even the voters' privacy. Software and apps that run on voters' computers and mobile devices contain untold software flaws and security vulnerabilities, as do most of the data networks comprising the Internet itself. Producing a paper record of a vote cast by electronic ballot return does not solve the problem, as an electronic man-in-the-middle attack changing the vote could be conducted from virtually anywhere in world, and at scale. Moreover, widespread voting via Internet would provide a target-rich environment for a distributed denial-of-service (DDoS) attack on election day(s), with botnets propagating massive data traffic jams and slowing down election activity. With Internet voting, there is simply too much risk for election officials to responsibly accept.
- **Call for Individual State After-Action Reports (AARs) on the 2020 Elections:** Just because the 2020 elections were the most secure in the American history does not grant us the luxury that every American citizen will accept that statement on its face value. One mistake that defenders of the November election's integrity and security can make is to simply dismiss or wave off the various claims of compromise, fraud, or "voting irregularities." While essentially none of those claims were successful in the court system, many of those allegations were never formally countered or discredited because of issues of standing, jurisdiction, procedure, or timing. While it is certainly true that some claims have no basis in fact and therefore do not warrant the time and resources of a formal investigation, after-action reports, or "AARs," are a very practical and reasonable vehicle for establishing factual details, clarifying misunderstandings, reconstructing event timelines, and explaining arcane vagaries of election procedures that do not necessarily lend themselves for sufficient explanation on 4–5 minute cable television hits. Several of the secretaries of state in contested states did an admirable job of debunking much of the disinformation and explaining many of the misunderstood election myths through press conferences and social media. But it is important to create a written record, for posterity alone, that addresses the full range of election accusations with a deliberate, factual, and thoughtful response. To be clear, what is *not needed* nor warranted is any type of blue-ribbon commission or independent investigation that would only give credibility to these made-up claims that are themselves incredible. Rather, the very practical and accessible nature of an AAR will be effective in establishing a dispassionate explanation and rebutting of the various charges of fraud and irregularity. The Biden Administration should press for each state secretary of state to conduct a review and publish an election AAR before the next election. These are generally not terribly expensive endeavors, but if necessary, the AARs should be deemed as allowable costs for EAC HAVA grants.
- **Reinvigorate National Civics Education:** The effectiveness of domestic disinformation exposed a fundamental weakness throughout the American electorate: the lack of meaningful knowledge about elections, how they work, federalism, the Electoral College, the role of the American president and the executive branch, and more. Basic civics, a core school subject that is often taken for granted among many of us and sometimes forgotten once we graduate from high school, is in crisis. Americans, at least in some quantity, do not necessarily know how their government—at all levels—is designed to function. A healthy representative democracy relies upon the presupposition that the people understand the basic mechanics of the institutions that govern them, including electoral laws and processes.

The "consent of the governed" cannot be properly conveyed if the governed do not sufficiently understand just to what, exactly, they have consented. The actor Richard Dreyfuss recognized this several years ago and established The Dreyfuss Civics Initiative. The Biden Administration, through the Department of Education, CISA, or other appropriate federal agencies, should find ways to partner with The Dreyfuss Civics Initiative, the Ad Council, and other organizations with a similar mission, to re-energize a national "refresher course" on elections and other elements of our democratic republic. "Schoolhouse Rock," the once popular and seemingly very effective (based on our peer group's ability to recite many of the songs and lessons forty years later), should be "re-booted" and applied to our nation's election system and procedures, including specific episodes focused on election security.

- **Protect Election Officials:** It is both troubling and depressing that this even needs to be an area of concern, let alone action, but given the myriad threats of violence that were levied against both federal and state election officials over the past few months, this is a legitimate problem. Attracting talented citizens to embark in a career in the election community, let alone recruiting election volunteers, is difficult enough without threats to their safety. While it is doubtful that any new laws need to be added to the books, the Biden Administration's Department of Justice should work with the States to aggressively pursue and prosecute any individuals who render threats against election officials, volunteers, or vendors. One foreseen challenge will be how we can increase transparency in election processes (i.e., voting tabulation and canvassing, ballot manufacturing and distribution, etc.) without putting election officials at greater risk. While many of our disinformed citizens were demanding viewing access to ballot counting, invariably the personal identity of election volunteers may be revealed by such a public accommodation, placing them in further jeopardy.

- **Break Down the Echo Chambers:** On January, 6, 2021 Senator Ted Cruz (R-TX) stood on the Senate floor and said that recent polling results indicated that "39% of Americans believe the election that just occurred was 'rigged.' You may not agree with that assessment, but it is nonetheless a reality for nearly half the country."[3] Whether or not those specific polling statistics are accurate, let us stipulate that there is, in fact, a sizeable constituency of the electorate that has lost faith in our national elections based on the electoral fraud they believe occurred in November. In the aftermath of the election and in the midst of the subsequent torrent of election disinformation, most all of the public officials and pundits who were offering the ground truth and factual clarifications to rebut the false claims of pervasive election fraud at scale were doing so on or in media platforms for whom the target audience was largely absent. And, upon our respective departures from CISA, this included me and other former CISA officials. Invitations for appearances or op-eds from MSNBC, CNN, *The Washington Post*, *60 Minutes*, and Washington, DC think tanks were offered and accepted. But the vast majority of people who believe the November elections were "stolen" or "rigged" are probably not watching these outlets. Defenders of the 2020 election's integrity spent most all of our time preaching to the proverbial choir on channels and in papers who already accepted the legitimacy of the election. Granted, as the saying goes, "it takes two to tango." And we are unaware of many, if any, invitations to election defenders to appear on FOX News, NEWSMAX, or One American News Network (OAN). But we should be asking for that airtime, not waiting to be asked. The fragility of our democracy will only be further stressed by the increasing polarization of political sensibilities. We have to take the election security case to those who doubt it, not just to those who already understand and accept it. And this is not just a post-election imperative. The Biden Administration, through CISA, should aggressively partner with the National Association of Secretaries of State (NASS) and the National Association of State Election Officials (NASED) to design and launch an election security information and education campaign in the run-up to the 2022 midterm elections. The audience is the American voter.

This campaign should target the full range of outlets and platforms, but it should conspicuously press networks, publications, and groups across various political beliefs to appear on their channels, write in their publications, and speak at their conferences about how election security works and how the integrity of every American's vote is validated and protected.

By taking action in these seven areas, we can both continue the momentum of election security that has been generated over the past four years while attempting to repair the most serious damage that has been inflicted on our election ecosystem since November. Clearly, when assessing the risk to election integrity—and to our democracy itself—the threats are no longer just from meddling nation-state actors who seek to favor a particular candidate or sow unrest or chaos. Nor are the threats solely through the vector of computer hacking. The risk to our election infrastructure will continue to be driven from both abroad and within, in both cyber and physical forms. But, as we are seeing now, perhaps the most insipid menace of all election threats is persistent disinformation from influential sources.

To protect our elections, we must continue acting to assert ourselves in a whole-of-society fashion and at all levels of government, but especially at the federal level where the national risk to our electoral system is best analyzed and understood. Eternal vigilance is the price of election integrity. It's the race with no finish line. And for the newly minted Biden Administration, the next heat has already begun.

7.3.5.1 ABOUT THE AUTHOR

Matthew Travis is the former deputy director of the Cybersecurity and Infrastructure Security Agency (CISA) within the US Department of Homeland Security.

NOTES

1. Joint Statement from Elections Infrastructure Government Coordinating Council and the Election Infrastructure Sector Coordinating Executive Committees, November 12, 2020.
2. In fact, the worst time to try to secure election infrastructure is right before an election. Tinkering with election technology or processes directly before an impending election actually introduces additional risk.
3. Election Infrastructure is a formal subsector within the larger Government Facilities sector as established in the *National Infrastructure Protection Plan* (NIPP).

REFERENCES

[1] "Background to "Assessing Russian Activities and Intentions in Recent US Elections": The Analytic Process and Cyber Incident Attribution", Intelligence.senate.gov, 2017. [Online]. Available: https://www.intelligence.senate.gov/sites/default/files/documents/ICA_2017_01.pdf. [Accessed: 02- Sep- 2021].
[2] "RUSSIAN ACTIVE MEASURES CAMPAIGNS AND INTERFERENCE IN THE 2016 U.S. ELECTION", Intelligence.senate.gov, 2020. [Online]. Available: https://www.intelligence.senate.gov/publications/report-select-committee-intelligence-united-states-senate-russian-active-measures. [Accessed: 02- Sep- 2021].
[3] P. Bump, "Ted Cruz's electoral vote speech will live in infamy", The Washington Post, 2021. [Online]. Available: https://www.washingtonpost.com/politics/2021/01/06/ted-cruzs-electoral-vote-speech-will-live-infamy/. [Accessed: 02- Sep- 2021].

7.4   THE STATE OF CAMPAIGN CYBERSECURITY

Brigadier General (ret.) Francis X. Taylor
Executive Director, US CyberDome

Joseph Drissel and Matt Barrett
Founder and Director, US CyberDome

7.4.1   INTRODUCTION

The US campaign community has a multitude of cybersecurity challenges facing it. The current and foreseeable challenge is that cybersecurity risk management activities are not well-matched to the significant cyber risks campaigns face. Addressing the out-of-phase nature of cyber risks and cybersecurity risk management is more difficult for the political campaigns based on factors such as short duration, timing of donor funding, independent operation, and campaign finance law.

7.4.2   THE WAKE-UP CALL

In 2016, the campaign community really became aware of the risks related to a network-based intrusion. The attack on the Clinton campaign demonstrated that nation-states and others would use their capabilities to try to influence the outcomes of one of the most important aspects of democracy, free and fair elections. This attack happened just five years ago, which is not very long from a cybersecurity perspective. The awareness of long-term exposure from a breach for a candidate or information about a candidate is only now becoming evident to the community. The weaponization of the stolen information in misinformation and disinformation has had a profound impact on our society.

7.4.3   WHAT'S AT-STAKE

The cyber threat to political campaigns has significant short- and long-term consequences. These include the targeting of politicians and their campaign staffs that will potentially hold significant positions of power within the US Government and the gathering of significant information about the US citizens, their political affiliations, and financial health. This stolen information can be used by the adversary for a variety of targeted actions such as, extortion of candidates and high-level government officials, theft or extortion of campaign funds; reducing votes through disinformation/misinformation campaigns; and weaponizing information to undermine confidence in the US election process.

7.4.4   THE THREAT IS STILL ACTIVE

Other adversaries have learned from what the Russians accomplished in 2016. In 2019, we have seen Iran, Russia, and North Korea conduct similar activities, as reported by Microsoft. While there are very few public reports of successful cyber-attacks against the 2020 US Presidential Elections, our adversaries prefer to operate in secrecy, and the presence of so many skilled national actors was ominous.

7.4.5   CYBER RISK MANAGEMENT USUALLY LAGS CYBER THREAT

In Figure 7.4.1, we superimpose the observation that Iran, Russia, and North Korea are actively targeting campaigns over key milestones from the Biden campaign. The presence of skilled national actors in September 2019 is out-of-phase with the most conspicuous outward sign that cybersecurity

FIGURE 7.4.1   2020 campaign cybersecurity timeline.

is being managed in the campaign, the hiring of a Chief Information Security Officer (CISO) in July 2020. This same statement is true of almost every 2020 US Presidential campaign. In fact, many campaigns did not have a CISO to lead their cybersecurity risk management activities. The absence of a CISO becomes most prevalent with US Congressional, state, and local campaigns.

7.4.6   TYPICAL CAMPAIGN LIFECYCLE

The campaigns typically underspend on cybersecurity in the early days of the campaign. Most campaigns get the largest amount of funding late in the campaign cycle leaving them exposed to a cyber-attack in the early phases of the campaign. This leads campaigns to operate as "start-ups" with minimal infrastructure and funding as they try to build the candidate's stature and support from voters. Staffing is minimal and there is little priority given to IT security, if at all. The focus is on getting voter support for the candidate to make the campaign viable. Only later when the campaign has secured additional funding is more infrastructure added when the campaign becomes viable and funds are prioritized. However, that infrastructure is focused on voter turnout and not the protection of information generated by the campaign or the campaign staff. This puts enormous pressure on the general Information Technology resources, which tend to already be stretched thin.

7.4.7   CYBERSECURITY LEADERSHIP IN CAMPAIGNS

The majority of US presidential primary campaigns did not have a Chief Information Security Officer in 2020. A CISO is typically a cybersecurity leader and expert whose full-time role is cyber-security risk management. The presence of a CISO is a key indicator that a campaign is serious enough about cybersecurity to allocate some dedicated resources. The CISO's responsibilities are to ensure that cyber risks are managed according to likelihood and consequence and that cyberse-curity is factored into broader campaign risk decisions. Currently, most campaigns manage cyberse-curity in isolation from other risk management decisions. This lack of integration into broader risk decisions typically occurs because of the reporting hierarchy and because of a common miscon-ception that cybersecurity can be managed in isolation from other risks. Even in campaigns where cybersecurity risk is well-integrated into overarching risk decisions, cybersecurity risk management is very complex given the short duration, wide variety of cyber awareness, highly distributed nature of the workforce, and a high usage of personal devices for campaign work.

7.4.8   CYBERSECURITY PROFESSIONALS ARE SCARCE

As is the case for the cybersecurity industry at-large, there is a cybersecurity resource gap within the political campaign community. The campaign community does not have a large/mature cyber-security labor force to identify qualified professionals, especially with the niche skill sets to address the complicated cybersecurity risks of a campaign. This lack of resources forces the community to look externally and compete for cybersecurity professionals in other communities that typically provide greater long-term financial stability and higher compensation. Further, the short-term and start-up nature of campaigns limits the number of cybersecurity professionals who can truly have an impact for campaigns.

7.4.9 FEDERAL GOVERNMENT HELP IS LIMITED

The government does not have a vehicle to directly reach and support the organizations and networks. The vast cybersecurity resources of the US government tend to sit on the sidelines when it comes to campaigns. While the US Government has made significant investment in the election infrastructure across the country since 2016, political campaigns were not beneficiaries of that investment. Non-incumbent federal campaigns avoid the use of federal agency services due to competitive sensibilities. Typically, the only time non-incumbent campaigns will engage federal organizations is for informational purposes, such as intelligence reports, or in response to a criminal or nation-state activity. This puts campaigns in a reactive position after a breach has occurred.

7.4.10 CAMPAIGNS OPERATE IN ISOLATION

The rapidly changing and completive nature of campaigns leads universally to independent cybersecurity operations for each campaign. Several factors contribute to this behavior. For instance, the dynamics of the community may make campaigns skeptical or hesitant to allow a potential competitive incumbent administration into the inner workings of the network. This current posture further isolates the campaign from the limited federal government cybersecurity resources that can be applied. Fierce competition through and including primaries lead to two additional isolating mindsets. Most campaigns resist assistance from their own major party committees until they have been chosen as the candidate. Additionally, rapidly changing political alliances early-mid campaign necessitate isolation. Frequently we see a greater wiliness to make alliances and receive external resources from party committees following the formal party nominations. These isolating circumstances erode cybersecurity risk management for all campaigns and place the leading organization for a party in the difficult position of managing cyber risk during the entire life cycle of a campaign.

7.4.11 LIMITED THREAT SHARING

Threat sharing is a critical component of a mature cybersecurity program. Up to date and advanced threat intel from the community can be used to properly allocate the very precious resources of the campaign. We have seen threat sharing have a positive effect on the defense industrial base and subsequently on US critical infrastructure. Inside the campaign community, there are limited community-driven threat-sharing options. Further complicating threat sharing, there are communication challenges among internal party lines and no formal threat sharing efforts across party lines, mainly due to the competitive nature of the industry.

7.4.12 A BIG TARGET WE AREN'T DISCUSSING

The vendor community that supports many of the internal operations of the campaigns are a major target for the adversaries. The vendors can be engaged by the adversary months before the election cycle even begins. This makes the vendors one of the most stable and consistent targets by hackers to maintain persistence between elections. Complicating the situation even more, the vendors do not have a cybersecurity validation/vetting requirement. This lack of cybersecurity of maturity again opens the door to the persistent cybersecurity threat. When campaigns launch, they can simply bring an intrusion event to their network by partnering with an election-focused vendor.

The sophisticated threat actors that affected the 2016 US Presidential election were still present, and joined by additional threat actors, in the 2020 elections. Despite this activity, campaigns are still waiting to address cybersecurity risk management in the final few months of their campaign. This misalignment of cyber threat and cybersecurity risk management leads to a big exposure, not just for the campaign, but for long-term national security. As campaigns become more conscious about this misalignment, there are a great many things that can be done to manage the cyber risk, as we will explore in the next essay, *Action Plan for More Secure Campaigns: Addressing the Gaping Hole in Our Electoral Process*.

7.5   THE PRICE OF LIBERTY—COUNTERING LONG-TERM MALICIOUS CYBER INFLUENCES ON DEMOCRATIC PROCESSES

José de Arimatéia da Cruz
Full Professor, Georgia Southern University

7.5.1   INTRODUCTION

In this article, the author postulates that long-term strategic and policy solutions are necessary to counter increasing malicious influences on free democratic elections. While short-term policies centered on protecting discrete portions of the electoral process have proven successful in recent years, nations must transition to an enduring security posture that includes cybersecurity of election equipment and infrastructure as well as counter-intelligence and thwarting cyberspace-enabled influence campaigns against democratic populations. The author starts with a review of infrastructure vulnerabilities discovered during recent "white hat" hacker activities and academic studies, recent foreign influence attempts against democratic elections, and provides an overview of lessons from recent policy actions within the United States. The author concludes with strategic recommendations for all democratic nations.

Election security has become a preeminent concern of national security in the twenty-first century. The scale and scope of the threat became evident to most US leaders following the 2016 election cycle but was known for some time to other nations susceptible to foreign influences and spy craft within their democratic process. Now, with the US 2020 presidential election fresh in the minds of lawmakers, it is time to take stock of successes, failures, and enduring challenges as we plunge headlong into the second decade of the Information Age.

The warning signs of foreign influences were there far before this became a national security crisis. Cybersecurity analysts, policy experts, and even the head of US intelligence have all expressed concern over the country's susceptibility to cyber-enabled influences and attacks on the election process (Lewis 2020; Coats 2019). US intelligence leaders warned lawmakers in public testimony that, following the perceived successful influence over the 2016 US presidential election, foreign actors would again employ "persistent and disruptive cyber operations" in 2018 and beyond, "using elections as opportunities to undermine democracy" (Zengerle and Chiacu, 2018a, b).

On the technical side, increasing reliance on insecure information technology infrastructure in the election process has alarmed cybersecurity experts. In August 2019, the annual hacker convention DEF CON held its 27th iteration with researchers from across academia collaborating to present a "hacking village" aimed at assessing multiple types of election equipment within the United States. Over two and a half days, cybersecurity experts from around the country tinkered with and noted severe compromises of touch screen direct recording electronic machines, topical scan paper and paper-ballot marking devices, and electronic poll books. The results were unsurprising to security experts but confirmed suspicions: virtually every device in use could be compromised with little or no advanced skill or laboratory time, the report noted specifically that "an attack that could compromise an entire jurisdiction could be injected in any of multiple places during the lifetime of the system" (Blaze et al., 2019). Many US states had not taken action to demand election equipment vendors close existing vulnerabilities that had been reported "over a decade earlier" (Blaze et al., 2019). The report urged all states to adopt paper ballots and post-election risk-limiting audits (RLAs), but few states so far appear willing to do so.

With election infrastructure vulnerabilities prevalent and foreign influence proven effective in the information age, all developed democratic nations must transition short-term election security plans into sustainable national security priorities. This essay examines the scope and method of malicious, cyber-enabled forces against free and democratic election processes. These forces take two primary forms: foreign interference with and influence over population by inserting falsehoods and manipulating perspectives ahead of an election, and the potential for cyberattacks and tampering that can alter results of voting processes during and after an election. First, an analysis of election infrastructure vulnerabilities will be presented, followed by a review of foreign attempts to manipulate elections outside of technical means, and an examination of recent US strategy and policy actions is presented to counter both threat vectors. The essay concludes with strategic recommendations for policymakers.

While US actions and influences are featured prominently in this essay, it should be noted that the recommendations and lessons learned from those influences can be applied to all democratic nations seeking a free and fair electoral process. The authors believe that democratic societies across the globe can and must become resilient in their cybersecurity measures, access controls, and prevention tools, or face existential threats to their very way of life.

7.5.2 ELECTION INFRASTRUCTURE VULNERABILITIES

Cyber interference in another country's election is becoming increasingly popular with both domestic and international actors. The use of cyber tools as a force multiplier is especially useful for weak or rogue nations in the post-Cold War international system of the twenty-first century. In his worldwide threat assessment testimony to the US Congress in 2019, then-Director for National Intelligence Daniel R. Coats put cyber effects and election interference as the top two global threats to national security (Coats, 2019). For cyber specifically, he states "our adversaries and strategic competitors will increasingly use cyber capabilities - including cyber espionage, attack, and influence - to seek political, economic, and military advantage over the United States and its allies and partners" (Coats, 2019). In short, our intelligence apparatus has been ringing the alarm bells for some time.

Returning to the DEF CON[1] 27 hacking village results, the report presents a number of troubling technical findings that lay bare the lack of security expertise used to set up automatic voting machines. Some devices come with out-of-the-box encryption but store keys in plain text on the device itself, rendering the encryption worthless. Other devices have default settings that bypass security measures or have been removed altogether. Several devices contained default commercial applications that come bundled with new devices, such as Amazon and Netflix, introducing potential third-party vulnerabilities. One device tested had hard-coded internet protocol addresses pointing to an overseas location, making the entire supply chain suspect.

Of all the technical vulnerabilities discovered during DEF CON 27, a common theme appears to present itself: a lack of standards and accountability. Many of the devices tested during the conference were used in as many as 27 states across the United States. It is not clear which states employ security professionals dedicated to election security measures, or if state policy exists that requires a defined security standard in device procurement and fielding. Additional research comparing state cyber defense preparations and responses would be valuable for the public policy community.

Such vulnerabilities within election technology infrastructure are well known to potential attackers, and attempts have been made to operationalize them. The Cybersecurity and Infrastructure Security Agency (CISA) released several alerts ahead of the election in which the US intelligence apparatus discovered plans by a state-sponsored advanced persistent threat (APT) group to target technical infrastructure at the US state level, including election websites. The evaluation determined that this threat made "an intentional effort to influence and interfere with the 2020 U.S. presidential election" (CISA, 2020a). Additional alerts have alarmed technical experts without pointing to a specific threat to election infrastructure, including the technique of "vulnerability chaining" which has the potential to endanger election equipment through unpatched or unmitigated vulnerability exploitation resulting in a confidentiality breach of voting or counting machines (CISA, 2020b).

This activity was not aimed at just voting machines, but government-owned websites that collect voter information. The definition of election infrastructure must encompass these sites as well. The key takeaway for all democratic election authorities is that foreign election interference includes multiple threat vectors, including using technical means to hack voting machines, counting machines, or breach registration websites to gather target lists for exploitation. While local governments are responsible for securing the infrastructure, they establish to manage these processes, such as a state-run website for voter information and registration, coordination and threat intelligence is needed at a national level to cue local electorates to dangers targeting their infrastructure.

7.5.3 FOREIGN INFLUENCES—ATTEMPTS AND SUCCESSES

A survey conducted by *The New York Times'* tracking web page for election disinformation and misinformation "Daily Distortions" finds that only four out of 165 articles contain any attribution for substantiated disinformation efforts from Russia, Iran, or China (*The New York Times*, 2020). This finding stands in stark contrast to the public's concern of foreign-based election disinformation and is combined within a larger context of newspaper reporting to understand foreign election interference in the 2020 United States presidential election.

Following pressure from the US Congress and the general public after the 2016 election, prominent social media platforms hired tens of thousands of workers and spent billions of dollars on combating foreign influence for the 2020 election (Alba, 2020). Relative success was reported and Russian operations were prominent (Frenkel and Barnes, 2020). After kicking off self-created accounts, Russian operatives began buying accounts from individual US citizens in order to post narratives under domestic identities. Political organizations' stand-alone websites were also bought off and served as a conduit for guiding users back to social media platforms through direct website links—a type of traffic sometimes undetected by automated flagging programs (Frenkel and Barnes, 2020; Wakabayashi, 2020). Russia also transitioned to more permissive platforms, such as Gab and Parler, which right-wing groups have also turned to after violating platform terms-of-use policies themselves (Alba, 2020; Bomey, 2020).

Though election disinformation was prevalent in the two previous US national elections, the 2020 presidential election saw a new level of integration between domestic and foreign actors as well as more sophisticated foreign techniques. This largely rides on a linear continuation of disinformation narratives exuded from the 2016–2020 US Head of State, who made an average of 19 false or misleading statements per day while in office by the run-up to the November election (Kessler et al., 2020). While this would normally be considered mere domestic disinformation, Russian interference campaigns integrated White House disinformation into a new strategy of acting as an amplifier to maximize the full extent of inaccurate propaganda—intertwining the two sources in a profound way (Sanger and Perlroth, 2020; Kanno-Youngs, 2020).

Despite numerous warnings from the Intelligence Community in 2019, President Trump's personal lawyer Rudy Giuliani was retained as counsel after cooperating with a Pro-Russian Ukrainian lawmaker Andrii Derkach who is long considered to be a Russian operative (Harris et al., 2020). Giuliani appeared with Derkach on One America News Network and used clips of the segment on his personal podcast to propagate a narrative of Trump's political opponent and President-Elect Joe Biden with unsubstantiated illegal corruption allegations in Ukraine (Lucas, 2020). Derkach was sanctioned for foreign intelligence interference by the US Treasury Department on September 10, 2020, some nine months following the impeachment of President Trump over withholding Ukrainian military aid against Russia's invasion of Crimea (with currently over 13,000 dead) and pressuring Ukraine to announce investigations into Biden (Cheney, 2020).

Pressure from the White House resulted in alleged malfeasance within the Intelligence Community, as well. The Office of Inspector General (OIG) is currently investigating the heads of the Department of Homeland Security who allegedly directed analysts to paint China and Iran as larger election influencers than Russia to help President Trump's reelection (Kanno-Youngs, 2020). As indicated by the presence of any need to modify the intelligence reports, this was largely a false narrative, yet some influence campaigns from China and Iran did take place. For China, three disinformation campaigns directly relating to the election were identified (though numerous were found in reference to COVID-19). The first was coined "Naval Gazing" and involved 155 accounts, 11 pages, and nine groups on Facebook with an additional six accounts on Instagram (Goldman et al., 2020). The influence campaign originally focused on Philippines-oriented information but then transitioned to early support for Democratic Party primary candidate Pete Buttigieg without gaining traction. Evolving its methods, pages for both presidential primary election candidates were later created to generate traffic, and most efforts focused on either polarizing voters or local and state elections. Google disclosed the second Chinese operation in June and Microsoft revealed another in September where Chinese hackers targeted Biden campaign staff members' email accounts (Sanger et al., 2020; Sanger and Perlroth, 2020). For comparison, attacks from Russia's military cyber operations unit known as Fancy Bear outshined the Chinese email attacks in a mere two-week period before Microsoft's announcement, though not enough detailed information was released for a direct comparison.

For Iran, Microsoft uncovered an attempt to identify email accounts of government officials, journalists, and Trump campaign workers that were likely a response to new US sanctions (Sanger and Perlroth, 2020). Publicly available information was then used to test passwords, successfully infiltrating at least four non-campaign targets' accounts. Additionally, the Democratic National Committee distributed emails warning of spear-phishing and false two-factor identification prompts that were propagating from fraudulent LinkedIn accounts.

Still, every report of cyber warfare must be treated with special care as attribution can be fleeting in disinformation operations. Reports indicate foreign cyber operatives have become more skilled in covering their tracks by deleting server logs, attacking from more advantageous vectors, and false flag operations are prevalent. Russia is already known to utilize "a proverbial grab bag of disguises" for its operations since 2014 and was discovered to be routing through Iran's cyber operations computers to attack at least 35 countries in previous years (Greenberg, 2019; Spaniel, 2022). Heeding this reality, this survey lacked evidence to link many new developments in the disinformation sphere specifically to foreign actors despite recognizing domestic-foreign alliances (wittingly or unwittingly) to have emerged as a clear foreign intelligence strategy.

However, trends continued for an overall representation of the disinformation and misinformation in the 2020 election, with notable findings such as politically conservative sources being the overwhelmingly predominant vector for misinformation and new developments were seen with tactics in mass texting, encrypted messaging, bots, and robocalls (Alba, 2020; Global Disinformation Index, 2022; Roose, 2020; Stolberg and Weiland, 2020). Numerous investigations into such developments were ongoing at the time of the study. The surveyed reports contained insufficient evidence to attribute these new disinformation practices to foreign actors; a fact also recognized by the reporters themselves, especially when considering the influx of domestic actors in the election cycle (*The New York Times*, 2020).

Foreign influence in the US's elections has continued despite warnings by the US government that any attempt to interfere in the elections would be tolerated and necessary actions would be taken. According to a recent classified intelligence report, as reported by *The Hill*, "classified version of the report from the Office of the Director of National Intelligence (ODNI) was presented to then-President Trump, congressional leadership and committees with oversight over intelligence operations on Jan. 7, 2021" and according to that report both Russia and Iran sough to influence the 2020 elections outcome. However, as *The Hill* reports, "We have no indications that any foreign actor attempted to alter any technical aspect of the voting process in the 2020 US elections, including voter registration, casting ballots, vote tabulation, or reporting results." the report concluded (Kelly and Chalfant, 2020).

7.5.4   LESSONS FROM RECENT US NATIONAL POLICY ACTIONS

Since the US Senate's intelligence committee concluded its investigation regarding likely Russian interference in the 2016 US election, and with the intelligence community's continuous urging, lawmakers, policy experts, and corporations alike have scrambled to build societal antibodies against such influence in the future. Indeed, a key recommendation from the committee's report stated that "the federal government should ensure they [states] receive the necessary resources and information" to reinforce states' responsibility for election security (SSCI, 2020).

Furthermore, testimony by senior intelligence officials in recent years has consistently pointed to online influence operations and election interference as a top global threat not just to the United States, but to democratic alliances and partnerships as well. Returning to DNI Coats' congressional testimony in 2019, he stated "U.S. adversaries and strategic competitors almost certainly will use online influence operations to try to weaken democratic institutions, undermine U.S. alliances and partnerships, and shape policy outcomes in the United States and elsewhere" (Coats, 2019).

Such congressional investigations and testimony have led lawmakers to use the National Defense Authorization Act (NDAA) as a vehicle for setting national policy supporting election security, however political forces and budgetary realities have hampered progress. Section 1238 of the fiscal year 2021 (FY21) NDAA conference report authorizes rewards for providing information on foreign election interference (United States Congress. H.R.6395, 2020). Previous appropriations and authorizations have done more for election security, such as increased funding for cyber vulnerability testing of state election systems, but larger bills or measures have been defeated within the legislature.

The US Department of Homeland Security took an active role in assisting states and districts across the United States with combating disinformation and cyber effects during the 2020 election, releasing a national strategy and several products designed for poll workers (CISA, 2020c). While CISA's strategy was limited to a single election cycle, such a framework can be scaled to become an enduring national strategy to protect the electoral process perpetually. Indeed, the entire US federal government was activated across several relevant agencies for the 2020 election, with the United States having learned to better coordinate efforts and focus on threat vectors since the 2016 influences. According to the US National Security Agency (NSA), the NSA's newly formed Cybersecurity Directorate coordinated with the Department of Homeland Security, US Cyber Command, the Federal Bureau of Investigation, and the Office of the Director of National Intelligence to share "insights on adversary cyber actors and activities, particularly regarding any indicators of intent to interfere" (USNSA, 2021).

Perhaps the most critical policy recommendations to emerge from the United States' election security efforts in recent years are those of the US Cyberspace Solarium Commission. Established by the National Defense Authorization Act of Fiscal Year 2019, the commission was charged with exploring a strategic approach to defend the United States in cyberspace, including election security. The commission's final report, released in early 2020, included a number of impactful recommendations and legislative proposals including improving the Election Assistance Commission to support states and localities to defend election infrastructure, promoting digital literacy, civics education, and public awareness at a national level to build resilience against cyber-enabled misinformation campaigns, strengthening public-private information sharing on cyber threats and intelligence, and increasing the level of coordination and leadership on cyber issues within the federal government (US Cyberspace Solarium Commission, 2020a).

7.5.5   STRATEGIC RECOMMENDATIONS

In order to strengthen critical election infrastructure from cyber-enabled attacks or espionage activity and build resilience against foreign influences, three strategic recommendations based on the extensive body of evidence that would be relevant for the Biden-Harris Administration are here suggested.

7.5.5.1   RECOMMENDATION 1: STANDARDIZE ELECTION INFRASTRUCTURE AND SUPPLY CHAIN MANAGEMENT ACROSS THE NATION, AND DEVELOP MANUAL METHODS TO ASSURE THE INTEGRITY OF THE VOTING AND COUNTING PROCESS

Before information security established itself in the corporate world as a professional discipline, and before "cyber" became an oft-overused and misunderstood buzzword, there was a more business-friendly concept called "information assurance." Since being largely discarded by security practitioners, it has rolled into the umbrella of governance, risk management, and compliance, or "GRC." The military, however, still keeps many of its principles; chief among them is assuring commanders in the field that the information they receive is accurate, timely, and comes from authoritative sources.

The core idea of information assurance is a perfect fit for election security, and it goes beyond technical methods to ensure votes are counted, and adversaries cannot tamper with results. A nation can develop cyber-secure technology infrastructure, but the public must feel assured that the process is secure or there will always be challenges to its integrity. In this case, all known technology methods fail to deliver such assurance, and new approaches (or perhaps, old approaches) are needed. It is a matter of trust: the public at large must be able to place absolute trust in the election process, and that can never happen with an infrastructure in which doubt can be cast based on technical vulnerabilities.

Thus, a national election security policy should be considered: return to manual methods of paper ballots, which can be counted with machines but then should be verified with human-driven auditing. In this case, where information assurance is paramount to acceptance, human-machine teaming must be tightly controlled and trusted. Whether information systems supporting election processes have been or could reasonably be exploited is not the primary issue here; simply the accusation that they could be is enough to cast doubt, and such doubt has no place in electoral proceedings.

A common dissent to a national election security policy this directive has been a possible infringement on states' rights. Article I, Section 4, Clause 1 of the US Constitution states: "The Times, Places and Manner of holding Elections for Senators and Representatives, shall be prescribed in each State by the Legislature thereof; but the Congress may at any time by Law make or alter such Regulations, except as to the Places of chusing Senators." Congress holds the power to pass laws that can be upheld by the courts in the interest of national security. Such a case can be made here, but it requires bipartisan support, which is sorely lacking in recent sessions of the legislature. A combination of incentives (such as federal funding), a common framework, and lowered barriers to entry will enable states to adopt manual methods, but to be completely assured of integrity, Congress must also act to cement it as the law of the land.

The United States, through the Cybersecurity and Infrastructure Security Agency (CISA), has done much to bring the resources of the federal government to bear in helping states conduct secure elections, but it lacks teeth to enforce standards and reduce supply chain risk across the republic. This is a national security problem, thus demanding federal action from lawmakers and coordination from the executive branch. Caution of treading on states' rights must be tempered by the need to ensure standards in technology, a job that the National Institute of Standards and Technology is well suited to accomplish. Coupled with coordination from CISA, the federal government has the means to employ technology solutions safer and more effectively, if only it would muster the political will to accomplish it in the name of national security.

7.5.5.2   RECOMMENDATION 2: CONTINUE TO IMPLEMENT ALL RECOMMENDATIONS FROM THE US CYBERSPACE SOLARIUM COMMISSION, EVEN THE ONES THAT ARE HARD

The US Cyberspace Solarium Commission's recommendations published in 2020 represent the best bi-partisan, study-based strategic approach to national cyber resilience in the nation's history. Each recommendation across its three strategic pillars—shape behavior, deny benefits, and impose costs—represents a critical link in the chain to achieve layered cyber deterrence, including inoculating the nation against foreign influence and cyber-enabled manipulation in the election process (US Cyberspace Solarium Commission, 2020b).

Some of the commission's recommendations will prove politically challenging, such as establishing new bi-partisan committees within Congress with new authority for oversight and lawmaking, and it would be tempting for an administration and session of Congress to "cherry-pick" some recommendations that are easier to implement. The author implores lawmakers and executives to come together to tackle the "hard" recommendations that require building bi-partisan partnerships to create a better cybersecurity workforce. Indeed, some may require longer than a single administration, but they must not be discarded.

7.5.5.3 Recommendation 3: Send Cyber-Focused Diplomats to Allied Summits and Conferences to Help Define Collective Defense, Attribution, and Reprisal Rules for Cyberattacks and Cyber-Enabled Intelligence Activity

The US Cyberspace Solarium Commission's influence should be expanded to reach allied and partner nations who are also falling under the influence of state-sponsored cyber operations against their critical infrastructure and election process. Outreach efforts, in partnership with the US Department of State and America's diplomatic allies, would put that same study-based methodology into the hands of other democratic governments who may not have found a winning strategy.

The Secretary of State, leveraging the Major Events Division and US ambassadors around the world, can bring together world leaders and senior security officials together in major summits and conferences with a robust agenda of collective defense topics. Additionally, the United States must advocate for adding collective election security to the agenda of many of these major events, such as the G7 (or perhaps G8, once again?) Summit, and the UN General Assembly. Sharing lessons learned, ideas, and policies—as well as potential public policy frameworks such as the Solarium Commission, will develop resilience among all democratic nations.

7.5.6 CONCLUSION

The ancient Chinese military strategist Sun-tzu stated that, "Subjugating the enemy's army without fighting is the true pinnacle of excellence. …Thus the highest realization of warfare is to attack the enemy's plans; next is to attack their alliances; next to attack their army; and the lowest is to attack their fortified cities" (Sun-tzu, 1994). Adversaries against free democracies understand the combined military might of the United States and her allies and partners; a kinetic military campaign against NATO nations would likely not yield an advantage. Thus, engaging in cyber-espionage and influence campaigns represents a viable attack vector to disrupt plans and alliances. Sun-tzu would be proud indeed.

Despite the threats facing democracy, there are reasons to be encouraged by progress thus far. Some US states are taking action to hire security professionals and cyber security-minded policy officials to oversee election security and coordinate with national authorities. For example, Minnesota hired a senior official and retired US military officer as its election cybersecurity leader within the Minnesota Department of State. The national policy arena, rife with complex challenges and hamstrung by bureaucracy and the machinations of politics, has rallied around a vehicle for change in the US Cyberspace Solarium Commission.

In another encouraging sign on the global stage, democratic nations have begun to take active measures against foreign interference in elections. In 2017, Sweden began a comprehensive public policy approach to combat Russian interference and disinformation in their electoral processes, building upon their understanding of what happened to the United States in the 2016 election cycle, including countering "fake news" through independent fact checking and educational reform to increase the population's resilience to disinformation, propaganda, and hate speech (Taylor, 2019). The world continues to look to the United States as an example, for better or worse.

Ultimately, lasting change in a democracy belongs to the people. It is a country's people that must demand change in a new digital world rife with both opportunity and peril. For America, that means peaceful activism, lobbying, and progressive action groups with the means and resources to effect change all play a key role in turning out voters and compelling lawmakers and executive leaders alike to be change-makers. The status quo means driving headlong into a dystopian future; careful policy and swift, bold actions by government and corporate leaders alike can ensure freedom and democracy endures into the twenty-second century and beyond.

An often-beloved quote in the defense and intelligence communities can be attributed to John Philpot Curran in the nineteenth century: "The condition upon which God hath given liberty to man is eternal vigilance." In a phrase, the price of liberty is eternal vigilance; vigilance that must take the form of an enduring strategy and smart policies to ensure the liberties enjoyed by democratic and free nations can continue to execute fair elections that their people can trust. Election security is not just a "cyber problem," it is a public policy problem, and one that must be met with expert judgment and decisive action.

7.5.6.1 About the Author

José de Arimatéia da Cruz, PhD/MPH, is Professor of International Relations and Comparative Politics at Georgia Southern University, Savannah, GA., Adjunct Research Professor at the US Army War College, Carlisle, PA., and Research Associate of the Brazil Research Unit at the Council on Hemispheric Affairs (COHA) in Washington, DC, and a visiting professor at the Prague University of Economics and Business, Department of International and Diplomatic Studies and a visiting Professor at the University of South Bohemia, Czech Republic.

The research, opinions, and recommendations herein are the author's own and do not represent his employers, the US Army War College, or the United States Government. The author would like to thank Travis Howard and Becky Kohler da Cruz for their comments and suggestions. Any errors or omissions are my own responsibility.

NOTE

1. DEF CON is one of the world's largest and most notable hacker conventions, held annually in Las Vegas, Nevada.

REFERENCES

Alba, Davey. "Robocalls Grab the Attention of Election Officials (Published 2020)." Nytimes.com, 2020 [Online], https://www.nytimes.com/2020/11/03/technology/robocalls-grab-the-attention-of-election-officials.html. Accessed 03 April 2022.

Auchard, Eric. "Macron campaign was target of cyberattacks by spy-linked group." *Reuters*, 24 April 2017, https://www.reuters.com/article/us-france-election-macron-cyber/macron-campaign-was-target-of-cyber-attacks-by-spy-linked-group-idUSKBN17Q200. Accessed 28 November 2020.

Blaze, Matt, Hursti, Harri, MacAlpine, Margaret, Hanley, Mary, Moss, Jeff, Wehr Rachel Spencer, Kendall, and Ferris, Christopher. "DEF CON 27 Voting Machine Hacking Village [report]." 2019, https://media.defcon.org/DEF%20CON%2027/voting-village-report-defcon27.pdf. Accessed 28 November 2020.

Bomey, N. "Parler, MeWe, Gab Gain Momentum as Conservative Social Media Alternatives in Post-Trump Age." *Usatoday.com*, 2020 [Online], https://www.usatoday.com/story/tech/2020/11/11/parler-mewe-gab-social-media-trump-election-facebook-twitter/6232351002/. Accessed 18 November 2020.

Bump, Philip. "Here's How Seriously You Should Take the Trump Legal Team's Conspiracy Theories." *The Washington Post* [Washington DC], 19 November 2020, https://www.washingtonpost.com/politics/2020/11/19/heres-how-seriously-you-should-take-trump-legal-teams-conspiracy-theories/. Accessed 28 November 2020.

Cheney, K. and Bertrand, N. "Treasury Sanctions Ukrainian Lawmaker Who Met with Giuliani to Smear Biden." *POLITICO*, 2020 [Online], https://www.politico.com/news/2020/09/10/treasury-designates-anti-biden-ukrainian-lawmaker-for-sanctions-for-election-interference-411750. Accessed 18 October 2020.

Coats, Daniel R. "Statement for the Record: Worldwide Threat Assessment of the US Intelligence Community." United States Government, 2019. *dni.gov*, https://www.dni.gov/files/ODNI/documents/National_Intelligence_Strategy_2019.pdf. Accessed 6 January 2021.

Cybersecurity and Infrastructure Security Agency. "Alert AA20-283A: APT Actors Chaining Vulnerabilities Against SLTT, Critical Infrastructure, and Elections Organizations." *U.S. Department of Homeland Security*, 2020, https://us-cert.cisa.gov/ncas/alerts/aa20-283a?fbclid=IwAR0hEg2yA-dP5j_94hXpSihmFJPtRF065IejiR3Zv2WRT7hYFqrGb6YvgzY. Accessed 28 November 2020.

Cybersecurity and Infrastructure Security Agency. "Alert (AA20-304A), Iranian Advanced Persistent Threat Actor Identified Obtaining Voter Registration Data." *U.S. Department of Homeland Security*, 2020a, https://us-cert.cisa.gov/ncas/alerts/aa20-304a. Accessed 28 November 2020.

Cybersecurity and Infrastructure Security Agency. "Election Disinformation Toolkit." *U.S. Department of Homeland Security*, 2020b, https://www.cisa.gov/sites/default/files/publications/election-disinformation-toolkit_508_0.pdf. Accessed 28 November 2020.

Cybersecurity and Infrastructure Security Agency. "#Protect2020 Strategic Plan." *U.S. Department of Homeland Security*, 2020c, https://www.cisa.gov/sites/default/files/publications/ESI%20Strategic%20Plan_FINAL%202.7.20%20508.pdf. Accessed 28 November 2020.

Fandos, N., Barnes, J., and Goldman, A. "Intelligence Officials Temper Russia Warnings, Prompting Accusations of Political Influence (Published 2020)." *Nytimes.com*, 2020 [Online], https://www.nytimes.com/2020/03/10/us/politics/election-interference-briefing-trump.html. Accessed 18 November 2020.

Frenkel, S. and Barnes, J.E. "Russians Again Targeting Americans With Disinformation, Facebook, and Twitter Say." *New York Times*, 1 September 2020 [Online], https://www.nytimes.com/2020/09/01/technology/facebook-russia-disinformation-election.html. Accessed 22 July, 2022. 2020.

Global Disinformation Index. "The Global Disinformation Index", 2022 [Online], https://www.disinformationindex.org/about/. Accessed 18 April 2022.

Goldman, A., Frenkel, S., and Barnes, J. "Facebook Takes Down Fake Pages Created in China Aimed at Influencing U.S. Election (Published 2020)." *Nytimes.com*, 2020 [Online], https://www.nytimes.com/2020/09/22/us/politics/facebook-china-election-interference.html. Accessed 18 November 2020.

Greenberg, A. "A Brief History of Russian Hackers' Evolving False Flags." *Wired*, 2019 [Online], https://www.wired.com/story/russian-hackers-false-flags-iran-fancy-bear/. Accessed 18 October 2019.

Harris, S., Nakashima, E., Miller, G., and Dawsey, J. "White House Was Warned Guiliani Was Target of Russian Intelligence Operation to Feed Misinformation to Trump." 2020 [Online], https://www.washingtonpost.com/national-security/giuliani-biden-ukraine-russian-disinformation/2020/10/15/43158900-0ef5-11eb-b1e8-16b59b92b36d_story.html. Accessed 18 November 2020.

Jankowicz, Nina, and Collins, Henry. "Enduring Information Vigilance: Government after COVID-19." The U.S. Army War College Parameters, vol. 50, no. 3, 2020, https://press.armywarcollege.edu/parameters/vol50/iss3/4. Accessed 28 November 2020.

Kanno-Youngs, Z. "Homeland Security Blocked Warnings of a Russian Campaign against Biden. (Published 2020)." *Nytimes.com*, 2020. [Online], https://www.nytimes.com/2020/09/03/us/elections/homeland-security-blocked-warnings-of-a-russian-campaign-against-biden.html Accessed 18 November 2020.

Kelly, Laura and Chalfant, Morgan, "US Intel Says Russia, Iran Sought to Influence 2020 Election," https://thehill.com/homenews/news/543460-us-intel-says-russia-iran-sought-to-influence-2020-election.

Kessler, G., Rizzo, S., and Kelley, M. "President Trump Has Made 6,420 False or Misleading Claims over 649 Days." *The Washington Post*, 2020 [Online], https://www.washingtonpost.com/politics/2018/11/02/president-trump-has-made-false-or-misleading-claims-over-days/. Accessed 18 November 2020.

Lewis, James A. "Can We Compete in Cyberspace?" *Center for Strategic and International Studies*, 2 November 2020, https://www.csis.org/analysis/can-we-compete-cyberspace. Accessed 28 November 2020.

Lucas, R. "GOP Report: Hunter Biden's Ukraine Job 'Problematic,' Effect on Policy 'Unclear'." *Npr.org*, 2020 [Online], https://www.npr.org/2020/09/23/916021299/gop-report-hunter-bidens-ukraine-job-problematic-effect-on-policy-unclear. Accessed 18 November 2020.

National Counterintelligence and Security Center. "Foreign Threats to U.S. Elections: Election Security Information Needs [brochure]." *U.S. Director of National Intelligence*, https://www.dni.gov/files/ODNI/documents/DNI_NCSC_Elections_Brochure_Final.pdf. Accessed 28 November 2020.

Roose, Kevin. "Misinformation Peddlers Start Early on Election Day (Published 2020)." *Nytimes.com*, 2020 [Online], https://www.nytimes.com/2020/11/03/technology/misinformation-peddlers-start-early-on-election-day.html. Accessed 18 July 2022.

Sanger, D. and Perlroth, N. "Chinese Hackers Target Email Accounts of Biden Campaign Staff, Google Says (Published 2020)." *Nytimes.com*, 2020 [Online], https://www.nytimes.com/2020/06/04/us/politics/china-joe-biden-hackers.html. Accessed: 18 November 2022.

Sanger, D., et al. "Russian Intelligence Hackers Are Back, Microsoft Warns, Aiming at Officials of Both Parties (Published 2020)." *Nytimes.com*, 2020, https://www.nytimes.com/2020/09/10/us/politics/russian-hacking-microsoft-biden-trump.html.

Senate Select Committee on Intelligence (SSCI). "Russian Active Measures Campaigns and Interference in the 2016 U.S. Election, Volume 1: Russian Efforts against Election Infrastructure with Additional Views [redacted report, public release]." *U.S. Senate*, 2020, https://www.intelligence.senate.gov/sites/default/files/documents/Report_Volume1.pdf. Accessed 28 November 2020.

Spaniel, D. "Returning to the Wilderness of Mirrors: How Great Power Competition and Cyberwarfare Could Precipitate a Digital-Age Cold War—ICIT (Institute for Critical Infrastructure Technology)." *ICIT (Institute for Critical Infrastructure Technology)*, 2022 [Online], https://icitech.org/digital-cold-war/. Accessed 18 March 2022.

Stolberg, Sheryl and Weiland, Noah. "Study Finds 'Single Largest Driver' of Coronavirus Misinformation: Trump (Published 2020)." *Nytimes.com*, 2020 [Online], https://www.nytimes.com/2020/09/30/us/politics/trump-coronavirus-misinformation.html. Accessed 18 April 2022.

Sun-tzu. The Art of War. Translated by Ralph D. Sawyer, Boulder, CO, Westview Press, 1994.

Taylor, Margaret L. "Combating Disinformation and Foreign Interference in Democracies: Lessons from Europe." *Brookings Institute: TechTank*, 31 July 2019, https://www.brookings.edu/blog/techtank/2019/07/31/combating-disinformation-and-foreign-interference-in-democracies-lessons-from-europe/. Accessed 11 March 2021.

United States Congress. H.R. 6395 *William M.* New York Times. "Tracking Viral Misinformation". The *New York Times*, 2020, https://www.nytimes.com/live/2020/2020-election-misinformation-distortions.

United States Congress. H.R. 6395 *William M. (Mac) Thornberry National Defense Authorization Act for Fiscal Year 2021 Conference Report.* United States Government, 2020. *Congress.gov*, https://www.congress.gov/bill/116th-congress/house-bill/6395. Accessed 6 January 2021.

US Cyberspace Solarium Commission (CISA). *Building a Trusted ICT Supply Chain (CSC White Paper #4).* United States Government, 2020a. *Cyberspace Solarium Commission Website*, https://www.solarium.gov/. Accessed 19 December 2020.

US Cyberspace Solarium Commission (CISA). *CSC Final Report.* United States Government, 2020b. *Cyberspace Solarium Commission Website*, https://www.solarium.gov/. Accessed 19 December 2020.

U.S. National Security Agency (USNSA). *2020 NSA Cybersecurity Year in Review.* United States Government, 2021, https://media.defense.gov/2021/Jan/08/2002561651/-1/-1/0/NSA%20CYBERSECURITY%202020%20YEAR%20IN%20REVIEW.PDF/NSA%20CYBERSECURITY%202020%20YEAR%20IN%20REVIEW.PDF. Accessed 14 January 2021.

Wakabayashi, Daisuke. "Election Misinformation Continues Staying Up on YouTube. (Published 2020)." *Nytimes.com*, 2020 [Online], https://www.nytimes.com/2020/11/10/technology/election-misinformation-continues-staying-up-on-youtube.html. Accessed 05 April 2022.

Zengerle, Patricia, and Doina Chiacu. "U.S. 2018 Elections 'Under Attack' by Russia: U.S. Intelligence Chief." *Reuters*, 23 February 2018a, https://www.reuters.com/article/us-usa-security-russia-elections/u-s-2018-elections-under-attack-by-russia-u-s-intelligence-chief-idUSKCN1FX1Z8. Accessed 28 November 2020.

Zengerle, Patricia, and Doina Chiacu. "U.S. 2018 Elections 'Under Attack' by Russia: U.S. Intelligence Chief." *Reuters*, 13 February 2018b, https://www.reuters.com/article/cnews-us-usa-security-russia-elections-idCAKCN1FX1Z8-OCATP. Accessed 10 January 2021.

8 Emergency Services

8.0 ABOUT THE EMERGENCY SERVICES SECTOR

Stanley J. Mierzwa
Director of the Center for Cybersecurity, Kean University

Lauren Spath-Caviglia
Lecturer, Kean University

When you consider industries that were reinvented in recent history, you will find companies that continued to morph and remain relevant and viable and those who started off valid and in favor, but alas, perhaps didn't make the sustainable cut. Consider, for example, Blockbuster Video, they were at the forefront of providing the legal rental of movies using physical media, such as a tape or DVD. They had the opportunity to transition from physical movie rentals to online—they had a customer base and name recognition. Do you see any Blockbuster Video stores around? Chances are you do not, and this may be for many reasons, but perhaps they did not take the opportunity to self-reflect and understand if they needed to change to remain a warranted provider for movie watchers.

In yet another example, consider the photography hardware companies who, for many years, provided cameras that allowed the masses to take photos to be shared and kept history. When the smartphone market was taking shape, these companies may not have taken the opportunity to self-evaluate and determine if they should entertain the smartphone product. Think about some of those companies, and I won't name names, but did they have the opportunity to reinvent themselves or migrate toward the up-and-coming smartphone market since they were experts in cameras already? Was there an opportunity, at some point along the way as the photography market changed for the general consumer, for these companies to re-evaluate areas in their business model and operations to learn more about certain new facets of the industry and stay abreast of the industry and a genuine industry leader?

As the role of Law Enforcement is currently undergoing scrutiny in the popular media and local governments and municipalities, this may be an excellent time period to consider areas that may benefit from greater attention to law enforcement and emergency services. During challenges to an industry or work segment, putting attention to align the necessary skills for the current demand or challenges will provide benefits and transition roles for the future.

In the following chapter, you will gather insights into the topical area of cybercrime investigations within the overarching Emergency Services Sector (ESS) of the Cybersecurity and Infrastructure Security Agency (CISA) identified sixteen defined critical infrastructure areas. A deep-dive focus into the National Initiative for Cybersecurity Education (NICE) Cybersecurity Workforce Framework will ensue surrounding the Investigate category. This category places emphasis on the tasks that take place to investigate cybersecurity events or incidents and crimes related to information technology and the associated components.

As you read the upcoming chapter, it is my hope that you are enlightened by the need for cybersecurity investigation knowledge in our emergency sector critical infrastructure. In our current environment, you cannot go a day without hearing about cybersecurity intrusions, exploits, hacking, and like incidents in the news. In this past year, the role of cybersecurity investigation made national headlines several times with the ransomware attacks that took place against our nations critical infrastructure categories. In progressing through the text, I ask you to resist the temptation

DOI: 10.1201/9781003243021-8

to consider that we should continue to reduce resources to our emergency services sector, but rather invest more and place greater emphasis to help reduce the number of cybercrime incidents plaguing our planet! Combine the growing cybersecurity incidents, with the call to challenge law enforcement, and you are provided with an opportunity to adjust the attention given to law enforcement investigations and aim for excellence. As the cybercrime landscape shifts and changes again in the years to come, again in habit, an opportunity will arise to adjust and reach excellence.

8.0.1   ABOUT KEAN UNIVERSITY

Kean University enrolls almost 16,000 students and offers more than 50 undergraduate majors and 60-plus graduate options, with four campuses in New Jersey and the only public university in America to have a campus in China. US News & World Report has recently ranked Kean University among the top universities in the northern United States for helping economically disadvantaged students enroll and graduate within six years. Kean is ranked 41st for social mobility out of 170 universities in the region.

8.1 CASE STUDY—LAW ENFORCEMENT DIGITAL FORENSICS AND INVESTIGATIONS REVIEW; RESULTS OF A CYBERSECURITY WORKFORCE READINESS SURVEY

Stanley J. Mierzwa
Director of the Center for Cybersecurity, Kean University

Lauren Spath-Caviglia
Lecturer, Kean University

8.1.1 INTRODUCTION

Critical infrastructures play an important role in the proper functioning and foundation of communities, cities, states, and countries and are relied upon by their constituents. At the time of this writing, there exist sixteen sectors that comprise the critical infrastructures of the nation that are vital and without could cause a debilitating effect on the country's economy, security, and public health and safety (Cybersecurity and Infrastructure Security Agency, 2021). Housed within the Emergency Services Sector (ESS) of the critical infrastructures is Emergency Management, Law Enforcement Emergency Medical Services, Fire and Rescue Services, and Public Works.

This research will explore if there are a general problem and lack of specialty skills and resources in the cybersecurity workforce concerning cybercrime investigations within the Law Enforcement component of the ESS. A rapid literature review is presented on the Investigate category's topics in the National Initiative for Cybersecurity Education (NICE) Cybersecurity Workforce Framework, the relevant cybersecurity certifications, and programs, and higher education relevance that align with this category.

Finally, the data results from a short electronic self-report survey on cybersecurity preparedness and resources provided to police departments in New Jersey is provided. Ultimately, the goal of this research is to bring greater awareness and attention to the Investigate category and, with deeper analysis, determine if changes are required in the specialty area and make recommendations for amending, adjusting, or adding to the NICE Cybersecurity Workforce Framework.

When considering the field of cybersecurity, one can look through many different lenses that provide varied perspectives. For example, at a 30,000 feet view, one could find the general areas of prevention, monitoring, and incident response. Evidence of these groups can be gleaned when reviewing the overarching groups of cybersecurity categories outlined in the NIST Special Publication 800-181, also known as the NICE Cybersecurity Workforce Framework. The Cybersecurity Workforce Framework was created to assist employers, workers, training and education providers, and technology providers with identifying needs and gaps with regard to specific cybersecurity roles (Mierzwa & Spath, 2021). There exist seven categories, thirty-three specialty areas, and 52 work roles inside the Cybersecurity Workforce Framework. When peeling away the onion further on the categories or functions, one will find items in Table 8.1.1. For the focus of this essay, it will deep dive into the Investigate (IN) category.

Examination of the CyberSeek supply and demand heat map made available by the NICE, the Computing Technology Industry Association (CompTIA), and Burning Glass Technologies provides a sense of where current cybersecurity roles are focused. It also shows where there are gaps in the workforce, what skills are required, and provides additional formative information. In doing a deeper dive into the information on CyberSeek concerning the Investigate category, it is the smallest segment of the cybersecurity workforce. Of the over 1 million job openings reported via

TABLE 8.1.1

NICE Cybersecurity Workforce Framework Categories

Category	Short Notation	Overview
Securely Provision	SP	Conceptualizes, designs, procures, and/or builds secure information technology systems, with responsibility for aspects of system and/or network development.
Operate and Maintain	OM	Provides the support, administration, and maintenance necessary to ensure effective and efficient information technology (IT) system performance and security.
Oversee and Govern	OV	Provides leadership, management, direction, or development and advocacy so the organization may effectively conduct cybersecurity work.
Protect and Defend	PR	Identifies, analyzes, and mitigates threats to internal information technology (IT) systems and/or networks.
Analyze	AN	Performs highly-specialized review and evaluation of incoming cybersecurity information to determine its usefulness for intelligence.
Collect and Operate	CO	Provides specialized denial and deception operations and collection of cybersecurity information that may be used to develop intelligence.
Investigate	IN	Investigates cybersecurity events or crimes related to information technology (IT) systems, networks, and digital evidence.

Source: National Institute of Standards and Technology (2021).

the Cyberseek heat map, just over 27,000 are aligned with the Investigate category reported as of February 11, 2021 (CyberSeek, Supply/Demand Heat Map 2021).

The smaller segment numbers surrounding the Investigate category have drawn the authors' attention to this information so that it can be further explored whether this is appropriate or not, given the increase in cybercrimes. If businesses and end-users begin to report the crimes more frequently to law enforcement, there is the possibility that more resources with the skills required for investigations will be essential. Given the upward trend in reporting of internet crime complaints, it is anticipated the number will grow as more and more members of society become more cyber smart, notice issues with awareness, and thus report in greater numbers. Many of the cybercrimes today involve the collection of cyber evidence, such as personal computers, email, cell phones, and other technologies such as wearables. With greater cybersecurity awareness, there is the potential for citizens to report cybercrimes just as easily as they do when their automobiles are stolen, for example.

Investigating cybersecurity incidents falls in line with activities when similar crimes or misconduct events or incidents occur. In such instances, the skills required to investigate dealings are specialized with proper data and information collection and forensic analysis. Such skills will align with tasks handled by those in police and law enforcement as well as staff in organizations assigned to such incidents with very modern and possibly complicated tools. However, the use of technology tools, be they hardware or software, will be required, and proper training to use these tools will be necessary. The concern from this chapter is that given the fact that the majority of police departments in the United States have 100 or less officers, are there properly trained and assigned staff to be able to perform the Investigate category tasks. Officers and staff assigned to perform digital investigations and with training will certainly aim toward greater successful outcomes. In one example, Herchenrader and Myhill-Jones (2015) discovered that by using Geographic Information Systems (GIS), police officers were enabled to be effective in preventing crimes based on spatial patterns related to crimes. Using new and modern approaches, with the budget investments, permits greater gains in policing.

The issue for smaller police departments, and those who do not have specialized expertise to perform cyber forensic investigations, is that their budgets are mostly spent on personnel issues, leaving less available for equipment, software tools, and training (Liou, 2019). In the current climate,

TABLE 8.1.2
NICE Cybersecurity Workforce Framework Investigate Specialty Areas

Investigate Category			
NICE Specialty Area	NICE Specialty Area Description	Work Role	Work Role Description
Cyber Investigation (INV)	Applies tactics, techniques, and procedures for a full range of investigative tools and processes to include, but not limited to, interview and interrogation techniques, surveillance, counter surveillance, and surveillance detection, and appropriately balances the benefits of prosecution versus intelligence gathering.	Cyber Crime Investigator	Identifies, collects, examines, and preserves evidence using controlled and documented analytical and investigative techniques.
Digital Forensics (FOR)	Collects, processes, preserves, analyzes, and presents computer-related evidence in support of network vulnerability mitigation and/or criminal, fraud, counterintelligence, or law enforcement investigations.	Law Enforcement/ Counterintelligence Forensic Analyst	Conducts detailed investigations on computer-based crimes establishing documentary or procedural evidence, to include digital media and logs associated with cyber intrusion incidents.
		Cyber Defense Forensic Analyst	Analyzes digital evidence and investigates computer security incidents to derive useful information in support of system/network vulnerability mitigation.

Source: NICE.

with police departments being asked to cut funding, it may be more difficult to obtain the required budget to properly train the smaller police departments that lack cyber investigations knowledge.

Specifically, the Investigate category includes within it the roles of Digital Forensics (FOR) and Cyber Investigation (INV), as detailed in Table 8.1.2 provided by NICE.

This chapter will identify if there is a general problem and, more specifically, lack of specialty skills, resources, and attention in the cybersecurity workforce concerning cybercrime investigations.

8.1.2 NICE CYBERSECURITY WORKFORCE FRAMEWORK KNOWLEDGE, SKILLS, ABILITIES (KSAS)

Each of the specialty areas in the NICE Cybersecurity Framework includes the faculties of Knowledge, Skills, Abilities, Tasks, and Capability Indicators. The National Initiative for Specific Cybersecurity Careers and Studies (NICCS) provides a subjective web application that allows close examination of each of these components to view key items included in the NICE specialty areas. For example, the Cyber Investigation (INV) specialty area includes the following specialty area abilities, as detailed in Table 8.1.3.

From the same NICCS web application, a listing of skills and the description or details of the skills are available detailing the Investigate specialty. A snapshot of the skills details can be found in Appendix 8.1.1 of this case study.

TABLE 8.1.3

NICCS—NICE Cybersecurity Workforce Framework—Ability Numbers of Investigate Specialty

Ability Number	Specialty Area	Description
A0174	IN-INV-001	Ability to find and navigate the dark web using the TOR network to locate markets and forums.
A0175	IN-INV-001	Ability to examine digital media on multiple operating system platforms.
A0005	IN-FOR-001	Ability to decrypt digital data collections.
A0175	IN-FOR-001	Ability to examine digital media on multiple operating system platforms.
A0005	IN-FOR-002	Ability to decrypt digital data collections.
A0043	IN-FOR-002	Ability to conduct forensic analyses in and for both Windows and Unix/Linux environments.

Source: NICCS.

8.1.3 METHODS

8.1.3.1 CURRENT METHOD/INVESTIGATIVE APPROACH

A literature review was performed to provide background about the intersection of cybercrime, police investigations team members and size, crime statistics, investigations-related employment openings, and financial impact. Literature was reviewed beginning from 2015 until the present to keep the content more current. In approaching recommendations to be considered for the next version or iteration of the NICE framework, an analysis of literature related to Investigate category was done. Included in this review was an investigation into the currently available certifications, training, and higher education programs were performed.

8.1.3.2 CURRENT CERTIFICATIONS RELATED TO THE INVESTIGATE CATEGORY

As with any technical profession, a number of professional certifications can be obtained. Certifications provide a means to ensure that individuals have obtained the requisite knowledge from the domains of the certifications to demonstrate their focused topic learning objectives. Professional certification confirms an individual has the minimum standard knowledge set to prove to employers, investigators, compliance agencies, and third parties that they can understand the core topic domains to do the job. As time and needs continue to arise, such certifications continue to grow in variety. Such certifications are made available from private for-profit and non-profit training, research organizations, and product/service vendors.

A review of the currently available certifications related to cyber investigations and forensics was performed and identified over seventeen available qualifications. The following certifications, identified with their full-text nomenclature included in Table 8.1.4.

Research and analysis were performed on each of these certifications related to cyber investigations. As part of the analysis in Table 8.1.5, special attention was given to determine if the certification was vendor or product-specific, was recognized, and the intended focus on the program.

Of particular note from the above-listed certifications include the Cybersecurity Forensic Analyst (CSFA), which requires an FBI background check. If a felony is observed on an individual's record, the exam cannot be taken. A majority of misdemeanor offenses will also disqualify the individual.

TABLE 8.1.4
Identified Investigate Related Certifications

Certification Name	Certification Acronym
Global Information Assurance Certification Forensic Examiner	GCFE
Global Information Assurance Certification Forensic Analyst	GCFA
Global Information Assurance Certification Network Forensic Analyst	GNFA
Global Information Assurance Certification Smartphone Forensics	GASF
Certified Digital Forensics Examiner	CDFE
Certified Forensic Computer Examiner	CFCE
Certified Advanced Windows Forensic Examiner	CAWFE
Access Data (FTK) Certified Examiner	ACE
Access Data (FTK) Certified Investigator	ACI
DoD Digital Forensic Examiner	DFE
Cyber Security Forensic Analyst	CSFA
Cellebrite Certified Mobile Examiner	CCME
BlackBag Technologies Certified Blacklight Examiner	CBE
BlackBag Technologies Mac and iOS Certified Forensic Examiner	MICFE
Certified Computer Examiner	CCE
Computer Hacking Forensic Investigator	CHFI
EnCase Certified Engineer	EnCE

TABLE 8.1.5
Review of Investigate Related Certifications

Name	Provider	Vendor Neutral	Product Specific	Nationally Recognized	Internationally Recognized	Certificate Focus
GCFE	SANS GIAC	Yes	No	Yes	Unsure	Computer forensic analysis
GCFA	SANS GIAC	Yes	No	Yes	Unsure	Incident investigations
GNFA	SANS GIAC	Yes	No	Yes	Unsure	Network forensic artifact analysis
GASF	SANS GIAC	Yes	No	Yes	Unsure	Forensic analysis of smartphones
GBFA	SANS GIAC	Yes	No	Yes	Unsure	Collection, acquisition, and triage
CDFE	Mile2	Yes	No	Unsure	Unsure	Cybercrime and fraud investigation
CFCE	IACIS	Yes	No	Unsure	Unsure	Computer/Digital Forensics
CAWFE	IACIS	No	Yes	Unsure	Unsure	Windows Forensics
ACE	AccessData	No	Yes	Unsure	Unsure	FTK Forensic Tools
ACI	AccessData	No	Yes	Unsure	Unsure	FTK Forensic Tools
DFE	DOD	Yes	No	Unsure	Unsure	Analysis of digital media
CSFA	Cybersecurity Institute (CSI)	Yes	No	Unsure	Unsure	Thorough forensic analysis
CCME	Cellebrite	No	Yes	Unsure	Unsure	Mobile device forensic investigation
CBE	BlackBag (Cellebrite)	No	Yes	Unsure	Unsure	Access forensic evidence with Blacklight
MICFE	BlackBag (Cellebrite)	No	Yes	Unsure	Unsure	MacOS and iOS forensic examination
CCE	ISFCE	Yes	No	Unsure	Unsure	Practice of digital forensics
CHFI	EC-Council	Yes	No	Yes	Yes	Computer hacking forensic investigation
EnCE	OpenText	No	Yes	No	No	Use of OpenText EnCase forensic examiner

8.1.3.3 GENERAL CYBERSECURITY CERTIFICATIONS RELEVANCE TO INVESTIGATE CATEGORY

Overarching or more general and popular cybersecurity certifications are available that one can often find as a requirement for many open or available jobs in the industry. Such generic certifications cover a huge gamut of a topic, meant to ensure that the student has an excellent broad understanding of the said topic domains. In reviewing the most popular certifications for cybersecurity, an analysis of their domains was performed to find relevance to the Investigated category.

The top 10 most popular cybersecurity certifications for 2020, as reported by *Forbes* (2020), include:

- Certified Information Systems Security Professional-Information Systems Security Management Professional (CISSP-ISSMP)—ISC(2)
- Certified Information Security Manager (CISM)—ISACA
- Certified in Risk and Information Systems Control (CRISC)—ISACA
- AWS Certified Security Specialty
- Certified Information Systems Auditor (CISA)—ISACA
- CompTIA: Security+
- Certified Cloud Security Provider (CCSP)—ISC(2)
- Certified Ethical Hacker (CEH)—EC Council
- CompTIA CySA+ (Cybersecurity Analyst)
- Google Cloud Platform Professional Security Engineer

A further analysis of the certification test content or exam overview for each of the top ten certifications indicated is in Table 8.1.6, with regard to including the Investigate category domains (digital forensics and cyber investigations).

Although the majority of the content from the top 10 cybersecurity certifications for 2020 did not demonstrate an abundance of content related to digital forensics and cybersecurity investigations, it should be noted that these certifications do provide background content that provides a core understanding of varied cybersecurity knowledge. As with any profession, the more and broad knowledge base can and will be helpful to one doing an investigation into a cybercrime incident. In searching for content related to the NICE Investigate category, a search on each of the outlined webpages above was done for the keywords of "digital forensic(s)" or "cybersecurity investigation(s)" to help increase focus for investigations.

8.1.3.4 LAW ENFORCEMENT SPECIFIC PROGRAMS RELEVANT TO THE INVESTIGATE CATEGORY

Law enforcement and agencies, such as the FBI, Secret Service, and Interpol, involved in the investigation and potential prosecution of technology-related crimes are afforded access to focused cybersecurity training programs. These programs are generally only offered to federal, state, and local law enforcement staff, or for those who obtain written approval or sponsorship to attend. In the cases of sponsorship, nominations need to be submitted to specific agencies, such as the United States Secret Service and National Computer Forensics Institute (NCFI). The NCFI is a federally funded training center that solely focuses on training state and local law enforcement staff and judicial professionals in comprehensive cybercrime trends, investigative methods, and prosecuting challenges. A review of such programs is provided in Table 8.1.7.

8.1.3.5 HIGHER EDUCATION PROGRAMS RELEVANCE TO INVESTIGATE CATEGORY

In addition to certificate and other education programs that provide knowledge related to the Investigate category in the NICE framework, United States higher education was examined for the presence of programs and their content. Resources available at the National Center for Education Statistics (NCES)

TABLE 8.1.6

Top 10 List of Cybersecurity Certifications with Investigation Related Content

Name	Vendor	Digital Forensics Content	Cyber Investigations Content	Source
CISSP-ISSMP	ISC(2)	Low	Low	https://www.isc2.org/-/media/ISC2/Certifications/Exam-Outlines/ISSMP-Exam-Outline-Effective-May-2018.ashx
CISM	ISACA	Low	Low	https://resources.infosecinstitute.com/category/certifications-training/cism/cism-domain-overview/
CRISC	ISACA	None	None	https://resources.infosecinstitute.com/category/certifications-training/crisc/crisc-domain-overview/
AWS Certified Security Specialty	Amazon	None	Low	https://d1.awsstatic.com/training-and-certification/docs-security-spec/AWS-Certified-Security-Specialty_Exam-Guide.pdf
CISA	ISACA	Low	None	https://www.isaca.org/credentialing/cisa/cisa-exam
CompTIA: Security+	CompTIA	None	None	https://www.comptia.org/certifications/security
CCSP	ISC(2)	Medium	Medium	https://www.isc2.org/-/media/ISC2/Certifications/Exam-Outlines/CCSP-Exam-Outline.ashx
CEH	ECCouncil	Low	Low	https://www.eccouncil.org/wp-content/uploads/2016/02/CEH-Exam-Blueprint-v2.0.pdf
CompTIA CySA+	CompTIA	Low	Low	https://www.comptia.org/certifications/cybersecurity-analyst
Google Cloud Platform Professional Security Engineer	Google	Low	Low	https://cloud.google.com/certification/guides/cloud-security-engineer

Source: Forbes (2020).

Table 8.1.6 Content Level Legend:
None—no content found
Low—minimal or may touch on content
Medium—more than minimal content
High—focused and high amount of content

were researched. The NCES is the primary federal organization and entity for collecting and analyzing data related to education in the United States and other nations. The NCES is located within the United States Department of Education and the Institute of Education Sciences (IES, NCES, 2020).

The NCES has available an online search application named College Navigator, which includes information on 7,000 colleges and universities in the United States. The information includes data on two-year, four-year, community colleges, liberal arts colleges, and large universities. A search was performed in College Navigator to determine programs that include cybersecurity forensic and investigations programs. The exact search terms included: Bachelor programs, Associate's programs, Advanced degrees, public, private non-profit, private for-profit, four-year, and two-year programs, and those with "Cyber/Computer Forensic and Counterterrorism." The search yielded 95 higher (95) education institutions or only 1.4% (95/7,000) from the data classified as having Cyber/Computer Forensic programs that are related to the NICE framework Investigate category. By comparison, a search for the same exact terms but supplanting "Cyber/Computer Forensic and Counterterrorism" program with "Computer and Information Systems Security/Information Assurance" program yielded over 500 named schools, or 7.1% of the 7,000 listed institutions (IES, NCES 2020).

TABLE 8.1.7

Cyber Investigations Law-Enforcement Related Programs and Certifications

Organization	Program(s)	Law Enforcement	Civilians Allowed
National Computer Forensics Institute	Variety of investigation courses	Yes (and prosecutor and judges).	No
National White Collar Crime Center (NW3C)	Certified Economic Crime Forensic Examiner (CECFE)	Yes (limited to US state, local, territorial, tribal and federal law enforcement, and regulatory personnel.	Yes. But limited offerings and fees apply.
National White Collar Crime Center (NW3C)	Certified Cyber Crime Examiner (3CE)	Yes (limited to US state, local, territorial, tribal and federal law enforcement, and regulatory personnel.	Yes. But limited offerings and fees apply.
National White Collar Crime Center (NW3C)	Certified Cyber Crime Investigator (3CI)	Yes (limited to US state, local, territorial, tribal and federal law enforcement, and regulatory personnel.	Yes. But limited offerings and fees apply.
Department of Defense Cyber Crime Center (DC3)	Digital Forensic Examiner (DFE)	Yes	Yes, but must be federal agency or under MOU.
Department of Defense Cyber Crime Center (DC3)	Cyber Crime Investigator (CCI)	Yes	Yes, but must be federal agency or under MOU.
Federal Law Enforcement Training Centers (FLETC)	Cyber Incident Response and Analysis (CIRA)	Yes	No. Must be law enforcement/agent with arrest authority.
Regional Computer Forensics Laboratory (RCFL)	Variety of investigation courses	Yes	No. Must be with a participating agency.

8.1.4   FINDINGS

8.1.4.1   DATA BACKGROUND

The top computer or cybersecurity certifications associated with the Investigate category are SANS/ GIAC Certification; Certified Information Systems Security Professional (CISSP), EnCase Certified Examiner, GIAC Certified Forensic Analyst, GIAC Certified Incident Handler. There are no national standards for digital forensic credentialing, and for that matter, no state-level ones. Some states have attempted to bring about such standards. Many of these states simply lump Private Investigator (PI) licensing and forensic credentialing into one in an attempt to add legitimacy to forensic investigators (Zahadat, 2019). While the NICE framework can be one of the solid starting points, there is still the egregious issue of credentialing and certification in digital forensics (Zahadat, 2019).

8.1.4.2   CYBERCRIME FINANCIAL IMPACT

The total financial losses by victim per state ranked in highest order first included: California, Florida, Ohio, Texas, New York, Illinois, New Jersey, Pennsylvania, Virginia, and Massachusetts (Internet Crime Complaint Center, 2019). Of note, the age group with the largest total loss and victim total count included the population aged over 60 years old. Estimates of cybercrime against vulnerable older adults can range as high as $37 billion (Lieber, 2018). The FBI had maintained that fraud against senior citizens is a target for cybercrime because they likely have savings, have excellent credit, and were born (1930s to 1950s) when they were raised to be polite and trusting (FBI. GOV. 2018). The US Census Bureau's population estimates of 2018 states that 52 million Americans are age 65 or older. Greater cybersecurity awareness, training, and outreach to the 60+ population would provide opportunities to minimize the total losses from cybercrime incidents to this group.

Current efforts exist in putting energy toward thwarting the prevention of cybercrime losses. One such effort is led by the United States Secret Service. In 2019, the Secret Service prevented $7.1 billion of cybercrime losses and returned over $31 million in stolen assets to victims of fraud (Verizon, 2010). This type of activity includes more than pure cybersecurity operations but operates through undercover operations, confidential informants, and partnerships with industry and the broader law enforcement community (Verizon, 2020). A key component relative to this research chapter of the Secret Service activities includes partnerships with industry.

There exist millions of businesses, and with that, the potential for cybercrime. Ensuring that cybersecurity professionals recognize the how and what of preparing for tasks included in the Investigate category should be a priority if increased solving of cybercrimes are to be tackled.

8.1.4.3 CRIMINAL CASES FILED

One can look at the number of legal cases filed related to cybercrime, in the United States to get a sense of the volume of cases actually being pursued. Given the amount of money being lost due to cybercrime one should expect a large number of cases. However, in reviewing the United States Department of Justice cases for 2016, you find approximately 114 cases filed at the federal level for computer fraud, 33 for advanced fee schemes, 59 for intellectual property violations, 274 for identity theft, and 337 for aggravated identity theft (Yar & Steinmetz, 2019). In total, this amounts to approximately 817 cases, and considering the scale of current cybercrime activity, this is not a large number. Cybercrime circumstances can be very complicated and time-consuming to pursue, and thus it is possible that the underreporting can be a result of the complexity involved and, therefore, not pursued.

8.1.5 CYBERSECURITY READINESS SURVEY BACKGROUND

An electronic survey was developed with the goal of obtaining data from New Jersey police departments. The survey questions included four sections: (1) Demographics and organization data; (2) cybersecurity posture, capabilities, needs; (3) cybersecurity resources available; and (4) open-ended perspectives and comments. The research questions were aimed at assessing the overall cybersecurity posture of the police departments. All responses were captured anonymously, and no identifying information, such as IP addresses, were collected. The police departments were contacted through the New Jersey State Association of Chiefs of Police (NJSACOP), who were kind enough to agree to submit the survey to their membership contacts. The survey was administered utilizing Qualtrics, a web-based electronic survey tool, during the first quarter of 2020.

A 21-question electronic web-based survey was created and circulated to police departments in the state of New Jersey. In order to reach the appropriate staff at the police departments, the survey was provided to chiefs of police organization and asked that the survey be sent to their constituents. A timeframe of several months was provided to allow participants to complete the survey at their convenience. Thirty-six surveys were completed.

8.1.6 CYBERSECURITY READINESS SURVEY RESULTS

The overall size of the team that provides cybersecurity efforts to the survey respondents was between 1 and 5 staff members for 83% of the police departments, as detailed in Table 8.1.8.

Given that in the United States 94.7% of police departments have fewer than 100 officers, this aligns with the figure on the smaller size of assigned cyber staff members [1, 2].

Respondents were queried on the type of police department they are a part of, with an option to select one. The majority of police departments are recognized as a local municipal police unit, as seen in Figure 8.1.1. This will align with the statistic that the greater percentage of police departments of smaller stature.

TABLE 8.1.8
Results of Query on Indicating the Size of the Team that Provides Cybersecurity Efforts

Police Cybersecurity Team Size			
Number	Answer	Percent	Count
1	None	0.00%	0
2	1–5	83.33%	30
3	6–10	11.11%	4
4	More than 10	5.56%	2
5	Unsure. Please Explain.	0.00%	0

When survey recipients were asked whom they receive support and guidance from for cybersecurity issues and efforts, allowing for selecting all that apply in their response, the top results were: 53% from the township or town IT consultants; 22% from township or town IT departments; 19% from specific municipal police IT department as detailed in Table 8.1.9.

This does suggest that the majority of cybersecurity tasks are handled by the township or town IT consultants and brings to question whether these staff members have the necessary experience and credentials required for cyber and digital forensic investigations. Furthermore, a deeper investigation may be warranted to determine if it would be advantageous to have internal staff of the police department handle cybersecurity-related tasks.

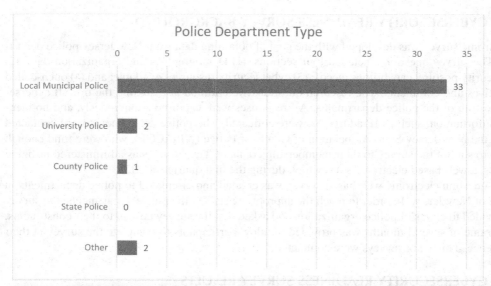

Police Department Type			
Number	Answer	Percent	Count
1	Local Municipal Police	86.84%	33
2	University Police	5.26%	2
3	County Police	2.63%	1
4	State Police	0.00%	0
5	Other	5.26%	2

FIGURE 8.1.1 Results of query on police department type.

TABLE 8.1.9

Results of Query on Indicating the Size of the Team that Provides Cybersecurity Efforts.

	Information Security Team Size		
Number	Answer	Percent	Count
1	Township or town Information Technology Department	17.78%	8
2	Township or town IT Security department	2.22%	1
3	Specific Municipal Police Information Technology department	17.18%	8
4	Specific Municipal IT Security department	4.44%	2
5	Township or town IT consultants	37.78%	17
6	Other: Please Explain.	20.00%	9

Note: Select all that apply were options in this self-report query

As shown in Figure 8.1.2, when asked which single person or position is considered the police organization's operational cybersecurity leadership, the top results, were: Township or town IT consultants—34%; Township or town Information Technology most senior person—22%; Township or town Information Security most senior person (CISO)—12.5%. Again, as seen in the previous survey question, further knowledge can be gained to determine if cybersecurity leadership can or should be populated by internal personnel in the police department.

Pertaining to staffing levels, on one question that asked if the police departments feel they have the appropriate amount of staff allocated/assigned to help protect from a cybersecurity event, 56% answered Yes, and 38% replied No. This can highlight that the police departments appear satisfied with the amount of staff allocated to respond to a cybersecurity incident in their facilities. However, this question does not necessarily address if the appropriate amount of staff is allocated to help analyze and perform adequate investigations.

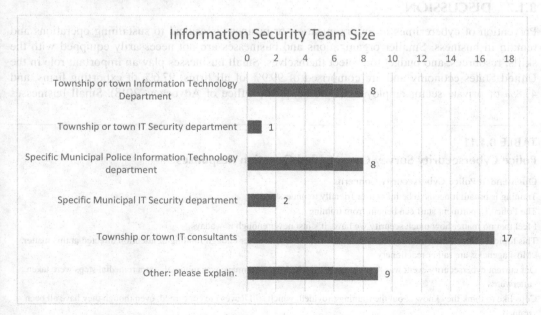

FIGURE 8.1.2 Results of query on who is considered the police organization's operational cybersecurity leadership—select one.

TABLE 8.1.10

Results of query on Technology Infrastructure and Operation Cybersecurity Risk Assessment Performed and Within What Timeframe

	Timeframe of Technology Infrastructure and Operation Cybersecurity Risk Assessment		
Number	**Answer**	**Percent**	**Count**
1	Within the past six months	25.00%	9
2	Within the past year	25.00%	9
3	Within the past two years	13.89%	5
4	Within the past five years	8.33%	3
5	Never	16.67%	6
6	Unsure: Please Explain.	11.11%	

Related to training, the participants were queried if they felt that adequate cybersecurity training has been provided to their police department. The response was 53% for No, not enough training has been provided and 44% for Yes.

As with any operation or organization, it is useful to include a routine, perhaps yearly, cybersecurity risk assessment. Risk assessments can take on very specific tasks, but during the course of the activity, there is the potential of uncovering issues of unmet needs. The said survey did query the respondents about the last such assessment, the results are outlined in Table 8.1.10.

An optional open-ended question was posed requests comments to share about concerns or problems that need to be further addressed regarding Cybersecurity, the following responses in Table 8.1.11 were recorded:

8.1.7 DISCUSSION

Prevention of cybercrimes to an organization or business is critical to sustaining operations and remain in business. Smaller organizations and businesses are not necessarily equipped with the skills, resources, and budget to protect themselves. Small businesses play an important role in the United States economy and are comprised of 99.9% of all firms, 97.6% of exporting firms, and 47.8% of private-sector employees (Romine, 2019; Office of Advocacy, 2018). Small businesses

TABLE 8.1.11

Police Cybersecurity Survey Open-Ended Question Responses

Open-Ended Police Cybersecurity Concerns

Training is broad. It needs to be more user friendly to understand.

The Police Department staff can benefit from training.

I feel that no matter how much security we have, it's just never enough nowadays.

This topic and associated training is absolutely critical. There is never enough funding or attention directed at this matter. Most agencies are rather reactionary.

Our current cybersecurity event was "caught early" and luckily the damage was minimal; extra remedial steps were taken afterwards.

Cops like to think they know about the training provided, which still leaves me concerned, even though they have all been trained.

Training is needed.

account for 61.8% of net new jobs from the first quarter of 1993 until the end of 2016 (Romine, 2019) [4]. Of special note is that small businesses created 1.9 million net jobs in 2015, with firms fewer than 20 employees experiencing the largest gains at 1.1 million net jobs (Office of Advocacy, 2018). If small businesses, which may be local entities, are not equipped well enough to protect themselves from cybercrime events, there is a potential that crimes will increase and thus require investigations. Without having specialized cybercrime prevention or analysis staff, these smaller businesses can potentially need to rely on local police departments to assist, but that would assume that the local police are trained and equipped to assist.

Consider greater awareness given to certifications in the Investigation category, such as the EnCase Computer Forensics Certified Examiner certification (EnCe). Other popular digital forensic certifications are available as well as newer ones are beginning to enter the market (Tittel, Lindros & Kyle, 2019). A job board search results with vendor-neutral certifications were done in 2019 resulted in top values for the GCFA (SANS GIAC) and GCFE (SANS GIAC), followed by CHFI (EC-Council) and EnCE (Encase). There appears not to be a standardized certification for investigation examiners (Srinivasan, 2013). Instead, professionals usually obtain tools or vendor-specific certifications. In a study supported by the National Institute of Justice (NIJ) indicated that first-responding officers often do not know how to properly secure digital evidence and that prosecutors have a tendency to request all information from devices without consideration of their physical storage size (Goodison et al., 2015). A future research study could include the evaluation of the number of those who perform cyber investigations and what certifications they hold to try and determine which are the most popular. It is possible that one of the more formative ones could become a de facto standard or could be retrofitted to make it a more global standard.

Cyber investigations will often deal with the efforts to research various entities and components after an incident takes place. Given investigations can include the use of law enforcement, the topic of prediction can come to mind. Predictive policing is a term applied to a range of analytic tools and law enforcement practices linked by the claimed ability to "forecast where and when the next crime or series of crimes will take place" (Hannem et al., 2019; Uchida, 2014).

Although this chapter does not address predicting as a way to thwart cybersecurity breaches, it can be a topic worth exploring in future research to determine it can be considered a future revision to the framework.

8.1.8   LIMITATIONS

In doing the review of the Investigate-related certifications, it is difficult to determine if the certification is nationally or internationally recognized without having the appropriate demographic information available. For example, there is a lack of a clearinghouse or database of all persons with Investigate related certifications and associated information such as home country.

Data and background were provided to help bring attention to cybersecurity investigations but with a focus on the domestic front, specific to the United States. It is virtually impossible to bring up cybercrime without thorough integration with the international crime community. The United Nations Office on Drugs and Crime Cybercrime Repository indicates that 159 countries have laws addressing cybercrime, amounting to 1,300 individual pieces of legislation (Yar & Steinmetz, 2019). There continues to be a movement to integrate the knowledge relating to cybercrime globally; however, it is challenging to enforce. Consider developing countries that face economic hardships, combined with health, poverty, and political issues, and it is easy to see that cybercrime may take a back seat during other priorities. The interesting dilemma is that with the simple tools of a computer, Internet connection, and willingness to commit crimes, it can happen virtually anywhere. Adding to the fervor is that if a country is enduring hardships, the population may be more inclined to consider cybercrime as a means for gain. As you can see, more attention can certainly be given to a whole gamut of international aspects, but for the purpose of the NIST 800-181 framework, the authors focused on the United States.

Concerning frameworks, this chapter focused on the National Cybersecurity Workforce Framework, which is promoted and updated by the NICE and developed by the National Institute of Standards and Technology. Other such frameworks exist that could have been explored, including the Institute of Information Security Professionals (IISP) and Skills Framework for the Information Age (SFIA), would have added a comparison with the NICE imitative.

8.1.9 CONCLUSION

Every one of the work roles that are identified in the NICE Cybersecurity Workforce Framework provides activities, services, and expertise required to help organizations to approach a comprehensive cybersecurity program. In this chapter, we focused on the Investigate category, which from our review is one of the smaller segments when compared to the other NICE categories. Our literature review of certifications and programs aligned with the Investigate category was outlined in this article to provide greater awareness of the options available. It should be noted that such certifications and programs are constantly being updated, added to, and may not be an exhaustive list provided in this chapter.

From the police cybersecurity survey, it was determined that departments received guidance and support and leadership for cybersecurity issues and concerns primarily from township IT consultants or township IT departments. This does correlate with the information that 94.7% of police departments have fewer than 100 officers and that in our survey, respondents reported that 84% have between one and five staff members allocated to cybersecurity efforts.

Related to adequate cybersecurity training, 53% of respondents reported they did not feel that they had enough training provided. Given the reliance on consultants for cybersecurity issues and concerns reported, this does align with the lack of training reported. Additionally, in the open-text question survey related to any other comments or concerns, a greater them surrounded the need for training.

8.1.9.1 ABOUT THE AUTHORS

Lauren Spath lectures on criminal justice topics at Kean University, including Victims of Crimes, Diversity & Criminal Justice, Comparative Criminal Justice Systems, and Research Methods. Spath received her MA in Criminal Justice at Kean University and is the Faculty Advisor for the Alpha Phi Sigma National Criminal Justice Honor Society.

Stanley J. Mierzwa is the Director of the Center for Cybersecurity and also lectures in topics including Cybersecurity Risk Management, Cyber Policy, Digital Crime and Terrorism, and Foundations in Cybersecurity at Kean University. Mierzwa received his MS in Management of Information Systems at the New Jersey Institute of Technology and his BS in Electrical Engineering at Fairleigh Dickinson University. Mierzwa is also a Certified Information Systems Security Professional (CISSP), member of the FBI Infragard, and currently pursuing a PhD Information Technology with a specialization in cybersecurity.

ACKNOWLEDGMENTS

This research study and report were supported by the Kean University Center for Cybersecurity, a multi-disciplinary collaboration between the School of Criminal Justice and Public Administration and the School of Computer Science and Technology. A special thank you to Dr. James Drylie, PhD and Dr. Patrick McManimon, PhD, Executive Director, for their unwavering support and envisioning the idea of pursuing a police cybersecurity readiness survey.

APPENDIX 8.1.1
NICCS—NICE Cybersecurity Workforce Framework Web Explorer—Investigate—Skill Numbers of Investigate Specialty

Skills	Specialty Area	Description
S0047	IN-INV-001	Skill in preserving evidence integrity according to standard operating procedures or national standards.
S0068	IN-INV-001	Skill in collecting, processing, packaging, transporting, and storing electronic evidence to avoid alteration, loss, physical damage, or destruction of data.
S0072	IN-INV-001	Skill in using scientific rules and methods to solve problems.
S0086	IN-INV-001	Skill in evaluating the trustworthiness of the supplier and/or product.
S0032	IN-FOR-001	Skill in developing, testing, and implementing infrastructure contingency and recovery plans.
S0046	IN-FOR-001	Skill in performing packet-level analysis using appropriate tools (e.g., Wireshark, tcpdump).
S0047	IN-FOR-001	Skill in preserving evidence integrity according to standard operating procedures or national standards.
S0062	IN-FOR-001	Skill in analyzing memory dumps to extract information.
S0065	IN-FOR-001	Skill in identifying and extracting data of forensic interest in diverse media (i.e., media forensics).
S0068	IN-FOR-001	Skill in collecting, processing, packaging, transporting, and storing electronic evidence to avoid alteration, loss, physical damage, or destruction of data.
S0069	IN-FOR-001	Skill in setting up a forensic workstation.
S0071	IN-FOR-001	Skill in using forensic tool suites (e.g., EnCase, The Sleuth Kit, FTK).
S0073	IN-FOR-001	Skill in using virtual machines. (e.g., Microsoft Hyper-V, VMware vSphere, Citrix XenDesktop/Server, Amazon Elastic Compute Cloud, etc.).
S0074	IN-FOR-001	Skill in physically disassembling PCs.
S0075	IN-FOR-001	Skill in conducting forensic analyses in multiple operating system environments (e.g., mobile device systems).
S0087	IN-FOR-001	Skill in deep analysis of captured malicious code (e.g., Malware Forensics)
S0088	IN-FOR-001	Skill in using binary analysis tools (e.g., HexEdit, command code xxd, Hexdump).
S0089	IN-FOR-001	Skill in one-way hash functions (e.g., Secure Hash Algorithm [SHA], Message Digest Algorithm [MD5]).
S0090	IN-FOR-001	Skill in analyzing anomalous code as malicious or benign.
S0091	IN-FOR-001	Skill in analyzing volatile data.
S0092	IN-FOR-001	Skill in identifying obfuscation techniques.
S0093	IN-FOR-001	Skill in interpreting results of debugger to ascertain tactics, techniques, and procedures.
S0032	IN-FOR-002	Skill in developing, testing, and implementing network infrastructure contingency and recovery plans.
S0047	IN-FOR-002	Skill in preserving evidence integrity according to standard operating procedures or national standards.
S0062	IN-FOR-002	Skill in analyzing memory dumps to extract information.
S0065	IN-FOR-002	Skill in identifying and extracting data of forensic interest in diverse media (i.e., media forensics).
S0067	IN-FOR-002	Skill in identifying, modifying, and manipulating applicable system components within Windows, Unix, or Linux (e.g., passwords, user accounts, files).
S0068	IN-FOR-002	Skill in collecting, processing, packaging, transporting, and storing electronic evidence to avoid alteration, loss, physical damage, or destruction of data.
S0069	IN-FOR-002	Skill in setting up a forensic workstation.
S0071	IN-FOR-002	Skill in using forensic tool suites (e.g., EnCase, The Sleuth Kit, FTK).

(Continued)

APPENDIX 8.1.1 *(Continued)*
NICCS—NICE Cybersecurity Workforce Framework Web Explorer—Investigate—Skill Numbers of Investigate Specialty

Skills	Specialty Area	Description
S0073	IN-FOR-002	Skill in using virtual machines. (e.g., Microsoft Hyper-V, VMware vSphere, Citrix XenDesktop/Server, Amazon Elastic Computer Cloud, etc.).
S0074	IN-FOR-002	Skill in physically disassembling PCs.
S0075	IN-FOR-002	Skill in conducting forensic analyses in multiple operating system environments (e.g., mobile device systems).
S0087	IN-FOR-002	Skill in deep analysis of captured malicious code (e.g., malware forensics).
S0088	IN-FOR-002	Skill in using binary analysis tools (e.g., Hexedit, command code xxd, Hexdump).
S0089	IN-FOR-002	Skill in one-way hash functions (e.g., Secure Hash Algorithm [SHA], Message Digest Algorithm [MD5]).
S0090	IN-FOR-002	Skill in analyzing anomalous code as malicious or benign.
S0091	IN-FOR-002	Skill in analyzing volatile data.
S0092	IN-FOR-002	Skill in identifying obfuscation techniques.
S0093	IN-FOR-002	Skill in interpreting results of debugger to ascertain tactics, techniques, and procedures.
S0131	IN-FOR-002	Skill in analyzing malware.
S0132	IN-FOR-002	Skill in conducting bit-level analysis.
S0133	IN-FOR-002	Skill in processing digital evidence, to include protecting and making legally sound copies of evidence.
S0156	IN-FOR-002	Skill in performing packet-level analysis.

Source: NICCS.

REFERENCES

Articles

Hannem, S., Sanders, C., Schneider, C., Doyle, A., Christensen, T. (2019). Security and risk technologies in criminal justice, critical perspectives. *Canadian Scholars.* 42–43.

Herchenrader, T., Myhill-Jones, S. (2015). GIS supporting intelligence-led policing. *Police Practice and Research—An International Journal.* 16(2), 136–147.

Liou, Kuotsai T. (2019). Technology application and police management: Issues and challenges. *International Journal of Organization Theory and Behavior.* 22(2), 191–208.

Mierzwa, S., Spath-Caviglia, L., Christov, I. (2021). Commentary or perspective: Opportunities to leverage the use of global public health innovative research and technology in combatting cybercrime. *Journal of Leadership, Accountability and Ethics.* 18(4), 35–43.

Romine, C., (2019). Cyber crime: An existential threat to small business. *United States Senate Committee on Small Business and Entrepreneurship.*

Zahadat, N. (2019). Digital forensics, a need for credentials and standards. *The Journal of Digital Forensics, Security and Law, 14(1).*

Books

Uchida, C. (2014) *Predictive Policing, Encyclopedia or Criminology and Criminal Justice.* New York. Springer-Verlag.

Yar, M., Steinmetz, K. (2019). *Cybercrime and Society,* (3rd Ed.). London. Sage Publishing.

Government

Cybersecurity and Infrastructure Security Agency (2021). Critical Infrastructure Sectors. Retrieved from: https://www.cisa.gov/critical-infrastructure-sectors

CyberSeek, Supply/Demand Heat Map (2021). CyberSeek. Retrieved from: https://www.cyberseek.org/heatmap.html

FBI.GOV, Scams and Safety: Fraud Against Seniors (2018). Retrieved from: https://www.fbi.gov/scams-and-safety/common-scams-and-crimes/elder-fraud

Internet Crime Complaint Center (2019). Internet Crime Report, United States Federal Bureau of Investigation. As retrieved from: https://www.ic3.gov/Home/AnnualReports

Institute of Education Services (IES), National Center for Education Statistics (NCES) (2020). CollegeNavigator Data Search System. Retrieved from: https://nces.ed.gov/collegenavigator/

National Institute of Standards and Technology (2021). NICE Framework Resource Center: As retrieved from: https://www.nist.gov/itl/applied-cybersecurity/nice/nice-framework-resource-center/resources

Office of Advocacy (2018). United States Small Business Profile. Retrieved from: https://www.sba.gov/sites/default/files/advocacy/2018-Small-Business-Profiles-US.pdf

Private Sector

Forbes (2020). Top 10 Most Popular Cybersecurity Certifications in 2020. As retrieved from: https://www.forbes.com/sites/louiscolumbus/2020/06/16/top-10-most-popular-cybersecurity-certifications-in-2020/#241f07f43f51

Lieber, N. (2018). How Criminal Steal $37 Billion a Year from America's Elderly. As retrieved from: https://www.bloomberg.com/news/features/2018-05-03/america-s-elderly-are-losing-37-billion-a-year-to-fraud

Tittel, E., Lindros, K., Kyle, M. (2019). Best Digital Forensics Certifications. Business News Daily. Retrieved from: https://www.businessnewsdaily.com/10755-best-digital-forensics-certifications.html

Verizon (2020). Verizon Data Breach Investigations Report. Retrieved from: https://enterprise.verizon.com/resources/reports/2020-data-breach-investigations-report.pdf

9 Energy

9.0 ABOUT THE ENERGY SECTOR

Chris Luras
Partner, Guidehouse

John Eckenrode
Director, Guidehouse

Donald Heckman
Director, Guidehouse

The Energy Sector is recognized as a uniquely critical enabler for the other 15 critical infrastructure sectors in Presidential Policy Directive 21. The Cybersecurity and Infrastructure Security Agency (CISA) has stated: "The US energy infrastructure fuels the economy of the 21st century; without a stable energy supply, health and welfare are threatened, and the US economy cannot function." Because of this, the Energy Sector's challenges are a priority and must be addressed to ensure our long-term prosperity as a nation.

The market landscape for utilities and energy companies is rapidly transitioning to one that requires a cleaner fuel supply, increased reliability, improved resilience, and more control over energy costs for customers. These factors, combined with the traditional requirements for safety, reliability, and low energy costs, will require utilities and energy companies to consider more rapid adoption of new business models, advanced technologies, and alternative rate designs and pricing options.

The Energy Sector can capitalize on the current movement to modernize and transform the technologies within its sector to provide greater efficiencies and resilience while addressing concerns around fossil-fueled, primarily coal-fired, generation plants. While these new technologies can improve current service, which taxes existing generation and transmission capacity during peak service times, they also have their own issues and concerns.

Clean energy replacements, such as dispersed solar and wind-powered generation sites, are often located in areas distant from load centers, which requires long transmission systems to deliver electrical energy to the demand. This means the generation sites are subject to adverse weather conditions, which can create operational difficulties in balancing generation and load during peak demand periods to maintain the 60 Hz frequency used across the North American electrical grid. Current efforts to build large-scale battery-storage facilities near load centers to address peak demand constraints are promising, although concerns are growing over the production, use, and eventual disposal of nickel-cadmium, lithium, and other hazardous materials. Operating perils, such as arc-flash incidents and thermal runaway associated with battery storage projects, must also be addressed to bring this promising technology to fruition. Environmental and other groups have also targeted renewable energy sources for various reasons, such as land use, challenges to wildlife and habitat, and hazardous materials involved in these green technologies.

And with the addition of new technologies, the grid, and energy infrastructure face increasing cyber and physical risks as cyberattacks and climate change impacts increase. Eighty-six percent of respondents of this year's State and Future of the Power Industry Pulse Survey consider cybersecurity to be a bigger risk to utilities than physical security. The SolarWinds hack in 2020 was a wake-up call for many industries and government agencies, including utilities. The Colonial Pipeline

DOI: 10.1201/9781003243021-9

cyber breach in 2021 was a direct shot at the US energy system. Utilities will need to anticipate similar attacks going forward and pre-emptively address security risks on both the grid and customer sides of the meter, especially as distributed energy resources continue to proliferate. While cybersecurity is certainly of major concern for utility executives, the past year saw widespread blackouts linked to fires, heat waves, hurricanes, and the Texas freeze. Increasing in frequency, these events are a reminder that the climate is changing before our eyes. Our energy system will need to be more flexible to deal with greater uncertainty.

9.0.1 ABOUT GUIDEHOUSE

Guidehouse is a leading global provider of consulting services to the public and commercial markets with broad capabilities in management, technology, and risk consulting. We help clients address their toughest challenges and navigate significant regulatory pressures with a focus on transformational change, business resiliency, and technology-driven innovation. Across a range of advisory, consulting, outsourcing, and digital services, we create scalable, innovative solutions that prepare our clients for future growth and success. The company has more than 10,000 professionals in over 50 locations globally. For more information, please visit www.guidehouse.com.

9.1 SECURING THE BACKBONE OF THE US CRITICAL INFRASTRUCTURE

Chris Luras, John Eckenrode, and Don Heckman
Guidehouse

9.1.1 INTRODUCTION

The Cybersecurity and Infrastructure Security Agency (CISA) recognizes 16 critical infrastructure sectors. The energy sector was recognized as a uniquely critical enabler for the other 15 sectors in Presidential Policy Directive 21 (PPD-21).[1] Stated another way by the Cybersecurity and Infrastructure Security Agency (CISA): "The US energy infrastructure fuels the economy of the 21st century." Cyber, physical security, and organizational challenges are common across all public infrastructure sectors, but energy's role as a key facilitator *sector requires requisite attention, resourcing, and diligence.* CISA also stated: "Without a stable energy supply, health and welfare are threatened, and the US economy cannot function."[2] *Because of this realization, the sector's technical and organizational challenges must be addressed to ensure our long-term prosperity as a nation.*

Recent events demonstrating challenges with the distribution of power in the face of both natural and man-made disasters have underscored the need for long-overdue infrastructure upgrades, both in generation and distribution.[3] The energy sector can capitalize on the current movement to modernize and transform the technologies within this sector to provide greater efficiencies, resilience, and cybersecurity while addressing concerns around fossil-fueled, primarily coal-fired, generation plants. These new technologies can improve current services that tax existing generation and transmission capacity during peak usage times. Environmental and other groups have also targeted renewable energy sources for various reasons, such as land use, challenges to wildlife and habitat, and hazardous materials involved in these green technologies.

Clean energy replacements, such as dispersed solar- and wind-powered generation sites, are often located in areas distant from load centers, which require long transmission systems to deliver electrical energy to the demand, and are subject to adverse weather conditions, which can create operational difficulties in balancing generation and load during peak demand periods to maintain the 60 Hz frequency used across the North American electrical grid. Current efforts to build large-scale battery-storage facilities near load centers to address peak demand constraints are promising, although concerns are growing over the production, use, and eventual disposal of nickel-cadmium, lithium, and other hazardous materials. Operating perils, such as arc-flash incidents and thermal runaway associated with battery storage projects, must also be addressed to bring this promising technology to fruition.

9.1.2 TECHNICAL CHALLENGES

9.1.2.1 AGING INFRASTRUCTURE

Aging infrastructure vulnerabilities, which are susceptible to cyberattacks, can have catastrophic consequences if exploited. This is perhaps best exemplified by the implication of transmission lines as a contributing factor in recent California wildfires.[4] Utilities have come under intense scrutiny by legal and regulatory authorities to determine the role transmission lines played in wildfire ignition. Potential outcomes may include liability and other legal issues, as well as utility restructuring due to bankruptcy or at the behest of regulatory bodies.

Other key factors that tax the capacity of aging infrastructure are increased loads and lack of local generation resources during peak periods. Older power lines and other transmission facilities often have a lower transfer limit than newer facilities—contributing to a loss in both efficiency and revenue. Current generation practices, and the nature of power flows, require that each transmission line be operated within its safe loading limit, which also constrains the total transfer capacity of the transmission system. Excessive power transfers cause overheated lines to sag or droop lower than designed. Several wildfires have been attributed to overloaded transmission wires sagging into vegetation. Every one of these factors could be affected by a cyberattack.

Aging power distribution infrastructure requires adequate planning and resourcing due to long lead times and expenses associated with addressing environmental issues prior to the process of siting and permitting. Effective planning must also include incorporation of advances in new technologies in construction materials and power distribution efficiencies. The entire energy sector needs to reduce its reliance on stop-gap measures such as planned outages to address systemic, sustained delivery issues. Planned and unplanned outages, and deliberate disconnection of certain load blocks, create a lose-lose situation, as power companies then become targets of angry citizens, governmental agencies, and regulatory bodies[5] for failing to meet consumer demand while simultaneously attempting to solve the wildfire ignition problem.

Holistic planning for the replacement of aging infrastructure with modern facilities that have greater power transfer capacities, along with a unified approach by grid participants, regulatory bodies, and environmental groups, is required to address the myriad of issues affecting the energy markets. This combined approach, along with interaction with consumers, ensures that the disparate equities of the stakeholders are effectively addressed. Integrating risk models into capital planning to optimize replacement cycles and drive investment priorities will lead to significant progress in this area.

9.1.2.2 INFORMATION TECHNOLOGY AND OPERATIONAL TECHNOLOGY INTEGRATION CHALLENGES

Resilient energy generation and delivery require balanced protection of both operational technology (OT) and information technology (IT) systems and effective integration of both organizational protections and governance to maximize efficiencies while reducing cybersecurity costs. Integration allows for a symbiotic relationship, with IT providing, for example, access to and protection of OT systems. This integration between IT and OT should not be viewed as a shared equipment schema or methods of minimizing security zones through the use of single physical systems but rather a means to allow the organization to benefit from the strengths of the multiple technology zones found in both IT and OT.

The issue of effective integration of IT and OT are rooted in the evolution of both systems, in general, and the gradual increase in global connectivity that has led to the interconnected workplace of today. Both IT and OT systems are woven into the fabric of today's energy market, each with different stakeholders, performance criteria, and expectations. Individual IT and OT systems both have Confidentiality, Integrity, and Availability ("CIA triad") protection needs that will vary, even within the same power company or business unit. Both technologies are key business enablers, and at the same time, either of these systems can act as a conduit for malicious actors.

The convergence between IT and OT is already taking place in many sectors, including new construction projects with intelligent buildings. However, IT and OT are still viewed in silos and the next steps in the energy system are as much cultural as technology driven. Multidisciplinary teams will help facilitate the convergence and move away from the current oil-and-water relationships of today. Failing to act in this area will delay cost savings and further establish inefficiencies in the interconnected systems.

9.1.2.3 LACK OF AUTOMATION

Cost considerations are usually the ultimate reason for utilities' IT and OT operations being "behind the curve" for adopting newer technology and automation. Automation across both areas can be expressed in the following categories:

1. Process automation
2. Server/system automation
3. Network automation

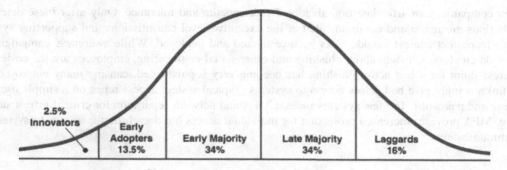

FIGURE 9.1.1   Utilities' IT and OT technology adoption.

Typically, energy sector companies operate behind the technology curve as either late majority or laggards as shown in Figure 9.1.1.

While this late majority/laggard approach offers some level of cost avoidance around "groundbreaking technology" adoption, this also impedes adoption of emerging and recently established technologies. Utility processes and procedures that continue to rely on manual methods are inefficient and error-prone—especially for processes supporting a utility's compliance (NERC CIP) program.

Lack of adoption of (real, integrated) automation is systemic in Supervisory Control and Data Acquisition (SCADA)/Energy Management System (EMS) and field systems, where many installations are several decades old. Initially considered "secure" due to their standalone "air gap" nature, over the years, IT has gradually connected to what used to be segregated systems. The National Institute of Standards and Technology (NIST) recognized a lack of guidance in this area and issued Special Publication 800-82, "Guide to Industrial Control Systems (ICS) Security." Updating these systems to the latest technology can be a significant endeavor that few utilities are willing to undertake; many companies lack the organic cyber expertise or capability to implement NIST guidance or industry best practices.

Human error introduces and accounts for a large amount of risk—both security and operational. By automating and leveraging human oversight of previously manual activities and processes, these risks can be reduced while decreasing labor costs.

9.1.2.4   THREATS: NATION STATES AND CRIMINAL ACTORS

Malicious activity and bad actors infiltrating any critical system are a concern. The derivative effect of malicious activity on energy systems can be grave for both the energy company and its customers. IT and OT both provide targets (customer data, and operational infrastructure, to name two) and threat vectors. These threat actors have improved their methodologies and are employing automation to increase the number of attacks and avoid detection. Current compliance mandates like NERC CIP alone cannot protect against today's threats, especially considering the constantly expanding threat surfaces due to increased reliance on the Internet of Things (IoT).

Three important factors are often overlooked regarding the protection of computer and network systems.

1. Understanding risk, risk tolerance, and risk appetite
2. Having a complete understanding of the IT/OT environment and the most probable ingress points for bad actors
3. Implementing top security methods to avoid bad-actor access (e.g., strong identity and access management using multifactor authentication (MFA), and implementing least privilege principles, segmentation, and continuous monitoring)

Few companies can articulate organizational risk appetite and tolerance. Only after these determinations are made and communicated at the executive level can missions and supporting systems to protect against outside risks be investigated and deployed. While awareness campaigns provide employees insight about phishing and other social engineering, employees are the easiest ingress point for a bad actor. Phishing has become very sophisticated, causing many employees to unknowingly give bad actors access to systems. Typical system access relies on a simple username and password. Too few systems include MFA and network separation for critical infrastructure. MFA provides increased protection for individual access but does little for system-to-system communications.

9.1.2.5 LACK OF COMMON SECURITY CONTROLS FOR ELECTRICAL DISTRIBUTION

NERC CIP provides a common set of compliance standards for the nation's bulk electrical system consisting of generation and transmission; however, distribution, microgrids, and other last-mile electrical service methods do not have common physical or cybersecurity controls. When providing electrical service, regardless of the method, protection of uninterrupted service is paramount. There is no success if the power cannot be utilized by the end customer, yet because of local and state regulations of electrical utilities, few discussions have focused on securing the last mile and none are concerned with a coordinated effort, either through security recommendations or required compliance.

As a starting point, utilities must assess and identify critical distribution equipment (i.e., equipment that is critical to the reliable production of electricity in major cities) and enhance the cyber and physical security processes and controls.

9.1.3 ORGANIZATIONAL CHALLENGES

9.1.3.1 AGING WORKFORCE

A recent article from the US Bureau of Labor Statistics[6] cited three major areas where an aging workforce may impact an organization: labor costs, productivity, and sustainability. Older employees tend to have higher salaries, more accrued leave time, and potentially more medical issues. As the workforce ages, many workers plan to work beyond their normal retirement ages due to longer life expectancies, insufficient planning or savings for retirement, and the gradual rise of the "normal" retirement age from 65 to 67 and beyond. The energy sector is seeing experienced workers leave the workforce in greater numbers than new workers are coming in. Electrical utilities tend to poach each other's workforces to fill empty positions, but this form of musical chairs is a self-defeating prospect. Loss of tacit knowledge as older workers leave an organization may be mitigated to some degree by succession planning, as well as mentoring and coaching programs that pair older and younger workers, but in the absence of sound knowledge-transfer practices, organizational sustainability may be at risk. The energy sector should partner with educational institutions and trade schools to establish effective training programs that meet the current and projected needs of the energy sector and create a strong pipeline of incoming talent to replace an aging and shrinking workforce.

As this has been highlighted as an industry risk for some time, the energy sector is already making strides here, but more work is needed. The energy sector should partner with educational institutions and trade schools to establish effective training programs that meet the current and projected needs of the energy sector and create a strong pipeline of incoming talent to replace an aging and shrinking workforce. Effective apprenticeships with shared resources that can fulfill multiple organizational ranks (for instance, within or across regional power pools, independent system operators (ISOs), and regional transmission organizations (RTOs) could increase expertise and reduce knowledge gaps. Likewise, additional public-private partnerships can drive workforce changes in this area.

9.1.3.2 ESCALATING TRAINING REQUIREMENTS

A Pew Research Center report[7] cited a "widespread feeling among US adults that the workplace is evolving, and they will have to continually update their skills and training in order to succeed." Pew reported the need to develop stronger training programs for effective skill development and retention is strongest in certain science, technology, engineering, and math (STEM)-related industries. The energy sector is heavily involved in STEM efforts as it continues to develop and implement specialized cyber systems to support and improve operations. It is imperative that employees are provided adequate training to maintain and develop their skills to be productive and successful in the heavily cyber environment of today's energy sector and forward into the future.

Martha Laboissiere and Monda Mourshed[8] described how energy sector participants can create workforce development programs to meet the divergent training needs of employee populations. They provided a graphic that described the roles played by a series of stakeholders in the US workforce-development system and included multiple learning and services loops to provide and sustain workforce development.[9] This exhibit also supports five principles that are a crucial foundation of workforce-development programs that should be pursued by policymakers, service providers, educational institutions, employers, and training participants. The five principles are adapted in the following list for energy sector training programs:

1. Define areas of need and identify target professions and desired skill sets
2. Deliver ROI to both the organization and its workforce
3. Support comprehensive, context-driven training methods
4. Assess and prepare learners prior to training
5. Provide central coordination of the workforce-development program

Operational training, safety training, and security training are currently built into the energy culture, but the regulatory focus is to mature both safety and risk management processes to exceed current NERC CIP (critical infrastructure protection) and NERC PER (operating personnel) requirements. This does not necessarily mean regulations should be tightened, but rather industry should continue to push its own best practices and move to robust knowledge management and knowledge transfer programs.

9.1.3.3 USING AUTOMATION IN THE WORKFORCE

Automation in the energy sector workplace has been a long-standing goal for power system operations, as well as compliance with regulatory standards, although the burden of implementing an automation strategy rests at the highest levels of the organization. Obvious cost reductions and operational improvements are key benefits, but there are intangible aspects such as creating better customer relations, optimizing the use of knowledge worker time, developing a stronger grasp on environmental issues, and increasing the pace and output of R&D activities. Two key roles filled by senior management in developing automation projects are (a) identifying which business systems may benefit from automation and (b) looking beyond current business systems to determine how automation will enable the organization to make bolder moves.[10] All these aspects are relevant to the energy sector as it seeks to implement automation in the workplace.

Guidehouse has worked with many stakeholders across the North American electrical grid and has noted over the years that unsuccessful automation attempts are typically driven by lower-level personnel, typically frontline technicians and managers, who identified localized benefits of automation, but did not have sufficient perspective, or influence, to successfully implement a strategic change initiative across the organization. Successful automation efforts, on the other hand, were supported by the senior management team and centered on managing documentation and periodic performance of compliance-related tasks. Successful automation projects in the energy sector generally involved the implementation of a robust system that included asset management, change configuration, and workflow management modules combined with task escalation and document management functionality. This allows staff to focus on core competencies, critical operational and compliance tasks, better customer service and compliance, and operational tasks performed smoothly and accurately.

Energy sector leaders should partner with learning-based organizations to develop robust training programs to instill automation skills across the existing workforce, recruit and retain new automation-savvy talent capable of development and implementation of new automated business systems, and identify concurrent roles that must be filled by human knowledge workers as automated systems fill other roles. Workforce displacement by automation is a major societal concern that should be addressed by policymakers in conjunction with energy sector leaders as automation projects become more prevalent.

9.1.4 RECOMMENDATIONS FOR THE FUTURE (2025) CYBERSECURITY LANDSCAPE FOR ENERGY SECTOR

These technical and organizational challenges must be addressed to avoid becoming significant problems for all other critical infrastructure sectors, which are heavily reliant on a stable, reliable, and secure electrical grid to optimize their own operations and services.

Utilities must adopt a comprehensive risk management approach to understand and mitigate risk to their facilities and operations. They should assess and identify critical distribution equipment (i.e., equipment that is critical to the reliable operation of major cities) and enhance the cyber and physical security processes and controls for those critical assets. Implementing top security methods to avoid bad actor access (e.g., strong identity and access management using MFA, implementing least-privilege principles, ensuring software is up to date and configured securely, and segmentation of mission-critical systems and continuous monitoring are all necessary to defend against today's cyber threats). They cannot be applied after deployment to support a recovery program.

The workforce needs to be retooled and instilled with a culture of cybersecurity where cybersecurity is everyone's responsibility, as most successful cyberattacks result from human error. When providing electrical service, regardless of the method, protection of uninterrupted service is paramount. There is no success if the power cannot be utilized by the end customer, and this will take a combination of people, technology, and operations to do it securely and reliably.

The NERC CIP and Operations and Planning Reliability Standards[11] need to constantly evolve to address new technologies and meet new cyber and physical security threats and ensure reliable operations across the North American electrical grid. Nevertheless, understanding that the standards process takes significant time, utilities need to develop deeper and stronger cybersecurity processes that go beyond the minimum threshold of compliance set by the NERC CIP. As new technologies are implemented within the sector, a common set of cybersecurity and compliance standards for the bulk electric system consisting of generation and transmission, as well as distribution, microgrids, and other last-mile electrical service methods, needs to be developed and uniformly applied to address the advanced persistent threat targeting this critical infrastructure sector.

Ensuring a reliable, secure, and environmentally sustainable energy supply and delivery systems as a critical component of the global economy is a major concern for everyone who depends on the 16 critical public infrastructure sectors. Meeting the needs of various factions while serving the public interest can only be addressed through a unified approach by grid participants across the energy value chain, regulatory bodies, and policymakers to make necessary investments to address aging infrastructure and cybersecurity challenges in today's market.

9.1.4.1 About the Authors

Chris Luras is a partner in the Guidehouse Risk, Regulatory, and Compliance practice. He brings more than 18 years of experience in the Energy Sector. He oversees the Risk, Compliance, and Security team and solutions within the Energy, Sustainability, and Infrastructure segment. He leads the development, management, and execution of tools and services aimed at Cyber Security and Reliability Compliance, Risk Management, Internal Controls, and Process Improvement within the Energy Sector.

John Eckenrode is a director in the Guidehouse Advanced Solutions Cybersecurity practice. He brings more than 30 years of experience supporting client cybersecurity challenges at the operational, mission, and strategic levels. He leads their energy cybersecurity business and heads up multiple cyber resilience offerings, as well as the development of the Industrial Control Security (ICS)/SCADA and Internet of Things (IoT) capabilities.

Donald Heckman is the director in the Guidehouse Advanced Solutions Cybersecurity practice. He is a cybersecurity subject matter expert and brings more than 36 years of experience in government leadership, spearheading cybersecurity and secure information-sharing initiatives across the Department of Defense, Intelligence Community (IC), and national security sectors. He is Guidehouse's Defense Cyber Solutions leader, as well as leading multiple data protection and privacy offerings for public and commercial sector clients.

9.1.4.3 Acknowledgments

A special thanks to contributing authors Matthew Moore and Keshav Sarin.

REFERENCES

1. President Barack Obama (February 12, 2013), "Presidential policy directive—Critical infrastructure security and resilience," White House Briefing, PPD-21, https://obamawhitehouse.archives.gov/the-press-office/2013/02/12/presidential-policy-directive-critical-infrastructure-security-and-resil.
2. Cybersecurity and Infrastructure Security Agency [CISA], "Critical Infrastructure Sectors: Energy Sector," October 2, 2020.
3. Union of Concerned Scientists, "Environmental impacts of renewable energy technologies," March 5, 2013, https://www.ucsusa.org/resources/environmental-impacts-renewable-energy-technologies.
4. Ted Goldberg, "California's largest utility providers face pressure as wildfires continue to burn," November 14, 2018, National Public Radio Podcast, "All Things Considered."
5. Rachel Sandler, "PG&E says faulty power lines may have sparked 2 California wildfires," Forbes, October 28, 2019, https://www.forbes.com/sites/rachelsandler/2019/10/28/pge-says-faulty-power-lines-may-have-sparked-2-california-wildfires/?sh=649b9f1d2584.
6. Charlotte M. Irby, "What to do about our aging workforce—The employers' response," Monthly Labor Review, US Bureau of Labor Statistics, August 2020, https://www.bls.gov/opub/mlr/2020/beyond-bls/what-to-do-about-our-aging-workforce-the-employers-response.htm.
7. Pew Research Center, "The State of American Jobs, Chapter 4, Skills and training needed to compete in today's economy," p. 63, October 6, 2016, https://www.pewsocialtrends.org/wp-content/uploads/sites/3/2016/10/ST_2016.10.06_Future-of-Work_FINAL4.pdf.
8. Martha Laboissiere and Mona Mourshed, "Closing the skills gap: Creating workforce-development programs that work for everyone," McKinsey & Company, February 13, 2017, https://www.mckinsey.com/industries/public-and-social-sector/our-insights/closing-the-skills-gap-creating-workforce-development-programs-that-work-for-everyone.
9. Second citation, "Exhibit 1."
10. Michael Chui, Katy George, and Mehdi Miremadi, "A CEO action plan for workplace automation," McKinsey Quarterly, July 10, 2017.
11. North American Electric Reliability Corporation, [NERC], "All Reliability Standards," https://www.nerc.com/pa/Stand/Pages/AllReliabilityStandards.aspx?jurisdiction=United%20States.

10 Financial Services

10.0 ABOUT THE FINANCIAL SERVICES SECTOR

Hitesh Sheth
CEO and President, Vectra AI

If the United States were a single human being, its financial system would be the bloodstream: circulating nutrients to the body's furthest extremities, facilitating essential biochemical exchanges, and inextricably blended with every other corporeal system. That is why vulnerabilities in the financial services sector, particularly cybersecurity issues, pose unique threats to American stability and national security.

Our national financial services infrastructure comprises banks, credit unions, and other depository institutions; investment and securities firms and the trading facilities they use, such as stock and commodity exchanges; insurance companies and other entities engaged in risk transfer and management; lenders of all sizes, serving customers from nervous newlyweds buying the first sofa to the largest multinational industrial enterprise; government-sponsored enterprises (GSEs) like Fannie Mae, tasked with improving economy-wide capital flow; and a multitude of financial utilities and service providers working to support all of the above.

About 8.7 million Americans were employed in finance industries in 2019, placing the sector among the nation's biggest jobs providers—bigger than construction, education, or energy.[1] But problems in financial services, cybersecurity-related or not, can endanger more than those jobs. They present some direct risk for virtually every American—for at least three reasons.

1. The trading economy depends on constant, ready access to capital. On the larger end of the scale, banks remain liquid and viable in part by lending each other short-term funds on the overnight market. At the micro end, a family's ability to go for pizza may hinge on locating a working ATM. Even a modest systemic interruption affecting capital transfer and delivery can mean lost revenue for a small pizzeria—or a liquidity crisis for a big bank.
2. Finance is a business of infinite global connections. Competitors are in constant, unavoidable contact, clearing one another's checks and loan payments in ways competing bus lines or apparel companies are not. Today's digital networks perform real-time miracles in nanoseconds: Using a credit card from a neighborhood credit union in Akron to buy souvenirs in Urumqi or dirhams at a Dubai currency exchange has long ceased to seem remarkable. But cybersecurity experts know data in motion is data at risk, and the US financial sector cannot be firewalled from the rest of the world.
3. Unlike businesses that manufacture goods or dispatch freight trains, financial providers sell nothing tangible. To entice the deposits or investments that keep the figurative bloodstream flowing, they must inspire faith, belief, and confidence. (Banks of yesteryear built stolid, classically styled branches of granite and marble to encourage this state of mind; recently launched virtual institutions, which in the customer's mind exist only as a logo on a phone app, must find other ways.) A crisis of confidence premised on little more than rumor and foreboding can spark depositor panic and a "run on the bank," with ripple-effect harm to other institutions perhaps quick to follow.

These characteristics of financial service providers not only underline their unique status in our system—their resilience and availability affect us not only economically, but psychologically—but

DOI: 10.1201/9781003243021-10

their equally unique appeal to cybercriminals. Taking down a department store chain with a ransomware attack makes an impression on those who pay attention, but most can shop elsewhere until the emergency is mitigated. Infiltrating a financial institution and cutting off depositors' access to capital, however, would be next-level: personal, frightening, and liable to inspire extreme reactions on Main Street.

Like energy, water systems, and health care, the US financial services sector is among 16 "critical infrastructure sectors" designated by the federal Cybersecurity and Infrastructure Security Agency (CISA). CISA publishes and updates a specialized defense plan for each critical sector, although years elapse between editions (the latest version covering the financial sector was issued in 2015). It points with pride to the sector's "shared security and resilience vision" and collaborative multi-agency initiatives, mounted in concert with private institutions, "to document critical systems, infrastructure, and institutions and use that information to inform security and resilience programs."[2]

Any degree of preparedness is welcome, but with financial services as important in some ways to the life of the nation as government itself, no degree may be sufficient. Yet, in addition to weighing omnipresent but usually abstract and unrealized threats of cyberattack, private interests controlling most financial providers also answer to shareholders pressing for profits as well as customers demanding greater speed and convenience at less cost. Management decisions on cyber defense posture and technology upgrades can therefore be products of compromise, which generates additional vulnerabilities.

Cyber threats evolve constantly. The financial services sector is in need of even greater focus on cybersecurity, and government programs and regulations can take us only so far. Without a fateful culture shift in the boardrooms and IT departments of the thousands of banks, credit unions, brokerages, mortgage lenders, payment processors, and more that comprise our national bloodstream, we risk more than temporary irritation when a cyber adversary succeeds. We risk the beating heart of the nation. A comprehensive takedown of critical financial infrastructure could be the equivalent of a national heart attack.

10.0.1   ABOUT VECTRA AI

Vectra AI solves the complex challenge of detecting hidden threats with AI-driven security that turns attackers' behaviors against them.

From the core to the cloud, we codify and correlate hidden attack behaviors to see and stop otherwise invisible threats before they can disrupt or do damage. By providing rich context and clarity in real-time, security teams can detect threats that have bypassed perimeter defenses, respond and remediate faster, and enhance existing security investments. Organizations can modernize their security posture and adapt to emerging opportunities across cloud, data center, IoT, and enterprise networks with speed, scalability, and confidence.

That's what happens when your security thinks. And why Vectra is the cybersecurity partner customers around the world trust to secure their business. www.vectra.ai.

REFERENCES

1. US Bureau of Labor Statistics, Employment by Major Industry Sector, 2019. https://www.bls.gov/emp/tables/employment-by-major-industry-sector.htm.
2. Department of the Treasury and US Department of Homeland Security, *Financial Services Sector-Specific Plan 2015*. https://www.cisa.gov/publication/nipp-ssp-financial-services-2015.

10.1 TIME FOR FINANCIAL PROVIDERS TO LEAD WITH CYBERSECURITY

Hitesh Sheth
CEO and President, Vectra AI

10.1.1 INTRODUCTION

On Monday, March 14, 2024, your morning started normally but changed quickly.

Clutching hot coffee, you flipped your laptop open and clicked to your online brokerage to check the Dow futures: your usual habit. Oddly, the website shook off your login. You double-checked the password. No error message, just paralysis. You couldn't recall that ever happening.

You shrugged and clicked over to Amazon to buy the kids' sneakers you browsed last night, but the checkout process rejected your credit card. Every card. You tried three and always saw: "We are having trouble authorizing your payment for your items. Please verify or update your payment method." Funny; they all worked fine yesterday.

The household was about out of food and Monday was shopping day. Driving to the supermarket, you spotted a gas station on your side of the arterial. Great; you were well below the quarter-tank mark. But a long line of honking cars sprawled into the street, and as you drew near, you saw a hastily spray-painted sign at the curb: CASH ONLY. Two blocks later, you passed a clutch of three banks, all with unmoving lines for the ATMs. As you rolled past you, saw people shoving each other, slapping dead ATMs in frustration, and raising fists at bank managers.

10.1.1.1 WHAT IS HAPPENING?

The store was teeming. In the produce section, you picked up anxious, hissed murmurs: "I can't get hold of Amex … Why would they cut us off? … Nothing works …" You tossed food into your shopping cart fast and unstrategically, preoccupied by your own credit card problems, but didn't size up the mob laying siege to the checkout tills until you joined it yourself. The swipe-and-PIN terminals were rejecting everybody's debit cards. Cash only.

You never carried money. Gave up grubby dollars years ago and became a dedicated digital wallet fan. Cash was dying, went the conventional wisdom, and you were pleased to help kill it. Now you thought wildly: *Is there any cash at home? After the last blackout I'm almost certain we put aside a couple of hundred. We could buy food.*

Shoppers were yelling at flustered clerks. Your ice cream was melting, and your heart began to pound. You abandoned your cart. Exiting the store, you trotted past shoplifters lugging armfuls of steaks, chuck roast, and bourbon.

You raced home through now-frenetic traffic, burning precious gas.

On arrival, you tried your brokerage website again on a whim. This time your login worked and took you to your portfolio summary. Total balance shown—your kitchen remodeling fund, the kids' college savings, and your Roth IRA: $0.00.

At the back of a cluttered kitchen drawer, behind whisks and spatulas, you found that envelope of emergency cash. It felt ominously thin in your hand. Later your spouse would admit to raiding it all winter to pay the neighbor kid for snow shoveling. At that moment in the kitchen, your stomach lurched. Your household's cash assets came to a ten-dollar bill and two ones $12.

That was when you finally turned on the TV and saw seasoned financial anchors, people accustomed to relaying bad news, fighting panic on camera. You flipped around; every channel was in wall-to-wall coverage. If you'd ever heard the phrase "critical infrastructure attack" before today, it had sailed over your head, but from what you could gather, you were amid one now. Wall Street and all banks were closed. Retailers, airlines, and fast food restaurants were paralyzed. The Social Security Administration could not do direct benefit deposits.

You tried calling your spouse at work, but the circuits were overwhelmed. Your impulse was to drive to their office, but there wasn't enough gas left in the SUV. Alone on the living room couch, a chill settled over you. You recognized the onset of psychologic shock. You hugged your knees to your chest and awaited a promised emergency statement from the White House. The CNN camera stayed trained on an empty podium. Outside on your street, you heard glass smashing, shouted threats, and the metallic crunch of cars colliding.

The 2024 cyber assault on the US financial system was less than four hours old. We could not claim we weren't warned.

10.1.2   STARK LESSONS FOR THE FINANCIAL SECTOR

The 2020 SolarWinds cyber breach was peak chaos—to that point, at least. A ruinous global supply chain attack afflicted dozens of organizations, from the United States Treasury to Intel and Cisco. The alarming difference from run-of-the-mill data theft cases: SolarWinds, like the Colonial Pipeline incident that followed in May 2021, was a successful assault on critical infrastructure, with the apparent aim of degrading victims' ability to operate. Targets in SolarWinds may have included American airports, hydroelectric dams and power plants, bridge and tunnel control networks—the nation's very circulatory system. "When nation-states target these networks, capable of powering machinery on or off or diverting resources from one portion of a system to another," said Kartikay Mehrotra of the cybersecurity coverage team at Bloomberg, "the results tend to be far more damaging than pure espionage."[1]

Financial providers hopefully took note of the SolarWinds attack's stark lessons. The unprecedented damage done with relative ease no doubt emboldened its architects to try for more. A motivated nation-state malefactor can infiltrate any data repository; at least, we shouldn't assume they can't. A SolarWinds-scale cybersecurity meltdown in the cloud is virtually inevitable, and the financial industry's critical digital infrastructure presents a particularly tempting target.

If an enemy aspires to terrorize the citizens of a connected digital society—a society increasingly enamored of more advanced, more esoteric fintech, as cash and coin lose favor—disabling critical financial infrastructure and inflaming economic anxiety is probably the most efficient method short of a kinetic attack.

Financial providers already suffer disproportionate interest from cybercriminals. Cybersecurity expert Earl Foote, CEO of Nexus IT Consultants, estimates the rate of cyber breaches in the financial sector increased by 300 percent from 2014 to 2019, to the point where cybercrime costs banks more than $1 trillion annually.[2] According to a Ponemon Institute study, 70% of financial services firms experienced a successful cyberattack in 2020—up more than 20% over 2019.[3] Even when the attack target is a client or customer, not the financial provider itself, the latter typically absorbs costs arising from fraudulent activity. The US Treasury has for years placed cyber threats atop its estimate of top threats to national financial stability.[4]

Work-from-home protocols arising from the 2020–2022 pandemic seemed to have made things worse. According to data from VMWare unit Carbon Black, from February to April 2020, as financial workers scrambled to reposition themselves at home, cyberattacks on the financial sector increased another 238% globally.[5] In the United Kingdom, where 90% of all data breaches in 2019 were attributed to human error,[6] 31% of financial firms' remote workers had access to critical sensitive data; 41% of the firms involved believed remote workers were putting the business in danger of a major breach.[7] Separate research from TrendMicro found remote workers engaged in riskier behavior: 39% used their own smartphones, tablets, and laptops to access corporate data, and half of the global remote workers had IoT devices on their home networks.[8]

But some of these perils are tried and true. Fat-finger keystroke errors, workers falling for phishing emails, and unsecured personal tech have bedeviled businesses for years, and not just financial providers. New threats particular to the financial sector, are swimming into focus. We have established that attacking financial infrastructure can potentially wreak a uniquely disruptive, frightening form of widespread, egalitarian havoc. Now let us turn to the four principal reasons the financial industry is at special, critical risk in the 2020s.

10.1.3   THE FINANCIAL SECTOR IS A PRIME TARGET

First, while banks and transaction networks have always been a prime quarry for cybercriminals—they are, after all, where the money is, and Verizon research says 71% of all data breaches are financially motivated[9]—SolarWinds suggested the stakes may now far exceed a mere cash jackpot.

Imagine a vertical hierarchy of cyber chaos. On the lower rungs of the chaos ladder: stolen personal credit or bank account data. Mobile personal banking via apps and less-than-secure wireless devices presents bandits with juicy, irresistible attack vectors. But while these common incidents are inconvenient and stressful, they are rarely crippling. They're the equivalent of petty theft at scale.

Higher up on the ladder come espionage campaigns against a single company or agency. Spies steal intellectual property: auto blueprints from manufacturers or specialized drug recipes from pharmaceutical companies. More commonly for financial companies, extortionists induce operational paralysis with ransomware.

"As fraud prevention and retail security have improved and the value of stolen credit card data and bank credentials has declined," said a Swift Institute report, "attackers have stepped up large-scale coordinated attacks on financial institutions' core networks, going for a few very large payouts instead of lots of small ones. Extortion is the number one concern for financial institutions, as internet of things (IoT) botnets and mass distribution of sophisticated crypto-ransomware threaten to take banks offline presents unique cybersecurity challenges. Regulatory demands are unique, and of course the potential for destabilizing financial losses is greater."[10]

But like petty theft, corporate espionage and extortion do not generally bring everyday life to a grinding halt. Given the success of SolarWinds, we must assume some malefactors' sights are shifting to bigger goals: not just destabilizing financial losses, but destabilization, period.

A critical infrastructure attack that affected our cluster of too-big-to-fail banks and transaction systems could panic Main Street America in a way unmatched by news of stolen health records or credit card numbers. The national stress level was already pinned at the start of the decade by the pandemic, economic distress, combative politics, and pervasive conspiracy theories. Were Americans to wake up to find their bank and brokerage balances at zero, ATMs suddenly dark coast to coast, and the loss of debit-transaction functions at the Kroger checkout counter, chaos would be too gentle a word for it. That possibility alone puts financial firms in a criticality category of their own.

SolarWinds showed us the possibility is anything but science fiction.

The second special risk factor in the financial sector: much of its critical infrastructure is consolidated, virtually impossible to replicate, and uniquely threatened by performance degradation. It's the nature of the business.

In the energy sector, the tempting cybersecurity attack surfaces are within industrial controls—command systems associated with a nuclear plant, hydro dam, or urban power grid. In the creative or manufacturing spheres, cybercriminals stalk intellectual property, stealing the new Bond movie script or the design for the next-generation Mustang. But in finance, where transaction speed and integrity are critical competitive differentiators, there is no dam to shut down, no car blueprints to steal. The value of a critical financial network lies in its efficiency—how quickly can it transfer money?—and secure nature. Compromise either, and your job as saboteur is done: the network is corrupted, which inhibits electronic transactions for banks that depend on it and therefore harms their customers.

A rather small handful of giant, ubiquitous network systems underpin financial providers large and small. In the United States, the Federal Reserve operates the Fedwire Funds Service, which banks use to make large-value, time-critical payments to one another.[11] The Fed also processes most payments run through the Automated Clearing House Network (ACH)—the national clearinghouse for electronic funds transfers, from direct payroll deposits to the mortgage payments and electricity bills you see debited from your checking account.[12] You can be a customer of nearly any bank under the sun, but still, you probably depend on the ACH Network without knowing it; it processes 27 billion discrete payments annually.[13] The principal alternative is The Clearing House Payments Company—a bank-owned entity and the country's sole private-sector ACH and wire operator, processing nearly $2 trillion in payments each day.[14]

There's a good chance you have never heard of the jauntily named Nacha (for National Automated Clearing House Association), which governs the ACH Network, or The Clearing House Payments Company. But it's hard to think of better examples of critical infrastructure: indispensable in daily life, dominant, and extremely hard to replicate.

No doubt their cybersecurity departments are on point. But even if networks like these deploy regional firewalls, knock them down, and you knock down essential economic activity. You might compare the American banking transaction landscape to an airline's hub-and-spoke route system, which funnels most passengers through a few high-traffic centers. Delta Air Lines, for example, serves dozens of cities in the southeastern United States, but to travel between nearly any two of them, a passenger must connect through Atlanta. Should thunderstorms close ATL, a customer heading from, say, Baton Rouge to Savannah is grounded. Atlanta is a network vulnerability for Delta. By routing virtually all transactions through a few processing "hubs," financial providers live with the same kind of risk as a weather-worried Delta dispatcher—even if The Clearing House Payments Company talks glowingly of its own "long history of operational resilience," with uninterrupted service since 1853.[15]

Data in motion is data at risk, to however slight a degree, and no network is invulnerable.

The third special risk factor besetting financial providers is their demanding regulatory environment. Financial concerns are policed heavily by federal and state agencies, and the rules change constantly. Those doing business beyond US borders face additional layers of international regulation, many new ones relating to digital privacy: the European Union's GDPR and PSD2 (Payment Services Directive 2), Brazil's General Data Protection Law, the development of Canada's Pan-Canada Trust Framework, and many more.[16] Evolution of the rules is almost always driven by noble motives, and non-compliance by financial firms is a fraught strategy in itself. But the compound effect of so many regulatory layers creates disadvantages too. Abiding by the rules is a massive undertaking, and cybercriminals don't have to follow suit.

"Ever-shifting regulations are a major obstacle to bank security," said Earl Foote of Nexus IT. "The nature of these regulations gives hackers an advantage. Criminals quickly adopt new technologies and discover how to exploit vulnerabilities without having to sort out the rules. Banks, on the other hand, must carefully abide by the rules, making it difficult to keep up with the bad guys."[17] Emerging new gray-area categories, such as sovereign digital currencies issued by central banks (exploration of which the Treasury Department is encouraging[18]) and cryptocurrency, present additional challenges and risks.

10.1.4 FINANCIAL SECTOR RISK INCREASES WITH CLOUD MIGRATION

There is a fourth risk factor, and in my mind, it is the most important and readily addressable: the data network configuration decisions made by financial providers.

Private financial concerns operate under constant shareholder pressure to maximize earnings per share. That means a constant hunt for opportunities to contain IT costs and drive efficiencies, which in turn drives these companies to migrate to cloud solutions.

On the one hand, financial providers realize a momentary competitive advantage from the cloud in the form of reduced on-premises IT expenses. On the other hand, they may no longer know precisely where much of their critical data resides; in a very real, vexing sense, they find themselves at the mercy of their vendors. (This is a particularly worrisome syndrome in the category of fledgling, mostly virtual consumer financial brands apt to outsource core services.) Embedded within what looks like a savvy cost-containment move is the chance of the ultimate competitive disadvantage: crippling data loss.

The cloud is a seductive solution. A client bank or brokerage gets to outsource not only the acquisition and maintenance of physical hardware but headcount dedicated to support. Data centers, and the task of securing them, are arguably not core competencies of a banking or mortgage business anyway, and all the major cloud solution providers promise built-in security.

So hybrid cloud solutions became standard scenery on the financial-provider landscape. But while the solution provider owns the servers, the client bank owns the risk—and the liability, recovery costs, and brand damage in the event of a breach. That risk resides in complex multi-cloud environments, where the specific locale of sensitive data can be hard to nail down, and SaaS applications that keep data in motion.

10.1.5   RECOMMENDATIONS FOR THE FINANCIAL SECTOR

Some of the prescriptive counsel for the financial sector is all too obvious and should be universally adopted. Basic best practices and cyber hygiene reinforce security on the lower rungs of the chaos-hierarchy ladder. More rigorous checks and balances should be applied to transactions. A distributed, post-pandemic workforce, prone to security mistakes when managing sensitive data from kitchen tables at home, should be subject to more stringent monitoring and oversight. And most of the reported 300,000 new malware threats created each day still have less ambitious goals than bringing society to its knees.[19] Some want nothing more than to swindle the unwary, like the old banking trojan Zeus Sphinx that resurfaced in 2020 in spam slugged "COVID-19 relief." Some set out merely to take a corporate hostage, like the PwndLocker ransomware unleashed in 2020 on ATM maker Diebold Nixdorf.[20]

And over and above the inevitable external malware assaults, financial providers will always be at risk of a bad apple, the all-too-human kind, pulling an inside job. In 2019, Capital One discovered the culprit behind 106 million hacked customer profiles was an employee who exploited a misconfigured web application firewall to infiltrate company servers.[21] In the category of petty theft, a little more cyber hygiene can reduce a lot of risks.

But we might label these nuisance breaches of an irritating but familiar type. Frankly, I worry more about risk exposure on the chaos ladder's higher rungs, where attack consequences are potentially far more severe, as SolarWinds made plain.

The bottom line is that although we know distributed data management infrastructure to be vulnerable, security is not always the top priority. The cybersecurity measures emphasized by cloud solution providers tend to favor endpoint defense and prevention, although it's long been clear that rapid detection and recovery tools are more effective. The SolarWinds example was all the more unsettling because invasive malware nestled within SolarWinds systems for months undetected and probably still thrived in some victim systems long after discovery.

The perpetrators worked from a venerable, well-understood cyberwar playbook. Nevertheless, defense mechanisms emphasizing endpoint detection splintered like wicker railroad bridges.

Despite this and other cases pointing to the inadequacy of firewalls and endpoint defense, a distressing 2018 Accenture report said much of the financial services sector had failed to adopt the most advanced technology to protect their data: "[O]nly 26% [of providers] have deployed AI-based security technologies and 31% advanced analytics."[22]

The argument made here is not for wholesale regression to on-premises proprietary data centers. In fact, overreliance on such facilities presents its own challenges: financial companies' in-house IT teams have been known to insist on writing their own home-brew security algorithms or generating one-off custom toolsets. Independently engineered, "orphan" cybersecurity solutions cause more grief, pound for pound, than laborious implementation of acquired best-of-breed tools.

The core argument is that a more thoughtful, security-first hybrid cloud topography must take hold within financial providers' critical infrastructure—with strategies predicated not on maximum cost containment but most stringent measures applied for most sensitive data, plus optimal threat detection. Data and transaction types can be stack-ranked for mission criticality. Not all of it should be in constant motion to and from parts unknown within a multi-cloud environment with subpar threat detection tools. Nor does all of it have to reside in a local fortress. Yes, a financial provider should have some bandwidth on the premises. In fact, owning it puts a financial company in a better negotiating position with a cloud provider. But for certain applications, the efficiencies offered by the cloud are too pragmatically tempting to pass up.

And while finance is far from the only business sector that pays too little heed, as an industry, to the virtues of rapid threat detection and remediation measures, it's particularly important that financial providers alter their focus. Overreliance on prevention, and subpar detection, allowed the SolarWinds malware to proliferate. A like incident within critical financial infrastructure could compromise a network so thoroughly, a torch-and-replace campaign might be the only prudent way to get back in business. The expense would more than exceed the savings associated with adopting the riskier strategy in the first place—and that is before estimating the reputational damage and squandered trust.

10.1.6 CONCLUSION

When it comes to cost-efficient infrastructure design and protection, it was said that the financial sector in 2021 entered a "trough of disillusionment." That sounds bad but may be a good, propulsive thing. Given the universal vulnerabilities exposed by SolarWinds plus the sector-specific risks we so clearly understand, it is to be hoped that disillusionment was never a more forceful motivator for corrective action. The United States has no choice but to act on existential cybersecurity threats in holistic, comprehensive terms—and secure financial networks are critical to national security. The financial industry must revisit its hybrid cloud strategies through the lenses of security and attack detection, not cost containment.

It took the loss of more than 1,500 souls aboard the *Titanic*, which sailed in 1912 with a criminally inadequate 20 token lifeboats,[23] to finally generate meaningful safety requirements for passengers at sea. From 1920 to 1960, the vehicular fatality rate in the United States doubled, to 22 deaths per 100,000 Americans, before seat belts became federally required in 1968.[24] Through history, people and institutions are usually moved to forceful action more by actual, costly catastrophes than hypothetical threats. But if SolarWinds ultimately bestows the gift of urgent thinking and revised priorities, it will be a silver lining to a terrible security episode.

We need not be constrained by bad precedent. Perhaps it is human nature to respond to actual disasters visible in our rearview mirror, not the theoretical ones in our windshield, up ahead—even when the latter are probable. But I hope we are better than that. Now is an excellent time for the financial industry to defy old, costly behavioral patterns and head off the cybersecurity catastrophe looming in our future.

10.1.6.1 ABOUT THE AUTHOR

Vectra AI CEO and President Hitesh Sheth has served since 2012 at the San Jose, California, security and network technology company. A veteran technology leader, Sheth previously held the position of COO at Aruba Networks and vice president or director roles at Juniper Networks, Cisco Systems, Liberate Technologies, and Oracle Corporation. Sheth grew up in Kenya and is proud of his status as an immigrant American CEO: "That's why I'm the CEO at Vectra here in America—I love my country and want to protect my homeland. And make the world a better place with technology." He earned a computer science degree from the University of Texas at Austin.

REFERENCES

1. Kartikay Mehrotra, "Critical Infrastructure Left in the Dark About SolarWinds Hack," Bloomberg News, 5 January 2021. https://www.bloomberg.com/news/newsletters/2021-01-05/solarwinds-hack-leaves-critical-infrastructure-in-the-dark-on-risks

2. Maine Li, "Cybersecurity in Banking," *Tech Times*, 21 October 2019. https://www.techtimes.com/articles/245785/20191021/cybersecurity-in-banking.htm

3. Louis Chunovic, "Hackers Hit 70% of Firms in 2020: Report," Financial Technologies Forum, 10 February 2021. https://www.ftfnews.com/hackers-hit-70-of-firms-in-2020-report/28542#:~:text=In%20a%20recent%20survey%2C%20fully,Institute%20LLC%20for%20Keeper%20Security

4. US Department of the Treasury, Office of Financial Research, "2017 Annual Report to Congress: Analysis of Threats to the Financial Stability of the United States," 5 December 2017. https://www.financialresearch.gov/annual-reports/2017-annual-report/

5. Sanne Wass, "Cyberattacks Rise in Pandemic's 'Perfect Storm'—Reminding Banks of Risks Ahead," S&P Global Market Intelligence, 26 June 2020. https://www.spglobal.com/marketintelligence/en/news-insights/latest-news-headlines/cyberattacks-rise-in-pandemic-s-perfect-storm-8212-reminding-banks-of-risks-ahead-59064396

6. Scarlett Phillips, "Five Biggest Data Breaches in Financial Services History: Lessons to Be Learnt," Six Degrees blog, 6 October 2020. https://www.6dg.co.uk/blog/biggest-data-breaches-financial-services/

7. Phil Muncaster, "Most Financial Services Have Suffered COVID-Linked Cyber-Attacks," InfoSecurity, 19 January 2021. https://www.infosecurity-magazine.com/news/financial-services-suffered-covid/

8. Sarah Coble, "39% of Employees Access Corporate Data on Personal Devices," InfoSecurity, 14 September 2020. https://www.infosecurity-magazine.com/news/corporate-data-on-personal-devices/

9. G. Dautovic, "Top 25 Financial Data Breach Statistics for 2020," Fortunly.com, 30 September 2020. https://fortunly.com/statistics/data-breach-statistics/#gref

10. William A. Carter, "Forces Shaping the Cyber Threat Landscape for Financial Institutions," SWIFT Institute Working Paper No. 2016-004. October 2, 2017. Center for Strategic and International Studies (CSIS) Strategic Technologies Program: https://www.csis.org/programs/strategic-technologies-program/cybersecurity-and-governance/financial-sector-cybersecurit-1

11. "Fedwire Funds Service," Board of Governors of the Federal Reserve System. Retrieved 23 February 2021. https://www.federalreserve.gov/paymentsystems/fedfunds_about.htm

12. "Automated Clearinghouse Services," Board of Governors of the Federal Reserve System. Retrieved 23 February 2021. https://www.federalreserve.gov/paymentsystems/fedach_data.htm

13. Nacha.org, "ACH Network Sees Record Growth in 2020 to 26.8 Billion Payments," 4 February 2021. https://www.nacha.org/news/ach-network-sees-record-growth-2020-268-billion-payments

14. ClearingHouse.org, "Our History," undated. https://www.theclearinghouse.org/about/history

15. Ibid.

16. Michael Magrath, "Top 2020 Banking Regulations & Security Compliance Requirements," OneSpan blog, 24 February 2020. https://www.onespan.com/blog/top-2020-banking-regulations-security-compliance-requirements

17. Maine Li, "Cybersecurity in Banking," *Tech Times*, 21 October 2019. https://www.techtimes.com/articles/245785/20191021/cybersecurity-in-banking.htm

18. PYMTS, "Digital Dollar Exploration Gets Backing from Treasury Secretary Yellen," PYMTS.com, 22 February 2021. https://www.pymnts.com/digital-payments/2021/digital-dollar-exploration-gets-backing-from-treasury-secretary-yellen/

19. "Antivirus and Firewall 'Security' Measures are OBSOLETE in 2021 – and It's Getting Worse," ModernDiplomacy.eu, 23 February 2021. https://moderndiplomacy.eu/2021/02/23/antivirus-and-firewall-security-measures-are-obsolete-in-2021-and-its-getting-worse/

20. Walter Contreras, "Cyberattacks on Financial Institutions: Data Breaches in 2020," Motiva.net, 2 December 2020. https://motiva.net/cyberattacks-on-financial-institutions-data-breaches-in-2020/

21. Scarlett Phillips, "Five Biggest Data Breaches in Financial Services History: Lessons to Be Learnt," Six Degrees blog, 6 October 2020. https://www.6dg.co.uk/blog/biggest-data-breaches-financial-services/

22. Accenture Security, "Cost of Cyber Crime Study: Insights on the Security Investments That Make a Difference in Financial Services," 13 February 2018. https://www.slideshare.net/accenture/cost-of-cyber-crime-financial-services-87930580

23. "The Titanic: Lifeboats," History on the Net, undated. https://www.historyonthenet.com/the-titanic-lifeboats

24. US Department of Transportation, Federal Highway Administration. https://www.fhwa.dot.gov/policy-information/statistics/2007/pdf/fi200.pdf

10.2 PUBLIC-PRIVATE PARTNERSHIP IN FIGHTING THE CYBER THREAT

Timothy L. Callahan
Senior Vice President, Global Security
Chief Security Officer, Aflac

10.2.1 INTRODUCTION

Our nation has a long history of public-private partnerships to enable us collectively to solve a problem with national implications either to security or commerce. The general practice is the government providing a forum, guidance, standards, and in some cases, financial backing to enable the private sector to solve the problem.

Most recently, in the pandemic crisis, we saw an example of the partnership between the government, research institutes, and pharmaceuticals in developing and delivering a vaccine for COVID-19. In this case, the government provided financial and research assistance and removed "yellow tape" requirements that delay the process of approval. In doing this, the government unleashed the power of private enterprise in solving the problem. Another example is all the manufacturing plants and distilleries that leveraged their facilities to produce protective equipment, medical equipment, and hand sanitizer to rapidly fill the needs brought on by the pandemic.

Throughout history, we have seen the use of the power of the federal government to protect private industry to enable commerce. This comes in trade agreements and treaties designed to provide access to foreign markets or protect US markets from unfair trade practices. Moreover, the early days of the US Navy can be traced to the need to protect US merchants from pirates and other threats to free and open trade. The government did not engage in the trade because of our fundamental belief in free enterprise, but the government did enable the trade by helping to provide a level playing field and protection from adverse forces or environments.

Now comes the modern commerce and support environment through the use of the web and digital infrastructure. We have seen rapid development and deployment of new technologies—machine learning, artificial intelligence, robotics, etc. The need today is to use the power of the government to protect and enable safe, secure, and fair practices over the digital environment. Innovation and growth of new technologies present cyber risk and outpace the time it takes to develop regulations for those industries that are regulated. In the absence of specific regulation, the government (national intelligence) may fill a vacuum in risk assessing new technologies and issuing guidance to Federal agencies as well as private industries.

Nearly every day, we read about, receive an alert, or hear of a cyberattack on a company, governmental agency, or the national defense structure. In recent years, municipalities have been devastated by such attacks. Cyberattacks manifest themselves in various scenarios. Among the major ones that affect municipalities are ransomware and distributed denial of service (DDoS) attacks. In these scenarios, the attack is designed to deny access to municipal services or to files needed to provide services to its constituency unless they pay the ransom.

Municipalities struggle to find the money to invest in a strong cyber security program and this weakness has led to succumbing to attacks, struggling to respond, and forcing, at times, an extended and expensive recovery phase. In the end, citizens suffer due to inaccessibility to services and increased taxes or fees to overcome the expense.

We have seen that agencies of the federal government, national defense agencies, and critical commercial infrastructure have also been the target of cyberattacks. The recent supply chain attack of SolarWinds was an example of an attack where the strong implication is that it was directed to Federal agencies and critical commercial infrastructure companies to give the threat actors access to intelligence and the technological environment. Some believe it was more than just intelligence gathering but an attempt to build in backdoors to critical components of the government to further a cyberwar advantage. "This is not just about an espionage attack," said Richard Clarke of Good Harbor Security Risk Management. "This is about something called preparation of the battlefield, where they're now able, in a time of crisis, to eat the software in thousands of US companies."[1]

The SolarWinds attack affected private companies and, most notable, cybersecurity companies. The threat actor here targeted the most used security companies to gain intelligence on penetration methods or to disable the protections provided by their products. They wanted to render ineffective the very controls cyber professionals use to detect and defeat malicious activity.

Private companies across the nation are collectively spending billions of dollars implementing protective measures due to the threat. The strong protective measures used to be primarily in financial industry firms but now are necessary for nearly all industries. The cost of these measures is passed on to consumers either directly in pricing the cost of products or services or indirectly in company overhead. Some of the hardest hit by the cost of cyber protection are the not-for-profit and charitable organizations—that can least afford nor have an avenue to recoup the cost.

Private citizens also suffer from malicious cyber activity, be it through their personal ecommerce activity or through criminals capturing their information to monetize. The point is that nearly every American is affected by cyber threats in one way or another. The government helping to overcome the threat serves the constituents. We need to provide an environment where companies are not spending inordinate amounts of resources against what is at times well-funded criminal or nation-state actors.

10.2.2   CATEGORIZATION OF CYBER THREAT ACTORS

Cyberattacks are launched by threat actors with various motivations. Motivations are important to understand in crafting a protection and response strategy. The threat actors and motivations also help inform in what areas the public-private partnership can help the best and thus the order and priority of partnership.

Understanding that sometimes the lines between the groups are blurred, below are primary threat actors with their key motivations:

- **Criminal:** This is by far the most prevalent threat in the private sector. In the pursuit of their goals, they use multiple techniques and vectors. The goal may be to take over a customer account, to take over and exfiltrate a database of sensitive information, extortion to prevent a denial of service attack or to trick employees into sending a wire transfer. There has been a tremendous growth in Ransomware attacks where the criminal encrypts an organization's data and demands payment to provide keys to decrypt the data. The motivation in a criminal attack is all about getting money.
- **Hacktivist/misinformation:** These tend to be threat actors with a social or political message. Their attacks usually manifest in taking over and defacing websites, hacking to release user lists or deceptively influencing social media platforms. Generally, there is no demand for money, but these attacks are designed to cause embarrassment, persuasion, or reputational hardships. Increasingly, we see conspiracy theories and misinformation as serving a similar political motivation.
- **Terrorism:** Terrorist organizations have become more tech savvy. Their motivation is generally to use harassment or denial of service to a political end. Terrorists may use cyber to attack or affect physical operations for disruption, such as attacking a power grid. They may also launch Ransomware and other extortion attacks as a revenue generator to fund their activity. In trying to influence a political ideology, Terrorism can be one of the more prominent blurred lines between hacktivist and nation-state.
- **Nation-state:** Typically, this threat actor is identified with motivations of cyberwar, espionage, and gaining intelligence. However, this threat actor can have motivations similar to

terrorists, and their intent may be to disrupt, similar to the hacktivist. The target could be data theft, similar to the criminal. Overall, the motive of the nation-state is to further their national interest and they act in the cyber domain to accomplish this. In some nation-states, where there is not a clear separation between business and government (China, for instance), the national interest may be to gain intellectual property, business secrets, or manufacturing advantage. This poses a unique challenge because this threat actor generally doesn't have the limitation of financial and personnel resources. They can act through their government employees, their military or use intermediaries to mask their cyber activity. This threat has the means and ability to be patient and persistent until they accomplish their goals.

Nation-states have proven their ability to attack throughout any point in the supply chain. They can penetrate legitimate companies and use that platform to compromise software or hardware that finds its way into companies and government agencies.

10.2.2.1 THE COMMONALITY OF THREAT ACTORS

The most significant threat to government and our national interests is certainly the nation-state and the most significant threat to private companies is the criminal threat. However, we have seen a blurring of these. Nation-states have been behind attacks on private companies to gain the information they can use for their national interests. As we look at ways to most effectively combat the threat, we are forced to look at what will have the greatest effect. While at one time, the tools, techniques, and maturity of cyberattacks between a criminal and a nation-state threat were recognizably different, with the nation-state attacks showing more maturity. Now, the signatures, techniques, tools, etc., are interchangeable and at times indistinguishable.

The fortunate part, if any, in all of this is that with that blurring, we can use similar tactics to combat them. As such, this is the area where the public-private partnership can prove the most effective. This is not to discount the other two threats. They are real. But the priority has to be the well-funded and executed criminal and nation-state threat. We acknowledge the key difference is generally the criminal will back off if it is costing more to attack than they will reap from success. The nation-state will not back off until their goals are accomplished.

10.2.3 RECOMMENDATIONS

10.2.3.1 PUBLIC-PRIVATE PARTNERSHIP

There are many ways the government and private sector can cooperate to secure our national defense and secure our business climate for national and global commerce. Some may require legislative, some may be accomplished through current law, but all must be the priority of the new administration, or they will not come about.

10.2.3.2 ATTITUDINAL

The Federal government can go a long way in fostering cooperation with the private sector in the standards promulgated and how breaches are handled. If a company is employing industry and commercially reasonable cyber security controls, has a "tops down" positive cyber security culture, and is not negligent yet is breached anyway, they should be seen as a victim, not criminally or civilly liable. The threat actors are the perpetrators and government resources such as Law Enforcement and Cyber Command must be directed at them. This attitude should be paramount in the drafting of legislation, policy, executive orders, etc. Companies that do not take appropriate measures should be held accountable, not for the attack but for their lack of preparedness. Our regulatory and enforcement structure must also accommodate this distinction. In the Senate, Senators Carper and Portman are working on a bipartisan bill that, as drafted, would provide indemnity to companies that have adopted a recognized security framework and have actively implemented it. This would provide an incentive for companies to adopt and maintain solid practices.

10.2.3.3 INFORMATION SHARING

Advances have been made in recent years in government agency and private company information sharing. The Cybersecurity Information Sharing Act of 2015 provided key protections to private companies when sharing vulnerabilities, indicators of compromise, and other essential information between companies and the Federal government. This has eased the concerns of companies' legal staff and permitted a better flow of information. (There may still be work needed in the liability space, but overall a better climate now.)

However, we don't see the same flow of threat information from government agencies to the private sector. Often when information is shared, it is of such a general nature that it is not actionable. The Administration can foster a better environment by getting actionable threat information out to the private sector in a timely manner. There is certainly acknowledgment that national intelligence agencies must protect sources and methods, but we believe there can be an accelerated program to evaluate, declassify (in part or in whole) and disseminate vulnerability and attack information to the private sector. The Department of Homeland Security Cybersecurity and Infrastructure Security Agency (DHS CISA) can help facilitate this through the relationships with the Information Sharing and Analysis Center structure.

Closely related is the ability for private sector cybersecurity executives and employees to obtain security clearances to have access to threat intelligence. There is presently a procedure, but it is lengthy and with little transparency on how to obtain the clearance. This is an area that may be solved administratively through executive action and may require greater resources dedicated to the process.

10.2.3.4 A NATIONAL FOCUS/NATIONAL LEGISLATION

Digital commerce is now, more than ever, a part of the daily lives of our citizens. Yet this environment is extremely exposed and our economic success is reliant on it. Our business climate and our national defense depend upon a secure digital environment. However, we don't have a comprehensive national focus that serves all sectors. Moreover, we have a patchwork of laws, regulations, and varying emphasis across the country. Some states are stricter than others in the area of data security and privacy. Some industries are more regulated than others, although they may have the same information on the consumers. We need to smooth out these inconsistencies. We need to acknowledge our economic reliance on digital commerce across government and private sector and ensure it is a national priority to ensure security and resiliency of this national resource.

Our US Constitution gives the federal government the authority to regulate interstate commerce. The digital world does not have boundaries—it is certainly interstate commerce. Yet, we continue to see this patchwork of regulation. Why is the same information, if it happens to be in a bank, regulated differently than that information in a retail company or a credit bureau? Why are the networks of regulated entities regulated and security mandated, yet the carriers that bring that networking capability are not required to secure the traffic? Why are service providers that host terabytes of sensitive information not regulated to the same degree as the companies they service?

We need unified National Data Security Breach Notification and National Privacy Law(s). We need a common definition of sensitive information with minimal standards for protection regardless of industry. *It must base protection requirements on the defined data not on industry.* Some part of this is how we define a "covered entity." The present definition in current law and regulations tends to hold the company dealing with the consumer as the covered entity. If we are serious about protecting the information, we should expand this definition to any entity that hosts, possesses, stores, transmits, or accesses the information. There should also be a clause that exempts a provider if they have a program that meets or exceeds industry standards, the data is encrypted, and the keys are held by the covered company (not in the service provider's custody). This would then incent hosting and service providers to adopt demonstrably strong security measures by indemnification.

In these conversations, enforcement is often the reason for the holdup in passing legislation. A solution would be to require/empower the existing regulatory structure or bodies to enforce the National standard. In the case of some industries, like insurance, where the existing regulatory structure is at the state level, this will require some incentive for States to adopt the enforcement aspects of federal legislation. If there is not a regulatory body for an industry, then (and only then) the Federal Trade Commission should be provided enforcement authority. Rulemaking authority should be provided to a dedicated council comprised of the various regulatory bodies, similar to how the Federal Financial Institute Examination Council (FFIEC) is composed.

Our federal government is also empowered in the Constitution to make international agreements and treaties. This is another area where we need global engagement for secure and resilient digital commerce across the globe. We need emphasis at the diplomatic level to ensure we have cooperation among nations. Some countries have an Ambassador for Cyber Security. Several lawmakers are pushing for this and believe this would be key to gaining influence on the international level.

10.2.3.5 SUPPLY CHAIN SECURITY

US Government Agencies and the private sector have been impacted by cyberattacks where threat actors have compromised hardware and software in the development and manufacturing process. The threat actor can use the compromise to gain access to protected sensitive information. This remains one of the most vulnerable areas of cybersecurity. The government at all levels, as well as private companies, are subject to these attacks with no real way to defend against this attack.

There are no national standards to which technology manufacturers are accountable, nor are there compliance requirements. It is common in the development process to pull open source code from the internet without knowing the security of the code. It is nearly impossible to discover "backdoors" that have been implanted in code, packaged into a product, new or updated and passed on to government or private companies. Once the compromised code is in the environment, threat actors have practically unfettered access to that network through these backdoors.

Software manufacturers have indemnification from liability for the security of their code. Private companies have little recourse or ability to negotiate with the largest software manufacturers to gain contractual liability. There is no structure in place to regulate the software industry expansively. With technology affecting nearly everything we do and all aspects of services, it is time to shore up this gap to ensure safety and security.

Companies must ensure they are taking appropriate measures to evaluate their supply chain for risk. However, software suppliers must be more transparent in their development process. Software manufacturers should have a set of standards they must attest to in any sales transaction. This can be fostered through a self-regulation protocol providing incentives for adoption—an Underwriters Laboratory type solution. This could also be regulated through an existing regulatory body or some combination of both. But the key is that the manufacturers must not have indemnification from liability for the products they provide. If manufacturers had a greater share of risk through liability, it would likely drive the industry to better practices.

10.2.4 CONCLUSION

This is a very high-level view of some of the ways to foster the public-private partnership in addressing cybersecurity threats. There are certainly more ways, but the most important factor is to create and sustain an environment of cooperation and collaboration between government agencies and the private sector. The Cybersecurity Advisory Committee Act, recently passed with the National Defense Authorization Act,[2] is a step in the right direction. This legislation authorizes the Director of the Cybersecurity and Infrastructure Security Agency to form an advisory committee of 35 cybersecurity professionals. This mixture of private industry CISOs with the government professionals in CISA will provide a solid foundation for an effective Public-Private Partnership.

10.2.4.1 ABOUT THE AUTHOR

Tim Callahan, CISSP, CISM, CRISC, joined Aflac in 2014 and currently serves as the Senior Vice President, Global Security, and Chief Security Officer. He brought more than 30 years of experience in information and physical security, business resiliency, and risk management. He was promoted to his current role in January 2016, where he is responsible for directing Aflac's global security strategy and leading the information security, business continuity, and disaster recovery functions across the company to prioritize security initiatives and allocate resources based on appropriate risk assessments.

REFERENCES

1. Deirdre Cohen, "The Threats Arising from the Massive SolarWinds Hack," CBS News, 3 January 2021, www.cbsnews.com/news/the-threats-arising-from-the-massive-solarwinds-hack.
2. United States, Congress. *William M. (Mac) Thornberry National Defense Authorization Act for Fiscal Year 2021*. U.S. Government Printing Office, 2020. 116th Congress. 2nd Session. Conference Report. https://docs.house.gov/billsthisweek/20201207/CRPT-116hrpt617.pdf.

11 Food and Agriculture

11.0 ABOUT THE FOOD AND AGRICULTURE SECTOR

Timothy Bengson
Vice President and Global CISO, Kellogg Company

Itzik Kotler
Co-Founder and CTO, SafeBreach

The Food and Agriculture Sector of the global economy provides the sustenance required to live and thrive. The Food and Agriculture Sector is almost entirely under private ownership and is composed of farms, food manufacturing, transportation, storage and processing, and production facilities, including restaurants. In the United States, there are an estimated 2.1 million farms, 935,000 restaurants, and more than 200,000 registered food manufacturing, processing, and storage facilities, according to CISA [1]. The sector accounts for roughly one-fifth of the economic activity of the United States. Globally, according to the World Bank [2], the sector makes up 4% of global GDP. The Food and Agriculture Sector has critical dependencies with many sectors, but particularly with:

- *Water and Wastewater Systems*, for clean irrigation and processed water
- *Transportation Systems*, for movement of products and livestock
- *Energy*, to power the equipment needed for agriculture production and food processing
- *Chemical*, for fertilizers and pesticides used in the production of crops

Aside from economic activity and providing food to the world, the Food and Agriculture Sector is considered a crucial element of economic development and global productivity. Nations that improve their food security and deliver reliable nutrition to citizens are far more likely to grow their economies and reduce poverty. Children that are well fed perform better in school and benefit from education. More efficient agriculture and food sectors also enable countries to benefit economically from exporting their bounty.

The Food and Agriculture Sector remains highly fragmented with varying levels of connectivity and digitization, both in the United States and in the rest of the world. The level of technological exposure ranges from small farms with very little dependence on technology for anything more than communications capabilities to large industrial processing plants and farms with highly automated sensors and control networks running on networked platforms.

A recent spate of ransomware attacks on the sector, which resulted in the shutdown of some of the largest food processing plants in the United States demonstrated the potential vulnerability of this sector; the attacks and shutdowns also validated the potential use of cyberattacks on the sector to impact a nation's food supply. Other cyberattacks in the past year on water infrastructure and energy systems, including a ransomware attack that took a large gasoline pipeline offline for an extended period, highlighted how upstream dependencies could hobble multiple sectors, including food and agriculture.

The rapid digitization of the Food and Agriculture Sector provides an expanded attack surface for bad actors. Factories and processing plants in the sector are deploying sensors and remote management capabilities to enable centralized management, control, and analysis of processes. While these efforts to digitize will yield greater efficiencies, digitization also exposes many software targets within the infrastructure of this sector including older industrial control systems and devices

DOI: 10.1201/9781003243021-11

and networks not originally designed to be exposed to the public internet. Newer systems, such as connected tractors and irrigation equipment, offer additional vectors for attacks.

Overall, this translates into a more and more complicated IT and network environment that requires greater sophistication to properly protect from cyberattacks. Food infrastructure is also an obvious target for asymmetric warfare and also for politically-motivated attacks by rogue states or non-state actors. For the coming decades, the Food and Agriculture Sector will need to improve its cybersecurity capabilities and create layers of security controls to deliver greater digital resilience and assurances that the food we eat will remain safe and readily available.

11.0.1   ABOUT SAFEBREACH

SafeBreach's mission is to change the way the industry deals with security and risk, and enable companies to use the security technologies they have invested into the fullest. By validating those technologies against attacks, from the known to the latest emerging threats, they will drive risk down—on a continuous basis. Companies will be able to invest smart and protect more. They will be able to quantify risks to the business and drive a security strategy aligned with the company's business growth. Changing the mindset of defenders to offensive and proactive will help us build a safer world.

REFERENCES

1. "Food and Agriculture Sector I CISA", Cisa.gov, 2020. [Online]. Available: https://www.cisa.gov/food-and-agriculture-sector. [Accessed: 18- Sep- 2021].
2. "Agriculture and Food", The World Bank, 2021. [Online]. Available: https://www.worldbank.org/en/topic/agriculture/overview. [Accessed: 02- Sep- 2021].

11.1 FOR CPG COMPANIES, A ZERO TRUST SECURITY STRATEGY IS THE BEST SUPPLY CHAIN DEFENSE

Timothy Bengson
Vice President and Global CISO, Kellogg Company

Itzik Kotler
Co-Founder and CTO, SafeBreach

11.1.1 INTRODUCTION

The SolarWinds and Microsoft Exchange attacks in 2020 and 2021 exposed the soft underbelly of the global software supply chain. These attacks made it clear that key components of that supply chain are likely compromised. The Solar Winds attack allowed unauthorized access to the most critical and widely used networking control tool for Microsoft Windows networks after the password for the system that delivered software updates was stolen. (The theft and resulting compromise were not detected for months.) The Microsoft Exchange attack allowed attackers to compromise email service and delivery for unpatched Microsoft mail servers, opening a path to further compromise of Microsoft applications or the use of trusted email to further penetrate corporate applications through the delivery of malware or phishing attacks.

We may never know precisely how many organizations and IT systems were impacted by the SolarWinds and Microsoft Edge attack campaigns in 2020 and 2021. The assessment of ramifications and the recovery processes for these attacks are still ongoing. Because the attacks leveraged trusted systems with broad access inside of organizations, the potential blast radius is wide. Due to the severity and wide reach of these attacks, threat actors may reap the rewards of their months of nearly unfettered access for many months to come. According to Brandon Wales, the acting director of CISA, the US Cybersecurity, the remediation effort for government networks will require at least 18 months [1].

It is highly likely that other similar compromises to trusted systems in the software and IT supply chain with respect to sensitive information have occurred and remain undiscovered on a global basis. The SolarWinds hack was carried out by skilled, sophisticated attackers intent on opening large-scale backdoors in the global technology infrastructure. The Microsoft Exchange hack was less artful but potentially quite damaging due to the omnipresence of this software and its access to critical and sensitive information.

Malicious actors have begun aggressively diversifying their targets to include critical infrastructure and manufacturing companies—so-called operational technology (OT). In an industrial facility, OT is the computing infrastructure that controls the systems overseeing the production of the actual resource. Information technology (IT) is the is technology infrastructure used to manage technology business functions such as email or communications and networks, rather than machinery or systems creating or controlling physical elements. In a cereal plant, for example, OT might be the controllers for the ovens used to dry and toast the cereal. IT powers email servers, networks, and phone systems. Increasingly, IT and OT overlap. The same network technology used to connect computers for finance and factory management teams is used to connect control systems of industrial equipment to technology systems running in the cloud, over IP networks. The increasing use of connected devices means that OT systems are vulnerable to attacks that in the past focused on IT systems. Today in many plants, OT systems are no longer air-gapped or segmented entirely from IT systems; a plant manager may receive information about machinery or product status on the same networks that also run the plant's IT systems.

The successful breach of a municipal water supply system in the United States in February, 2020, underscored the latent risk [2]. For the most part, these attacks on infrastructure and manufacturing are targeting a weak point in the global technology armor—the overlap of OT and IT systems and the technology used to directly control industrial processes. Those controllers are likely running an outdated operating system such as Windows XP or Windows 95, which are no longer supported by Microsoft.

Even as the security community continues to focus so much energy and effort is on identifying and combating Zero-Day attacks, the reality is that novel attacks are both less likely and likely to be less of a risk than software supply chain compromises of trusted actors in the IT ecosystem. We should further expect that supply chain attacks will expand to target not just the IT systems but also the OT systems and subsystems of consumer packaged goods (CPG) and other industrial companies.

To address this, we must plan for combined OT and IT attacks by building a list of attack assumptions and testing against those assumptions to evaluate readiness. With these assumptions and a clearer picture of our potential weaknesses, we can move toward a Zero Trust mentality and architecture. There is no way to identify all possible breach or failure scenarios because the ecosystems we protect are too complex with too many moving parts. We can identify better ways to contain the blast radius of an attack by testing and validating our controls against classes of attacks to see whether our defenses are up to the task. Adversarialsimulation must include both IT and OT to be effective, just as any solution should be holistic across both realms.

11.1.2 SUPPLY CHAIN AND RANSOMWARE ATTACKS ARE CHANGING THE GAME

The SolarWinds and Exchange attacks certainly had political and industrial espionage goals. At the same time, supply chain breaches are likely correlated with increased volumes and severity of ransomware attacks. APTs that are likely responsible for the more serious supply chain breaches are now funded from a multitude of sources. Those sources include state funding and also online fraud and illicit activities. As ransomware has become more profitable, APTs have shown more interest in using these attacks as a funding mechanism. In the past two years, ransomware adversaries have broadly recognized that attacking the supply chain to access targets with hard-to-defend yet critical systems, such as health care and manufacturing organizations, can yield seven or even eight-figure payouts in a matter of days. The victimized organizations make the inevitable calculus that fighting the attackers potentially for weeks or months to regain control of their infrastructure is more damaging than just paying them off.

The only viable response to these hacks is to accelerate the move toward the adoption of Zero Trust architectures on a wide scale. This is especially true in the CPG industry. Unlike a bank or an automaker, CPG companies make food that people eat. This means that we play a crucial role in feeding the world. We saw during COVID that interruptions in the supply chain resulted in soaring food prices in many countries. This can create dangerous conditions and civil unrest.

In this article, we will take you through the unique and growing cybersecurity challenges facing CPG organizations and why Zero Trust along with continuous adversary simulation and control validation is the inevitable and only option to maintaining robust security for manufacturing organizations in the face of a growing cascade of sophisticated and potentially lucrative attacks.

11.1.3 HOW OT HAS LAGGED IT IN CYBER RISK MITIGATION

In the world of manufacturing and industrial processes, there are always two distinct technology universes. One is traditional IT, which maintains connectivity and networks, ensures that email works, and enables productivity, communications, and data security for company information and assets. IT Cyber security in the CPG world is on par with security even in advanced technology companies.

A second and less developed universe is OT. This is the universe of the factory floor, of massive multi-million-dollar machines that make the things we need to live and survive. In food and CPG, this is a world of ovens, mixers, conveyor belts, packaging systems, and endless other types of industrial equipment used to make a lot of food as quickly as possible with the highest degree of precision. This world includes systems such as programmable logic controllers (PLCs), an industrial, ruggedized computer designed specifically to withstand the stresses of operating in manufacturing or industrial environments. Operational Technology is a parallel universe where until very recently, many of the systems were not even connected to each other or to internal networks, let alone exposed to internet-facing systems. Most OT systems today do have some type of computer systems controlling their operations. Those systems, however, tend to run dated operating systems that are no longer supported with patching and system updates. Typically, industrial control computing runs on Windows XP or even Windows 95 operating systems with even older systems running SCADA-based operating systems that are both brittle and poorly understood and hard to monitor for signs of cyberattack.

Updating OT systems to more current computing and operating capabilities is challenging. Most OT systems were designed with multi-decade lifecycles in mind. The giant ovens required to make cereal, for example, may cost millions of dollars. Many of them were designed and installed before the Internet of Things was even in its earliest stages. So little thought was given to designing upgrade pathways for the associated computing systems.

After all, these systems were not connected to the external networks and many were never intended to be connected to internal networks. As time wore on, this perceived "air-gap" served as justification for allowing these systems to remain in operations despite risking cybersecurity risk. In reality, the systems were not effectively air-gapped. Operators or technicians began to link OT assets to data lakes, analytics tools, and diagnostic tools. Companies began the process of upgrading plants to "smart factories" by adding sensors that linked to both the processors of these assets and the outside world to push useful data into analytics and monitoring packages.

Even if the data connections were episodic, they have become inevitable. Technicians logging into these systems remotely are they themselves connected to both IT and OT networks. Usually, the device they are using to connect to an IT or OT asset is also connected to the public Internet. The COVID-19 pandemic forced CISO's to allow OT support organizations to punch holes in perimeter-based security defenses because they could not be present in the factories and needed to be able to monitor and control production runs from their homes or via mobile devices. Remote connections present enhanced risks such as effective use of VPNs and reliance on consumer networking gear such as home Wi-Fi routers. These routers may be more challenging to harden and may even have known vulnerabilities or are still using factory default network administrator passwords.

These realities underscore the need to upgrade CPG production assets to more modern operating systems and better security, and the urgent need to push upgrades more quickly to vulnerable systems. Despite this realization, CISOs struggle to secure upgrades. Security teams cannot simply order downtime for a system upgrade. In food plants, factories run 24 hours a day for weeks on end. The rare maintenance windows are a few hours, at most, and in those windows, security teams must compete with all other teams for time and resources during this brief period.

What's more, large changes to operating systems or anything else are risky for manufacturing operations with a low tolerance for outages. The calculation for many factory managers is that it is better to continue running consistently on time and meet production schedules with dated and dangerous systems and risk the unknown rather than incur the risk of a self-inflicted wound should an upgrade or other change cause a large-scale outage. This concern is understandable in the realm of CPG consumables. Interrupting production means interrupting the world's food supply. Introducing unknowns can not only lead to production outages but also might lead to unforeseen weaknesses and holes in the new OT fabric. The business logic of leaving well enough alone was hard to argue with in the past. These OT systems do what they were designed to do and with a higher degree of uptime and efficiency. There had been no logical business reason to swap them out or change them. That risk equation has forever changed; in the spring and early summer of 2021, ransomware attacks on a major gasoline pipeline and the world's largest meat producer halted operations for weeks, resulting in heavy damages.

In addition, sensitivities around food production are also higher than in almost any other industry. Food is an emotional subject and food security concerns evoke visceral reactions. This injects yet another barrier to change and innovation in the industry.

11.1.4   THE ZERO TRUST IMPERATIVE FOR MANUFACTURING

All of the above challenges facing CPG and food manufacturing are addressable if the industry can move swiftly toward a Zero Trust infrastructure. In reality, most CISOs today would admit that the legacy model of establishing a secure perimeter with trusted internal enclaves has been quickly dying for several years now and is no longer an effective way to maintain a security posture.

Ongoing shifts in how employees and organizations use technology make the perimeter defense strategy less effective. The software has moved from hosted to SaaS and running in the cloud, delivered via the web. More and more companies are storing their essential data hosting, mission-critical, business applications in public or virtual private clouds located far from their offices or factories. Employees seek to access their information from many more devices and often they use the same device for personal and work tasks. Organizations that have become more fluid now require porous boundaries to enable collaboration across groups of employees, contractors, and freelancers. More and more business applications connect to each other via application programming interfaces API(s), a standard mechanism to allow applications to communicate. These connections result in more potential pathways into an organization, putting more stress on the traditional firewall-based perimeter defense models.

Lastly, the growing spectrum of connected devices, including wireless peripherals, IoT systems, and sensors, makes the perimeter nearly impossible to define. With the Fourth Industrial Revolution in full swing, analysts now anticipate that trillions of IoT devices will be connected via IP address to public or private networks within the next few years. The sheer number of connections and the constant changes in status and state overwhelm the idea of a perimeter.

The manufacturing and food processing sector suffers the same problems with fluid perimeters and the growing number of connected devices applies. This challenge is made even greater by the fact that every manufacturing plant has a unique OT footprint. In manufacturing, plant managers often commission their own custom software and firmware upgrades to meet specific needs. Plants also have a wide variety of applications and specialized equipment to perform the same task. Two plants producing the same SKU might have different ovens for baking, different mixers for mixing, and different extrusion machines. If that weren't challenging enough, the data flows might vary from plant to plant. Some plants may have connected certain assets to censors and out to a data center storage pool in a public cloud. Others keep their assets offline but periodically remote access them to check status or see error codes.

All in all, it is a uniquely challenging environment for building a Zero Trust architecture. The challenges in controlling this environment also highlight why a ransomware or other form of automated attack could prove so damaging. Once inside of a traditional perimeter defense of OT systems, an attacker would meet a particularly soft environment. Because these systems run software that is no longer supported, getting patches and fixes running in a timely fashion would be exceptionally difficult. This would leave attackers time and space for horizontal traversal and to more deeply embed themselves into the OT stack so they could mount persistent attacks.

11.1.5   WHAT NEEDS TO BE DONE TO MAKE ZERO
TRUST A MANUFACTURING REALITY

Cyber security leaders that want to bring Zero Trust into their OT stack and their production assets can follow a set of logical and non-controversial steps to create an incremental program that eases their organization towards a more secure future without disrupting ongoing operations and workflows.

11.1.5.1   MAKE CYBER PART OF THE INITIAL IoT AND DATA CONVERSATION

Every CPG company is now executing on a data strategy and digital transformation to upgrade and modernize their plants and manufacturing operations. Cybersecurity must not be an afterthought for plants wiring up for IoT. Adding new types of connectivity and data flows should trigger an analysis of security implications. It also brings up new opportunities to make system changes that put in place simple steps for Zero Trust such as more frequent authentications, consolidated logging, and putting in place specific controls mapped to IoT systems. An organization that might not otherwise embrace Zero Trust might find the concept more compelling when framed as a necessary step for IoT initiatives.

11.1.5.2   DESIGN TO CONTROL THE BLAST RADIUS

Segmentation and compartmentalization have long been cornerstones of security. That said, most businesses have struggled to enforce these principles, in part due to increasingly porous perimeters. As we saw with the WannaCry supply chain attacks, pernicious malware that is smartly designed can propagate widely in a matter of minutes. Even seemingly benign actions like updates from accounting software can deliver devastating, fast-spreading attacks. In CPG, any attack that takes a plant offline is catastrophic, costing millions of dollars in downtime and lost revenues. For this reason, controlling the blast radius of any attack against a CPG organization is of paramount importance. This means injecting authentication handshakes in more places and setting privilege bars higher for reauthentication, or even inserting continuous authentication for more critical capabilities. For many OT environments, the concept of blast radius control was not part of the system design because plants, and manufacturing assets within plants, were not connected to each other or to the outside world. To control blast radius, all potential vectors for ingress must be noted, mapped, and controlled. In most cases, existing security controls can be easily expanded to accommodate this practice. In addition, CISOs with a seat at the table should include "blast radius impact" into design considerations and modifications for evolving OT applications and IoT installations.

11.1.5.3   PICK AND CHOOSE YOUR ENTRY POINTS AND EXPANSION PATH

While putting a Zero Trust architecture in place to cover all OT systems is ideal, the reality is this almost never occurs in a single stroke. OT teams will want to see how Zero Trust changes their processes and validate that it does not add unacceptable friction. OT teams are by nature conservative, and rightly so, given the stakes of disruption. Effective CISOs recognize this and adopt a go-slow approach by picking a few specific systems on which to put in place Zero Trust initially and test the waters. With a clear win, CISOs can then seek to expand Zero Trust along a well published and predictable path to give OT confidence that they are being consulted in the process.

11.1.5.4   CONTINUOUSLY TEST AND VALIDATE EFFICACY OF ZERO TRUST
AND SECURITY CONTROLS

To date, adversarial simulation has largely been confined to IT environments. This is a mistake. OT systems are likely even more valuable targets than traditional IT systems precisely because they are so much closer to the actual production and value generation (the actual physical good). In infrastructure such as utilities, we are already seeing a greater focus by APTs on compromising our water supply and power grid. The same is likely underway for our manufacturing plants. In this light, CPG and food manufacturing CISOs must identify ways to better test the efficacy of their Zero Trust architecture and, more generally, the vulnerability of their IT and OT systems to the latest attacks. Speed is of the essence. A CPG CISO should be able to run an adversarial simulation to validate their security controls within days of an exploit release or breach revelation.

Running continuous or very frequent control validations is still not standard practice for most IT security organizations. In point of fact, most security organizations treat control validations as an extension of penetration testing exercises, which they run once or twice per year. The technology for adversarial simulation has improved significantly in the past five years, making it now possible to run continuously and on demand without significant preparations for your testing environment. This makes it viable to add continuous security control validation to the checklist for standard security hygiene procedures. This type of continuous validation can not only test the efficacy of controls but also highlight areas where existing controls can be better utilized or, worst case, where additional controls might be needed. In addition, continuous validation and simulation give us the rare ability to be proactive versus reactive to potential gaps or risks in our environments.

11.1.5.5 Demonstrating That Cyber Brings Value, Not Just Cost

For CISOs at CPG and other manufacturing organizations, the biggest challenge is demonstrating clearly that cybersecurity brings value and strategic benefit rather than just friction and cost. The cost of a lightweight Zero Trust policy should be manageable in additional licenses or security controls; CISOs and their teams may be able to implement this with existing controls and authentication systems. So, the question of outlays should be easy to address. This is half the battle.

The other half is demonstrating that cyber is generating actual value in terms of either increased revenues or decreased risks. Demonstrating increased revenues is challenging but CISOs working closely with OT teams can make a strong case that the type of resilience and agility required to implement Zero Trust can yield improved uptime and continuity. The COVID-19 crisis proved this. During the crisis, manufacturing companies scrambled to put in place remote monitoring, third-party vendor access, and control systems that would be far simpler with a Zero Trust architecture already laid out.

Decreasing risk is best indicated by generating a series of risk metrics based on measurable improvements in security hygiene. Continuous security control validation is a good way to establish these benchmarks using the ever-evolving realm of real-world cyberattacks. Standard metrics might be time-to-remediation, attack block rate, proper control utilization rate, and block rate of novel attacks due to common sense security control deployment.

11.1.6 CONCLUSION

For CPG and food manufacturing companies, the coming decade will likely bring far more cyber security challenges than the past decade. We are entering an inevitable rush towards omni-connectivity, where every system is de facto connected to other systems and to large networks. Omni-connectivity means the perimeter will dissolve over time, leaving behind a collection of systems to verify identity and intent for all transactions that carry risk. Entering this era of omni-connectivity with eyes wide open is crucial for CISOs if they hope to pre-empt the next supply chain attacks.

Heading off those attacks will require improved security for dated and no-longer supported control systems. CPG CISOs will need to adjust their strategy to move away from perimeter defense and towards a strategy that relies more on Zero Trust and constant verification. Part of this will include more frequent control validation to ensure that existing controls are optimized to minimize blast radius. There is no perfect solution. The manufacturing plant of the future will be a mix of old and new—old OT assets and new security strategies. It will never be possible to remediate all possible risks. For that reason, CISOs and their teams must systematically and continuously identify the greatest risks. They must address those risks as effectively and quickly as possible without interrupting production activities in order to maintain the critical supply of what society needs to survive.

11.1.6.1 ABOUT THE AUTHORS

Timothy Bengson serves as the Vice President, Global Chief Information Security Officer (CISO), Kellogg Company. Tim is responsible for building and maintaining the security program that protects Kellogg's global critical assets, manufacturing, and supply chain, enabling business capabilities. He is responsible for all aspects of information security—operations and cyber defense; governance, risk, and compliance; identity and operational technology; and security transformation. Before joining Kellogg, Tim was with MasterCard for 13 years, where he held various leadership roles within infrastructure and security organizations. Tim frequently speaks on cybersecurity topics and is on the advisory board of several companies, including SafeBreach, CyberArk, Forcepoint, and Claroty.

Itzik Kotler is the CTO and Co-Founder of SafeBreach. Itzik has more than a decade of experience researching and working in the computer security space. He is a recognized industry speaker, having spoken at DEFCON, Black Hat USA, Hack in the Box, RSA, CCC, and H2HC. Prior to founding SafeBreach, Itzik served as CTO at Security-Art, an information security consulting firm, and before that he was SOC Team Leader at Radware. (NASDQ: RDWR).

REFERENCES

1. P. O'Neill, "Recovering from the SolarWinds hack could take 18 months", MIT Technology Review, 2021. [Online]. Available: https://www.technologyreview.com/2021/03/02/1020166/solarwinds-brandon-wales-hack-recovery- 18-months/. [Accessed: 02- Sep- 2021].
2. A. Greenberg, "A Hacker Tried to Poison a Florida City's Water Supply", Wired, 2021. [Online]. Available: https://www.wired.com/story/oldsmar-florida-water-utility-hack/. [Accessed: 02- Sep- 2021].

11.2 SOFTWARE HELPS FEED AMERICA—HOW DO WE KEEP IT SECURE?

Rusty Sides
Public Sector Technical Sales Director, Checkmarx

Justin Ruth
Lead Sales Engineer, Checkmarx

Will Berriel
Sales Engineer, Checkmarx

Scott McBain
Sales Engineer, Checkmarx

Michael Deck
Regional Sales Manager, Checkmarx

11.2.1 INTRODUCTION

It may seem strange to say that software feeds America. But that is increasingly the case as technology continues to make its way into every aspect of the agriculture and food supply chain.

Today, we are seeing the emergence of a concept called precision agriculture, were, as the USDA's National Institute of Food and Agriculture explains, "… sensing, information technologies, and mechanical systems enable sub-field crop management." However, this concept extends beyond crops, with technology even enabling the management and monitoring of livestock and forests [1].

Because of the capabilities and tools that precision agriculture solutions enable, the global precision farming market size is anticipated to reach $16.35 billion by 2028, according to research by market analyst, Grand View Research, Inc. These projections illustrate the incredible demand for technologies that can help farmers increase yields, decrease risk, and maximize their crops' profit [2].

A new generation of IoT sensors and connected devices are rolling out to farms across America with the intended goal of increasing the information available to farmers and decreasing the uncertainty that has always existed in farming. Weather sensors that connect to irrigation systems are making it possible to more accurately and precisely water crops. Crop management systems are being embraced in fields to monitor crop growth better and identify disease or other issues that could harm crop yields so that farms can take proactive steps to rectify problems. There are even cattle management and monitoring solutions designed to monitor the health and wellbeing of farm animals. As these IoT devices gain acceptance and increase in adoption, the security of these devices—and the firmware and applications that enable them—becomes increasingly paramount to securing the supply chain that ultimately results in feeding Americans.

The digital transformation that makes America's food supply chain vulnerable to cyberattacks by those looking to harm our country or generate a profit is not limited to just the farm. From water treatment plants, our electrical grid, and our transportation infrastructure, America's entire critical infrastructure is also increasingly becoming network-enabled and reliant on software. One could say the same for the industrial devices and manufacturing equipment within the nation's food processing and distribution facilities.

To make remote access and management possible and enable proactive and preventative maintenance, owners increasingly connect their industrial equipment to networks. This connectivity allows the devices to have their settings, operational information, and maintenance schedules monitored via applications and dashboards both within and outside the facility. It makes it possible for operators to access critical device and system settings remotely. It also makes these critical systems vulnerable to cyberattacks that could have significant impacts—both direct and indirect—on our food and agriculture supply chain.

The drive to modernize agriculture, food processing, food distribution, and the critical infrastructure that enables it has drastically increased the importance of software in feeding Americans. While this modernization has significant benefits to operational efficiency, food production, and risk mitigation for America's food producers, it makes application security of paramount importance.

11.2.2   TODAY'S APPLICATION SECURITY THREAT LANDSCAPE

In June 2021, it was disclosed that JBS USA Holdings, Inc. paid an $11 million ransom to cybercriminals in an attempt to restore their data and systems and avoid further disruptions to their operations. The plants impacted process approximately 20 percent of the meat consumed in their country and are a vital part of our nation's agricultural and food supply chain [3].

The ransomware attack on JBS USA Holdings, Inc. is one of many attacks that occurred in the first half of 2021, targeting critical infrastructure in our nation. It is also a stark reminder that our nation's food supply is not only susceptible to ransomware and other attacks but actively being targeted.

If IoT sensors with embedded firmware and corresponding software and dashboards are going to increasingly make their way into the agriculture and food processing industry, the universe of attack vectors that can be leveraged by malicious actors will only increase. This means that application security needs to be a priority. The large farms and agricultural companies purchasing IoT solutions need to take the security of their vendors into account. And the companies manufacturing these devices need to ensure their firmware and software solutions are secure. And for very good reason.

While much of the focus of cybersecurity professionals is on network and endpoint security, software remains one of the most significant vectors for cyberattacks. According to the analyst firm Gartner, "Over 70 percent of security vulnerabilities exist at the application layer, not the network layer." This number was even higher in findings by the National Institute of Standards and Technology (NIST), which found that "… 92 percent of reported vulnerabilities are in applications not in networks" [4].

Application-layer cyberattacks include more than the usual retail and financial service sector targets. Software vulnerabilities have been the entrance point for malicious actors in multiple notable security breaches against government agencies and critical infrastructure. A poignant and painful recent example is the 2020 SolarWinds attack. This breach, which impacted as many as ten different government agencies, including the Departments of Commerce and the Treasury, directly resulted from vulnerabilities in a network management software application that was offered as a "freemium" solution and used widely across many public and private sector organizations.

While it's evident that software and application vulnerabilities are a significant cyber risk across enterprises, the changing nature of software and applications is making that risk larger and more complex by the day. Today's application development teams are under pressure to develop software at an incredibly rapid pace to keep up with the speed of innovation. Simultaneously, the adoption of microservices and new architectures and platforms—such as containers and the platforms necessary to manage and orchestrate containers—has given these teams the tools they need to develop and deploy software updates and patches on accelerated schedules.

While accelerated updates and patches also accelerate identified vulnerability remediation in software and applications, they also can breed more vulnerabilities as development teams speed through the software development lifecycle (SDLC) to add new features and capabilities to their solutions. Containers can also add to security concerns as they are often created independently and tend to pile up, creating a security and management concern that is becoming known as "container sprawl."

Ultimately, the independent services and components that comprise software and applications today—and the larger ecosystem of endpoints that access applications—are making it harder to keep track of, manage, and patch applications. These independent services carry a more critical role but are more accessible than ever due to their connectivity to networks and the Internet. Therefore, it's more crucial to update and patch applications than ever before—and significantly more challenging to do so. Worse, two major changes in software structure, development, the infrastructure on which it's deployed are creating a new set of security vulnerabilities that were never concerns in the past.

11.2.3   THE NEW THREAT—INFRASTRUCTURE AS CODE

We've established that farmers, factory farms, food producers, and food processing companies are beginning to rely more on IoT devices, sensors, and software to optimize their operations, we've also discussed why application security then needs to be a priority—as it remains one of the largest vulnerabilities that can be exploited by malicious actors. But it's not enough to simply check the boxes for application security. The vendors creating IoT solutions and software applications that will be used in the vital agriculture and food processing supply chain that feeds America also need to ensure that they're staying up to date on the latest application security vectors and vulnerabilities.

And one of the largest new vulnerabilities has resulted from evolutions in the cloud and how we both provision and configure the infrastructure that runs our applications.

In the past, applications were developed and deployed on hardware that was most likely on-premises. The rise of the cloud and the emergence of cloud-native technologies, containerization, and container orchestration solutions marked a new software development era. Today, applications are no longer all managed on a single server—or even a group of servers. Instead, they're deployed across several containers that are all managed by the development team independently. The infrastructure that runs these containerized applications consists of private clouds or public cloud resources, such as those made available by one of the large cloud solution providers, including Amazon Web Services (AWS), Google Cloud, Microsoft Azure, and several other providers.

The infrastructure needed to run those applications is no longer defined and configured by an organization's IT department in a physical data center. In most cases, it is provisioned in the cloud—defined and managed by software. The rise of the cloud also gave rise to the concept of "self-service," which often involves development teams provisioning, defining, and configuring their own cloud infrastructure. Together, these technology changes and trends have given rise to a new phenomenon known as Infrastructure as Code (IaC), which is another term for the automation of the deployment of infrastructure in modern, dynamic environments—such as public, private, and hybrid clouds.

IaC, empowers application development teams to utilize scripting code that functionally sets up the network necessary to host and run their applications. Teams repeatedly leverage and share scripting code created by application developers who are not experts in provisioning and configuring secure networks. But what happens when a script configures the infrastructure and cloud resources in an unsecured way? When a malicious actor identifies a script vulnerability, they will indeed look for it in the IaC across the entire organization or industry. Furthermore, if previous experience tells us anything, zero-day vulnerabilities are weaponized and spread quickly among malicious actors.

We would be remiss not to point out that IaC is in no way less secure than physical infrastructure. Traditional physical infrastructure and hardware can be just as unsecured as IaC. But the vulnerabilities in physical infrastructure are often identified earlier because people trained to build and configure secure infrastructure are at the helm. Vulnerabilities in physical infrastructure are also less likely to be repeated across the organization since the process is less automated and repeatable.

Teams use IaC to develop and deploy dashboards and applications across the agriculture and food supply chain, including developing and hosting the applications that allow remote management and monitoring of farm and food processing equipment and devices. Unfortunately, IaC is just one of the two new cyber risks facing organizations due to changing software development technologies and trends.

11.2.4 THE OTHER NEW THREAT—APIs

The applications of the past were built as individual, monolithic solutions that took years upon years to create and additional years to update and patch. Today's applications—such as the firmware and applications that encompass modern precision agriculture solutions—are a combination of smaller parts known as microservices, smaller applications responsible for specific jobs, functions, or capabilities.

Take a grocery delivery application as an example. One microservice might check stock when a customer places an order while another runs the credit card processing. Yet another microservice might pair that order with a shopper in a geographic location close to both the customer and the store, then another tracks the status and location of the shopper to notify the customer when their order arrives.

While all these microservices have distinct functions and capabilities, they all need to talk to each other and interact to complete the entire task. The code that allows these microservices to interact and connects them is known as an API. It's unmistakable that APIs will be utilized in the construction of advanced precision agriculture solutions and applications. In fact, they're most likely already being utilized by the developers coding those tools today. These APIs are already becoming increasingly numerous in today's modern applications. Unfortunately, with organizations leveraging more APIs to connect these microservices for complex functions, they're creating a new security vector. And that vector could be creating vulnerabilities in precision agriculture solutions.

According to the Open Web Application Security Project (OWASP), a nonprofit foundation that works to improve the security of software, "By nature, APIs expose application logic and sensitive data such as Personally Identifiable Information (PII) and because of this have increasingly become a target for attackers" [5]. Noting that innovation would be impossible without secure APIs, OWASP has aggregated a top ten list of API vulnerabilities. This top ten list includes several known software attacks and vulnerabilities, including injection and authentication flaws. However, it also contains several vulnerabilities that are either unique to APIs or exacerbated by APIs' access and exposure to PII.

According to the State of API Security annual report released by SALT, approximately 90 percent of respondents claimed to have experienced an API security incident in the previous year. The report also found that 66 percent of respondents delayed the launch of an application due to an API security concern [6]. As APIs become increasingly essential in key software and applications running America's farms, food processing facilities, and food distribution centers, they also become an increasingly large cyber risk. If ignored, bad actors could hack them to shut down our critical food and agriculture supply chain.

With software taking an outsized role in the agriculture and food supply chain, developers moving faster to create applications at the speed of innovation, software vulnerabilities among the most exploited in cyberattacks, and two new vectors in the form of IaC and APIs, it may seem like securing our critical infrastructure and supply chains is impossible. However, organizations can leverage certain technologies in the application development process to make applications more secure. There are also new approaches to application development that help teams deploy software quickly without sacrificing security.

11.2.5 DevSecOps AND SHIFTING LEFT

With the application layer already being one of the most exploited for cyberattacks—and new vulnerabilities emerging because of advances in how we build and deploy applications—the vendors creating precision agriculture solutions and IoT devices for use in our agriculture and food processing supply chain clearly need to take AppSec seriously. And one of the best ways to build secure applications is to bake security into the entire application development process.

The past decade has seen a movement toward an efficient and scalable approach to application development. In the past, organizations used the "waterfall approach" to develop applications and software, which entailed discrete steps in a process that resembled successive plateaus in a waterfall and corresponded to an application moving ever forward from one team to the next as it progressed through the SDLC. In the waterfall method of application development, the development team would work to develop the application. Then the operations team would be responsible for provisioning and configuring the infrastructure needed to run the application upon deployment. From there, the application and the requisite infrastructure would progress to the security team for vetting and testing for vulnerabilities.

This approach to application development reserved the responsibility of the application's security for the very end of the SDLC. Essentially, security was "tacked on." The waterfall method also slowed application development and deployment down considerably. The security team became a bottleneck or roadblock to deployment, often slamming the breaks on applications that the development and operations team thought were ready to be deployed.

Not only did this approach slow down the development process, but it also made it less efficient. By identifying security vulnerabilities at the end of the process, the entire application would have to be sent back to the development team for remediation. Often, deep-seated vulnerabilities within the application would require long hours to fix, increasing the time and cost necessary to develop and deploy it.

Thankfully, many application development teams and organizations are evolving away from the waterfall method of application development and adopting a new method called DevSecOps. In the DevSecOps model or method of application development, all the parties—the development team, operations team, and security team—work in unison to develop software. DevSecOps ensures that the infrastructure needed to run the application is defined in advance and configured correctly at the time of deployment. It also shifts security left within the SDLC to happen earlier in the process.

Shifting security left effectively bakes security into all new applications and software as soon as possible during the development process. It also ensures that vulnerabilities are identified earlier in the SDLC, requiring less time and effort to address them. The DevSecOps approach to development removes the large speedbump or obstruction that previously stopped application deployments right as they approached the finish line. With security testing and vulnerability remediation a continuous process, there are no surprises that keep new applications, services, capabilities, or updates from deploying to the user.

The most important result of the move toward DevSecOps is accelerating the SDLC and developing applications faster without sacrificing security or releasing vulnerable software. Applying DevSecOps within the software development of IoT devices, sensors, and applications that are increasingly prevalent in the agriculture and food supply chain can ensure that new functionalities and capabilities can launch at the speed of innovation without introducing exploitable vulnerabilities. Failing to do so could disrupt a critical part of our nation's infrastructure. Yet embracing this approach to application development is just one step toward making applications more secure. There are also emergent technologies in the marketplace that can help secure the software that helps feed America.

11.2.6 AUTOMATING SECURITY TO PROTECT CRITICAL SOFTWARE

In addition to embracing a DevSecOps approach to application development, organizations can shift security left by adopting security automation solutions on the market that function to scan code for known vulnerabilities. Today's next generation of application security testing (AST) solutions enables security to become an intrinsic part of development instead of security as a post-development add-on.

AST allows organizations and their developers to start scanning source code as early as possible in the SDLC: when developers write code. AST is about making security part of the process—baking it into development—instead of an additional step post-process. There are multiple types of AST solutions available for application development teams that can work in tandem to ensure the software they're developing is secure and free of vulnerabilities.

The first solution is static analysis security testing (SAST), which identifies potential security vulnerabilities in custom code. SAST is an essential vulnerability identification and remediation tool for applications that are being custom coded. However, many of today's applications rely on Open-source software tied together with custom code.

For identifying and remediating the vulnerabilities in third-party code, there are software composition analysis (SCA) solutions. These tools scan software projects to enumerate the open-source components and third-party libraries used by the projects and identify any known vulnerabilities in the third-party code. SCA is essential as many Open-source vulnerabilities are known to malicious actors and, as we discussed, known vulnerabilities are among the first to be exploited.

Both SAST and SCA solutions are essential for automating security testing and identifying vulnerabilities early in the SDLC. It's also important, however, to identify vulnerabilities that arise as the application is running. Interactive application security testing (IAST) fills that role by leveraging existing functional testing activities to automate the detection of vulnerabilities in running applications. And while all three of these solutions can combine to make the applications that development teams are creating secure from the jump, there is still the problem of IaC security to address.

Suppose the cloud infrastructure that has been provisioned and configured for the application is insecure. In that case, it can undercut the work that these applications and the development teams have put into building a secure application. However, a new generation of automated security solutions called IaC Scanning solutions can help ensure that all cloud and virtual infrastructures and configurations are secure. Utilizing these IaC Scanning solutions, application, operations, and security teams working together in a DevSecOps environment can scan their IaC to ensure that everything meets their intended security standards.

To ensure that the IaC that's running next-generation software solutions and applications is secure, some AST solution providers—including Checkmarx—have developed IaC Scanning solutions and making them available at low or no cost to users. The Checkmarx solution, called Keeping Infrastructure as Code Secure (KICS), is an open-source solution for static code analysis of IaC. Checkmarx is committed to keeping both the scanning engine and security queries clear and open for the software development community.

If embraced when developing the IoT devices and applications utilized within the agriculture and food supply chain, these tools can help identify exploitable security vulnerabilities during the SDLC and not after being deployed. This security can make all the difference between our nation's critical food supply chains being compromised or standing firm against those that would look to disrupt them. But making secure software is about more than just finding vulnerabilities in third-party code, custom code, IaC, and running applications. It's also about keeping those vulnerabilities from being written into the code in the first place.

11.2.7 TRAIN TO DEVELOP SOFTWARE SECURELY

In a DevSecOps environment and with security automation and scanning tools being used in the SDLC, the application developer takes on a much more significant role in fighting against malicious actors and cyberattacks. Unfortunately, application developers infrequently have sufficient training in cybersecurity and cyber best practices. Keeping up with the constantly evolving and shifting cybersecurity threat landscape is difficult. And surveys of application and software developers show that approximately seven out of ten claim to lack the necessary application security training to secure the software they develop adequately.

If application developers are going to stop committing code with common vulnerabilities, they need training on how hackers attack applications and how to design and develop software without common vulnerabilities. To accomplish this end, organizations must educate their application developers. There also needs to be a cultural shift to ensure that application security becomes a key mission across the entire organization.

Cybersecurity needs to become a priority, and developers need secure coding education to ensure secure code from the beginning of the process. Organizations need to instill good cyber hygiene and habits, continue to assess the employees' skills, and train based on the results of those assessments.

Application security education needs to be mandatory and a priority. But it also must be effective, and that's where things like gamification can play a role.

Studies show that hands-on, interactive training solutions that fit into developers' daily routines are more effective than whole-day training sessions about out-of-context security vulnerabilities. Instead, these organizations should be embracing developer training offered in on-demand sessions that are relative to the specific challenges they are facing in their code. Training solutions are also most effective when they integrate with the organization's SAST solution. In this environment, the SAST solution's vulnerabilities are linked to practical training lessons, providing quick and pointed remediation guidance. This just-in-time learning teaches the developer why the problem happened, how to fix it, and, more importantly, how to prevent making the same mistake again.

By training the developers responsible for creating the apps and software used within the food and agriculture supply chain, we can prevent them from developing vulnerable, exploitable software and help protect the farms, food processors, and food distributors that feed Americans.

11.2.8   RECOMMENDATIONS FOR SECURING THE US FOOD AND AGRICULTURE SUPPLY CHAIN

The organizations that comprise America's critical agriculture and food supply chain will embrace new technologies. They'll adopt IoT devices that increase their transparency into their operations and help them operate more effectively. They'll also embrace network-enabled systems and equipment so that they can enable proactive, preventative maintenance and maximize their investments in essential tools and equipment. We can't ask them to go back to how things were—to their own detriment—simply because embracing network-enabled IoT devices and the software that comes with them increases their cyber risk and opens them up to cyberattacks.

However, software vulnerabilities are among the most exploited in cyberattacks. There is much at stake should a malicious actor compromise the software and firmware that is gaining adoption across our food and agricultural supply chain. IoT and network-enabled irrigation systems could be compromised and instructed not to water crops, leading to the loss of revenue for farmers and the loss of critical food resources for Americans. Hackers could compromise equipment at food processing and food distribution plants leading to shutdowns or failures, creating delays or stoppages in food production.

Just like the ransomware attack that debilitated JBS USA Holdings, Inc., attacks against our agricultural and food supply chains and infrastructure can and will happen again.

Software will continue to play an outsized role in producing and distributing the food that gets on American tables, so we need to ensure that the applications are secure and free of the vulnerabilities that would virtually welcome malicious actors to abuse them. The solution and equipment providers servicing the food and agriculture supply chain need to be aware of what is at stake should they develop and deploy unsecured applications into the marketplace. They need to be encouraged to develop with a DevSecOps approach and methodology to ensure that they are not just developing at the speed of innovation but developing secure applications. And they need to be incentivized to embrace the technologies and training necessary to ensure that the code coming from their developers is sound and free of vulnerabilities.

However, it is potentially too damaging to our nation's food supply to wait until a high-profile breach shames these equipment and solution providers into taking application security seriously. Whether through certification processes or mandates, these organizations need to be held accountable for securing their applications. It is not enough to take a "check-the-box" approach to AST by relying on downstream mitigations or requiring security scans in the SDLC. These vendors and solution providers need to be impelled to implement a robust application security program including security testing. They should be encouraged to conduct threat modeling for their solutions and applications and embrace the application security measures commensurate to the threat they face.

Requiring cultural changes that prioritize security, scanning and automation tools that can improve application security, and training to turn application developers into cyber warriors should be essential for any solution provider that interacts with our nation's critical infrastructure.

Software helps to feed America. Keep it safe.

11.2.8.1 ABOUT THE AUTHORS

Rusty Sides, Public Sector Technical Sales Director, Checkmarx. Rusty has 26 years of software engineering, team management, and security consulting experience. He has aided global organizations in industries ranging from finance, entertainment, and Silicon Valley technology leaders in the private sector to public sector organizations within the DoD, Civilian and Intel communities implement solutions to secure software development life cycles. His background in application security, wide range of programming languages, software architectural design, DevSecOps expertise, Federal compliance, and Public Sector knowledge has been an asset to many speaking engagements at government, technology, and security conferences internationally.

Scott McBain, Sales Engineer, Checkmarx. Scott McBain has developed commercial software and systems for over 20 years. He led and managed teams for many years building security-conscious software systems for KYC/OFAC compliance, payment efficiency, and data publishing solutions for SaaS and on-premises.

Justin Ruth, Lead Sales Engineer, Checkmarx. Justin Ruth is an Offensive Security Certified Professional (OSCP) with over seven years of experience in Application Security and vulnerability exploitation. In his current role as a Lead Sales Engineer at Checkmarx, Justin guides engineers in providing security solutions to global enterprises. In his previous role, Justin led a Product Security team responsible for supporting the global development practices of over 1,000 developers. Justin actively participates in various bug bounty programs, vulnerability research, and cyber security audits.

Michael Deck, Regional Sales Manager, Checkmarx. Michael Deck has been in the Application Security industry for the past seven years supporting US Civilian Agencies. His focus is software vulnerability remediation.

William Berriel, Sales Engineer, Checkmarx. William Berriel is an engineer who has been involved in networking, security, and Internet of Things for over 20 years. He just received his MS from NYU in Cybersecurity and currently lives in Brooklyn, New York.

REFERENCES

1. "Adoption of Precision Agriculture", National Institute of Food and Agriculture, 2020. [Online]. Available: https://www.nifa.usda.gov/adoption-precision-agriculture. [Accessed: 02- Sep- 2021].
2. "Precision Farming Market Size Report, 2022–2030", Grandviewresearch.com, 2020. [Online]. Available: https://www.grandviewresearch.com/industry-analysis/precision-farming-market?utm_source=prnewswire&utm_medium=referral&utm_campaign=ICT_22-Apr-21&utm_term=precision-farming-market&utm_content=rd. [Accessed: 02- Sep- 2021].
3. J. Bunge, "JBS Paid $11 Million to Resolve Ransomware Attack", The Wall Street Journal, 2021. [Online]. Available: https://www.wsj.com/articles/jbs-paid-11-million-to-resolve-ransomware-attack-11623280781. [Accessed: 26- Jul- 2022].
4. M. Morana, "How to start a software security initiative within your organization: a maturity based and metrics driven approach", Owasp.org, 2009. [Online]. Available: https://owasp.org/www-pdf-archive/OWASP-ItalyDayEGov09_04_Morana.pdf. [Accessed: 02- Sep- 2021].
5. "OWASP API Security Project I OWASP Foundation", Owasp.org, 2019. [Online]. Available: https://owasp.org/www-project-api-security/. [Accessed: 02- Sep- 2021].
6. "2021 API Security Trends", Salt.security, 2021. [Online]. Available: https://salt.security/api-security-trends. [Accessed: 02- Sep- 2021].

11.3 TRUST IN THE FOOD AND AGRICULTURE SUPPLY CHAIN STARTS IN THE DIRT AND ENDS ON OUR TABLES

Joyce Hunter

Executive Director, Institute for Critical Infrastructure Technology (ICIT)

11.3.1 INTRODUCTION

In many instances, technology has equal potential to create value as it does to cause harm. Some risk and harm are offset through rules and regulations, but much is dependent on the actions of the individual. In cybersecurity, we are our own worst enemies. Most instances of compromise or data loss are the result of user behavior. Digital threat actors are more opportunistic than targeted. Most breaches still rely more on social engineering than on sophisticated malware. In this regard, the food and agriculture sector is no different than any other critical infrastructure.

The four areas in agriculture of greatest value to an attacker are:

- Access to services (e.g. Tractor firmware),
- Personal privacy (e.g. PII),
- Proprietary information (e.g. company forecasting), and
- Intellectual Property (IP) (e.g. seed blends and new technologies).

The majority of assets and attack vectors in food and agriculture can be defined by these four areas [1].

Smart agriculture depends on smart technology, data, and cybersecurity awareness. Cybersecurity is a balancing act between resources and perceived risk. Informed action and a comprehensive strategy to secure assets are rooted in how aware stakeholders are of emerging cyberthreats and how accurately they perceive the risk to the aforementioned areas. As with any sector, food and agriculture has unique threats to specific assets that may not be easily understood or appreciated by experts outside the sector. An estimated 20 percent of the threats to crops are specific to a particular crop. The type of crop, its use, and the distribution chains might be different compared with another crop. The distribution system for apples is different than corn or soybeans, but each is critical for their markets, downstream third parties, and the public [1].

Agriculture cybersecurity is very young compared to other sectors. The business of using technology to help increase yield, reduce labor costs, or add improve quality are fairly new to the industry. Even drones, which are one of the faster-growing ag technologies, have only recently been introduced [1].

Risk assessment in food and agriculture is normally focused on crop yield, seed development, climate patterns, market trends, and planning cycles. As technology becomes more ubiquitous and pervasive in the sector, opportunistic and geopolitical adversaries will attack America's agriculture along the path of least resistance. The sector needs to become more sophisticated in providing similar analyses to data, technology, and cybersecurity [1].

11.3.2 EMERGING THREATS TO AGRI-FOOD BUSINESSES

The Food and Agriculture sector is transforming into a more data-driven and complex ecosystem. Advances in automation, mobility, machine learning, cloud computing, IoT, and big data present major opportunities and challenges for the sector. Food and agriculture acts as the backbone of the nation; the critical supply chain that fuels the people and families that operate all other critical infrastructure. However, as the adage goes, "a [secure] chain is only as strong as its weakest link." The complex constellation of networks that comprise the sector are dependent on third parties and many risks are obfuscated or outside of the governance of agriculture businesses information security. A successful cyber or cyber-kinetic attack on a critical third party could hobble one or more vital supply chains and lead to cascading impacts across the sector. The increasing threat of disruptionware—malware deployed with the intent of rendering systems inoperable or causing significant downtime—also poses a significant socioeconomic threat as targeted attacks could lead to shortages in essential food or production resources [2].

Adversaries vary in motivation and sophistication, but most have discernable motives to target the Agriculture sector. Hacktivists may launch targeted attacks due to ideology or conspiracy theories such as the Anonsec attacks a few years ago (chemtrail-based conspiracy). Cybercriminals may target individuals or production plants such as in the May 2021 ransomware attack against JBS, the world's largest meat supplier. Even just criminals being able to digitally identify and track trucks could have a major impact on regions' access to food and goods. For instance, recent data from Transported Asset Protection Association (TAPA) suggests that cargo theft has increased by 114 percent over the last 12 months. According to a survey conducted by LoJack Mexico, cargo theft of trucks increased 25 percent during the coronavirus pandemic period. If cybercrime advances in the sector, entire shipments could be redirected and stolen and production facilities could be held for ransom or rendered permanently inoperable. The impact of the threat increases in consideration of the rapid spoilage of stored foods and the lack of national redundancy stock. With much of the food industry comprising small local businesses, ransomware will often become a question of paying or closing—and this equation will attract additional attackers. Worse, more sophisticated advanced persistent threat groups might attempt to steal proprietary seeds, compromise essential equipment, or disrupt supply chain and storage systems [2].

Unlike cybercriminals, APTs, which are often sponsored by nation-states, and which operate to achieve geopolitical and socioeconomic impacts, may be more intent on harming Americans than on monetary theft. The importance of the food supply chain is a hallmark of military conflict. For example, in 1812, the Russian army repelled Napoleon via a scorched earth policy to deny food supplies to the French. Without supplies, Napoleon was forced to retreat from Moscow, which arguably and ultimately led to his downfall. The pandemic has highlighted the fragility of the global food chain and the insight will not be lost on opportunistic cyber attackers. "It is a well-known fact," comments the Information Security Forum's Dan Norman, "that during times of conflict, the party that can destroy the food supply chain will inevitably win. It is therefore conceivable that cyber-attacks from nation state-backed actors and terrorist groups will begin targeting organizations dependent on new technologies, disrupting global supply chains" [3]. Short-term interruptions to the food supply chain demoralize the population, inflate prices, and lead to political turmoil. As we saw during the COVID-19 pandemic, sustained interruptions and shortages, even those lasting only weeks or months, may lead to protests, riots, or looting. An adversary may be able to exert a small amount of effort and resources to disrupt a supply chain and cause a long series of cascading impacts. We collectively joke now about toilet paper and pasta shortages from the pandemic, but will we still be joking if coffee, wheat, or flour are in short supply?

Food and agriculture supply chains are vulnerable at every stage. Farmers use GPS technology and robotics to customize fertilizer and seed their land to optimize yield. What if these systems are hacked—without their knowledge—resulting in crops that underperform expectations across the nation. If an attacker wants to disrupt the supply chain, they may also target transportation networks, critical manufacturing and production facilities, or food safety labs and academic research institutions. As much as portrayals of cyberattacks in the media focus on the theft of data, we need to be much more worried, especially in the food and agriculture sector, about threats that damage equipment or poison supplies.

11.3.3   THE SKY ISN'T FALLING QUITE YET

The Biden administration announced in June 2021, the formation of a new task force to address supply chain disruptions, which will include the Departments of Commerce, Transportation Secretary, and Agriculture. That is a start, but it should also include the Environmental Protection Agency and the Food and Drug Administration. I would also recommend seriously adopting, executing (it does no good if it is not appropriately funded and becomes shelf-ware), and requiring the following for everyone in the supply chain. That includes academics and research organizations.

1. **Secure Privileged Access Management:** Attackers move laterally through networks in search of privileged accounts so that they can access sensitive resources and establish persistence. An effective Privileged Access Management (PAM) framework will disrupt this common attack trajectory, but to further mitigate the chances of a supply chain attack, the PAM itself needs to be protected. A PAM should be protected by both external and internal defense. Reinforcing PAM security could prevent supply chain attacks and improve compliance with President Biden's Cybersecurity Executive Order [4].
2. **Implement a Zero Trust Architecture:** Zero Trust assumes all network activity is malicious by default and only permits connections that verify against a strict Policy Engine (PE), Policy Administrator (PA), and a Policy Enforcement Point (PEP). The PE decides whether network traffic should be permitted by following the rules set by the Trust Algorithm. The PA communicates the PE's decision (pass or fail) to the PEP. The PEP is the final gatekeeper that either blocks or permits network requests based on the PE's decision [4].
3. **Evaluate Third Party Networks:** If vulnerabilities remain unremediated, they may be exploited and leveraged in supply chain attacks. A foundation of any service level agreement of partnership that involves network interaction should include clear security metrics, roles, responsibilities, expectations, and incident response and recovery policies.
4. **Prepare for the Worst, Hope for the Best:** Adopt an Assume Breach mindset that assumes that a data breach will happen, as opposed to hoping it won't happen. This subtle shift in mindset encourages the deployment of proactive cyber defense strategies across all vulnerable attack vectors in an organization. The three attack surfaces at the highest risk of compromise are—people, processes, and technologies. Identify and prioritize critical assets and secure them according to their value or what assets an adversary could laterally compromise from them.
5. **Remove BYOB and Shadow IT:** Shadow IT refers to all devices that are not approved by an organization's security team. IT security departments should enforce the registration of all IT devices alongside strict guidelines about what can and cannot be connected. All permitted devices (especially IoT devices) should be monitored to identify Distributed Denial of Service (DDoS) attacks being launched from the supply chain.

11.3.4   CONCLUSION

For time immemorial, food has been the foundation of human connection, interaction, and socialization. Roads, villages, towns, nations, and empires have been built and destroyed based on their food and agriculture sector. Just as science has reduced the meteorological and biological threats to food supply and advances in production have improved access, the threat of cyber and cyber-kinetic impacts looms large. We must do more to educate the sector about disruptionware threats, cyber-hygiene, and cybersecurity best practices.

11.3.4.1 ABOUT THE AUTHOR

Joyce is the Executive Director of the ICIT. Previously, she served as both the Interim CIO and Deputy CIO of the US Department of Agriculture and held other senior leadership roles within the federal government, Lotus Development Corp, Lawson Software, and Computer Sciences Corporation (CSC). She's managed multi-billion dollar IT budgets and established or led several data governance and PMO initiatives. She understands how to communicate with and across diverse communities and how to forge relationships that enable those stakeholders to succeed. She regularly uses these skills in both her TEDx talks and publications.

Joyce has a BA from Villanova University and an MBA in Marketing from the University of Pennsylvania, Wharton School of Business. She holds certificates in Emotional Intelligence, Design Thinking, Technology Business Management (TBM), and Scaled Agile Framework (SAFe). She sits on multiple industry boards and is active in several philanthropies focused on advancing STEM and Data Science education for underserved and underrepresented youth.

REFERENCES

1. L. Manning, "What Is the Cybersecurity Threat in Agriculture? AFN," *AFN*, 2022. [Online]. Available: https://agfundernews.com/what-is-the-cybersecurity-threat-in-agriculture. [Accessed: 05 March 2022].
2. B. Boyce, "As Agriculture Gets More High-Tech, Is Cybersecurity a Concern? | AGDAILY," *AGDAILY*, 2018. [Online]. Available: https://www.agdaily.com/technology/as-ag-gets-more-high-tech-is-cybersecurity-a-concern/. [Accessed: 05 March 2022].
3. D. Norman, "Influencing Security Behaviour—Information Security Forum," *Information Security Forum*, 2021. [Online]. Available: https://www.securityforum.org/spotlight-on/influencing-security-behaviour/. [Accessed: 05 March 2022].
4. V. R. Viool, "Cybersecurity in the Agrifood Sector," 2021. [Online]. Available: https://www.wur.nl/upload_mm/4/6/a/f74a893e-c829-4bf3-9884-e357929ff5d6_Cybersecurity%20in%20the%20agrifood%20sector.pdf. [Accessed: 05 March 2022].

12 Government Facilities

12.0 ABOUT THE GOVERNMENT FACILITIES SECTOR

Donald Maclean

Chief Cyber Security Technologist, DLT

I have had the privilege of working with ICIT almost since its inception. Its dynamic personnel (Parham Eftekhari, Drew Spaniel, Joyce Hunter, Catherine Squeo, and Kathryn McIver, to name just a few) share a common and essential drive: to protect our nation from cybersecurity attacks. The goal is enormous in scope and complexity and success will require active and avid participants from all sectors of society including government, industry, academia, non-profits, health care, and more.

The Cybersecurity and Infrastructure Security Agency (CISA) has categorized US infrastructure into 17 sectors (including election security), each playing an indispensable role in our well-being, each requiring stringent and comprehensive protection from our adversaries. The question, of course, is how to protect ourselves?

To seek answers to this broad question, ICIT reached out to its Fellows, a "who's who" of thought leaders in cybersecurity representing all sectors of society. Each contributed their insights and recommendations, and reviewed the work of their peers, and the result is a blueprint for improving our nation's cybersecurity defenses for the immediate, mid-term, and long-term future.

According to CISA, the Government Facilities Sector [1]:

> Includes a wide variety of buildings, located in the United States and overseas, that are owned or leased by federal, state, local, and tribal governments. Many government facilities are open to the public for business activities, commercial transactions, or recreational activities while others that are not open to the public contain highly sensitive information, materials, processes, and equipment. These facilities include general-use office buildings and special-use military installations, embassies, courthouses, national laboratories, and structures that may house critical equipment, systems, networks, and functions. In addition to physical structures, the sector includes cyber elements that contribute to the protection of sector assets (e.g., access control systems and closed-circuit television systems) as well as individuals who perform essential functions or possess tactical, operational, or strategic knowledge.

Technology continues to evolve and advance. At the time of this writing, we are facing an upsurge in aggressive "disruptionware" campaigns that range in sophistication from simple ransomware to complex, multi-layered cyber-physical attacks that leverage custom malware. Intrusions such as the Sunburst hack, Kaseya, Colonial Pipeline, and more once were known only to cybersecurity insiders but now seize the front page of newspapers, headlines of cable news programs, top billing in online news sources, and spread virally on social media. Such attacks are consistently increasing in frequency, sophistication, and scope.

Such attacks are merely increasing in frequency, sophistication, and scope. They show how our adversaries watch us closely, have enormous technical knowledge, are patient, and have financial and logistical backing from nation-states that seek our demise. The Sunburst hack is the strongest evidence of this: the team of engineers who devised and executed the intrusion likely consisted of more than 1,000 top-quality engineers. (For comparison, the security team at one major government agency where I worked consisted of five engineers and some administrative personnel). This group compromised the software supply chain at its source, and showed that even technology companies with strong security programs and well-trained staff are vulnerable to intrusion.

DOI: 10.1201/9781003243021-12

Clearly, our enemy is dangerous and their willingness and ability to compromise the supply chain are a threat to our national security. Even so, a more disturbing paradigm shift is in play. Many attacks are going beyond the abstract world of bits and bytes, and into the real physical world. The Colonial Pipeline attack resulted in gas shortages and price increases. Although the damage to our economy in this case was minor and short-lived, the Colonial Pipeline was a clear harbinger of more pernicious and widespread harm looming in the future.

No single technology, or even a single security philosophy such as Zero Trust can solve these problems. We must come together as a nation, as patriots dedicated to the safety and welfare of our fellow citizens, to face these threats. Success requires disciplined thought, innovation, and careful planning. The essays presented here represent a crucial first step in this process, upon which our national security depends. I am honored that my work is included in this compilation, and I hope that my work, and the work of others, will be of value in our vital effort to protect the country. ICIT's work here, as always, is of the highest quality, and I thank them not just on my own behalf, but on behalf of our nation, for this invaluable contribution. I hope that you will not merely read these essays, but put them into practice to help achieve our common goal.

12.0.1 ABOUT DLT

DLT Solutions is the premier government solutions aggregator that specializes in understanding the IT needs of the federal, state, local, and education markets. We help simplify the process for independent software vendors, federal systems integrators, and value-added resellers doing business in the public sector. Leveraging a robust cybersecurity portfolio, an extensive array of public sector contract vehicles, and dedicated channel and enablement services, DLT provides government agencies and channel partners with the means to rapidly and cost effectively transform technology and secure technology stacks to achieve mission success. For more information, please visit www.dlt.com.

REFERENCE

1. "Government Facilities Sector", Cisa.gov, 2020. [Online]. Available: https://www.cisa.gov/government-facilities-sector. [Accessed: 02- Sep- 2021].

12.1   ZERO TRUST: BUZZWORD OR PANACEA?

Donald Maclean
Chief Cyber Security Technologist, DLT

12.1.1   AN INTRODUCTION TO ZERO TRUST

The cybersecurity industry is abuzz with the term "Zero Trust": the term appears constantly in webinars, e-mail blasts, and advertising on industry websites. The concept, however, is amorphous, and can become an empty buzzword instead of a reference to a substantive approach to security. It makes sense, then to pose fundamental questions about Zero Trust (hereafter called "ZT," for brevity).

- What Is ZT?
- What problem(s) does ZT solve?
- What does a successful ZT implementation require, and is it worth the cost?
- How does ZT align with current industry trends such as cloud, hybrid cloud, containerization, and work-from-home?

To explore these questions, I will examine the salient features of the major frameworks and initiatives around Zero Trust, to understand Zero Trust from multiple perspectives, and to identify common themes that emerge in all of these approaches. Specifically, this chapter will describe:

- National Institute of Standards and Technology (NIST) SP800-207 [1]
- Forrester ZTX [2]
- Google BeyondCorp [3]

Gartner promulgates a framework dubbed "CARTA" (Continuous Adaptive Risk and Trust Assessment), but a discussion of CARTA is beyond the scope of this chapter. Moreover, information on CARTA is difficult and expensive to obtain. I mention it briefly, however, for the interested reader who may wish to delve into it on their own.

In brief, CARTA's primary tenets are [4]:

- Adaptive attack protection
- Micro-segmented networks
- Contextual access control/security management for agentless devices
- Automated device control
- Ongoing cyber and operational risk assessment

12.1.1.1   IMPLEMENTATION CONCERNS

ZT is a comprehensive program, so implementation can be complicated technically and managerially. Major implementation concerns include:

1. Cost, schedule, performance
2. Culture shift, managing change
3. Management Support
4. Quantifying return on investment (ROI)

To synthesize these concepts and definitions, I will identify key elements arising in all of the frameworks and initiatives (except CARTA), to answer the question posed in the title: Zero Trust: Buzzword or Panacea?

12.1.1.2 What Is ZT?

ZT is a philosophy about security, based on realistic (some might say "pessimistic") assumptions, and rooted in changing dynamics of computer networking and communication. The ZT philosophy recognizes that many security technologies, particularly those based on the "moat and castle" architecture, are at best only partially effective. Firewalls, intrusion detection/prevention (IDS/IPS) systems are basically "speed bumps" for determined hackers: they slow them down a bit, but do not keep them from their goals. Moreover, since more and more employees are working from home and using their own devices to access business systems, the concept of a network perimeter has lost relevance.

The fundamental tenet, then, is that: *the internal network is just as vulnerable as the Internet.* Network location does not connote safety or security, all traffic is assumed to be malicious, all devices assumed to be hostile, and all systems are assumed to be compromised. This attitude may appear overly pessimistic (it is not always true), it provides the foundation for a strict, "safety-first" approach to security.

ZT is also a holistic philosophy, encompassing all aspects of security, from encryption to identity and access management to user awareness to phishing protection. The comprehensive nature of ZT creates some confusion in the market: ZT is not a single product, technology, or architecture, and is thus difficult to pigeonhole. It also allows nearly all vendors of security products to claim they are "ZT," since almost any product can find a home somewhere in the large landscape of ZT.

Such claims are generally valid but rarely complete, and their variegation can add "noise" to the "signal." When an identity vendor says they are "Zero Trust," and an encryption vendor also says they are "Zero Trust," both are correct, but to the audience, the message is perplexing: "Is ZT an identity approach, or an encryption technology?" In truth, ZT encompasses both (and more).

While ZT is new to many, it does not abjure the use of traditional security methods and technologies. In many cases, it simply urges a different way of using those technologies, or even just a more aggressive implementation.

After an organization begins a ZT implementation, it can lose sight of the purpose of ZT. Understandably, the ZT implementation begins to become the goal when it is really a means to an end. The purpose of ZT is not simply to implement ZT. The purpose of ZT is to improve the security posture of an organization.

To jump ahead a bit to the Google BeyondCorp discussion, I will provide the following quotes, which beautifully summarize the philosophy behind ZT security:

> … most enterprises assume that the internal network is a safe environment …, Google's experience has proven that this faith is misplaced. Rather, one should assume that an internal network is as fraught with danger as the public Internet and build enterprise applications based upon this assumption. [1]
>
> All access to enterprise resources is fully authenticated, fully authorized, and fully encrypted based upon device state and user credentials. As a result, all Google employees can work successfully from any network, and without … a VPN connection. [1]

12.1.1.3 What Problems Does ZT Solve?

Since ZT is a comprehensive security architecture, it ultimately seeks to solve all security problems. That lofty goal, however, is too broad and unachievable to be relevant. Instead, I'd like to focus on four major problems in the crosshairs of the ZT arsenal.

1. **Securing a disappearing perimeter:** Three significant trends are causing the traditional network perimeter to disintegrate, diminishing the relevance of security tools designed for that architecture. Cloud adoption continues unabated, employees use their own devices for enterprise access ("BYOD"), and working from home is much more common, especially with COVID-19 restricting many of us to our homes.

Since it is difficult to surround systems with protection, it makes sense instead—at least in the ZT methodology—to place security measures at or near the assets of value, typically the organization's most sensitive data.

2. **Mitigating inevitable intrusions:** Mathematical proofs exist showing that all non-trivial software contains bugs. A certain percentage of these bugs relate to security, so preventing intrusion is essentially impossible. ZT recognizes this unfortunate reality, and thus recommends security measures that mitigate the effect of inevitable intrusions and treat all traffic and all system interactions as hostile until proven otherwise.

A recent major hack attributed to Russian operatives and targeting two major security firms is but one example of how breaches are unavoidable, even for organizations with a high degree of security awareness and technical acumen.

3. **Long dwell times/lateral movement:** Since intrusions are inevitable, it follows that the intruders will generally try to remain inside target systems as long as possible. Again, the ZT philosophy acknowledges this hard truth, and thus recommends active threat hunting to find breaches and remediate their ill effects.

4. **Securing a growing attack surface [5]:** The diminishing perimeter has an equal and opposite effect on the attack surface: it expands it. The concept of "attack surface" seems simple and intuitive, but there is a considerable body of research on this notion. A full discussion is of attack surface is beyond the scope of this paper, but the work of Manadhata and Wing [5] is worthy of a brief look; interested readers can do further research at their discretion.

These researchers define three major components in the attack surface [5]:

   a. **Methods (M):** Methods describe *how* the attackers operate, with a focus on their Tactics, Techniques, and Procedures ("TTPs"). While many attackers install their own malware, many control and misuse the victims' resources also.
   b. **Channel (C):** The Channel element defines *where* the attack comes from, and how it arrived at the victim's system. The most common channels are
      • External network traffic: ZT makes no real distinction between "external" and "internal" traffic, so this channel could be consolidated with the next.
      • Internal network traffic
      • Phishing: Phishing is by far the most prevalent attack vector, since it is easy to implement and effective for the attacker.
      • Insider threat: Many people believe that ZT focuses primarily or exclusively on elimination of the insider threat. Identification of insider threats is certainly a component of ZT but is by no means its only aim.
   c. **Untrusted data items/input (I):** This element refers to malicious external input, and includes common methods such as buffer overflows, code injection, SQL injection, and other attacks using the victim's input systems.

12.1.2   FRAMEWORKS AND INITIATIVES

To simplify the large, complex scope of ZT, several organizations have promulgated ZT frameworks, and Google has implemented its own recommendations. Here is a look at the most significant of these initiatives, from which I will distill common features.

I. **National Institute of Standards and Technology NIST SP800-207 [1]:** In August 2020, NIST published a guide to ZT, SP800-207 "Zero Trust Architecture." It is a helpful framework that enumerates seven tenets of ZT.

   a. **Tenet #1:** The first tenet defines all data sources and computing services as *resources*, a unifying concept and simplifying term. (I am reminded of the way *nix operating systems view everything as a file). This tenet is little more than an exercise in terminology and has no real equivalent in other frameworks.

b. **Tenet #2:** The second tenet is that *all communication is secured regardless of network location.* This principle speaks directly to the phenomena of the disappearing perimeter and permeable network defenses discussed above. This tenet, and tenet #3 below, are substantive and appear in other ZT rubrics.

c. **Tenet #3:** The third tenet is essentially the premise of the second (I would reverse the numbering of these two tenets): *network location alone does not imply trust.* This means that all traffic is untrustworthy, and thus should be secured.

d. **Tenet #4:** This tenet states that "Access to resources is determined by dynamic policy—including the observable state of client identity, application/service, and the requesting asset—and may include other behavioral and environmental attributes." A "policy" in this context consists of a set of rules based on a resource's attributes. These attributes can include identity, behavioral attributes, and the state of the asset, such as:

- device characteristics, e.g., software/firmware versions, device type
- network location
- time/date of request
- credentials

Moreover, access should be granted on a per-session basis, and use multiple in-depth evaluation criteria such as:

- Least privilege/job role
- Recency of access
- Geolocation
- Time of day
- Group membership/job role

This principle is fundamental and will re-emerge in other ZT frameworks.

e. **Tenet #5:** This principle holds that the enterprise should monitor and measure the integrity and security posture of all owned and associated assets. The key aspect of this tenet is that such monitoring should be continuous and dynamic. Many government agencies perform measurements only periodically, often only tri-annually, in accordance with the NIST Risk Management Framework (RMF).

This tenet is commensurate with the sixth (and often neglected) phase of the Risk advocates continuous diagnostics and mitigation. Continuous diagnostics and mitigation are difficult or impossible without real-time measurement and evaluation of the security posture of an enterprise's resources, and such measurements typically require expensive and complex technology.

Successful implementation of this component of ZT requires complete visibility into the system: traffic, devices, users, cloud connections, etc. Visibility is a central element in other ZT frameworks; it seems odd that NIST subsumed it to other concepts.

Tenet five, however, will re-appear under different nomenclature in the frameworks to be discussed below.

f. **Tenet #6:** This principle requires authentication and authorization to be dynamic and strictly enforced. This is an important element of ZT, but in my view, could be incorporated into tenet four. In practical terms, this implies multi-factor authentication, among other IAM technologies.

g. **Tenet #7:** This element in the NIST doctrine calls for the enterprise to collect information about assets, network infrastructure, and communications and use it to improve its security posture. This practice is undeniably worthwhile but is not unique to ZT. Its presence in the document, however, underscores the point that much of the ZT approach is to ensure or expand on standard security practices.

II. **Forrester Zero Trust eXtended (ZTX) [2]:** The Forrester ZTX framework is extremely comprehensive, and claims as its founder Jon Kindervag, who coined the term "Zero Trust," and to whom many credit the invention of the entire concept of ZT. This is an area of some dispute, on which I will remain neutral since the exploration of ZT in general, and ZTX in particular, is more important than the disputation of their origins. (I will mention that I am certified as a Forrester ZTX Strategist, but I have no financial or other relationship with Forrester).

The Forrester ZTX framework charter consists of the following seven components, which I will examine in more detail below:

1. Data Encryption
2. Networks
3. People
4. Automation
5. Visibility
6. Devices
7. Workloads

1. **Data Encryption:** Data encryption is hardly new, but in a ZT world, its implementation should be as aggressive and comprehensive as possible. Remember that ZT assumes that systems have been compromised, so the purpose of encryption is to minimize or eliminate the value of purloined data.

    For data in place, encryption can, and should, be implemented at all appropriate levels:
    • File level
    • Disk level
    • Database
        • Row
        • Column
File integrity monitoring is not only an encryption method but is also a prudent ancillary technology for encryption.

    Forrester also advocates encryption of all traffic (data in motion), in keeping with the premise that there is no safe haven and no impervious network. Encryption of mail messages, and other messaging protection systems such as DMARC, are also methods of protecting data in transit.

2. **Networks:** Forrester specifies three main aspects of network security, the third overlapping with the previous recommendation.

    a. **Micro-segmentation:** This may be the most "pure-play" technology associated with ZT. Micro-segmentation allows the use of some traditional firewall technologies at a granular level. Far more salient, however, is micro-segmentation's ability to respond automatically to (inevitable) breaches, denying traffic to or from an affected system, except perhaps for an administrative virtual local area network (VLAN). This method of isolation accelerates incident response and mitigation and facilitates investigation of infected systems.

    b. **Conditional access/network access control (NAC):** Since all devices are considered untrustworthy until proven otherwise, Forrester's ZTX approach recommends NAC. This technology ensures the proper presence, configuration, and timeliness of security technologies on all devices before they are permitted access to resources (data, networks, or other computing devices). Again, this recommendation aligns with the central tenets of the ZT security rubric.

3. **People:** While other approaches include the human element implicitly, by reference to behavior, Forrester ZTX offers an explicit and comprehensive examine of people. Specific components include:

   a. **Identity:** Securing user identity includes everything from stringent background checks to biometrics to multi-factor authentication. As with any security program, organizations should have a solid inventory of their user base and should be able to identify the minimum privilege level each user needs to perform their duties.

   b. **Behavior analytics:** In its simplest form, behavior analytics can allow or prevent access based on a user's expected behaviors: time of access, geolocation, failed login attempts. More sophisticated systems can examine and analyze how a user typically behaves in more subtle ways, everything from typing speed and patterns of mouse movement to seasonal patterns of system access, and—importantly—frequency, volume, and duration of data downloads. Such data can be difficult to obtain and manage but can also be an important way of stopping insider threats.

   c. **Authentication/least privilege:** These concepts are inextricably linked to identity: without proper identity, it is impossible to know if someone should be authenticated. However, ensuring the least privilege, particularly for IT staff, can be a difficult administrative and managerial task.

   d. **Continuously monitoring access and privileges:** To monitor access, an organization must first determine what is allowable, but must also monitor access and privileges to identify violations. After initial access, an intruder's first order of business is privilege escalation, so real-time awareness of system access and changes to privileges are essential to ZT.

   e. **Securing/protecting users' interactions:** Identifying illicit access is essential, but protecting legitimate transactions is equally important.

   f. **Training/security awareness:** Too often, security training is a perfunctory, "click-through" exercise. To be effective, training should not be simply rigorous but should include follow-up activity to measure its value: did training truly change user behavior? If so, is the change measurable and was it worth the money?

   g. **Phishing*:** Phishing is the most effective and widely used attack method. However, training users to detect phishing attacks is notoriously ineffective. The work of Arun Vishwanath, here, is highly recommended: http://bitly.ws/atjI

   h. **Background checks:** Here we see the comprehensive nature of ZT in full force: background checks are well outside the purview of security personnel but fall well within the broad range of ZT security.

4. **ZTX: Automation:** Given the profusion of attacks, the huge population of attackers, the enormous quantity of data to process, and a security staff that is typically overburdened, automating security operations is a central facet of the ZTX framework. Software defined networks (SDN) is a key technology in automated incident response, as it allows immediate isolation of infected systems. Of course, almost any aspect of security defense is suitable for automation: detection and response, evidence collection and analysis [6, 7].

5. **ZTX: Visibility:** As my company says, security is a combination of foundations plus innovation. Too often, vendors focus on the new and exciting technology at the expense of the bread-and-butter systems that enable those technologies. Visibility is perhaps the foundational requirement of all: it is impossible to secure a system if it is invisible to those responsible for it.

   The Forrester ZTX framework outlines visibility requirements in detail, specifying three broad categories:

6. **Devices:**
   - (including virtual devices such as VMs and containers
   - IOT devices

- Mobile devices (phones, tablets)
- Desktop & laptop machines

Device visibility also encompasses accurate inventory, mobile device management (MDM), and device configuration visibility.
- User behavior
- Traffic
  - "active-to-network"
  - "active-to-device"

7. **ZTX: Workloads:** Unique among the frameworks outlined here, the ZTX framework includes the concept of the workload, which comprises the entire application stack: the application itself, the operating system(s) on which it runs, any virtual platforms such as VMs or containers, and even the hypervisor. The concept even includes the application development process, with an emphasis on DevSecOps.

Although each of the underlying elements gets individual attention in the ZTX approach, it makes sense to look at workloads in their totality, especially regarding their role in the business of the organization. This holistic approach aligns with the comprehensive philosophy of ZT and helps to correlate business needs to security requirements.

III. **Google BeyondCorp [4]:** To secure their own systems, Google has developed BeyondCorp, a proprietary implementation of ZT. Unlike the NIST document and the ZTX approach, BeyondCorp is a real-world, functional implementation of ZT. Ward and Beyer give a good overview in *BeyondCorp: A New Approach to Enterprise Security* [4]. Here are the main pillars of BeyondCorp.
   a. **Securely Identifying the Device:** In the BeyondCorp implementation, devices and their configuration—collectively designated a managed device—are inseparable. Only managed devices may access resources, and device inventory (which includes configuration information) is stored dynamically in databases that Google manages centrally.
   b. **Securely Identifying the User:** Google systems integrate tightly with HR systems, and generate short-term use tokens for resource access. Google has also implemented Single Sign-On (SSO) to facilitate access.
   c. **Removing Trust from the Network:** The BeyondCorp system takes an interesting approach to network architecture. Their "unprivileged" network uses a private address space and uses an ACL to limit connections to specific internal services (DNS, DHCP, and some configuration management systems), and to the Internet.
   d. **Externalizing Applications and Workflows:** Google uses an Internet-facing access proxy that enforces encryption for all enterprise applications.
   e. **Inventory-Based Access Control:** BeyondCorp uses its Access Control Engine to infer trust for both users and devices. The engine correlates assertions about the user and their group memberships, device certificates, geolocation, and data from the device inventory. Each request is authorized (or denied) on a per-request basis.

12.1.2.1 Zero Trust: Implementation Concerns

As with any major undertaking, the primary concerns are cost, schedule, and performance. Successful ZT implementation will require careful tracking of costs and resulting benefits, a structured schedule, and ensuring that it does not diminish system performance, or impede the business significantly. Quantifying the return on investment is difficult—security value is often based on hypothetical events—but it will contribute significantly to executive buy-in and management support.

TABLE 12.1.1
Zero Trust Model Alignment

Feature	Forrester ZTX	NIST	CARTA	BeyondCorp
Networks/micro-segmentation	X	x	x	x
Encryption in place	X			
Encryption in transit	X	x	x	x
Network access control	X	x	x	x
Automated response	X		x	x
Continuous access control/monitoring	X	x	x	x
Visibility: devices	X	x	x	x
Visibility: activity	X	x	x	x

In addition, since ZT is based on a relatively new and different philosophy about security, it entails a culture shift, particularly for the security staff. Consequently, change management becomes a critical element for a successful ZT implementation.

12.1.2.2 ZERO TRUST: COMMON FEATURES

As may be apparent from the foregoing discussion, ZT is an amorphous concept, subject to interpretation by those who conceive it, try to standardize it, or implement it. It makes sense, then, to identify features and priorities common to all. Readers wishing to implement a ZT program can prioritize these in alignment with their organization's needs as shown in Table 12.1.1.

12.1.3 BUZZWORD VS PANACEA

After reviewing the salient aspects of the various frameworks and initiatives, and identifying their common features, we can now address the theme of this paper: "Zero Trust: Buzzword or Panacea?" Table 12.1.2 summarizes some key aspects of these two extremes, but I think ZT is clearly much more than an empty buzzword. More and more organizations, in both the private and public sectors, have recognized that traditional safeguards are inadequate. The recent discovery of a massive hack of numerous government agencies and private businesses—including cybersecurity firms—is clear evidence of this problem. In response, these organizations are accelerating efforts to implement ZT. For example, the US Department of Defense has released a ZT reference guide and the Defense Information Systems Agency (DISA) is implementing a ZT lab in conjunction with the US cyber command.

There is clearly no panacea for cybersecurity defense, but ZT is clearly much more than a buzzword as shown in Table 12.1.2. I urge all professionals in the field to take a close look at ZT. Even without a full-fledged ZT program, many of its principles and recommendations are germane to any organization and warrant serious consideration.

TABLE 12.1.2
Defines and Contrasts a Cybersecurity "Buzzword" versus "Panacea"

Buzzword	Panacea
Loosely defined	Comprehensive
• Vendors exploit the "gaps" in language, market knowledge	• Covers nearly all aspects of security • Encourages a holistic view • Upper management involvement
Not a single product or technology	Realistic
• "Bandwagon" phenomenon: everyone's a Zero-Truster	• Acknowledges likelihood/certainty of intrusion • Acknowledges changing landscape • Acknowledges failure of traditional perimeter defenses
Complex implementation	Complex implementation
• Cultural, technical, performance issues	• Cultural, technical, performance issues

12.1.3.1 ABOUT THE AUTHOR

As Chief Cybersecurity Technologist for DLT, Don Maclean formulates and executes cybersecurity portfolio strategy, speaks and writes on security topics, and socializes his company's cybersecurity portfolio. Don has nearly 30 years' experience working with US Federal agencies. Before joining DLT in 2015, Don managed security programs for numerous US Federal agencies, including DOJ, DOL, FAA, FBI, and the Treasury Department. This experience allowed him to observe the strengths and limitations of traditional cybersecurity defenses, leading to his interest in innovative technologies such as those featured in this article. In addition to his CISSP, PMP, CEH, and CCSK certificates, Don holds a BA in Music from Oberlin, an MS. in Information Security from Brandeis Rabb School, and is a recipient of the FedScoop 50 award for industry leadership. An avid musician, Don organizes a concert for charity every year, and has been known to compete in chess and Shogi (Japanese chess) tournaments, both in-person and online.

REFERENCES

1. Rose, S., Bortchert, O., Mitchell, S., & Connelly, S. (August 2020). *Zero Trust Architecture SP 800-207.* https://csrc.nist.gov/publications/detail/sp/800-207/final
2. Blankenship, Joseph, et al. "Zero Trust Security Playbook For 2021". *Forrester Blogs and Podcasts.* Forrester, 2 July 2020, https://www.forrester.com/report/Defend±Your±Digital±Business±From±Advanced±Cyberattacks±Using±Forresters±Zero±Trust±Model/-/E-RES61555
3. Ward, R., Beyer, B. (2014). *BeyondCorp: A New Approach to Enterprise Security.* Login, Vol. 39, 6th ser., pp. 6–11.
4. Forcepoint (2017). *"A Risk-Adaptive Approach"*, https://www.gartner.com/teamsiteanalytics/servePDF?g=/imagesrv/media-products/pdf/Forcepoint/Forcepoint-1-4YCDU8P.pdf
5. Manadhata, P. K., & Wing, J. M. (2011). *A Formal Model for a System's Attack Surface*, Advances in Information Security Moving Target Defense, pp. 1–2. (Not available for download.)
6. T. Miller, "THREAT INTELLIGENCE: AUTOMATING THREAT DETECTION & RESPONSE", I.blackhat.com, 2020. [Online]. Available: https://i.blackhat.com/webcasts/2020/01-23-black-hat-webcast-automated-threat-detection-and-response.pdf. [Accessed: 02- Sep- 2021].
7. V. Stross, "CLOUD-NATIVE NETWORK DETECTION & RESPONSE", I.blackhat.com, 2020. [Online]. Available: https://i.blackhat.com/webcasts/2020/01-23-black-hat-webcast-cloud-native-network-detection-and-response.pdf. [Accessed: 02- Sep- 2021].

12.2   OUTDATED AND LEFT BEHIND: IMPROVING AND INNOVATING OUR GOVERNMENT FACILITIES

Dr. Nikki Robinson
Security Architect, IBM
Adjunct Professor, Capitol Technology University

12.2.1   INTRODUCTION

The government facilities sector, as defined by the Cybersecurity and Infrastructure Security Agency (CISA), are the buildings located both in and outside the United States owned by federal, state, local, and tribal governments (CISA, 2020). These buildings are generally open to the public for business or recreational activities, but some are also used to hold extremely sensitive data (CISA, 2020). Special facilities that are not open to the public include military installations, national laboratories, or embassies (CISA, 2020). Given the sensitive nature of these facilities, which hold critical systems and networks, it is crucial to keep these facilities updated and protected. This paper identifies several challenges observed within the government facilities sector, including vulnerability management, resource allocation, and associated budgets.

12.2.2   CHALLENGES FACING GOVERNMENT FACILITIES

12.2.2.1   VULNERABILITY MANAGEMENT

The first challenge, and potentially most critical, to be addressed in the government facilities sector is vulnerability management and prioritization of remediation efforts (Oltsik, 2019). Typically, vulnerability management is handled in the context of individual vulnerabilities in systems, or more specifically, patch management. In this chapter, vulnerability management represents the holistic view from the top-down of the organization. Vulnerability management encompasses security controls, end-of-life software, unsupported hardware, outdated physical systems, and architecture/design flaws. As organizations and facilities work toward cloud implementations and closures of on-premise data centers, they must simultaneously upgrade antiquated equipment.

Vulnerabilities are not solely a missing patch or security control in hardware or software. These vulnerabilities can represent a camera pointed in the wrong direction, a workstation that does not lock when a PIV card is removed, or a server room that is not cooled at the correct temperature. In government facilities, especially older and outdated buildings, may have more vulnerabilities than newer and updated spaces. Specifically, in outdated federal buildings, the most prevalent vulnerabilities include outdated security equipment (cameras, monitors, etc.), unsecured windows, gaps in doors and door sensors, lack of physical security training, and unmonitored camera or alarm systems (GMSC, 2018). A security system is only as good as the monitoring and review conducted by personnel, and alerting notifications set in the system.

The COVID-19 pandemic has pushed agencies and organizations to move to telework environments such as Virtual Private Network (VPN), virtual desktops, remote applications, or hybrid environments. This requirement for impromptu hardware and software upgrades occurred rapidly, and most organizations implemented solutions without a chance to develop a robust plan. Rearranging people, processes, functions, and assets left gaps in security controls or partial security assessments. The transition could leave some end-of-life applications vulnerable by opening access to telework environments.

Additional challenges in vulnerability management and the future of government facilities networks will appear. End-of-life software and hardware may still exist in many on-site facilities. The risk of exploitable vulnerabilities with legacy applications and hardware cannot be remediated.

The recent revelation of the SolarWinds breach in the supply chain, leaving unpatched systems for even 30 days, represents ripe targets for sophisticated attackers. There must be an inventory collected of each network to determine which systems to upgrade first, and where the risk is highest in the organization.

12.2.2.2 RESOURCE ALLOCATION

The second major challenge to the government facilities sector is resource allocation of both information technology (IT) and cybersecurity professionals. Patch management continues to be a time-consuming and challenging task (Oltsik, 2019). If on-premise systems, workstations, and physical hardware still exist in an environment, it could take additional time to track down individual vulnerabilities. If patch management solutions are not 100 percent effective, other strategies must be explored to reduce patch management efforts. IT and cybersecurity personnel spend an excessive amount of time working on manual tasking, where automation could alleviate repetitive tasks.

Resource allocation applies not only to IT and cybersecurity personnel but also to the physical security in government facilities. As mentioned in the previous section, untrained personnel can lead to major vulnerabilities and gaps in physical security. With the increased use of third-party software, Supervisory Control and Data Acquisition (SCADA) systems, and the Internet of Things (IoT), come more sophisticated exploits to gain access to those systems. These systems also expand the connectivity between physical devices, the complexity of the networks, as well as the attack surface for the organization. Vulnerabilities in SCADA systems exist from the Human-Machine Interface (HMI) to mobile and web applications (TrendMicro, 2019).

12.2.2.3 BUDGET DISTRIBUTION

In combination with resource allocation and management, budgets for IT and cybersecurity teams are usually tight and constrained based on numerous factors. Cybersecurity teams work closely with IT teams on infrastructure tasks like engineering, architecture, and project management. IT projects and upgrades are an essential component for any government facility or organization but can very possibly end in failure (Yaraghi, 2015). Management must balance the IT budget between upgrading the physical systems, migrating current systems to a cloud environment, or upgrading desktops and laptops. Prioritizing items in a limited budget is complicated by security requirements (tools and resources) that must compete with the need to manage upgrades and maintain older systems.

12.2.3 AREAS FOR INNOVATION

12.2.3.1 SECURITY TRAINING AND AWARENESS

Security awareness starts from the top of any organization. Government organizations must embrace a "security first" attitude at the Executive level. Directors, management, and team leadership must understand the organizational and strategic vision, as well as where security fits into the business. Security training can be tailored for each area of the organization, including executive management, finance, human resources (HR), and IT operations. Customized training improves the ability for security objectives to be outlined in a meaningful way for each department. By improving security awareness and creating customized training, security becomes an integral part of each government facility.

12.2.3.2 DIGITAL TRANSFORMATION

For this paper, digital transformation refers to integrating technology into all areas of government facilities, intending to improve operations (Brandon, 2019). To help improve operations of government facilities, requirements must be defined and analyzed, followed by understanding risks throughout the enterprise (Brandon, 2019). With this holistic view, gaps may be identified, and plans can be put in to place to evaluate current tools and infrastructure, and finally evaluate emerging technology. New solutions could integrate technology for automation and increase mobility for employees and executives.

12.2.3.3 MOBILITY

Mobility is the cornerstone of technological advancement for any organization. Businesses use mobility to increase collaboration with partners and improve the functionality of their employees. Government facilities should continue to seek improvements for the mobility of employees and services. Given the global pandemic and increased telework presence, our government entities have no choice but to embrace a mobile workforce. This increased mobility allows employees to be in any location while still accomplishing the mission and goals of the organization. The significant benefits of using a mobile workforce include working from anywhere, hiring talent in any location, and allowing employees to improve productivity by reducing the need for driving to a physical location (Newman, 2015). Government facilities could consider scaling back on plans for new brick-and-mortar facilities and encourage telework. Lowering government facilities' physical footprint would expand budget allocation for more digital transformation and mobility.

12.2.3.4 CLOUD CONSIDERATIONS

While lowering physical government facilities' footprint could allocate additional budgeting for IT and cybersecurity budgets, removing on-premises data centers may also be a cost-saving measure. Depending on the scope of the cloud environment required, there are many viable options to move these physical data centers to cloud or hybrid environments. Through the digital transformation strategy session, antiquated systems may be identified for either cloud migrations or removal. Removing old equipment or migrating to cloud environments may increase security and lower overall risk while saving space and resources. But cloud migrations must be done with care and security input from the onset of the project, when done incorrectly, cloud systems can increase vulnerabilities in the network. A cloud migration is an ideal time to re-evaluate security controls, data loss prevention, and identify and access management (IAM) practices.

As government facilities consider converting to cloud or hybrid environments, another area for innovation is consolidating applications and equipment. Most government entities have accumulated many different applications over time. As mentioned before, many of these systems may require updates, which provides an opportunity to consolidate or virtualize those environments while simultaneously removing risks. Virtualization consolidates physical servers, improves administration through a standard interface, and reduces the need for physical rack space in the data center. Innovating with digital transformation, virtualization, and mobility strategies are all essential to improving government facilities.

12.2.4 RECOMMENDATIONS FOR THE FUTURE

12.2.4.1 TOP-DOWN SECURITY

There are several recommendations to consider as government facilities, including using a top-down security approach, utilizing private sector partnerships, and involving partnering with academic institutions for research. An academic collaboration can also bring fresh talent into the organization through internships. Organizations should consider involving security leadership, such as CISOs and Security Operations Center (SOC) managers in architectural, strategic, and design meetings. Security leadership can bring a "security-first" attitude to the meetings so that all new projects and designs include risk management from the onset. This provides several benefits, including increased security, improved project timelines, and enhanced communications between teams. Allowing security leadership into all facets of government facilities improves both physical security and cybersecurity objectives.

While considering security leadership in project management and engineering tasking, other directors and officers must gain insight into security threats and the risk landscape. If Executive meetings should include CISO briefings on current threats, security mitigation efforts, and vulnerability management priorities. Creating broader awareness and visibility into the security program allows executive leadership to appreciate the scale and scope of security efforts. Future efforts should include increased collaboration with security leaders to address concerns and improve communication throughout government facilities.

12.2.4.2 STRATEGIC PRIVATE SECTOR PARTNERSHIPS

Another major theme of improvement in the future is the integration of emerging technology from private sector companies. Major technology companies can create and innovate at a much faster pace than government facilities. Increasing the number of Federal Risk and Authorization Management Program (FedRAMP) available partners, and even those without FedRAMP certification, should be considered with complete security assessments. While FedRAMP offers a level of comfort of security with a vendor, a thorough security assessment should be completed to ensure compliance with federal standards. However, without these strategic partnerships with private sectors, transforming technology and identifying innovative solutions is far more complicated. When considering future physical government facilities, the public sector should investigate potential private sector partnerships or areas of advancement.

12.2.4.3 COLLABORATION WITH ACADEMIA

Working with an academic partner can provide the best opportunity for improvement in government facilities. Many technical institutions are working on research to improve cybersecurity and identify problems within the private and public sectors. Researchers have developed tools, new frameworks, and even identified unknown issues through their research. These researchers and professors can guide executive leadership, security analysts, and IT administrators. They may be able to identify security risks, assist in enterprise architecture, and create innovative solutions for complex problems surrounding government facilities. With federal regulations and procedures in mind, there are still many ways to improve government facilities, both physically and technically. There is a proven history of positive interaction and modernization when major academic institutions and public sector entities work together (Causey, 2016).

12.2.5 CONCLUSION

The government facilities sector requires major innovation and technological advancement to meet emerging security challenges. Government entities must embrace change and mobility to improve efficiency across all government sectors. The transition can be accomplished by leveraging private industry and academic partnerships, using mobility and digital transformation strategies, and involving security leadership in significant decisions. While not all-inclusive, this paper outlines areas of improvement and an outline for where to start to enhance government facilities.

12.2.5.1 ABOUT THE AUTHOR

Nikki Robinson holds a Doctor of Science in Cybersecurity from Capitol Technology University. Her specialization is in vulnerability management and the challenges around it. She has over 12 years in both the IT and Security fields as a cybersecurity engineer with an IT background, which brings technical descriptions to each presentation. Dr. Robinson holds certifications in both IT and Security, including the CISSP, CEH, CNDA, MCITP, and CCAA. Her goal is to help people to solve issues around vulnerability management and lower their organization's risk profile.

REFERENCES

Brandon, J. (2019). *What is a digital transformation strategy?* Retrieved from https://www.techradar.com/news/what-is-a-digital-transformation-strategy#:~:text=The%20basic%20idea%20with%20a,with%20the%20new%20technologies%2C%20and

Causey, M. (2016). *Federal government and private sector collaborations.* Retrieved from https://federal-newsnetwork.com/causey/2016/07/federal-government-and-private-sector-collaborations/

CISA (2020). *Government facilities sector.* Retrieved from https://www.cisa.gov/government-facilities-sector

GMSC (2018). *Five common security vulnerabilities.* Retrieved from https://gmscsecurity.com/common-security-vulnerabilities/

Newman, D. (2015). *Five important ways mobility empowers the workforce.* Retrieved from https://fowmedia.com/important-ways-mobility-empowers-workforce/

Oltsik, J. (2019). *Vulnerability management woes continue, but there is hope.* Retrieved from https://www.csoonline.com/article/3385083/vulnerability-management-woes-continue-but-there-is-hope.html

TrendMicro (2019). *One flaw too many: Vulnerabilities in SCADA systems.* Retrieved from https://www.trendmicro.com/vinfo/us/security/news/vulnerabilities-and-exploits/one-flaw-too-many-vulnerabilities-in-scada-systems

Yaraghi, N. (2015). *Doomed: Challenges and solutions to government IT projects.* Retrieved from https://www.brookings.edu/blog/techtank/2015/08/25/doomed-challenges-and-solutions-to-government-it-projects/

12.3 RECOMMENDATIONS FOR SECURING GOVERNMENT FACILITIES

Dr. Ron Martin
Professor of Practice for Critical Infrastructure, Capitol Technology University

12.3.1 INTRODUCTION

In a press release issued by the Federal Bureau of Investigation (FBI) on January 7, 2021 regarding the violent activity at the US Capitol, FBI Director Christopher Wray stated that "… The violence and destruction of property at the US Capitol building yesterday showed a blatant and appalling disregard for our institutions of government and the orderly administration of the democratic process …" (Wray 2021). This wanton attack on the United States Capitol Building will be studied for years to come. What is known is the Capitol Police Department, and the Sergeant of Arms was not prepared to turn back the hordes of people from assaulting the three facilities that comprise the US Capitol Complex. The President Biden administration will need to issue governance and policies that guide to protect all government facilities.

On May 22, 1998, President William J. Clinton issued Presidential Decision Directive 62 (PDD 62)—Protection Against Unconventional Threats to the Homeland and Americans Overseas. PDD-62 established the framework that provided the protection protocols to protect national significance events (PPD-62 1998).

Homeland Security Presidential Directive 7 (HSPD-7) prescribes in section 26 that "The (DHS) Secretary, after consultation with the Homeland Security Council, shall be responsible for designating events as 'National Special Security Events' (NSSEs) (HSPD-7 2003)." In the wake of the events of January 6, 2021, additional measures are needed to plan for the protection of our democracy.

12.3.1.1 RECOMMENDATION ONE

The administration issues an Executive Order and a Policy Directive requiring to expand the National Special Security Event (NSSE) Program to include events where domestic and International intelligence present a clear danger to human life and the United States democracy.

The presidential election of 2020 was a predicate of the US Capitol events of January 6, 2021. The members of Election Infrastructure Government Coordinating Council (GCC) Executive Committee—Cybersecurity and Infrastructure Security Agency (CISA) on November 12, 2020, released the following statement "… There is no evidence that any voting system deleted or lost votes, changed votes, or was in any way compromised …" (Cybersecurity & Infrastructure Security Agency, 2020). In the wake of individual members of the losing political party not accepting the presidential election results, there is a need to establish elections as an entire sector under the National Infrastructure Protection Plan (NIPP). In January 2017, the Department of Homeland Security Under Secretary J. Johnson made the following Critical Infrastructure Declaration: "By 'election infrastructure,' we mean storage facilities, polling places, and centralized vote tabulations locations used to support the election process, and information and communications technology to include voter registration databases, voting machines, and other systems to manage the election process and report and display results on behalf of state and local governments" (DHS 2017). The declaration assigned the elections as a sub-sector under the Government Facilities Sector (GFS).

12.3.1.2 RECOMMENDATION TWO-A

The administration issues an Executive Order and a Policy Directive requiring the elections sub-sector elevated as a separate and distinct sector under the NIPP.

12.3.1.3 RECOMMENDATION TWO-B

The administration issues an Executive Order and a Policy Directive recommending that each state, tribal and territorial assign an appropriate elections employee to a Government Coordinating Council. The sector coordinating Committee will consist of industry representatives with interest in the elections industry.

The GFS must be revised to reflect the protection imperatives our country requires. But first, let us briefly review the origins of the United States Infrastructure program.

The origins of the United States critical infrastructure program (CIP) program is a systematic and evolutionary process that started with the US Presidential Commission on Critical Infrastructure Protection (PCCIP) of 1997. The PCCIP Report of 1997 recognized that individual facilities or infrastructures are critical to our way of life. As such, we found that many of these facilities were susceptible to various threats (PCCIP, 1997). The PCCIP report led to 1998, Presidential Decision Directive No. 63 (PDD-63) (CRS 2015, p. 3). The terrorist attack on September 11, 2001, moved our Executive Branch to take action to implement the findings of the PCCIP Report. Presidents, G.W. Bush, and Obama Administrations issued executive orders and directives that provided the basis of our nation's current Critical Infrastructure Protection (CIP) program (CRS 2015 PPS 7–14). This governance laid the groundwork for the NIPP of 2013 and the 16 Sectors. Since the 2013 NIPP release, the nation has not issued any additional CIP governance requiring the revision of the NIPP.

It will be necessary for the Biden administration to assess and implement measures to enhance the sector's security posture. The new administration has direct authority to provide policies for the executive branch of government. The legislative and judicial branches receive policy direct from a law or legislative action. That said, the Biden administration must propose legislative action to protect all governmental facilities.

12.3.1.4 RECOMMENDATION THREE

The administration issues an Executive Order and a Policy Directive requiring the NIPP revision in 180 Days. This NIPP revision will require the integration of cybersecurity within the plan.

12.3.1.5 RECOMMENDATION FOUR

Issue or include in the Executive Order and a Policy Directive requiring DHS and Executive Agencies to revise Agency-Specific Sector Plans with six-months after the release of the NIPP revision (Recommendation 3).

12.3.2 GOVERNMENT FACILITIES SECTOR OVERVIEW

The GFS includes a wide variety of buildings, located in the United States and overseas, owned or leased by federal, state, local, and tribal governments. Many government facilities are open to the public for business activities, commercial transactions, or recreational activities. In contrast, others are not open to the people that contain sensitive information, materials, processes, and equipment. These facilities include general-use office buildings and special-use military installations, embassies, courthouses, national laboratories, and structures that may house critical equipment, systems, networks, and functions. In addition to physical facilities, the sector includes cyber elements that contribute to protecting sector assets (e.g., access control systems and closed-circuit television systems) and individuals who perform essential functions or possess tactical, operational, or strategic knowledge. The initial GFS plan was not available for public viewing due to individual Federal Facilities' sensitivity. Therefore, the Department of Homeland Security (DHS) opted not to publish a sector plan until 2015. The GFS has subsectors that reach beyond the facilities owned, leased, or controlled by the United States Government.

The Education Facilities Subsector of the GFS covers pre-kindergarten through 12th-grade schools, higher education institutions, and business and trade schools. The subsector includes government and private sector entities (Education Facilities Subsector Snapshot 2011). The preponderance of these facilities is non-federal. The oversight governance resides within the US Department of Education.

An ancillary initiative was enacting the Jeanne Clery Disclosure of Campus Security Policy and Campus Crime Statistics Act (20 US C. § 1092 (f)). The Office of Safe and Drug-Free Schools (OSDFS), an organization of the US Department of Education (ED), serves as the Sector-Specific Agency for the Education Facilities Subsector Sector (EFS). The Education Department published the Handbook for Campus Safety and Security Reporting (ED Handbook 2016) to help organizations understand and meet the various Higher Education Act of 1965 (HEA) requirements. The Clery Center was founded in 1987 by Howard and Connie Clery, following the murder of their 19-year-old daughter, Jeanne, in her dorm (CRS 2014 p 1). The ED 2016 Edition of the handbook for campus safety and security reporting describes the Clery Act (ED Handbook 2016). Numerous laws predicated the Clery Act. The Higher Education Act of 1965 (HEA) required all postsecondary institutions participating in HEA's Title IV student financial assistance programs to disclose campus crime statistics and security information (ED Handbook 2016, p. 1-1). In October 2020, The Clery Act requirement was moved to the United States Department of Education's Federal Student Aid (FSA) Handbook.

12.3.2.1 RECOMMENDATION FIVE

The Biden Administration must issue or include in the Executive Order and a Policy Directive requiring the Education Facilities' designation as a separate sector with the US Department of Education as the Sector-Specific Agency.

The National Monuments and Icons Subsector encompasses a diverse array of assets, networks, systems, and functions located throughout the United States. Many National Monuments and Icons assets are listed in either the National Register of Historic Places or the List of National Historic Landmarks (National Monuments and Icons Subsector Snapshot 2011).

The GFS covers the two additional subsector plans and guidance for Embassies, Courthouses, National Laboratories, and structures that may house critical equipment, systems, networks and functions, general-use office buildings, and special-use military installations.

12.3.3 GENERAL RECOMMENDATIONS

All infrastructures are conceived, built, maintained, and replaced using a specific process. The capital equipment installed within the facility has a shorter life cycle than constructed facilities. Facilities contain various types of building and access control systems. A 2019 US Department of Energy Inspector General Report found that physical and logical access security controls did not always provide sufficient restrictions over information technology (IT) resources. This section provides a high-level view of converged protocols to enhance the security posture of infrastructures. The NIPP and sector-specific plans do not offer governance or policy guidance for the planning, deployment, and maintenance of facility control systems. A 2014 Government Accountability Office (GAO) report titled DHS and GSA Should Address Cyber Risk to Building and Access Control Systems. This report recommended that the DHS develop and implement a strategy to address the cyber risk to building and access control systems. And The Interagency Security Committee (ISC), a DHS Office, revise its *Design-Basis Threat* report to include cyber threats to building and access control systems (GAO 15-6, p. 1). Presidential oversight is limited to the executive branch. However, the Biden administration should recommend the United States Congress enact laws that mirror executive action in certain facility protection instances.

As reported by the GAO report, the ISC is an organization within DHS. The ISC was established by President Clinton in 1995 via Executive Order 12977 to enhance the quality and effectiveness of physical security in federal facilities, is responsible for developing physical security standards for nonmilitary federal facilities. The *Design-Basis Threat* report is an appendix to ISC's physical security standard, *The Risk Management Process for Federal Facilities (RMP)*, with which federal executive branch agencies must comply. The RMP includes standards for agencies' facility risk assessment methodologies (GAO 15-6 p. 19). The legislative and Judicial Branches are not bound to adhere to the Executive Branch Directives.

12.3.3.1 RECOMMENDATION SIX

The Biden Administration must issue or include in the Executive Order and a Policy Directive requiring DHS and GSA to implement the GAO Recommendations from GAO-15-6. Specifically, (1) To develop and implement a strategy to address the cyber risk to building and access control systems and (2) direct ISC to revise its Design-Basis Threat report to include cyber threats to building and access control systems.

12.3.4 GFS SPECIFIC RECOMMENDATIONS

Much has been said about the importance of a building control system. Yet, there is little information about these systems, and there is even less information about the security protocol to protect them. These control system architectures are use-case models of building control systems, and general security measures to protect them. System life cycle planning and identity management highlight protocols that will enhance buildings' security posture. In the ASIS International Foundation 2017 Project, Building Automation and Control Systems (BACS) highlight the importance of these systems. The BACS provides an Investigation into Vulnerabilities along with current practice & security management best practices. One premise of the BACS report was to identify the many terms used, such as Building Automation Systems (BAS), Building Management Systems (BMS), Building Energy Management System (BEMS), Intelligent Buildings (IB), and increasingly, Smart Buildings and even Smart Cities, 5G, fifth-generation cellular standard and the Internet of Things have elevated the need to converge BACS. The report's contents are holistic approaches that can serve as a baseline Body of knowledge for BACS. In essence, they have become embedded into the contemporary built environment and its facilities (BACS 2017 p. i). As our nation embraces the Internet of Things (IoT) with 5G bandwidth connectivity, the systems will become susceptible to threat actors here and abroad. Now, our facilities must plan for attacks on the physical, information, and operational systems.

The National Institute for Standards and Technology (NIST) highlights the need to guide the security requirements in the draft Special Publication (SP) 800-213. The Draft NIST SP 800-213, titled IoT Device Cybersecurity Guidance for the Federal Government: Establishing IoT Device Cybersecurity Requirements, this publication identifies IoT device cybersecurity requirements (SP 800-213. 2020. pp 1-4). In April 2020, NIST initiated a 5G cybersecurity project to prepare for a secure evolution to 5G. This project recognizes the need for increased device cybersecurity preventative measures as the nation evolves toward full 5G implementation (5G Cybersecurity 2020).

The GAO report recommendations and the 2017 ASIS BACS report provide additional guidance for the GFS and other sectors. These reports, as well as the NIST initiatives, are essential elements in Facility protection. Additionally, these systems should adhere to the security requirements of NIST SP 800-82, Guide to Industrial Control Systems (ICS) Security.

The Public Building Service issues the PBS-P100, "Facilities Standards for the Public Buildings Service," which is GSA's mandatory facilities standard. It does not prescribe Information Communication Technology (ICT) Guidance. The absence of this recognition prevents a holistic view of total facility protection. Therefore, GSA's Public Building Service must include ICT governance within PBS-P100 Standard.

12.3.4.1 RECOMMENDATION SEVEN

The Biden Administration must issue or include in the Executive Order and a Policy Directive requiring DHS and GSA (PBS) revise the PBS-100 "Facilities Standards for the Public Buildings Service," BMS and BACS recognize these systems as control systems.

The GFS includes a wide variety of facilities owned or leased by Federal, state, local, territorial, or tribal governments, located domestically and overseas. Some of the government facilities are governmental. However, many GFS facilities are open to the public. Therefore, this article provides general and sector-related recommendations that will enhance the GFS security posture consistent with the draft SP 800-213.

12.3.4.2 RECOMMENDATION EIGHT

The Biden Administration must issue or include in the Executive Order and a Policy Directive requiring DHS to provide guidance consistent with SP 800-213. Federally owned or leased facilities will increasingly employ IoT devices using 5G technology.

12.3.4.3 ABOUT THE AUTHOR

Dr. Ron Martin is a Professor of Practice at Capitol Technology University in the following functional areas: Critical Infrastructure, Industrial Control System Security, and Access and Identity Management. Through his consultancy, Dr. Ron Martin maintains professional relationships with a diverse mix of businesses. He served as a board of directors for-profit and non-profit organizations. Dr. Martin retired from the United States (US) Army in 1999 and the US Government in 2011. In between his tours of Federal Service, he served five years as a civilian police officer in the Commonwealth of Virginia. During his Federal Service, he served with the US Department of Health and Human Services as the program director for the development and implementation of the department's Identity, Credentialing, and Access Management (ICAM) Program.

He now serves on the Security Industry Association and ASIS International Standards Committees. Dr. Martin is a member of the ASIS International's Commission on Standards & Guidelines Commission. He is a voting member of the United States Technical Advisory Group to International Standards Organization (ISO) which works to develop and articulate the United States' position by ensuring the involvement of US stakeholders from the private and public sectors. While on active duty, he served as Military Comptroller, Provost Marshal, Security Manager, and a Doctrine Literature Writer and Instructor. Dr. Martin served as a member of the Federal Identity, Credentialing and Access Management (FICAM) Roadmap Development Team and provided FICAM Subject Matter Expertise by regularly providing advice and assistance to Federal agencies and organizations engaged in Identity Credentialing activities. Dr. Martin was recognized as an International Fire Security Exhibition and Conference (IFSEC) Global influencer in Security and Fire for 2020. He is also a published author of Critical Infrastructure articles for John Jay College of Criminal Justice's Encyclopedia of Security and Emergency Management and the International Foundation for Protection Officers, Second Edition of The Professional Protection Officer.

REFERENCES

5G Cybersecurity (2020). https://csrc.nist.gov/publications/detail/white-paper/2020/02/20/5g-cybersecurity-preparing-a-secure-evolution-to-5g/draft
Abrams, M., Hahn, A., Lightman, S., Pillitteri, V., Stouffer, K. (2015). Guide to Industrial Control Systems (ICS) Security, NIST Special Publication 800-82. Gaithersburg, MD: National Institute of Standards and Technology. Guide to Industrial Control Systems (ICS) Security (nist.gov).
BACS (2017). https://www.securityindustry.org/wp-content/uploads/2018/08/BACS-Report_Final-Intelligent-Building-Management-Systems.pdf

Bartock, M., Cichonski, J., Souppaya, M. (2020). 5G Cybersecurity Preparing a Secure Evolution to 5G. Rockville, MD: National Cybersecurity Center of Excellence. 5G Cybersecurity: Preparing a Secure Evolution to 5G (nist.gov).

Brady, K., Cuthill, B., Fagan, M., Herold, R., Marron, J., Megas K. (2020). IoT Device Cybersecurity Guidance for the Federal Government: Establishing IoT Device Cybersecurity Requirements. Gaithersburg, MD: National Institute of Standards and Technology. https://nvlpubs.nist.gov/nistpubs/SpecialPublications/NIST.SP.800-213-draft.pdf

Brooks, D., Coole, M., Griffiths, M., Haskell-Dowell, P., Lockhart, N. Building Automation & Control Systems an Investigation into Vulnerabilities, Current Practice & Security Management Best Practice. Alexandria, VA: ASIS Foundation. BACS-Report_Final-Intelligent-Building-Management-Systems.pdf (securityindustry.org).

Bush, H. (2003). Homeland Security Presidential Directive 7. Washington, DC: Office of the President. https://www.cisa.gov/homeland-security-presidential-directive-7

CRS (2014). https://crsreports.congress.gov/product/pdf/R/R43759

CRS (2015). https://irp.fas.org/offdocs/pdd/pdd-63.htm

Cybersecurity & Infrastructure Security Agency. (2020). Joint Statement from Elections Infrastructure Government Coordinating Council & the election Infrastructure Sector Coordinating Executives' Committees. Washington, DC: US Department of Homeland Security. Joint Statement from Elections Infrastructure Government Coordinating Council & the Election Infrastructure Sector Coordinating Executive Committees | CISA.

Clinton, W. (1995). Executive Order 12977: Interagency Security Committee. Washington, DC: Office of the President. Homeland Security Digital Library (hsdl.org).

Clinton, W. (1998). Protection against Unconventional Threats to the Homeland and Americans Overseas. Washington, DC: Office of the President. https://www.hsdl.org/?view&did=758094

Department of Homeland Security (2017). Election Infrastructure Security. Washington, DC: Author. Election Infrastructure Security | CISA.

ED Handbook (2016). https://www2.ed.gov/admins/lead/safety/handbookfsa.pdf

Higher Education Act of 1965. 20 USC § 1001 et seq (1965). TOPN: Higher Education Act of 1965 | US Law | LII/Legal Information Institute (cornell.edu).

Jeanne Clery Disclosure of Campus Security Policy and Campus Crime Statistics Act, 20 USC § 1092 et seq. (1991). Microsoft Word—WPM$68DB.doc (owens.edu).

Moteff, J. (2015). Critical infrastructures: Background, Policy, and Implementation (CRS RL30153) Congressional Research Service. Washington, DC. Retrieved from https://fas.org/sgp/crs/homesec/RL30153.pdf

National Monuments and Icons Subsector Snapshot (2011). https://www.dhs.gov/xlibrary/assets/nppd/nppd-ip-national-monuments-and-icons-snapshot-2011.pdf

National Press Office (2021). Director Wray's Statement on Violent Activity at the US Capitol Building. Washington DC: Federal Bureau of Investigation. https://www.fbi.gov/news/pressrel/press-releases/director-wrays-statement-on-violent-activity-at-the-us-capitol-building

Office of Financial Student Aid (2020) Clery Act Appendix for Federal Student Aid (FSA) Handbook. Washington, DC: US Department of Education. https://ifap.ed.gov/sites/default/files/attachments/2020-10/CleryAppendixFinal.pdf

Office of Infrastructure Protection (2013). National Infrastructure Protection Plan (NIPP) (2013) Partnering for Critical Infrastructure Security and Resilience. US Department of Homeland Security. Washington, DC. Retrieved from https://www.dhs.gov/sites/default/files/publications/national-infrastructure-protection-plan-2013-508.pdf

Office of Infrastructure Protection (2011). Education Facilities Subsector. Washington, DC: US Department of Homeland Security. https://www.dhs.gov/xlibrary/assets/nppd/nppd-ip-education-facilities-snapshot-2011.pdf

Office of Infrastructure Protection (2011). National Monuments and Icons Sector. Washington, DC: US Department of Homeland Security. https://www.dhs.gov/xlibrary/assets/nppd/nppd-ip-national-monuments-and-icons-snapshot-2011.pdf

Office of Infrastructure Protection (2011). Embassies, Consulates, and Border Facilities. Washington, DC: US Department of Homeland Security. http://www.hsdl.org/?view&did=775444

Office of Inspector General (2019). Security over Industrial Control Systems at Select Department of Energy Locations Audit Report DOE-OIG-19-34. Washington, DC: US Department of Energy. Retrieved from https://www.energy.gov/sites/prod/files/2019/06/f63/DOE-OIG-19-34_1.pdf

Office of Postsecondary Education (2016). The Handbook for Campus Safety and Security Reporting 2016 Edition. Washington, DC: US Department of Education. The Handbook for Campus Safety and Security Reporting: 2016 Edition.

Presidential Commission on Critical Infrastructure Protection (PCCIP) (1997). The Report of the President's Commission on Critical Infrastructure Protection. Washington, DC: The White House. Retrieved from https://fas.org/sgp/library/pccip.pdf

Public Building Service (2018). P100 Facilities Standards for The Public Buildings Service. Washington, DC. General Services Administration. PBS-P100 Facilities Standards for the Public Buildings Service (wbdg.org).

US Government Accountability Office (2014). DHS and GSA Should Address Cyber Risk to Building and Access Control Systems GAO-15-6. Washington, DC: Author. GAO-15-6, Federal Facility Cybersecurity: DHS and GSA Should Address Cyber Risk to Building and Access Control Systems.

Wray, C. (2021). https://www.fbi.gov/news/pressrel/press-releases/director-wrays-statement-on-violent-activity-at-the-us-capitol-building-010721

13 Healthcare and Public Health

13.0 ABOUT THE HEALTHCARE AND PUBLIC HEALTH SECTOR

Krishnan Chellakarai
CISO, Gilead Sciences Inc.

Itzik Kotler
Co-Founder and CTO, SafeBreach

The Healthcare and Public Health Sector provides health care and services to the world population. The sector includes a variety of components including health care delivery and services, pharmaceutical research and manufacturing, medical device research and manufacturing, and pharmaceutical, medical device, and healthcare equipment distribution. The sector also participates in the response and mitigation of unforeseen hazards such as infectious disease outbreaks, natural disasters, and acts of terrorism. The ownership and operation of the physical assets and organizations delivering the goods and services generated by the health care sector vary from country to country; in the United States, the sector is primarily privately operated and owned. In other countries, the sector has a greater component of publicly owned providers of health care services.

The Healthcare and Public Health Sector is arguably the most important economic sector in the world today because it provides critical services and goods that keep us alive and healthy. From disease response to basic prevention, from novel drugs and devices to app-based care programs, the healthcare and public health sector interacts with nearly every person on the planet. The sector is also one of the largest economic drivers of the global economy, comprising US$7.8 trillion in spending in 2017 and 10% of the global GDP, according to the World Health Organization.

Because it relies on modern technology to function effectively and efficiently, the health care and public health sector depends on many other economic sectors including communications, energy, transportation, technology, and manufacturing. Increasingly, public health and health care sector infrastructure is digital. The sector is a frequent target of cyberattacks. Large-scale ransomware attacks have shut down portions of national health care systems in Ireland and the United Kingdom, and large hospital chains in the United States, forcing delays in the delivery of critical care and procedures such as surgeries and chemotherapy. The effectiveness of these attacks could also make ransomware a form of "denial of service" attack and a key weapon in asymmetric campaigns against developed nations by terrorist groups or even state-sponsored groups.

Because the research portion of the healthcare sector creates valuable intellectual property, pharmaceutical development firms, in particular, have become the target of attackers seeking to exfiltrate sensitive research and development data. This represents a threat of both economic espionage but also data blackmail; attackers that have successfully breached systems and exfiltrated personally identifiable data now routinely threaten to publish that data online unless they are paid. Like all other portions of the economy, the healthcare sector has undergone disruptions and shifts due to the COVID-19 pandemic; the digitization of the sector was accelerated by the mandate for remote work. This shift increased the potential attack surface by increasing the needs for accessing critical systems from home networks and from personal or less strongly secured devices.

The rapidly evolving threat landscape facing the healthcare and public health sector is forcing sector CISOs to explore innovative approaches to securing their networks and their data against cyber-attacks. This section addresses how CISOs are changing their thinking about securing their data and networks and new approaches they are adopting or considering improving security posture given the realities of modern cyberwarfare and cybercrime.

DOI: 10.1201/9781003243021-13

13.0.1 ABOUT SAFEBREACH

SafeBreach's mission is to change the way the industry deals with security and risk, and enable companies to use the security technologies they have invested in to the fullest. By validating those technologies against attacks, from the known to the latest emerging threats, they will drive risk down—on a continuous basis. Companies will be able to invest smart and protect more. They will be able to quantify risks to the business and drive a security strategy aligned with the company's business growth. Changing the mindset of defenders to offensive and proactive will help us build a safer world.

13.1 HOW TO NAVIGATE A NEW ERA OF THREATS TO THE HEALTHCARE SECTOR

Krishnan Chellakarai
CISO, Gilead Sciences Inc.

Itzik Kotler
Co-Founder and CTO, SafeBreach

13.1.1 INTRODUCTION

Cyberattacks against the healthcare sector have been escalating for the past decade. A recently released report by IBM X-Force shows healthcare *cyberattacks doubled in 2020* and 28% were ransomware attacks. Extraordinarily damaging ransomware attacks struck dozens of healthcare institutions amid the worst pandemic in 100 years. A number of those institutions quickly paid seven-figure ransoms in a desperate hope of resuming operations quickly and recovering invaluable and sensitive data [1].

On the whole, 23% of security incidents in 2020 involved ransomware, which increased from 20% in 2019. Twenty-eight percent of all cyberattacks on the medical field utilized ransomware. These attacks usually involved data theft before encryption of files to force victims into giving ransom payments to stop the exposure or sale of stolen information. Around 59% of ransomware attacks documented in 2020 employed this double-extortion technique [1].

Twenty-two percent of ransomware attacks used Sodinokibi. The analysts estimate that the Sodinokibi gang's collection of ransom money reached $123 million in 2020. Some other remarkably active ransomware campaigns were Netwalker, Ryuk Ragnarlocker, and Maze, each of which are credited with perpetrating 7% of the attacks [1].

Ransomware was the top attack type, followed by data theft and server access. Data theft went up by 160% year-over-year, with a substantial percentage of the attacks using the Emotet Trojan. Server access went up by 233% last year; they generally involved vulnerabilities exploitation and usage of stolen credentials.

While cyberattacks on healthcare institutions and pharmaceutical companies have occurred in the past, rarely have we seen mass disruptions and successful attacks impacting both patients and organizations on such a wide scale. Large clinical organizations have been forced to curtail operations and postpone lifesaving procedures due to disruptions from cyberattacks. State actors have also significantly increased attacks aimed at stealing research and trial data in hopes of gaining a competitive advantage in the race to create the most effective vaccine against COVID-19. Attacks against the "cold chain" of entities required to bring temperature-sensitive vaccines to injection locations have demonstrated that attackers seek to exploit every possible weakness in the healthcare supply chain.

More broadly, state actors and APTs have intensified their focus on penetrating and compromising key technology supply chain tools such as SolarWinds and Microsoft Exchange. This affords them a broad capability to breach nearly any type of industry and organization. As the technology and software supply chain has grown both in size and complexity, the focus has shifted from finding "zero day" attacks to recycling existing attacks paired with more innovative phishing and social engineering attacks. The SolarWinds attack, for example, appeared to be a simple password compromise for DevOps teams running the software server update.

13.1.2 THE BIG SHIFTS DRIVEN BY COVID-19

The onset of the COVID-19 pandemic incited a new and more precarious era of cyber risk for businesses and organizations across the healthcare industry. The disadvantageous risk-reward ratio in even attempting to resist many types of cyber-attacks has become clear. While the US Federal

Government has long mandated that organizations should not (and are legally proscribed from) paying ransom in ransomware attacks, in most cases, victims are paying, and paying quickly. The sad truth is, for a major research institution or even a national healthcare system, government responses might span months and may never result in the full unlock and recovery of systems and data. This presents an unacceptable cost.

The pandemic further highlighted that clinical data for potential treatments and research in progress is extraordinarily valuable, both in terms of geopolitics and financial upside. At the same time, protecting critical and highly valuable intellectual property has become a far more difficult task. The pandemic sent much of the workforce home but their work continued online and in the cloud. The pandemic proved that many of the activities of healthcare organizations could be effectively conducted remotely. Much of the work of sequencing and analyzing COVID-19, for example, occurred in the digital realm rather than in the physical laboratory. Organizations such as Moderna have created new ways to produce vaccines and medications that rely heavily on robotics, meaning they are more susceptible to cyber sabotage.

For healthcare providers and their patients, the pandemic brought a mass shift to video consultations and delivery of information via apps and the Internet, with healthcare providers working from home. While creating a more resilient system for conducting research and providing care, this shift created a more distributed attack surface with many more potential points of exploitation and a more convoluted supply chain and chain of custody. While some of the activities and workflows of the healthcare sector will logically revert back—doctors and patients will come together in offices, researchers will come back to laboratories—the remote option will continue to exist. In attacks outside the healthcare sector, as well, we saw indications of even more serious risks.

The 2020 attack on a Florida water treatment plant aimed at modifying the chemistry of drinking water clarified that the long-feared possibility of using cyber to conduct attacks against civilians is now in the arsenal of terrorists and state actors. In the realm of healthcare, there are many ways to potentially access and modify critical treatment modalities to harm not both systems and patients. Modifying recipes during drug production runs, shutting down dialysis machines, and sabotaging key life support systems are real possibilities.

In this new and more dangerous environment, the question for healthcare organizations is no longer what an incident will cost, but rather how long an organization can survive an attack—and whether an attack might undermine the long-term viability of that organization. In short, we were rushed into a new era of cybersecurity for healthcare and there is no going back. How we prepare, respond and improve our capabilities and procedures to deal with this new reality will determine how secure healthcare will be today and in the future.

13.1.3   THE NEW REALITIES OF CYBERSECURITY

In light of the changes that have emerged in threat variety and risk severity, the healthcare and pharmaceutical sectors must rethink many of their approaches to cyber security. While the changes that transpired in the past year had long been building, the pandemic accelerated the shifts. This is forcing healthcare organizations to move quickly and embrace new tactics and techniques to achieve a better security posture and stop threat actors early.

13.1.3.1   THE EVOLUTION OF RANSOMWARE

To understand how quickly the threat environment has evolved, let's consider the rapid evolution of ransomware. Various types of ransomware have existed for over a decade. The primary modus operandi was to freeze systems to induce payment. Until very recently, running a ransomware operation required some technical acumen. In the past few years, we saw radical shifts in that landscape. Ransomware-as-a-Service operations emerged, giving the capability to anyone who could upload a list of email addresses for targeted phishing attacks. (The DarkSide gang that shut down the Colonial Pipeline with ransomware offered this service until bad publicity caused them to terminate the offering.)

The environment of COVID also redefined the war against ransomware for healthcare organizations. Ransomware attackers quickly realized that the data they had frozen might be more valuable if exfiltrated and sold to interested parties; those parties might be interested either in the personally identifiable information for use in direct fraud or indirect social engineering attacks targeted later, or for the content of the data (experimental data or production techniques, for example). This created additional profitable markets for ransomware gangs, inducing them to amp up their efforts. A third vector for profits was simply threatening to post data online, violating privacy concerns of healthcare organizations. Organizations serving patients directly risked significant reputational damage and remediation cost should the patient or other clinical data be posted online. With COVID-19 upping the value of healthcare organization activities, the attackers recognize this opportunity for what it was and piled in.

13.1.3.2   APTS LIKELY TO REMAIN FOCUSED ON HEALTHCARE TARGETS

In the past, advanced persistent threat (APT) groups, often sponsored and funded by state actors, have focused more energy on targets with traditional political, military or financial value. The pandemic demonstrated clearly that healthcare can be crucial to national security. As scientists from dozens of nations raced to develop a vaccine, data from ongoing trials or research compiled during vaccine development processes suddenly became a matter of life and death. While the attacks on healthcare organizations seeking to exfiltrate vaccine development data will likely recede, all countries that maintain significant cyber espionage programs now see the value of maintaining access to healthcare sector systems. For this reason, APTs are likely to continue attempting to breach and implement a backdoor or compromise IT systems and data storage platforms where crucial data might be readily accessed in case of the next crisis.

13.1.3.3   CYBER ATTACKERS SEEKING LESS PROTECTED PATHWAYS

As we saw during the pandemic, multiple large pharmaceutical companies partnered either with other pharma giants or with smaller biotech companies that had particularly strong research capabilities or pipelines in SARS respiratory treatments and vaccines. Because the perceived value of information about vaccine development was so high, attackers expanded their attempts to focus on partners or organizations that enjoyed a high degree of trust with the target organization. For an attacker, a smaller biotech company that probably did not have a full-time CISO or cyber security team likely presented a softer target than a large multinational.

In COVID times, with so much research and collaboration shifted online and into the cloud, partners presented enticing pathways for potential social engineering or API attacks on better-defended targets. Another attack vector that appeared for the first time was breach and attack efforts against the extended "cold chain" required to distribute and preserve (through refrigeration) key vaccine types. In this development, attackers sought to compromise elements of the cold chain either to gain intelligence about plans, volumes, and movements, or to identify potential high-value ransomware targets. The level of sophistication in target selection was high, showing strong strategic initiative. A new research report by IBM X-Force shows that these cold chain attacks were in fact much more extensive than first reported. They targeted at least 44 companies in 14 countries in Europe, North America, South America, Africa, and Asia. The expanded scope of precision targeting includes key organizations likely underpinning the transport, warehousing, storage, and ultimate distribution of vaccines.

The attack on the cold chain echoed what was probably the most alarming development in cyber security over the past year—successful supply chain attacks that compromised widely used—almost ubiquitous—technology tools. The damage from the SolarWinds compromise, which may have gone undetected for months, may take years to finally understand. A similarly damaging supply chain attack, on Microsoft Exchange, may take as much time to unravel. It is highly likely that savvy attackers have exploited these serious vulnerabilities to plant compromise mechanisms in numerous—potentially hundreds of thousands—of IT systems. SolarWinds was used for network administration for a large percentage of Windows networks and systems; government and health-care institutions frequently deploy Windows.

13.1.4   NEAR TERM CONSIDERATIONS AND PATHS TO IMPROVEMENT

There are several ways that CISOs could shore up their security posture to specifically address weaknesses illuminated by the attacks of the past year.

13.1.4.1   ACCURATELY MAP YOUR ATTACK SURFACE

Due to the increasing use of cloud computing platforms and SaaS offerings, the attack surface has grown and diversified. Workers also are more likely to access organizational networks from personal devices over the public Internet, often using unsecured Wi-Fi. It is no longer viable to demand that all access be gated by proximity or location within a perimeter. COVID accelerated the widening of the attack surface by creating an even more distributed map of access and forcing even broader permissions for access. To properly defend an organization, the attack surface should be mapped in as much detail as possible. This is a thankless and never-ending task but it also generates far better awareness of where attacks may originate and allows red and blue teams to better test and secure networks, devices, and infrastructure.

13.1.4.2   IDENTIFY AND LOCK-DOWN TOOLS THAT COULD AMPLIFY ATTACK DISTRIBUTION

Everyone from leaders in state, federal, and local government to the CISOs or healthcare organi-zations can catalog and rate by risk the touchpoints inside their IT architectures that can have a broader impact. SolarWinds is a perfect example of one of these touchpoints—a widely used tool that can gain trusted access to all networks and therefore to all systems. For CISOs, this catalog will likely contain many IT platforms such as those used for configuration and endpoint management, and even cybersecurity systems that are broadly distributed such as VPN systems (client-server).

13.1.4.3   ANALYZE AND IMPROVE SYSTEMIC RESILIENCE

Related to the previous point, CISOs and security leaders in the sector should analyze how their systems will respond in case of attack and how long it might take to bring them back up. Based on this analysis, CISOs can lay out plans to improve resilience. This might mean putting in place additional architectural redundancy or identifying ways to restrict the blast radius of an attack to better preserve other parts of IT systems and networks. CISOs could even take this to an extreme like the country of Estonia, with full backups of all systems ready to deploy as cloud servers. Make no mistake, there is a price to resilience but in the wake of the past year and the ongoing attacks, the cost of ignoring resilience has become crystal clear and clearly unacceptable.

13.1.4.4   STEP UP ADVERSARIAL SIMULATIONS AND OTHER CONTINUOUS TESTING OF SECURITY CONTROLS

The only way to be prepared for a continuous onslaught is to take the initiative and get ahead of the attackers by continuously running adversarial simulations to validate security controls. Newer technologies, such as breach and attack simulation (BAS), also referred to as continuous security control validation, make it both economical and less disruptive to simulate attacks and identify security gaps early. This is different from traditional penetration testing because it can run through hundreds or even thousands of attack playbooks using data pulled from Common Vulnerability and Exposure (CVE) databases or custom playbooks designed by in-house red teams or consultants. Adversarial testing is also a strong method to validate which security controls are effective, and determine how to improve resilience by creating a layered approach to security.

13.1.4.5 IMPLEMENT MORE ROBUST AND MORE CONTINUOUS AUTHENTICATION

In most cases, breaches and bad actors could be more easily detected and blocked if authentication systems were more robust and more continuous. Much of the healthcare sector still relies on a dated model of perimeter security with additional authentication for sensitive systems that usually is required only once per session. Too often, those systems only require password and username combinations; two-factor authentication is being used more but implementing 2FA on older systems common in many healthcare settings is challenging. Nevertheless, healthcare organizations need to follow the lead of the financial services and telecommunications sectors by deploying authentication that requires multiple factors and is more continuous. In addition, CISOs should be moving away from 2FA, which relies on SMS and text messages because of the ease of compromising SMS-based authentication.

This shift can take various forms to be effective. A CISO may gradually decrease the frequency of authentication requirements for parties whose actions indicate they can be trusted. Alternatively, a CISO can implement full Zero Trust protocols by insisting on authentication prior to starting any new transaction on systems, even within sessions. This usually requires some sort of token. More generally, the old reliance on passwords should be reduced. This will not only improve the user experience but also improve security; passwords are the glaring weakness of most security postures.

13.1.4.6 DEVISE WAYS TO IMPROVE SECURITY AWARENESS FROM THE BOARDROOM TO THE LUNCHROOM

Cybersecurity is only as good as people's awareness of the risks and their ability to respond. Executive sponsorship of cybersecurity efforts is essential. Include executives from all business lines in annual or semi-annual cyber wargames. Education efforts to help line employees better grasp the potential risks of their actions can reduce security slipups significantly. Running phishing education programs and randomized phishing response testing by sending users simulated phishing attempts are excellent ways to engage all employees in cyber security thinking. In healthcare organizations, cyber risk covers not only computing devices but also the numerous platforms that might have embedded systems which are at even higher risk due to the challenges in updating and patching those systems. For example, many medical devices run older Windows operating systems on their embedded computing platforms. As well, in healthcare, human eyes and awareness are crucial to identifying signs of anomalous behaviors in these systems, which may not be obvious to network and security operations teams.

13.1.5 OVER THE HORIZON: SECURITY OF THE FUTURE FOR HEALTHCARE

Even as CISOs improve security in the present, the healthcare sector and patients stand to benefit tremendously from newer technologies that are not widely adopted yet or not yet ready for commercial use.

13.1.5.1 AUTOMATION OF SECURITY ORCHESTRATION, RESPONSE, AND PATCHING

Security alerts come in fast and furious. If an analyst spends two minutes per incident alert in an hour, they can only analyze 30 incidents. That assumes no serious incidents which require more time.

Machine learning systems can today assess the risk of each incident alert and prioritize incident response queues accordingly. Businesses can use this to implement risk-based vulnerability management and to guide continuous adversarial simulation, as well; security operations teams should test the efficacy of controls against the most serious and likely risks and attack types. The machine learning engine can also be trained to focus on the "crown jewels" holding the most potential for horizontal traverse of the most important information and data. Organizations can also automate patching by integrating patch engines and vulnerability management tools with continuous integration/continuous development pipelines. This allows for patches flagged as "critical" to automatically be deployed with an assurance that IT teams can roll back the code or configuration changes to an earlier version should the patch cause problems. Accelerating and automating patching is particularly critical because criminal gangs and APTs know that many organizations may take weeks or months to deploy patches and they focus attacks on recently released vulnerabilities to take advantage of this security gap. Closing the patch gap should be a top priority for healthcare organizations.

13.1.5.2 ENHANCED FORMS OF ENCRYPTION

At present, encryption is usually a binary state. A file or piece of data is either encrypted or unencrypted. When it is encrypted, it is not readable or usable. We are in the early stages of seeing newer encryption systems that allow computation to be performed against encrypted data without first decrypting the data. These so-called homomorphic encryption systems will be a step-change improvement in security. In the near future, healthcare organizations should adopt these newer forms of encryption to create workflows where data is encrypted all the time, not only when it is at rest.

13.1.5.3 PRODUCTS THAT IMPROVE BOTH SECURITY AND UX

It is possible today to use an Apple Watch on your wrist to authenticate yourself on Macs and iPhones. A watch is a form factor that is easy to carry and relatively unobtrusive. The watch can also continuously validate—perhaps even with biometric data—that the wrist is that of the approved user. Waving a watch is a far better user experience than struggling with password and username combinations. A healthcare CISO might try a pilot program where these watches become the primary multi-factor authentication mechanism. Doing so would likely reduce help desk calls, improve efficiency and make for a smoother user experience. This is one hypothetical example but the reality is, today's users expect the same experience in a business setting as they obtain with consumer applications. This expectation and willingness to embrace consumer-grade experiences can be powerful leverage to drive improved security compliance and understanding.

13.1.6 CONCLUSION: ADDING MORE CONTROLS AND COMPLEXITY IS NOT THE ANSWER

The typical security operations team already has too many solutions to manage. They are also unlikely to realize the full value of their controls. In some instances, two or more sets of controls may actually be canceling each other out. Most security operations teams also have an incomplete view of risk (and how to manage risk.) Creating a well-thought-out risk model and assigning systematic risk ratings to key systems and to types of incidents can yield tremendous benefits by allowing security teams to better focus and to optimize their controls to mitigate the most serious risks. Building ways to quantify, visualize, and report on both risks and outcomes is the most essential skill to staying safe in this new era of threats. What is not measured is not improved, even with the best intentions and large budgets for tools and personnel. For healthcare, creating greater resiliency and security agility will only become more crucial as threats continue to evolve and the importance of healthcare in our lives continues to grow.

13.1.6.1   About The Authors

Krishnan Chellakarai is the Chief Information Security Officer at Gilead, located in Foster City, California. He has over 28 years of experience in Information Security across various industries and close to 15 years in the pharmaceutical and biotechnology industries. Mr. Chellakarai has been the CISO at Gilead for six years, and he is responsible for Cyber Security strategies, architecture, engineering, and cyber security operations. Prior to Gilead, Krishnan has worked as the Chief Security Architect at Roche/Genentech for nine years and had a similar role in various organizations including Stanford Hospital, CNA Trust, Reuters America, and ABN Amro.

Itzik Kotler is the CTO and Co-Founder of SafeBreach. Itzik has more than a decade of experience researching and working in the computer security space. He is a recognized industry speaker, having spoken at DEFCON, Black Hat USA, Hack in the Box, RSA, CCC, and H2HC. Prior to founding SafeBreach, Itzik served as CTO at Security-Art, an information security consulting firm, and before that he was SOC Team Leader at Radware (NASDQ: RDWR).

13.1.6.2   About Gilead Sciences, Inc.

Gilead Sciences, Inc. is a biopharmaceutical company that has pursued and achieved breakthroughs in medicine for more than three decades, with the goal of creating a healthier world for all people. The company is committed to advancing innovative medicines to prevent and treat life-threatening diseases, including HIV, viral hepatitis, and cancer. Gilead operates in more than 35 countries worldwide, with headquarters in Foster City, California.

REFERENCE

1. IBM Security X-Force Threat Intelligence Index", Ibm.com, 2021. [Online]. Available: https://www.ibm.com/security/data-breach/threat-intelligence/. [Accessed: 02- Sept- 2021].

13.2   DIRECT PATIENT CARE SUBSECTOR CYBERSECURITY STATE OF THE UNION

Joey Johnson
CISO, Premise Health

13.2.1   INTRODUCTION

The US healthcare ecosystem represents a sector that is both critically important and highly complex. The data assets in play are sensitive and directly targeted by threat actors ranging from cybercriminals to fraud entities, to skilled individual hackers, to nation states. Each with their own motivations and intents. As we have experienced this past year through the COVID-19-pandemic, intellectual property data assets such as vaccine research are highly coveted, and their compromise has both economic and national health stability consequences. We are highly adept at innovative research but less adept at protecting this data where interested nation state adversaries could abscond with said data and mass produce at labor costs we struggle to compete with or control supply chain distribution in manners that may be disadvantageous to the United States.

But to fully grasp the complexity of the entirety of the healthcare sector and its associated threat profile, it is necessary to recognize the distinctions of the formally defined sub-sectors as defined by Healthcare and Public Health Sector-Specific Plan (HPH-SSP) [1]. Each subsector functions differently, having unique threat profiles, varying levels of cybersecurity maturity and resourcing, and distinct critical assets to protect.

The primary intent and focus of this paper will be exclusively on the largest of these subsectors in the Direct Patient Care subsector and the current and forthcoming cyber threats with which it must contend. The Direct Patient Care subsector is comprised of front-line healthcare professionals in the practice of patient treatment and the business operations that surround them. This is inclusive of hospitals, urgent care centers, ambulatory and emergency responders, primary care and family practice centers, dentistry, employer-sponsored wellness centers, pharmacies, mental and behavioral health practices, and specialty practices. In certain circumstances, this may also extend to less traditional practices such as physical therapy, medical fitness, occupational health, massage and acupuncture, and nutrition and wellness coaching. Per the 2015 drafting of the HPH-SSP, this subsector employed over 12 million Americans, supported 5,686 recognized healthcare facilities with 900,000 staffed beds; and it admitted over 35 million Americans for care annually.

In evaluating the subsector holistically, it is critical to recognize that the subsector itself is highly fragmented and has traditionally grown at scale through merger and acquisition activity. Small private practices are frequently absorbed into larger conglomerates and regional hospitals consolidate or are acquired by national hospital groups. However, often this consolidation activity leaves the organizations' existing technology infrastructure intact as the cost of replacing a fully functional technology infrastructure simply for the purpose of obtaining a singular enterprise architecture is often not justified. The resulting outcome of this can be wildly disparate technology fiefdoms with no singular overarching enterprise architecture. This creates significant challenges in establishing and maintaining cybersecurity standards and baselines.

Furthermore, dedicated funding and focus on cybersecurity within the subsector have historically been challenged. With regard to the Direct Care Provider subsector, many of these organizations are recognized as existing below the "cyber poverty line." This lack of resourcing and focus is further exacerbated by the lack of strong cybersecurity leadership within the provider practices. While the larger nationally recognized hospital groups and those attached to university research centers tend to have both strong cybersecurity leadership and strong cybersecurity programs, the drop off from there is steep and concerning. Nascent programs combined with wildly disparate and fragmented technology architectures result in a healthcare provider ecosystem that is highly vulnerable. These collective challenges were detailed by the HPH Cybersecurity Task Force in 2017, with a progress update issued in 2018 [2]. They were identified both as areas where some progress had occurred but also as areas where much opportunities remained.

13.2.2 DATA AT RISK: MEDICAL RECORDS

Given the concerns detailed above, we need to then contemplate the specific threats to this ecosystem and their impacts on a national scale. The most obvious data asset of value is medical record data. From a pure cybercrime perspective, the value of medical record data is its permanency and ubiquity. Unlike a compromised credit card, a medical record cannot simply be deleted and re-issued. It is a permanent artifact representing an individual, and it is often combined with additional sensitive personal information such as social security numbers and payment card data. It is also highly decentralized. There is no one place an individual can go to get their full medical record. It is scattered across all the hospitals, urgent care centers, private practices, and medical insurance providers that an individual has engaged with throughout their lifetime. Additionally, sector imperatives such as interoperability and health information exchange frameworks ensure that the data is ubiquitously available across the ecosystem, regardless of the cybersecurity postures of the various hosting entities. So, when this data is compromised, it cannot simply be deleted and re-issued. It is a permanently viable copy of a valuable dataset. Further complicating matters, due to the ubiquitous presence of the data, fraudulent activity takes a long time to detect and trace back to the source of compromise.

As previously stated, the threat is even further complicated by the challenge of the typically immature and highly fragmented nature of healthcare provider institutions, whose monitoring and detection capabilities are challenged to uncover such complex fraudulent access scenarios. Understanding where the data was compromised from can be extremely daunting, as the same critical record elements (insurance numbers, social security numbers, date of birth, address, specific medical condition(s)) may exist in the databases of Hospitals A, B, C, and D. Not to mention the insurers and smaller specialty private practices. So, when it is used maliciously, where was it stolen from originally? Is that provider group even aware?

For these reasons, medical record data can be stolen and resold on the black market to facilitate medical-oriented fraud activities. According to the 2020 Trustwave Global Security Report, estimates for the value of a medical record on the black-market hover around $250, whereas the next highest value record (a payment card) is only valued at $5.40 [3, 4]. So, the delta in value is measured in orders of magnitude. Health care fraud costs insurers between $70B and $234B each year (between three and ten percent of annual healthcare spending), which ultimately harms both patients and taxpayers. These fraudulent activities also directly fund national healthcare epidemics such as the opioid crisis.

13.2.3 MEDICAL INTERNET OF THINGS: THE INTERSECTION OF CYBER RISK AND THE PROTECTION OF HUMAN LIFE

Medical devices, even those with built in compute capability, are nothing new. Within large care provider environments, there have typically been some version of a "clinical engineering" team that was accountable for maintaining, calibrating, and generally managing these devices. What brought about great change in this space was network connectivity. In one of the first largely publicized breaches, we witnessed the infiltration of one of the largest US retailers in Target. The Target breach demonstrated that the source entry point for an attacker could be through a third-party facility supplier. In this case, the entry coming through their Internet connected HVAC system, used by their facility maintenance supplier, brought awareness to the threat vector of having industrial management devices connected to the Internet.

Today we face that same challenge with medical devices, but the problem statement is actually more complex. Prior to network connectivity, hospital information technology teams had no real concern with or oversight of medical devices. Once they became network-enabled devices suddenly, IT teams became, at least in theory, accountable for these devices in the same way they would be accountable for any other device connected to the network. This introduced some challenges in the industry where clinical engineering teams were reluctant to provide access and control of these devices to technology departments for fear that they could be taken offline at inappropriate times, modified in some way that inhibited functionality, or otherwise generally took them out of the full purview of the clinical engineering team. Conversely, technology engineering teams expressed concerns over accountability for ensuring device uptime, bandwidth allocation, consistent connectivity of other medical systems, and needing continued autonomy to generally manage the enterprise network without having to coordinate downtime and maintenance operations with non-technology teams. Technology teams felt both distinctly accountable for success and acutely disadvantaged to ensure successful outcomes.

The narrative was tense, and the conflict was palpable. Then came the onslaught of security concerns. Parties accountable for security began expressing concern that these connected devices, many of which relied on legacy compute systems, presented significant security vulnerabilities. Vulnerabilities which, beyond the traditional cybersecurity risk concerns, in a breach scenario could facilitate the exact patient safety concerns that clinical engineering teams fretted. The crux of the conflict tipping point had emerged—Critical lifesaving devices cannot be taken offline or made unavailable and cannot be modified or manipulated in any capacity. At the same time, these devices introduce serious security risks that can affect entire hospital enterprises and their patient communities if they are not patched, updated, configured with limited access, and otherwise protected.

Across the globe, the Internet of Things (IoT) has dramatically and irreversibly reshaped the cyber risk landscape. Expert estimates vary on exact prediction metrics, but conservative estimates hold that as of 2020, in the United States, there were ten connected devices per household [5]. This is compared to 1.03 devices per person in 2010, with the growth curve expected to spike dramatically and exponentially in the next five years [5]. The specific reference here to consumer devices, while seemingly a disparate set of facts from the device footprint in patient care facilities, is very deliberate. This is because looking forward, the associated advent of telehealth, home-based healthcare, and the explosion of wearable devices are dramatically extending the traditional "healthcare practice perimeter." It is ushering in a change in the foundational manners in which patient data is both generated and consumed. This is a topic we will explore in greater depth later in this essay.

However, for the purposes of this section, the key callout is that, whether in traditional patient care facilities or within patient homes, the majority of these devices are connected as they are configured out of the box (with default login username, passwords, administrative credentials left intact). It's a trivial exercise to pull up an Internet search engine, type in an IoT device name, and discover the default login credentials from the online user manual. From a cyber risk perspective, this effectively means creating exponentially more breach entryways into an environment.

For a moment, let's explore what the actual cyber risks are. Stated succinctly, the intersection of provider healthcare and connected devices represents the point at which cybersecurity threats have direct impacts on the protection of human life. The ability to alter the calibration and control points of medical devices can directly result in compromise of human life if blood types are changed, insulin delivery is increased, respiration cadence is changed, pulmonary rhythms are altered, etc. These are just a few examples, and in true patient care, both manual and out-of-band monitoring and care delivery safety precautions currently exist to prevent these types of dramatic adverse outcomes. But as technology adoption and reliance outpaces humans' ability to provide granular oversight, this challenge will be more difficult to manage.

Also, consider altering a lifesaving or life-preserving device's basic functionality. If a respiration machine can be made non-functional, the result may be loss of life. As we have witnessed historically with political figures of note, if a pacemaker can be compromised wirelessly, the result may be loss of life. These types of "manipulations" are extremely trivial to execute. Again, as we embark on an era where there is a rapid uptake in adoption of both connected and human-embedded devices, these threats need to be recognized as having much greater potential for actualization than in any prior period. This would be especially concerning in scenarios where the health posture and wearable or medical device reliance of key political, military, or otherwise important figures could be compromised.

This deluge of device growth is both ubiquitous and irreversible, and in the context of healthcare provider organizations, even greater complicating factors exist which exacerbate this threat profile. The first challenge to recognize is a fundamental economic problem. Technology hits obsolescence points at a remarkably aggressive pace. There is a profound security implication to this reality. Newer technology generally improves in its security posture over time, building on the deficiencies of the technology which it replaces. Meanwhile, older technology hits stages where it is no longer supported, and its inherent security shortcomings are no longer addressed or patched by the vendor. This is a typical software and technology lifecycle where, to a certain degree, the eradication of security concerns is self-policing as newer technology replaces older technology. Like an old vehicle, there is a tipping point at which continued maintenance and replacement of expensive parts is no longer a practical approach.

However, within the healthcare provider ecosystem, an inherent disparity exists. Connected medical devices can be extremely costly and historically were not manufactured like "technology devices" with an expectation that their usefulness ages out quickly like a laptop might. Rather they are manufactured to last decades, with price tags to match. Predictably, these devices are becoming more and more connectivity oriented. And this connectivity is frequently reliant upon whatever technology was current at the time of manufacture. In this capacity, a hospital may be riddled with numerous medical devices that are critical and expensive and continue to function and perform well but are bound to old PC operating systems that cannot be upgraded. Thus, the devices are ripe for malicious compromise.

Further complicating matters is the fact that not only may the device be connected to a very old PC using very old software, but the physical device itself may have very old computer hardware with its own set of critical vulnerabilities. These vulnerabilities cannot be directly remediated as attempts to patch or upgrade the device frequently void the manufacturer's warranty and willingness to provide technical support. Worse still is the fact that these medical devices may be deemed critical and, as such, cannot be taken offline at any time. This further inhibits the ability to provide appropriate protective technical support. That means hospital groups are encumbered with insecure devices where those security risks are difficult to effectively address.

Further complicating matters, it is frequently the underlying Original Equipment Manufacturer (OEM) supply-chain components that harbor the vulnerabilities. The outcome of this is that the discovery of a single firmware level weakness in an OEM component can present itself across a vast array of devices that were constructed using that component. As recently as December 2020, medical device security research firm CyberMDX discovered vulnerabilities in a range of GE Healthcare radiological devices [6]. The Cybersecurity and Infrastructure Agency (CISA) swiftly issued an advisory on the discovery reflecting a critical and broadly-impacting severity because the vulnerability could allow an attacker to gain access to sensitive PHI data, alter the data, and impact the availability of the machine [7]. Over 100 device types were impacted by this singular vulnerability, including CT Scanners, PET machines, Molecular Imaging Devices, MRI Machines, Mammography Devices, X-Ray Machines, and Ultrasound Devices. The vulnerability also impacts certain affiliated workstations and imaging devices used in surgery.

Medical device security has been a top security concern since the early 2000's and should have been considered a mission-critical priority since at least 2016 [8]. The cybersecurity product market moves rapidly, and over the past several years, several cybersecurity products have emerged with a focus on IoT security, a subset of which have a primary focus on medical IoT (MIoT) devices.

So, solutions are now present to meet the need. However, procurement and implementation of these solutions, unfortunately, remains out of reach for many of the neediest healthcare provider organizations. The solutions may be expense to procure, may have long and complex implementation timelines, and maintenance and support require workforce resources that many organizations simply do not possess and cannot afford.

13.2.4   RANSOMWARE IN PROVIDER HEALTHCARE

Several years ago, ransomware was just one more obscure cybersecurity threat. However, since then, it has revolutionized the organized criminal market. The reason for this is simple: Prior to the advent of ransomware, an adversary had to successfully infiltrate an organization, then determine which data assets within that organization held value. After that, the adversary still had to find a way to stealthily exfiltrate the valuable data and then find a market for the stolen data in order to monetize it. From a threat actor perspective, the associated timelines are long, the effort to discover valuable assets is complex and risks discovery, and the need to then monetize the compromised data requires undesirable levels of criminal activity exposure.

Ransomware changed all of that. An adversary now only needs to infiltrate an organization through a mechanism as simple as a phishing scheme to compromise login credentials. With access to the environment, an adversary can arbitrarily encrypt data and/or systems at will. It is no longer important if that data has "value" or black-market appeal. Whatever the data is, it is likely important to the company who owns it, even if it's entirely unimportant to anyone else. Additionally, file structures necessary to support systems operations can be encrypted, thus rendering critical systems unavailable. So, the attack play is bigger than just data. And the need to reclaim that data or system under conditions of duress creates an immediate and direct buyer/seller arrangement between attacker and victim. Prior to this, the victim was not involved post-breach. They were simply victimized, and the attacker needed to generate a "customer" for their recently hijacked data trove. This paradigm shift has driven a rapidly monetized and high organized cybercrime ecosystem.

Ransomware aggression is sector-agnostic; however, the threat has created a uniquely perfect storm for direct patient care organizations. The intent of this section is simply to highlight the particular ramifications of this broad problem set on the direct patient care subsector and why this subsector is so uniquely vulnerable. As previously stated, the direct patient care subsector has traditionally been behind the curve in terms of cyber maturity. The organizations tend to be highly fragmented, and investment in cybersecurity is insufficient to meet the risk level. This has resulted in an environment that is inherently insecure.

This has been the case for some time. But in 2020, with the emergence of COVID-19, an already security-challenged sector was pushed to its breaking point. Hospitals were shuttered for all but critical patient treatment, and multiple revenue streams eroded. Simultaneously these same hospitals were flooded with COVID patient management needs and struggling to keep up with protective equipment needs such as masks, sanitizer, gowns, gloves, goggles, etc. This critical state further required the introduction of new and unvetted technologies that had to be implemented under duress, which typically has a direct correlation to introduced security vulnerabilities in said technologies. The provider workforce was exhausted and themselves succumbing to increased COVID contraction rates, which further constricted an already razor-thin critical workforce. Many workers went home, and numerous providers tried to rapidly adapt to telehealth, which had a particularly high learning curve as, telehealth aside, many providers were not acclimated to spending multiple hours a day on a computer to begin with.

So, the threat landscape was set—a critical US sector, replete with sensitive data, already immature on a cyber front, working under unprecedented conditions of extreme duress. Where one can at the same time be both highly financed and morally bankrupt, then one can take advantage of a considerable set of circumstances. And that proved to be the case in the ransomware campaigns this past year. In 2020, it was estimated that 50 percent of healthcare breaches were the result of ransomware, with no less than 560 healthcare provider organizations being compromised. The subsector was and continues to be, targeted directly and relentlessly. It is a disproportionate degree of cyber aggression with which the subsector cannot contend.

Further adding to the gravity of the situation, in the healthcare provider industry, the consequences of a ransomware attack can have life-threatening results. We have not yet reached the point where there have been confirmed incidents of loss of life due to ransomware. But a notable case from Germany in September 2020 provides a clear warning of the imminent threat. A German hospital was affected by a ransomware attack, and with key systems unavailable, a woman died. Numerous initial reports and speculation indicated that this represented the first clear case of a ransomware cyberattack being directly responsible for a loss of life event. However, German law enforcement authorities ultimately determined that the woman's health was in such a poor state that her death was likely inevitable, and the delay introduced by systems' unavailability due to ransomware could not be deemed as the directly responsible factor in her death [9]. But with slightly altered conditions, with a healthier patient, in more direct and immediate need of a lifesaving device, it could be determined that the ransomware attack was, in fact, the key contributor to the loss of life situation.

One month later, in October 2020, as the COVID-19 epidemic was breaking records in the United States, a wave of ransomware attacks targeted the US direct patient care subsector. This collective event was significant enough that a joint advisory titled Ransomware Activity Targeting the Healthcare, and Public Health Sector was collectively issued by CISA, FBI, and HHS (alert AA20-302A), warning healthcare groups about this active threat [10]. Per cybersecurity firm Check Point, there was a 71% increase in ransomware attacks against the healthcare sector in just a month of October 2020 [11]. If systems and critical lifesaving device availability are compromised, ambulances are re-routed to alternate facilities, and overcrowded hospitals have no capacity, the chances of loss of life as a direct result of ransomware-based attacks dramatically increase. Dishearteningly, the critical and desperate state of these healthcare provider entities only exacerbates the aggression. This concern, and the associated US response by the US Cyber Command in late 2020, are well documented [12, 13]. The ransomware concern is generally recognized to have reached a state of criticality that it has become a national security concern.

13.2.5   TOMORROW HAPPENED YESTERDAY: HELLO TELEHEALTH!

Telehealth solutions have been around for quite some time. But seemingly overnight, the global COVID-19 pandemic acted as an unprecedented catalyst for the massive and rapid adoption of telehealth out of pure necessity. Much of the technology itself is not new, but for reasons as simple convenience and reluctance to embrace and learn a new technical platform, in the absence of a forcing agent, adoption for telehealth lagged on both the provider and patient side of the equation.

However, per a 2020 research report issued by McKinsey & Company, since the start of the pandemic, providers are now seeing 50 to 175 times more patients via telehealth than at any time prior [14]. The adoption rate is staggering and introduced an undeniable paradigm shift in care delivery that will persist even once the COVID-19 pandemic has passed. Numerous estimates anticipate that telehealth will drive a $250 billion industry in virtualized care management. Simply the nature of so dramatically shifting human-to-human interaction scenarios to occurring via technology solutions increases security risk due to increased exposure alone [15].

The telehealth platforms themselves have matured quickly during the global pandemic, but there have been significant ancillary effects as well. Due to the inherent ability for telehealth to extend the reach of quality healthcare into the home and out to remote and underserved areas, previously underserved communities can now access care. Furthermore, as care is delivered electronically, via both audio and video Internet-based connections, an associated mass adoption of patient care connected devices and wearable technology has occurred.

While this brought forth undeniable positive outcomes in healthcare delivery, the rapid adoption of new technology is outpacing the ability to ensure its security posture. This is further complicated by the fact that, like most consumer technology, the onus for securing the devices is ultimately on the patient. And while typically, there are some limited configuration options available to the end user, in a broader sense, the security posture of wearable technologies and at-home medical devices is beyond the control of the consumer. Furthermore, the paradigm shift of an individual generating their own patient data presents a regulatory "gray area" regarding accountabilities for how that sensitive data must be protected.

13.2.6   THE NEXT CHAPTER: UNREGULATED PERSONAL HEALTH AND WELLNESS DATA

Medical devices and wearable technologies, and the data they collect, remain somewhat unregulated from a healthcare perspective. Privacy-oriented regulations such as the California Consumer Privacy Act (CCPA) and the US Global Data Protection Regulation (GDPR) make efforts to address end-user privacy rights. But at the true data and device security level, regulations have gaps. The US Food & Drug Administration (FDA) has done an honorable job attempting to tackle this problem and set the foundation for regulation [16]. But much of this focus is on the device types procured and used by patient care organizations and those developed by the recognized device manufacturers. However, from a patient and/or end-user perspective, the field is largely unregulated.

A key concern here is that "device" and "data" classification in a consumer context is elusive to define. Contemplate for a moment that a connected medical device within a hospital that measures and records glucose levels and then imports that data into a medical record application is clearly regulated. The data generated by a licensed medical practitioner is definitively Protected Healthcare Information (PHI) under the Health Insurance Portability and Accountability Act of 1996 (HIPAA), and the collection device is most likely classified and regulated by the FDA. Conversely, a mobile application on an individual's smartphone that connects to a wearable device that the individual wears, which also collects the same exact data elements, is unregulated. A critical distinction being that the consumer is ultimately accountable for the generation of their own dataset.

In the context of direct consumer-facing devices, there is no reasonable assurance of security provided. The data may be stored locally on the smartphone in an insecure fashion. It may remotely accessible by unknown entities. The collecting application itself may have a very weak security posture, allowing for the data it processes to be accessed and manipulated. The mobile application may export and store data to an unknown cloud hosting environment in a foreign nation with entirely different or non-existing personal data protection requirements.

Currently, many of the more recognized manufacturers such as Fitbit, Samsung, and Apple (among numerous others), have made proactive efforts to design products in a manner that could meet HIPAA requirements. However, this is entirely up to the manufacturer's discretion and interpretation of which regulations should be in scope and how to interpret the demands of said regulation. But for each responsible manufacturer, there are many who do not aim to achieve those standards of accountability, and there are no concrete regulations, classifications, or standards for them to necessarily strive toward. This is not to infer that absolutely none exists, but rather that an overarching collectively agreed-upon framework to govern the full end-to-end product development lifecycle (of hardware-level security and then the subsequent firmware/software that a secondary manufacturer puts on top of that hardware to take the product to market) currently does not exist. As these devices and mobile applications interface and exchange data with the electronic systems hosted and managed by direct patient care entities is the point at which they hit upon the theoretical "HIPAA boundary" where data becomes defined as PHI and those regulatory requirements take effect. But in principle, any maliciously intended developer could create a fitness or wellness application that centrally collects numerous health metrics directly from a consumer, and that environment is wholly unregulated.

13.2.7 THE ROLE AND EFFICACY OF REGULATION

The cybersecurity challenge is, by its very nature, perpetually outpacing what regulation can address directly with any level of granular efficacy. Technology innovation and adoption are outpacing organizations' ability to govern and manage it. There is an ever-present delta between the set of technology an organization can effectively manage and govern and that which they are newly embracing and determining how to manage and govern. In that delta lies the most technology cybersecurity risk.

Threat actors are imminently aware of this delta and focus efforts on attack vectors to exploit this delta, increasingly leveraging powerful automation and artificial intelligence capabilities to exacerbate both the speed and efficacy at which they are able to achieve their desired outcomes. In this capacity, they are inherently and perpetually ahead of the protection curve. While it may take a threat actor minimal funding to determine these exploit pathways, organizations must determine what the deltas are to be protected and then try to allocate resourcing and funding to address those gaps. This takes time.

In the absence of a regulatory position on risk scenarios involving emergent technology lead organizations develop risk control mechanisms and collaborate to strengthen those approaches. This is the nature of the emergence of best-practice approaches within cybersecurity. After a long enough period, those best practices gain widespread acceptance among industry leaders and then eventually make their way into baseline regulatory requirements. However, this process typically takes several years to come to fruition. These requirements determine the low-watermark baseline for compliance. But compliance is not equivalent to security when many primary threat exposures are occurring in areas that the regulation doesn't yet speak to.

Within the direct patient care arena, we have witnessed this with the structure of HIPAA [17]. At its core, HIPAA has both "required" and "addressable" controls. The intent of this being to have a singular framework that can provide guidance to both large mature organizations and much smaller practices who have neither the resources nor the technical aptitude to implement complex security controls.

Due to this flexibility, demonstrating HIPAA compliance can still result in an environment that is lagging from a security best-practice perspective across a variety of critical control areas. It is important to recognize that the initial intent of HIPAA was not one primarily focused on data privacy and security. Those elements were later added to the mandate and, since that addition, have not been materially updated to speak to the risk areas called out in this essay.

Specifically, numerous "gray areas" have emerged that are formally outside the scope of HIPAA governance but still involve data elements that are similar to, if not exactly the same as, those formally defined PHI elements. The rapid adoption of consumer-based mobile computing has ushered in a world of consumer-generated data in the areas of nutrition, fitness, wellness, behavioral health, and the like. More recent modalities such as wearable consumer devices, virtual reality, and consumer-facing genetics applications have introduced even more areas of formally ungoverned personal healthcare data grey areas.

For these emergent technologies, data can be generated and stored on insecure devices, hosted within cloud computing environments across multiple nationalities, and potentially shared or marketed in manners in which the individual has no visibility or control. Even in the context of user acceptance of privacy terms, these are, perhaps deliberately, complex and non-negotiable. Recent regulation such as the CCPA has made some initial progress in governing these areas, but there is still much left to address.

A more recent addition to the healthcare cybersecurity governance structure has been the introduction of the HITRUST Cybersecurity Framework (CSF) and the associated HITRUST accreditation process. The intent of the HITRUST framework is both unique and well-intended. Between the private and public sectors, there are multiple well-intended security and privacy governance structures, which get even more specific and unique at the State regulatory level. And as has been famously attributed to Andrew Tanenbaum, "The nice thing about standards is that there are so many to choose from." The intent of HITRUST, while initially healthcare sector focused, is to pull multiple different regulatory and best-practice standards into a single common controls framework and enhance that by ensuring that the HITRUST CSF requirements evolve aggressively year over year in line with the rapid technology advancements across industry sectors. The ambition of this framework is progressive, but it is ultimately led as a not-for-profit entity. This means that while setting a high bar for maturity and compliance, it is not mandated in any formal manner. The entities most likely to subject themselves to HITRUST CSF compliance are those entities who are already operating at some level of security maturity and pursuing HITRUST as some form of a competitive differentiator to evidence a level of "advanced maturity" to their leadership or board. But the organizations that most need a mandated maturity measuring stick are not subjected to CSF adherence. So in this capacity, an effective model exists, but its voluntary nature limits its broad efficacy. Additionally, the not-for-profit operating model is distinctly different from any other mandated regulatory framework.

Looking back a bit, though, we are fortunate in that we are not starting from scratch. In the Cybersecurity Act of 2015, Congress established the Health Care Industry Cybersecurity (HCIC) Task Force to address healthcare industry cybersecurity challenges. The task force comprised a number of private and public sector leaders representing the breadth and depth of the healthcare industry sectors. The outcome of their efforts resulted in the Task Force's 2017 *Report on Improving Cybersecurity In the Healthcare Industry* [18]. While the full set of discoveries and recommendations presented in this report is beyond the scope of this essay, it is important to recognize that the report identified as a primary imperative the need to "Define and streamline leadership, governance, and expectations for healthcare industry cybersecurity." The full report itself is strongly recommended reading any audience interested in the content of this specific essay. But for brevity, and because it is relevant to this essay, the six imperatives the report presented as recommendations were:

1. Define and streamline leadership, governance, and expectations for healthcare industry cybersecurity.
2. Increase the security and resilience of medical devices in health IT.
3. Develop the healthcare workforce capacity necessary to prioritize and ensure cybersecurity awareness and technical capabilities.
4. Increase health care industry readiness through improved cybersecurity awareness and education.
5. Identify mechanisms to protect research and development efforts and intellectual property from attacks or exposure.
6. Improve information sharing of industry threats, weaknesses, and mitigations.

When speaking to the regulatory environment at the time, the HCIC report calls out that multiple federal entities play a multi-pronged role in the healthcare regulatory environment, and this can introduce complexity [18]:

> Within the HHS, the Office for Civil Rights (OCR), CMS, the Food and Drug Administration (FDA), the Office of the National Coordinator (ONC), and the Office of the Assistant Secretary for Preparedness and Response (ASPR) play important and diverse roles in cybersecurity. Other administrative agencies and independent commissions, for example, the Federal Trade Commission (FTC) also play a role in setting expectations for privacy and security of health information. The multiplicity of actors in this space is often necessary to address a wide range of cybersecurity challenges and system types, and can be helpful in allowing these challenges to be viewed and addressed from multiple perspectives. It also has the potential to create complications. Some entities may be subject to regulation and oversight by multiple federal government entities, each with their own rules, which may be difficult to reconcile. Product and technology innovations for medical devices and health IT outpace the development and creation HEALTH CARE INDUSTRY CYBERSECURITY TASK FORCE 12 of regulations. While many regulations that apply to cybersecurity in health care are wellmeaning and individually effective, taken together they can impose a substantial legal and technical burden on health care organizations.

These organizations must continually review and interpret multiple regulations, some of which are vague, redundant, or both. In addition, organizations must dedicate resources to implement policy directives that may not have a material impact on reducing risks.

At the same time, gaps in protections can leave key health care unaddressed and create holes in cybersecurity infrastructure for health information. Consider, for example, the different roles of FDA and OCR with respect to health information cybersecurity. FDA is charged with ensuring approved and cleared medical devices are safe and efficacious, whereas OCR is charged with oversight of the privacy and security regulations under HIPAA, which applies only to "covered entities" (e.g., most health care providers, health plans, and health care clearinghouses), and contractors acting on their behalf, known as "business associates." With the recent publication of the FDA's final guidance for manufacturers on device cybersecurity, the FDA has taken more steps to address the patient safety concerns generated by cybersecurity risks to medical devices. However, FDA oversight is limited to patient safety and does not extend to patient privacy. HIPAA's regulations focus on both privacy and security; however, medical device manufacturers may not be covered entities or business associates under HIPAA. This leaves a health care provider using a medical device with potentially greater responsibility for assuring privacy and security protections for health information created and shared by the device. While many stake-holders agree that protecting against cybersecurity threats should be a shared responsibility, to date, health care providers have shouldered an inordinate amount of the burden even when actions needed to improve security in the device have been outside their control.

At the time of the writing of this essay (September 2021), we are nearly five years past the issuance of that initial report from the HCIC. And while significant discussions have ensued, and some progress has been made since that time (continued FDA guidance on medical device security standards, continued maturity of the private/public sector Healthcare Information Sharing Analysis Center (H-ISAC)), we have also faced the realities of the rapid growth, availability, and adoption of new technologies in that span which perpetuate the lagging ability of regulation to keep pace with technology and data risk emergence.

13.2.8   CALL TO ACTION RECOMMENDATIONS

The healthcare direct patient care sector in remains under-resourced in an alarming number of areas. It is a sector struggling with rapid technology adoption and change and the associated security implications that accompany that adoption rate. It represents an inherently fragile ecosystem, and one that amid a global COVID healthcare crisis is being pushed to the brink. The workforce is fatigued and depleted and highly susceptible to the tactics of cyber-adversaries. But there are key areas where federal aid can provide tangible support.

Perhaps the most easily attainable option for healthcare provider organizations to rapidly mature their cybersecurity operations is participation with the Healthcare Information Sharing and Analysis Center (H-ISAC [19]). An ISAC is a nonprofit entity that exists to support threat intelligence sharing and security community relationship development within a critical sector. This environment provides a confidential and open forum for the exchange of ideas and intelligence to support participant organizations in establishing, operating, refining, and optimizing their cybersecurity programs. The ISAC provides members direct access to sector-specific thought leadership working groups focused on key topics such as medical device security, third party risk management, cybersecurity awareness education, cloud computing security, security incident response, and preparedness, among other topics. The ISACs also function as the critical intersection point between federal and private sector threat intelligence sharing.

Membership costs to participate in the H-ISAC vary based on organizational revenue but hover between $2,500 and $15,000 for smaller organizations [19]. The return on investment for this participation is immense, but the cost commitment and/or lack of awareness still present challenges to many of the under-resourced "below the poverty line" healthcare institutions. A full value-proposition overview of the H-ISAC is beyond the scope of this essay, but for the purposes of this writing, it is the author's view that H-ISAC membership is one of the most effective and consumable change agents available to healthcare provider organizations to dramatically improve their security maturity and efficacy. Federal support mechanisms to provide awareness and assist under-resourced provider organizations with the opportunity to attain membership would be one of the most pivotal, rapid, and highly effective mechanisms to fortify the resilience of the sector. Any efforts to incentivize member participation would yield exponential benefits to the provider ecosystem security posture in its entirety.

13.2.8.1 About the Author

Joey Johnson is currently employed as the Chief Information Security Officer (CISO) with Premise Health, the nation's largest Direct Patient Care provider, exclusively serving the nation's largest employer groups with over 800 onsite and near-site clinics and wellness centers, as well as local and nationally focused telehealth programs. Premise Health operates in forty-six states and several US Territories. Premise Health clients operate as recognized "Fortune level" industry leaders across multiple sectors to include finance, defense, healthcare, pharmaceutical/biomedical, technology, energy, transportation, manufacturing, agriculture, retail, higher education, and state and regional governments and municipalities. Johnson has served in this capacity for over 11 years with Premise Health.

As the processor and custodian of personal healthcare records for a patient community of roughly eleven million employees, Premise Health has been subjected to high degrees of security scrutiny from its multi-sector, highly regulated clients, as Premise undergoes hundreds of in-depth client security audits annually. This audit activity has forced Premise Health to operate at a level of cybersecurity maturity and efficacy that meets not only HIPAA but also the multiple independent sector-specific cybersecurity compliance regulations and frameworks. This represents a degree of external scrutiny that is differentiated from most traditional Direct Patient Care entities.

Prior to his time with Premise Health, Johnson held cybersecurity leadership roles within the US Department of Commerce, as well as with various government contracting institutions over a 20-year cybersecurity career. Additionally, Johnson has served for over seven years in an advisory capacity with the Health Information Sharing & Analysis Center (H-ISAC), a cyber best-practice and threat intelligence sharing community comprised of critical infrastructure owners and operators within the Healthcare and Public Health (HPH) sector. The H-ISAC also functions as the key critical infrastructure private/public sector threat intelligence sharing operation for the HPH sector. In this advisory capacity with the H-ISAC, Johnson has worked with H-ISAC senior leadership to help evolve aspects, efficacy, and maturity of the ISAC in providing value and maturity opportunities for the ISAC membership. During this time, has had the opportunity to observe the distinct challenges and cyber threat profiles specific to each of the eight distinct HPH critical subsectors.

Additionally, Johnson serves in an advisory capacity with multiple cybersecurity technology investor groups, serves as a direct advisor and board member to numerous cybersecurity technology software manufacturers, and also serves in a thought leadership advisory capacity to various medical device manufacturing organizations. These collective facts are presented as they are relevant in understanding both the context and perspective of the author.

Given this background, this essay will focus heavily on the HPH Direct Patient Care subsector. Chronologically, given the time of this essay development in April 2021, an emphasis will be put on topics of relevance since the issuance of the 2015 Healthcare and Public Health Sector-Specific Plan and the subsequent 2017 Healthcare Cybersecurity Task Force issuance of findings to Congress.

REFERENCES

1. "Healthcare and Public Health Sector-Specific Plan", *CISA*, 2016. [Online]. Available: https://www.cisa.gov/sites/default/files/publications/nipp-ssp-healthcare-public-health-2015- 508.pdf. [Accessed: 20- Jul- 2022].
2. "Public Health Emergency: Cybersecurity Year One Activity Update", *Phe.gov*, 2018. [Online]. Available: https://www.phe.gov/Preparedness/planning/CyberTF/Pages/OneYearUpdate.aspx. [Accessed: 20- Jul- 2022].

3. "2020 Trustwave Global Security Report", *Trustwave*, 2020. [Online]. Available: https://www.trustwave.com/en-us/resources/library/documents/2020-trustwave-global-security-report/. [Accessed: 20- Jul- 2022].
4. T. Taylor, "The Value of Healthcare Data | SecureLink", *SecureLink*, 2022. [Online]. Available: https://www.securelink.com/blog/healthcare-data-new-prize-hackers/#:~:text=According%20to%20a%20Trustwave%20report,record%20(a%20payment%20card). [Accessed: 20- Jul- 2022].
5. B. Safaei, A. Monazzah, M. Bafroei and A. Ejlali, "Reliability side-effects in Internet of Things application layer protocols", *2017 2nd International Conference on System Reliability and Safety (ICSRS)*, 2017. Available: 10.1109/icsrs.2017.8272822 [Accessed 20 July 2022].
6. "CyberMDX Research Team Discovers Vulnerability in GE LightSpeed, Revolution, and other CT, MRI, and X-Ray imaging systems", *CyberMDX*, 2020. [Online]. Available: https://www.cybermdx.com/vulnerability-ge-radiology-201208/. [Accessed: 20- Jul- 2022].
7. "ICS Medical Advisory (ICSMA-20-343-01): GE Healthcare Imaging and Ultrasound Products", *Us-cert.cisa.gov*, 2020. [Online]. Available: https://us-cert.cisa.gov/ics/advisories/icsma-20-343-01. [Accessed: 20- Jul- 2022].
8. C. Sherman, M. Maxim, E. Pikulik, M. Flug and P. Dostie, "The Forrester New Wave: Connected Medical Device Security", Forrester.com, 2020. [Online]. Available: https://www.forrester.com/report/The-Forrester-New-Wave-Connected-Medical-Device-Security-Q2-2020/RES157303. [Accessed: 26- Jul- 2022].
9. P. Howell O'Neill, "Ransomware did not kill a German hospital patient", *MIT Technology Review*, 2020. [Online]. Available: https://www.technologyreview.com/2020/11/12/1012015/ransomware-did-not-kill-a-german-hospital-patient/. [Accessed: 20- Jul- 2022].
10. "Ransomware Activity Targeting the Healthcare and Public Health Sector | CISA", *Us-cert.cisa.gov*, 2020. [Online]. Available: https://us-cert.cisa.gov/ncas/alerts/aa20-302a. [Accessed: 20- Jul- 2022].
11. "Hospitals Targeted in Rising Wave of Ryuk Ransomware Attacks - Check Point Software", *Check Point Software*, 2020. [Online]. Available: https://blog.checkpoint.com/2020/10/29/hospitals-targeted-in-rising-wave-of-ryuk-ransomware-attacks/. [Accessed: 20- Jul- 2022].
12. B. Krebbs, "Report: U.S. Cyber Command Behind Trickbot Tricks – Krebs on Security", *Krebsonsecurity*.com, 2020. [Online]. Available: https://krebsonsecurity.com/2020/10/report-u-s-cyber-command-behind-trickbot-tricks/. [Accessed: 20- Jul- 2022].
13. E. Nakashima, "Cyber Command has sought to disrupt the world's largest botnet, hoping to reduce its potential impact on the election", *The Washington Post*, 2020. [Online]. Available: https://www.washingtonpost.com/national-security/cyber-command-trickbot-disrupt/2020/10/09/ 19587aae-0a32-11eb-a166-dc429b380d10_story.html. [Accessed: 20- Jul- 2022].
14. O. Bestsennyy, G. Gilbert, A. Harris and J. Rost, "Telehealth: A quarter-trillion-dollar post-COVID-19 reality?", *Mckinsey & Company*, 2021. [Online]. Available: https://www.mckinsey.com/industries/healthcare-systems-and-services/our-insights/telehealth-a-quarter-trillion-dollar-post-covid-19-reality. [Accessed: 20- Jul- 2022].
15. T. Henry, "After COVID-19, $250 billion in care could shift to telehealth", American Medical Association, 2020. [Online]. Available: https://www.ama-assn.org/practice-management/digital/after-covid-19-250-billion-care-could-shift-telehealth. [Accessed: 26- Jul- 2022].
16. "Device Advice: Comprehensive Regulatory Assistance", *U.S. Food and Drug Administration*, 2021. [Online]. Available: https://www.fda.gov/medical-devices/device-advice-comprehensive-regulatory-assistance. [Accessed: 20- Jul- 2022].
17. "HIPAA Security Series: Security Standards: Technical Safeguards", *HHS*, 2007. [Online]. Available: https://www.hhs.gov/sites/default/files/ocr/privacy/hipaa/administrative/securityrule/techsafeguards.pdf. [Accessed: 20- Jul- 2022].
18. "HEALTH CARE INDUSTRY CYBERSECURITY TASK FORCE: REPORT ON IMPROVING CYBERSECURITY IN THE HEALTH CARE INDUSTRY", *Phe.gov*, 2017. [Online]. Available: http://www.phe.gov/Preparedness/planning/CyberTF/Documents/report2017.pdf. [Accessed: 20- Jul- 2022].
19. "Health Information Sharing and Analysis Center | *H-ISAC*", H-ISAC, 2021. [Online]. Available: https://h-isac.org/. [Accessed: 20- Jul- 2022].

14 Information Technology

14.0 ABOUT THE INFORMATION TECHNOLOGY SECTOR

John Fanguy
CTO, Micro Focus Government Solutions

CISA defines the Information Technology Sector as "central to the nation's security, economy, and public health and safety as businesses, governments, academia, and private citizens are increasingly dependent upon Information Technology Sector functions. These virtual and distributed functions produce and provide hardware, software, and information technology systems and services, and—in collaboration with the Communications Sector—the Internet. The sector's complex and dynamic environment makes identifying threats and assessing vulnerabilities difficult and requires that these tasks be addressed in a collaborative and creative fashion."

Information Technology Sector functions are operated by a combination of entities—often owners and operators and their respective associations—that maintain and reconstitute the network, including the Internet. Although information technology infrastructure has a certain level of inherent resilience, its interdependent and interconnected structure presents challenges as well as opportunities for coordinating public and private sector preparedness and protection activities.

Governments are being driven to rapidly expand digital services to their citizens, reduce cybersecurity incidents and breach impacts, and lower operating costs. Often, citizen's and agency personnel's expectations are being driven by rapidly evolving—yet often not secure—consumer technology offerings.

Cybersecurity is typically viewed as just necessary spending to stay ahead of the attackers by employing increasingly stronger defenses. This mindset leads to cybersecurity competing with mission systems enhancements, which ultimately makes systems less secure and less mission-ready.

The typical breach-response-remediation approach for most agencies ultimately yields costly duplication of overlapping cybersecurity defenses, as well as gaps due to legacy versus new software platform components. Simply put, breach response and remediation are urgent and costly; evolving agency applications are slow and measured by functions rather than security improvements. The Federal government spent over $90B on IT broadly and $17B on cybersecurity specifically.

And the problem is growing: The US government is a prominent target for cybercrime. In 2018, US government agencies reported 31,107 cyber incidents, an approximately 11.8% increase from the previous year.

Building with the right technologies and standardized processes has been proven to reduce cybersecurity risks and impacts while dramatically improving overall system resilience at no additional cost and often reduced costs due to efficiencies of process integration. This approach is known as "Zero Outage" and has been driven and proven by some of the largest technology organizations in the world. Successful Zero Outage implementations bring together and align the priorities of the three main pillars of IT spending in agencies: CIOs, CISOs, and program leaders. Zero Outage concepts allow all three to find common ground for investments.

Zero Outage is a growing global approach and framework that emphasizes standardization in the quality of IT platforms, people, processes, and security throughout the whole lifecycle. Doing this

DOI: 10.1201/9781003243021-14

will enable organizations to minimize errors, increase availability, ensure security, and operate more cost-effectively. Common proven benefits for organizations include:

- Reduce the cost of fixing security issues by 90%.
- Reduce incident recovery times by over 50%.
- Reduce the time-to-effective for new IT personnel.

You might not find excitement with your agency leadership if you want to request the purchase of the latest security tool, but you probably will if you talk about fewer outages, faster deployments, and lower manpower costs. And that's the key: if you focus your stakeholders and budget keepers on reducing outages, you'll get beyond just talking about fighting security-related issues.

The three basic concepts of Zero Outage are:

1. Reusable components including micro-services … imagine a Lego approach to IT development
2. Security end-to-end with the DevSecOps approach to system development
3. Situational Awareness and Automation using user and entity behavior analytics and automation

Zero Outage mirrors the requirements in the recent Executive Order on Cybersecurity, as well as the recently required Trusted Internet Connection (TIC) 3.0 requirements. Specifically, the four key principles are:

1. Limiting access greatly limits breach impacts
2. Automating to improve resiliency and reduce exposure window
3. Reducing the value of exfiltrated data
4. Managing risks inherent in using open source components (securing your software supply chain)

And the key technology concepts which are very prominent in both the EO and TIC 3.0 are:

1. Least privilege access management, also known as Zero Trust
2. Data privacy and protection
3. User and entity behavior analytics, or UEBA
4. Security orchestration and response, or SOAR

14.0.1 ABOUT MICROFOCUS GOVERNMENT SOLUTIONS

MFGS, Inc. – the Master Supplier to the US Government for Micro Focus enterprise-grade, scalable software solutions – helps organizations and agencies leverage MFGS' best in class portfolio of enterprise-grade scalable software solutions to solve mission-critical IT challenges, foster digital transformation, strengthen cyber resilience, run and transform business, provide critical tools to build, operate, analyze, and secure data, applications, and identities.

14.1 CYBERSECURITY AND ZERO OUTAGE: WHERE CISOs AND MISSION LEADERS ALIGN

John Fanguy
CTO, Micro Focus Government Solutions

14.1.1 INTRODUCTION

The May 2021 Cybersecurity Executive Order has re-focused all Federal agencies on formalizing and accelerating many cybersecurity goals and mandates, including the new TIC 3.0 and various existing and pending legislation including the Information Transparency and Personal Data Control Act [1, 2, 3, 4]. As agencies move to modify programs and plans to achieve compliance with the executive order, there is an additional perspective to consider which would deliver operational improvements without additional costs: Zero Outage. Zero Outage is an approach to delivering and evolving IT is proven to help large IT organizations reduce development and support costs, improve responsiveness to mission needs, and reduce the inherent security risks in development and operations. Zero Outage concepts can help Federal agencies achieve significant reductions in costs and reduced cyberattack exposure. Key features include cloud management with consumable services, built-in security governance during development, and achieving real-time monitoring, scalability, etc. [5]

Outages of IT services are most often associated with the misbehavior or errors of operating personnel or with technical problems—which might, for example, be attributed to errors in the design. Analysis has shown that over the past five years, 76% of all published cyber vulnerabilities were from applications. Given this radical shift in attacker focus, it's time to embed security from design, through development, and into production. The best way to do this is to focus on building safer code during initial development rather than waiting for a security acceptance test late in the development cycle [6].

Zero outage is a growing global approach and framework that emphasizes standardization in the quality of IT platforms, people, processes, and security throughout the whole lifecycle [5]. Doing this will enable organizations to minimize errors, increase availability, ensure security, and operate more cost-effectively. This enables government agencies to:

- Reduce the cost of fixing security issues by 90%.
- Reduce incident recovery times by over 50%.
- Reduce the time-to-effective for new IT personnel.

Over 45% of federal agencies' security breaches are now indirect, as threat actors target the weak links in their extended operation. This is modestly higher than global responses, where indirect attacks represent 40% of security breaches. This shift to indirect attacks blurs the true scale of cyberthreats. Organizations should look beyond their four walls to protect their operational ecosystems and supply chains. Fully 85% of federal respondents, in line with the global responses (82%), agreed their organizations need to think beyond securing their enterprises and take steps to secure their ecosystems to be effective.

Surveyed organizations, on average, spend 11% of their IT budgets on cybersecurity programs (10% exactly for federal agencies). Leaders spend slightly more at 11.2%, which is insufficient to account for their dramatically higher levels of performance [7].

Often, CIOs, CISOs, and program leaders in agencies have diverging or different priorities. As you can see from industry-leading recent surveys of Federal executives in IT and mission areas, there are similar but different priorities. Zero Outage concepts allow all three to find common ground for investments [8].

TABLE 14.1.1
Ranked Leadership Priorities

Rank	CISO Priorities *Gartner* Top Priorities IT Leadership	CIO Priorities *IDG State of the CIO*	Program Manager Priorities *CIO.gov*
1	Protecting Assets with Least Privilege	Security management	Deliver smarter, better, faster service to citizens
2	Shifting Identity Management	Improving IT operations performance	Efficiency: Maximize value of federal spending
3	Integrating DevSecOps	Aligning IT initiatives with organization goals	Deploy a world-class workforce and create a culture of excellence
4	Continuous Auditing and Reporting	Aligning IT initiatives with business goals	Support innovation, economic growth, and job creation
5	Moving to Proactive vs. Reactive	Driving innovation	

Source: [9, 10, 11].

In the following sections, we present four actionable initiatives that are already mandated by legislation or executive orders yet have not gotten enough priority within agencies to implement, and hence the government remains exposed to—and recently attacked successfully by—threats unnecessarily. Additionally, these 4 initiatives alone address 6 of the top 14 priorities of key leaders within Federal agencies, featured in Table 14.1.1 above.

In the sections below, we outline specific cybersecurity initiatives included in the Executive Order, which are specifically aligned with the benefits of a Zero Outage perspective.

14.1.2   LIMITING ACCESS GREATLY LIMITS BREACH IMPACTS

"Trust, but verify" is an old Russian proverb made famous by Ronald Reagan. With the growing number and increasing aggressiveness of nation-state actors, the Federal government is dangerously relying only on verification for access to IT systems. Trust is the missing component.

In 2008, the US Department of Defense suffered a significant compromise of its classified military computer networks. It began when an infected flash drive was inserted into a US military laptop at a base in the Middle East. The flash drive's malicious computer code, placed there by a foreign intelligence agency, uploaded itself onto a network run by the US Central Command. That code spread undetected on both classified and unclassified systems, establishing what amounted to a digital beachhead from which data could be transferred to servers under foreign control. Effectively, a rogue program was inside the wire, poised to deliver active military defensive plans to an unknown adversary [12].

Moreover, in 2020 and 2021, all five branches of the US Military, The US Pentagon, State Department, NASA, NSA, Department of Justice, and other Federal agencies were compromised by the recent SolarWinds/Microsoft Breach through a variety of sophisticated attack methods including significantly exploited credentials of both administrators and system processes [11].

These two of many incidents demonstrate that even though perimeter- and application-level security are the current standards in Federal, lateral movement and privilege escalation allow virtually unlimited access to data through an application, regardless of the in-transit, application, and at-rest encryption methods and tools used.

The resulting Zero Trust architecture means exactly that: Nothing is trusted inside or outside the network. Entry requires strict access controls, user authentication, and continuous monitoring of networks and systems, among many elements. Users and devices that request access to resources are continually authenticated.

Zero Trust focuses on protecting resources (assets, services, workflows, network accounts, etc.), rather than network elements because the data within the networked assets is at risk once the network perimeter has been breached. While it's a large effort in total, beginning to address Zero Trust with practical, tactical investments can yield significant reductions in both the frequency of breach and breach impacts.

Authentication and authorization, both subject and device, are discrete functions performed before a session to an enterprise resource is established. Zero Trust is a response to enterprise network trends that include remote users, bring your own device (BYOD), and cloud-based assets that are not located within an enterprise-owned network boundary.

In December 2018, the White House released an updated draft of its Trusted Internet Connection policy (TIC 3.0), which is a program created by the federal government to consolidate the number of external internet connections within agencies so that IT teams can more efficiently manage security efforts. While the prior versions of TIC, 1.0 and 2.0, centered on network and endpoint security, TIC 3.0 addresses the new reality: data access and user/entity behaviors within Federal systems are the real concern [4].

TIC 3.0 recognizes perimeter-based security is no longer sufficient. This is due in part to so many users or systems working outside the perimeter, and malicious actors have become far more proficient at stealing credentials and getting inside the perimeter [4].

Consequently, the best policy is to trust no one. The Zero Trust security model ensures security in an environment in which cloud, mobility, and related technologies have diminished the effectiveness of perimeter-based security. Zero Trust also recognizes that in this era of phishing attacks and stolen credentials, there is no meaningful distinction between internal and external threats. Everyone on the network must be seen as a potential threat. Practically speaking, that means every time a user (or system) requests access to applications, data, or other network resources, the network should verify identity and privilege and whether the user or system should have access to that resource.

14.1.3 AUTOMATING TO IMPROVE RESILIENCY AND REDUCE EXPOSURE WINDOW

Mission effectiveness requires highly reliable and continuous availability. Guaranteeing uptime beyond 99.5% can be a challenge when a system is under attack or even during peak usage hours, as we experienced in national emergencies. Figure 14.1.1 shows the discrepancies between leaders',

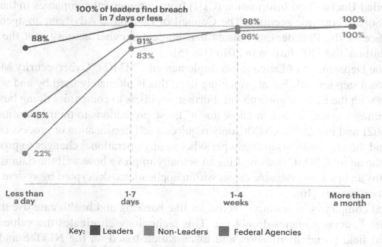

FIGURE 14.1.1 Average time to detect a security breach. (*Source*: [7].)

agencies', and non-leaders' ability to detect a security breach a different time points. Automating mundane and repetitive tasks with workflow processes can be a significant force multiplier for human assets, which can drive much higher system availability. According to Accenture, on average within the first day of a breach, 88 percent of leaders, 45 percent of Federal agencies, 22 percent of non-leaders can detect a security breaches. Within a week, 100 percent of breaches against leaders, 91 percent of breaches against Federal agencies, and 83 percent of breaches against non-leaders were detected. The last decade of rapidly evolving operations orchestration software (aka, robotic process automation) has now begun to help SOC personnel and can handle up to 50% or more of incident response tasks. Workflow automation and AI can interrogate endpoints, configure the setting on network hardware, isolate devices, and lockout or modify permissions on user and even system accounts. These technologies also assist human analysts by gathering data to speed analysis and undertake remediation. In use case studies, integrated AI and machine learning can speed the investigation of and response to incidents by a factor of 10 [7].

At present, organizations routinely respond to large volumes of alerts and threat data requiring immediate attention. To manage the unrelenting flow of increasingly complex event information, agencies are now leveraging machine-driven automated activities. Agencies moving toward TIC 3.0 and Zero Trust will benefit from technologies that help organizations to have a central place for collecting alerts and threat feeds—and to respond and remediate incidents at machine speed.

A recent Forrester *study* concluded that by implementing an integrated enterprise SOAR platform, organizations would experience benefits of [13, 14]:

- Saving an average of more than one hour of analyst time for each security incident
- Reduction of hardware and software tool maintenance costs by elimination of duplicate products
- Increased end-used productivity by reduction in cyber incident-related remediation downtime
- Improved audit efficiency

14.1.4   REDUCING THE VALUE OF EXFILTRATED DATA

The most recent breaches involving third party software products, both commercial and open-source, have proven that eventually, data will be exfiltrated. Data exfiltration is the primary target for hackers, whether it be PII, credit card and social security info, health records, or in the case of the OPM breach, foreign contacts of US citizens applying for a security clearance. The aggregate loss of Controlled Unclassified Information (CUI) from commercial companies in the US increases the risk to national economic security. The Council of Economic Advisers, an agency within the Executive Office of the President, estimates that malicious cyber activity cost the US economy between $57 billion and $109 billion in 2016 [14, 15].

Recently, the Department of Defense has implemented CMMC ("Cybersecurity Maturity Model Certification) as a step towards better protecting data; this is ultimately used by and with companies doing business with the Federal government. Further, suppliers to companies doing business with the Federal government will also have to "flow down" those protections to their operations. Practically speaking, in 2021 and into 2022, CMMC only requires a self-certification of process controls around data usage. And the certifications are only periodic, so any operational changes to processes or software obviate the audit. CMMC does nothing to actually improve how well the data is protected. So the data remains an open and valuable target within applications, decrypted by system processes and applications continuously [16].

Commercial companies in sensitive industries like banking and health care use this technology pervasively, but Federal agencies do not yet. This technology eliminates the value of stolen data through partial field pseudonymization and tokenization based on the NIST Standard 800-53G, Format Preserving Encryption (FPE) [17, 18].

These solutions encrypt partial fields of sensitive data like social security numbers or medical information but allow the data to be used by applications and data analytics.

Applications, users, malware, and bad actors all have access to the data, but only authorized users/apps can decrypt the de-identified fields on an exception basis. In many cases, data does not need to be de-identified, for example, such as the first five digits of a social security number when using the last four for user identification. And because the data maintains referential integrity, analytics can be run against even the encrypted data.

14.1.5 MANAGING RISKS INHERENT IN USING OPEN SOURCE COMPONENTS (SECURING YOUR SOFTWARE SUPPLY CHAIN)

The inside threat today exists largely in the form of application code. Third-party components make up a significant portion of many applications' codebase, making Software Composition Analysis (SCA) a "must-have" AppSec capability. On average, applications used by government agencies are 80% custom code or open-source code, and over 60% of cybersecurity data breaches can be traced to software defects. They're not from a vendor that has enterprise-grade software testing capabilities. Cyber incidents and breaches are, 85% of the time, the 90% of applications that rely on third-party libraries that comprise up to 70% of code [6].

14.1.5.1 ABOUT THE AUTHOR

John Fanguy is a former Federal technology executive who has spent 30 years serving Federal and Fortune 1,000 organizations in both consulting and operational roles. During his 14 years at Accenture, he served clients globally, designing, developing, and operating innovative solutions in customer care, infrastructure operations, financial systems, and logistics. John has more than a decade of helping deliver innovative Federal programs to agencies throughout the Federal government including DoD, DHS, Commerce, and HHS. John received his Bachelor's and Masters of Electrical Engineering from Georgia Tech. He is an active mentor to early-stage, leading-edge software technology companies.

REFERENCES

1. "Executive Order on Improving the Nation's Cybersecurity | The White House", *The White House*, 2021. [Online]. Available: https://www.whitehouse.gov/briefing-room/presidential-actions/2021/05/12/executive-order-on-improving-the-nations-cybersecurity/. [Accessed: 20- Jul- 2022].
2. "TIC | CISA", *Cisa.gov*, 2021. [Online]. Available: https://www.cisa.gov/trusted-internet-connections. [Accessed: 20- Jul- 2022].
3. S. Delbene, "H.R. 1816 - Information Transparency & Personal Data Control Act", *Delbene.house.gov*, 2021. [Online]. Available: https://delbene.house.gov/uploadedfiles/delbene_privacy_bill_final.pdf. [Accessed: 20- Jul- 2022].
4. "Achieve Zero Trust with TIC 3.0", *Mfgsinc.com*, 2021. [Online]. Available: https://www.mfgsinc.com/resources/security-risk/achieve-zero-trust-with-tic-30. [Accessed: 20- Jul- 2022].
5. "CIO Council Priorities - The President's Management Agenda (PMA)", *Cio.gov*, 2021. [Online]. Available: https://www.cio.gov/pma/. [Accessed: 20- Jul- 2022].
6. "Resilient Digital Public Sector and Government Services", *CyberRes*, 2021. [Online]. Available: https://www.microfocus.com/media/ flyer/resilient-digital-public-sector-and-government-services-flyer.pdf. [Accessed: 20- Jul- 2022].
7. L. Oliver and P. Hartley, "Building government resiliency with strategic foresight", *Accenture.com*, 2022. [Online]. Available: https://www.accenture.com/us-en/industries/afs-index?c=psv_us_accenturefedera_10490752&n=psgs_brand_0119&gclid=EAIaIQobChMIuYa1hrq18AIVGfbjBx0mtwCxEAAYASAAEgLtu_D_BwE&gclsrc=aw.ds. [Accessed: 20- Jul- 2022].
8. E. Kedrosky, "New CISO Priorities of 2021", *Sonrai | Enterprise Cloud Security Platform*, 2021. [Online]. Available: https://sonraisecurity.com/blog/new-ciso-priorities-of-2021/. [Accessed: 20- Jul- 2022].

9. C. Howard, "Top Priorities for IT: Leadership Vision for 2021", *Gartner*, 2021. [Online]. Available: https://emtemp.gcom.cloud/ngw/globalassets/en/publications/documents/top-priorities-for-it-leadership-vision-for-2021-security-risk-leaders-ebook.pdf. [Accessed: 20- Jul- 2022].

10. "CIOs Take the Reins in the Year of the Pandemic", *IDG*, 2021. [Online]. Available: https://f.hubspotusercontent40.net/hubfs/1624046/2021_SoCIO_ExS_R2.pdf?__hstc=164992608.531c4f260a9b7f7e61425e50e68cf365.1620318667221.1620318667221.1620318667221.1&__hssc=164992608.2.1620318667222&__hsfp=294629276&hsCtaTracking=d5d69771-7907-455f-a6ad-492f22bb39b7%7Caf29282a-9ef0-4d13-bfea-9b7e6a1caea7. [Accessed: 20- Jul- 2022].

11. "Zero Outage Layered Model - Zero Outage", *Zero Outage*, 2021. [Online]. Available: https://zero-outage.com/the-standard/architecture/zero-outage-layered-model/. [Accessed: 20- Jul- 2022].

12. W. Lynn III, "Defending a New Domain: The Pentagon's Cyberstrategy", *Foreign Affairs*, 2010. [Online]. Available: https://www.foreignaffairs.com/articles/united-states/ 2010-09-01/defending-new-domain. [Accessed: 20- Jul- 2022].

13. A. Mellen, "Planning Is Paramount When Adopting SOAR", *Forrester*, 2022. [Online]. Available: https://www.forrester.com/blogs/planning-is-paramount-when-adopting-soar/. [Accessed: 20- Jul- 2022].

14. "The Total Economic Impact Of IBM Security SOAR", *Ibm.com*, 2021. [Online]. Available: https://www.ibm.com/downloads/cas/ADBYOMO4. [Accessed: 20- Jul- 2022].

15. "The Cost of Malicious Cyber Activity to the U.S. Economy", *Hsdl.org*, 2018. [Online]. Available: https://www.hsdl.org/?view&did=808776. [Accessed: 20- Jul- 2022].

16. "The CMMC – Myths and realities", *SecureCyber Defense*, 2021. [Online]. Available: https://securecyberdefense.com/ the-cmmc-myths-and-realities/. [Accessed: 20- Jul- 2022].

17. "SP 800-53 Rev. 5 Security and Privacy Controls for Information Systems and Organizations", *Csrc.nist.gov*, 2020. [Online]. Available: https://csrc.nist.gov/publications/detail/sp/800-53/rev-5/final. [Accessed: 20- Jul- 2022].

18. "New NIST Security Standard Can Protect Credit Cards, Health Information", 2016. [Online]. Available: https://www.nist. gov/news-events/news/2016/03/new-nist-security-standard-can-protect-credit-cards-health-information. [Accessed: 20- Jul- 2022].

14.2 MANAGING GLOBAL SUPPLY CHAINS AND THEIR IMPACT ON US CRITICAL INFRASTRUCTURE: WHAT DO CRITICAL INFRASTRUCTURE SECTORS NEED TO DO, NOW AND IN THE FUTURE?

Donald R. Davidson Jr.
Director Cyber-Supply Chain Risk Management (C-SCRM) Programs, Synopsys

The US must ensure its Supply Chains are reliable, safe and secure to include the hardware, software and services that enable all of our US Critical Infrastructure Sector capabilities. This essay will address:

1. CHALLENGE: Information Communications Technology (ICT) is not always trustworthy.
2. What is the overall problem with Cyber-SCRM in US Critical Infrastructure Sectors?
3. VISION: Supply Chain Illumination
4. Can US Critical Infrastructure see into its Supply Chain & Manage Associated Risk?
5. Gaining supply chain visibility and discerning when and where it's needed to inform risk decisions
6. WAY-AHEAD: What do the Sectors need to do?

14.2.1 CHALLENGE: INFORMATION COMMUNICATIONS TECHNOLOGY (ICT) IS NOT ALWAYS TRUSTWORTHY

14.2.1.1 WHAT IS THE OVERALL PROBLEM WITH CYBER-SCRM IN US CRITICAL INFRASTRUCTURE SECTORS?

In today's globally sourced, hyper-connected, and information-enabled world, the "nail" (below) could be a hardware (HW) or software (SW) sub-component anywhere in the supply chain of the design manufacture and delivery process or the supply chain of the operations and sustainment lifecycle.

> For want of a nail, the shoe was lost;
> For want of the shoe, the horse was lost;
> For want of the horse, the rider was lost;
> For want of the rider, the battle was lost;
> For want of the battle, the kingdom was lost;
> And all for the want of a horseshoe nail …

This poem (or an earlier version of it) is attributed to Benjamin Franklin. Its earliest known appearance was in the Poor Richard's Almanack of 1758 [1].

> These chips are a wonder of innovation and design that power so much of our country and enable so much of our modern lives…. We need to make sure these supply chains are secure and reliable.
>
> **—President Biden, Feb. 24, 2021**

The same can be said for the software that enables it all.

The US must ensure its Supply Chains are reliable, safe, and secure. by evaluating the hardware, software, and services that enable all of our US Critical Infrastructure Sector capabilities. 2021–2022 Executive Orders have emphasized the need to secure America's Supply Chains and improve the

Nation's Cybersecurity [2]. On February 24, 2021, the White House issued "Executive Order on America's Supply Chains." This Supply Chain Executive Order asked for a quick-turn report within 100 days on four "critical" industries and their associated supply chains. Specific government agencies were assigned to lead the quick-turn review as follows [3]:

Industry/Supply Chain Issues	Responsible Agency
Semiconductor manufacturing	Department of Commerce
High-capacity batteries (including for electric vehicles)	Department of Energy
Rare earth elements	Department of Defense
Pharmaceuticals	Department of Health and Human Services

All critical infrastructure sectors should be doing this same 100-day quick review internally, identifying their most critical capabilities, systems, and associated enabling HW, SW, and Services and following up with a year-long study/report on the supply chains of those critical capabilities, systems, and components. Ultimately. Sectors should develop a full C-SCRM Plan in accordance with NIST SP 800-161 and a C-SCRM/Cybersecurity "Controls Overlay" based on NIST 800-53 rev5 [4].

On May 12, 2021, the White House issued an "Executive Order on Improving the Cybersecurity" The EO says: "… the Colonial Pipeline incident is a reminder that federal action alone is not enough. Much of our domestic critical infrastructure is owned and operated by the private sector, and those private sector companies make their own determination regarding cybersecurity investments. We encourage private sector companies to follow the Federal government's lead and take ambitious measures to augment and align cybersecurity investments with the goal of minimizing future incidents." Tenets of the executive order include:

- Remove Barriers to Threat Information Sharing Between Government and Private Sector.
- Modernize and Implement Stronger Cybersecurity Standards in the Federal Govt.
- Improve Software Supply Chain Security.
- Establish a Cybersecurity Safety Review Board.
- Create a Standard Playbook for Responding to Cyber Incidents.
- Improve Detection of Cybersecurity Incidents on Federal Government Networks.
- Improve Investigative and Remediation Capabilities.

14.2.1.2 Events in Early 2021 Highlight Software and Supply Chain Threats to US Critical Infrastructure

In January and February 2021, hackers attempted to sabotage water treatment facilities servicing San Francisco and Tampa [5], respectively;

Moreover, the early 2021 Dark Side attack on Colonial Pipeline is just one example of the more frequent, more lethal software and supply chain attacks on the US energy sector [6].

This Information Communications Technology (ICT)/Cyber Supply Chain Risk Management (C-SCRM) challenge has been evolving over the last few decades, where ICT developers, providers, and consumers have been more focused on cost and schedule (how do I get it fast and cheap) to gain a desired functional capability—often, unknowingly, trading-off security, and sustainability of those capabilities [7]. It now appears that the United States is getting serious about developing a stronger but still risk-based approach to Cyber-SCRM to better include sustainability and security concerns in our ICT development and acquisition processes.

In April 2021, Semiconductor Industry Association and Boston Consulting Group (SIA & BCG) published "Strengthening the Global Semiconductor Supply Chain in an Uncertain Era," calling for government actions to promote long-term supply chain resilience [8]:

1. Guarantee a level global playing field for domestic and foreign firms alike, as well as strong protection of intellectual property rights;
2. Promote global trade and international collaboration on R&D and technology standards;
3. Invest in basic research, STEM education, and workforce development;
4. Advance immigration policies that enable leading global semiconductor clusters to attract world-class talent; and
5. Establish a clear and stable framework for targeted controls on semiconductor trade that avoid broad unilateral restrictions on technologies and vendors.

In April 2021, US National Institute for Standards and Technology and Cybersecurity and Infrastructure Security Agency (NIST & CISA) published "Defending Against Software Supply Chain Attacks," providing [9]:

an overview of software supply chain risks and recommendations on how software customers and vendors can use the National Institute of Standards and Technology (NIST) Cyber Supply Chain Risk Management (C-SCRM) framework and the Secure Software Development Framework (SSDF) to identify, assess, and mitigate risks.

A likely first step is developing a Software Build of Material (SBOM, not yet fully defined); this is basically an asset/SW inventory of what makes up your enterprise.

On April 20, 2021, the Center for New America Security (CNAS) published "Trust the Process: National Technology Strategy Development, Implementation, and Monitoring and Evaluation," calling for a new National Strategy on Technology, embracing four pillars of "Promote, Protect, Partner and Plan" [10].

On May 19, 2021, the Center for Strategic and International Studies (CSIS) published, "Mapping the National Security Industrial Base: Policy Shaping Issues," addressing the National Security Industrial Base, past, present, and future [11].

On May 20, 2021, Dark Reading published "How 2 New Executive Orders May Reshape Cybersecurity & Supply Chains for a Post-Pandemic World," stating [12]:

The biggest risk emerging from these orders is the inherent tendency to look backward and revert to paradigms of previous eras. In fact, the strong economic nationalism spreading across the globe is a great example of this risk. The complexity and interdependence of today's supply chains, coupled with the global and dynamic threat landscape, render economic nationalism a self-defeating strategy. These executive orders, fortunately, balance inward investment with outward collaboration. Each is essential to promote competition, security, and innovation domestically while leveraging the comparative advantages of democratic allies and movement toward trustworthy and secure products and networks....

Both executive orders address the need for collective economic and national security with allies, like-minded countries, and the private sector as essential to the collective security of all.

14.2.3 WHAT IS ICT/CYBER-SCRM?

14.2.3.1 KEY DEFINITIONS

From NIST [13]:

The ICT supply chain infrastructure is the integrated set of components (hardware, software and processes) within the organizational boundary that composes the environment in which a system is developed or manufactured, tested, deployed, maintained, and retired/decommissioned. Whereas C-SCRM covers the full lifecycle [13].

ICT Supply Chain Risk are (r)*isks that arise from the loss of confidentiality, integrity, or availability of information or information systems and reflect the potential adverse impacts to organizational operations (including mission, functions, image, or reputation), organizational assets, individuals, other organizations, and the Nation.*

ICT Supply Chain Risk Management, (now called Cyber-SCRM) *is the process of identifying, assessing, and mitigating the risks associated with the global and distributed nature of ICT product and service supply chains.* NIST has since defined cyber supply chain risk management (C-SCRM) as *the process of identifying, assessing, and mitigating the risks associated with the distributed and interconnected nature of [IT] product and service supply chains.*—This definition distinguishes C-SCRM as an ongoing activity, rather than a single task, and accounts for the procurement and maintenance of hardware and software. With growth of the Internet-of-Things (IoT), C-SCRM is not limited to information systems/networks; it extends to all Information technology and operational technology (IT / OT) components, leveraging hardware assurance (HwA), software assurance (SwA) and assured services.

14.2.3.2 BACKGROUND: THE GLOBAL SUPPLY CHAIN

Supply chains consist of people (to include both individuals and organizations), processes, and technologies. The ICT ecosystem has rapidly evolved to be a globally connected, interdependent supply chain network delivering relatively inexpensive ICT in a rapid fashion; unfortunately, most of these ICT products often do not adequately consider end users' security needs. Products often function "as intended," but little is done to evaluate if they function "only as intended." Consumers often unknowingly trade off security requirements for fast acquisition of less expensive ICT products. Increasingly there are governmental (US and others) regulations weighing in to bring more balance to ICT lifecycle cost, schedule, and performance trades (with security being an often under-valued performance characteristic until recently). Sometimes individual National Security concerns will precipitate more severe restrictions on products, companies, and possibly countries; hopefully, we can identify mitigations that fall short of this generalized "blacklisting."

ICT supply chains are complex interconnected ecosystems that span the entire lifecycle of hardware, software, and managed services from third-party vendors, suppliers, service providers, and contractors. As the adage goes, "a supply chain is only as strong as its weakest link." Gaining comprehensive visibility of any supply chain is challenging but a "Zero Trust" risk-based-approach to C-SCRM may prove effective and practical provided that it focuses on functional resiliency that includes a whole of lifecycle approach and continual data collection and analysis [14]. Risk exists on a spectrum; just because a vulnerability exists does not mean that it will be exploited. It behooves managers to prioritize vulnerabily mitigation and remediation according to the likelihood an adversary will leverage an exploit to inflict a harm on a critical system.

Threat actors target government and industry ICT supply chains to steal, compromise, alter, and destroy sensitive information and they may compromise vendor or downstream systems to laterally compromise the supply chain. CISA advises, "Vulnerabilities may be introduced during any phase of the product life cycle: design, development and production, distribution, acquisition and deployment, maintenance, and disposal. These vulnerabilities can include the incorporation of malicious software, hardware, and counterfeit components; flawed product designs; and poor manufacturing processes and maintenance procedures" [15]. Attackers may not be cognizant of the defensive posture of compromised systems and the uncertainty creates the potential to leverage purposefully embedded vulnerabilities to detect and expose adversarial efforts. Adversarial campaigns against valuable systems should be resource intensive if defensive technologies are properly deployed. The chance of exposure and loss of resources should be weaponized as a deterrent against attackers seeking to mass compromise technology (i.e. an entire commercial-off-the-shelf, COTS, product line)—but may drive them to pursue specific tailored supply-chain attacks against deliberate targets instead.

NIST Special Publication 800-161 on ICT-SCRM provides guidance to federal agencies on how they can align C-SCRM with an organization's existing risk management framework [13]. Activities for risk management include cataloguing current systems and business practices, surveying systems for vulnerabilities, and developing processes to mitigate those vulnerabilities on an ongoing basis [13]. C-SCRM needs to be incorporated in an organization's overall enterprise risk management process.

Conceptualizing risk depends on the availability of dynamic threat information, an assessment and appreciation of vulnerabilities in deployed systems, and a framework that makes security decisions according to prioritization of risk and available resources. Supply chain entities may lack the expertise or IT threat information necessary to properly manage risk or thwart supply chain threat actors. Federal agencies, private sector leaders, and upstream supply chain partners should collaborate with their partners to prioritize risk management, help entities assess vulnerabilities, identify threats, and determine why they may be targeted, who or what may target them, and how. In order to extend these principles to their supply chain, entities will also need information on their vendors and suppliers, threat tactics, and best practices to mitigate risk [13].

Risk profiles (e.g., risk tolerance, resource allocations, vulnerabilities, threats, etc.) and effective management are unique and vary from one entity or sector to another [13]. This makes managing risk an activity which is individualized for each entity or sector. However, there are policy areas in which any organization may act with regard to C-SCRM that can affect their supply chain risk decisions.

14.2.4   VISION: SUPPLY CHAIN ILLUMINATION: CAN US CRITICAL INFRASTRUCTURE SEE INTO ITS SUPPLY CHAIN AND MANAGE ASSOCIATED RISK?

USG and Critical Infrastructure commercial partners facilitate and enable an ecosystem that delivers safe, secure, high quality, state-of-the-art technology in a timely manner at affordable prices enabling critical infrastructure capabilities. Each sector manages its internal processes and works with supply chain partners to tailor risk-based processes to deliver products to customers that meet or exceed their specific requirements and needs.

Critical Infrastructure Section Leaders and Communities of Practice/Interest define and implement their own C-SCRM requirements and plans but share information with USG and other Sectors as appropriate; Sectors incorporate/leverage C-SCRM best practices, and lessons learned from supply chain partners, trade associations, standards development organizations, and other applicable governmental laws, regulations and contracts, as appropriate.

Most sectors already have some form of Quality and Configuration Management (QCM) and Safety policy, program/plan, and process. Sectors can leverage these QCM and Safety successes to evolve and improve their Third-Party Risk (3PR) programs, ensuring their Sector (and others') information is protected by supply chain partners. QCM and 3PR programs should already have a good start on confidentiality and availability. New Critical Infrastructure ICT or Cyber-Supply Chain Risk Management (C-SCRM) policy/program(s) need to focus more on the integrity of the products or services they consume or build into their sectors.

Critical Infrastructure C-SCRM policy/program(s) will improve visibility into their supply chains, with the ability to illuminate their supply chains when and where necessary, enabling better C-SCRM and the ability to best address customer questions/requirements on C-SCRM. Sectors should strive to achieve and maintain a full HW/SW Bill-of-Materials (BOM, yet to be fully defined) for all functional capabilities and products. This may not be possible initially, and functional capability and product owners may have to adopt a risk-based approach to their supply chain visibility and their HW/SW BOM and initially focus on their more critical functions and systems.

14.2.5   PLAN OF ACTION AND MILESTONES (POAM): WHAT DO THE SECTORS NEED TO DO? (HIGH LEVEL)

1. **Conduct Criticality Analysis:** Identify the Sector's most critical functions/capabilities & enabling systems and components.
2. **Illuminate Supply Chains:** Begin a risk-based approach to illuminate the Sector's supply chains of those critical systems and components.

3. Identify Risks associated with the People, Processes, and Technologies developing, delivering, and sustaining those critical systems and components of the Sector.
4. Develop Mitigations for the development, delivery, use, and sustainment of those critical systems and components of the Sector.

Simplistically, Critical Infrastructure Sectors need to follow guidance from US National Supply Chain Integrity month May 2021 website, by the Office of the Director for National Intelligence (ODNI) ICT/Cyber-SCRM "Best Practices" [16]

- Obtain Executive Level Commitment for Supply Chain Risk Management Program
  - Build and Integrated Enterprise Team
  - Communicate across the Organization
  - Establish Training and Awareness Programs
- Identify Critical Systems, Networks, and Information
  - Exercise Asset Management
  - Prioritize Critical Systems, Networks, and Information
  - Employ Mitigation Tools
- Manage Third-Party Risk
  - Conduct Due Diligence
  - Incorporate SCRM Requirements into Contracts
  - Monitor Compliance

Sectors should develop a PLAN OF ACTION & MILESTONES (POAM) for their C-SCRM activities and track their progress to mature their C-SCRM capabilities.

NIST SP 800-161 suggests a F-A-R-M interactive model for practicing/implementing C-SCRM depicted below in Figure 14.2.1.

Frame + Assess + Respond + Manage = FARM, which is similar to Synopsys' Plan-Do-Check-Act model in the QA/CM policy/plan.

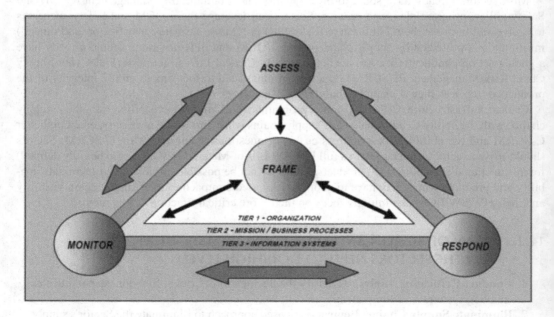

FIGURE 14.2.1   NIST F-A-R-M model.

TABLE 14.2.1
Supply Chain Risk Management Stakeholders (NIST SP 800-161)

Tier Name	Generic Stakeholder	Activities
Organization	Executive Leadership (CXOs)	Define corporate strategy, policy, goals, and objectives
Mission (& Product Lines)	Business Management, Program Management [PM], & Systems Development Life Cycle (SDLC) ... (including) management related to reliability, safety, security, quality, etc.)	Develop actionable policies and procedures, guidance, constraints, and implementation (day-to-day activities).
Information System	Systems (Risk) Management (throughout the SDLC)	Policy Implementation, requirements, constraints and implementations (day-to-day activities).

The steps in NIST SP 800-161's C-SCRM process—Frame, Assess, Respond, and Monitor—are iterative and not inherently sequential in nature. Different individuals may be required to perform the steps at the same time, depending on a particular need or situation. Organizations have significant flexibility in how the risk management steps are performed (e.g., sequence, degree of rigor, formality, and thoroughness of application) and in how the results of each step are captured and shared—both internally and externally. The outputs from a particular risk management step will directly impact one or more of the other risk management steps in the risk management process.

Below is extracted from Table 14.2.1.

The ICT/C-SCRM process should be carried out across the three risk management tiers with the overall objective of continuous improvement in the organization's risk-related activities and effective inter-tier and intra-tier communication, thus integrating both strategic and tactical activities among all stakeholders with a shared interest in the mission/business success of the organization. Whether addressing a component, a system, a process, a mission function, or a policy, it is important to engage the relevant ICT (Cyber) SCRM stakeholders at each tier to ensure that risk management activities are as informed as possible.

Generically, an effective Cyber-SCRM policy and program encompasses the following key points:

- **Foundational Practices:** C-SCRM lies at the intersection of cybersecurity and supply chain risk management. Existing cybersecurity and supply chain practices provide a foundation for building an effective C-SCRM program.
- **Organization-wide:** Effective C-SCRM is an organization-wide activity that involves each organizational tier (Organization, Mission/Business Processes & *Products*, and Information Systems), various organizational functions (cybersecurity, supply chain management, acquisition/procurement, legal, engineering, etc.), and is implemented throughout the system development life cycle.
- **Risk Management Process:** C-SCRM should be implemented as part of overall enterprise risk management activities. Activities should involve identifying and assessing applicable risks, determining appropriate mitigating actions, developing a C-SCRM Plan to document selected policies and mitigating actions, and monitoring performance against that Plan. Because cyber supply chains differ across and within organizations, the C-SCRM Plan should be tailored to individual, organizational contexts.
  - **Risk:** Cyber supply chain risks are associated with a lack of visibility into, understanding of, and control over many of the processes and decisions involved in the development, acquisition, and delivery of IT/OT products and services.

- **Threats and Vulnerabilities:** Effectively managing cyber supply chain risks requires a comprehensive view of threats and vulnerabilities. Threats can be either "adversarial" (e.g. tampering, counterfeits) or "non-adversarial" (e.g. poor quality, natural disasters); vulnerabilities may be "internal" (e.g. organizational procedures) or "external" (e.g. part of an organization's supply chain).
- **Critical Systems:** Cost-effective supply chain risk mitigation requires agencies to identify those systems/components that are most vulnerable and will cause the greatest organizational impact if compromised.

14.2.5.1 CRITICAL INFRASTRUCTURE SPECIFICS

Critical Infrastructure Sectors should begin to document, assess and report on their Cyber-SCRM practices; documenting the people/organizations, processes, and technologies involved in the design, build and delivery of hardware (HW), software (SW), and services supporting Sector-specific capabilities/systems and most specifically HW, SW, and services that enable those capabilities/ systems.

Each Sector can develop their own C-SCRM metrics and plans to support their capabilities and products, influencing how they mitigate risks in their C-SCRM efforts. These Sector-specific C-SCRM Plans and activities should be presented and discussed periodically in Sector Coordinating Councils (SCCs), Government Coordinating Councils (GCCs), and Information Sharing and Analysis Centers (ISACs). SCCs, GCCs, and/or ISACs will be used to share C-SCRM best practices and lessons learned to continuously improve enterprise-wide Sector-specific C-SCRM capabilities in each sector. Additionally, DHS/CISA should add C-SCRM as a regular Agenda-Item for the Cross-Sector Cybersecurity Working Group (CSCSWG).

Sectors should Initially start with USG C-SCRM requirements.

C-SCRM assessments will consider *People, Processes, and Technology* in the supply chain:

- the *People/Organizations* "touching" the design, delivery, or maintenance of product; what are their qualifications/credentials, what laws and rules must they follow, are there any other allegiances identified;
- the organizational *Processes* used in design, delivery, or maintenance of the product: (what processes are documented/certified) and,
- the importance of the *Technology* in the product (how critical is this technology/this product to the overall ecosystem, parent-product, or overall capability, as identified in criticality analysis; which components and sub-components critically enable capability).

Is the technology being assessed *hardware, software, or an enabling /supporting service?* What weaknesses and/or vulnerabilities might exist in the HW or SW? Has the providing organization provided any data from tests performed in their process; does the organization have any certifications for their product, for their people, their organization, or its processes?

C-SCRM processes are designed to prevent or minimize impact in loss/breach of confidentiality, integrity, or availability. (*Confidentiality, Integrity, and Availability* as defined in ISO/IEC 27002):

- **Confidentiality:** Ensuring that information is accessible only to those authorized to have access.
- **Integrity:** Safeguarding the accuracy and completeness of information and processing methods.
- **Availability:** Ensuring authorized users have access to information and associated assets when required.

Some other sector specific C-SCRM "requirements" may be developed from representative International standards with C-SCRM applications listed here (not a comprehensive list)

- ISO/IEC 27036 on Information Technology—Security techniques—Information security for supplier relationships
- ISO/IEC 20243 Information technology—Open Trusted Technology Provider Standard (O-TTPS)—Mitigating maliciously tainted and counterfeit products
- SAE/G32 on Cyber-Physical Systems Security

US Critical Infrastructure C-SCRM policies/programs will improve visibility into supply chains, enabling better C-SCRM and the ability to best address customer questions/requirements on C-SCRM. Sectors will strive to achieve and maintain a full HW/SW Bill-of-Materials (BOM, yet to be fully defined) for all Sector-specific functional capabilities and systems. This may not be possible initially, and functional capability and system owners may have to adopt a risk-based approach to their supply chain illumination/visibility and their HW/SW BOM, focusing on only the most critically enabling HW/SW and some percentage of their Tier 1 suppliers/providers. Additionally, there will be a judgment, by those owners, on whether it is more important to drill deeper into those Critical Tier 1 component providers (i.e. Tier2s, 3s, etc.) or is it more important to gain full visibility and analysis of the Tier1 providers. Ultimately there is a Sector goal of full supply chain visibility (or at least an ability to "illuminate" the supply where needed, identifying HW.SW BOM for Tiers 1, 2, and 3 (maybe more TBD for the most critical products and/or functional capabilities).

14.2.6   CONCLUSION

The United States has been working on this Cyber-SCRM Challenge for a while, and there is a wealth of information already published about this challenge and recommended ways to develop C-SCRM capabilities and how to manage global supply chain risks.

In April 2020, a response to Executive Order 13873 was published: "Methodology for Assessing the Most Critical Information and Communications Technologies and Services."

On May 15, 2019, the President signed Executive Order (EO) 13873: Securing the Information and Communications Technology and Services Supply Chain. This EO addresses the threat posed by the unrestricted acquisition or use of Information and Communications Technology (ICT) and services "designed, developed, manufactured, or supplied by persons owned by, controlled by, or subject to the jurisdiction or direction of foreign adversaries," and declares a national emergency with respect to this threat.

The DHS response to the EO says:

Information technology and communications technology intersects almost every aspect of operations essential to national security, the Nation's critical infrastructure, and National Critical Functions (NCFs). NCFs are those functions of government and the private sector so vital to the United States that their disruption, corruption, or dysfunction would have a debilitating impact on national security, national economic security, national public health or safety, or any combination thereof." Assessments "shall include an evaluation of hardware, software, or services relied upon by multiple information and communications technology or service providers, including the communications services relied upon by critical infrastructure entities identified pursuant to Section 9 of Executive Order 13636.

The DHS Fact Sheet on Executive Order 13636, "Improving Critical Infrastructure Cybersecurity," says:

Facing threats to our Nation from cyber attacks that could disrupt our power, water, communication and other critical systems, the President issued the Executive Order (EO) on Improving Critical Infrastructure Cybersecurity and Presidential Policy Directive (PPD) on Critical Infrastructure Security and Resilience. These policies reinforce the need for holistic thinking about security and risk management. Implementation of the EO and PPD will drive action toward system and network security and resiliency, and will also enhance the efficiency and effectiveness of the US government's work to secure critical infrastructure and make it more resilient.

The DoD and GSA response to EO 13636 says:

When the government purchases products or services with inadequate: 'built -in' cybersecurity, the risks persist throughout the lifespan of the item purchased. The lasting effect of inadequate cybersecurity in acquired items is part of what makes acquisition reform so important to achieving cybersecurity and resiliency. Purchasing products and services that have appropriate cybersecurity designed and built-in may have a higher up-front cost in some cases, but doing so reduces total cost of ownership by providing risk mitigation and reducing the need to fix vulnerabilities in fielded solutions.

And recommends:

I. Institute Baseline Cybersecurity Requirements as a Condition of Contract Award for Appropriate Acquisitions.
II. Address Cybersecurity in Relevant Training.
III. Develop Common Cybersecurity Definitions for Federal Acquisitions.
IV. Institute a Federal Acquisition Cyber Risk Management Strategy.
V. Include a Requirement to Purchase from Original Equipment Manufacturers, Their Authorized Resellers, or Other "Trusted" Sources, Whenever Available, in Appropriate Acquisitions.
VI. Increase Government Accountability for Cyber Risk Management.

Building cybersecurity into your acquisition processes goes hand-in-glove with Cyber-SCRM.

All of these *Recommended Critical Infrastructure C-SCRM Processes* are a start point for consideration. Sector-specific Functional Capability and Critical Systems Owners should develop their own Cyber-SCRM practices that best fit their overall Sector Risk Management.

14.2.6.1 ABOUT THE AUTHOR

After 44 years in the US Department of Defense (DoD), **Don Davidson** transitioned to Synopsys in the private sector. He is an Experienced Leader working with military, whole-of-government, and public-private partnerships with industry, academia, and international partners. He is skilled in STEM, Enterprise Risk Management, and M&S/data-analytics for both governmental and commercial organizations. He is a Strong Professional with a Master of Science (MS) degree in National Security Strategy from the US National Defense University and a Bachelor of Science in Engineering from the United States Military Academy at West Point.

REFERENCES

1. R. Williamson, "A Little Neglect May Breed Great Mischief", Citadel.edu, 2008. [Online]. Available: https://www.citadel.edu/root/images/commandant/assistant-commandant-leadership/for-the-want-of-a-nail.pdf. [Accessed: 21- Jul- 2022].
2. "Executive Order on America's Supply Chains | The White House", The White House, 2021. [Online]. Available: https://www.whitehouse.gov/briefing-room/presidential-actions/2021/02/24/executive-order-on-americas-supply-chains/. [Accessed: 21- Jul- 2022].
3. N. Snyder, T. Bourne and D. Gallacher, "At a Glance: White House 100-Day Supply Chain Report", The National Law Review, 2021. [Online]. Available: https://www.natlawreview.com/article/glance-white-house-100-day-supply-chain-report. [Accessed: 21- Jul- 2022].

4. "SP 800-53 Rev. 5: Security and Privacy Controls for Information Systems and Organizations", NIST, 2021. [Online]. Available: https://csrc.nist.gov/publications/detail/sp/800-53/rev-5/final. [Accessed: 21- Jul- 2022].

5. R. Fremery, "The Growing Threat of Water Supply Hacks - The LastPass Blog", The LastPass Blog, 2021. [Online]. Available: https://blog.lastpass.com/2021/07/the-growing-threat-of-water-supply-hacks/. [Accessed: 21- Jul- 2022].

6. J. Steele, "Energy Sector Cyberattacks: Threats Growing, Defenses Available - OILMAN Magazine", Oilmanmagazine.com, 2021. [Online]. Available: https://oilmanmagazine.com/article/energy-sector-cyberattacks-threats-growing-defenses-available/. [Accessed: 21- Jul- 2022].

7. "Executive Order on Improving the Nation's Cybersecurity", The White House, 2021. [Online]. Available: https://www.whitehouse.gov/briefing-room/presidential-actions/2021/05/12/executive-order-on-improving-the-nations-cybersecurity/. [Accessed: 21- Jul- 2022].

8. S. Ravi, "Strengthening the Global Semiconductor Supply Chain in an Uncertain Era", Semiconductor Industry Association, 2022. [Online]. Available: https://www.semiconductors.org/strengthening-the-global-semiconductor-supply-chain-in-an-uncertain-era/. [Accessed: 21- Jul- 2022].

9. "Defending Against Software Supply Chain Attacks", Cisa.gov, 2021. [Online]. Available: https://www.cisa.gov/sites/default/files/publications/defending_against_software_supply_chain_attacks_508_1.pdf. [Accessed: 21- Jul- 2022].

10. L. DeJonge Schulman and A. Riikonen, "Trust the Process", Cnas.org, 2021. [Online]. Available: https://www.cnas.org/publications/reports/trust-the-process. [Accessed: 21- Jul- 2022].

11. J. Lewis, "Mapping the National Security Industrial Base: Policy Shaping Issues", Csis.org, 2021. [Online]. Available: https://www.csis.org/analysis/mapping-national-security-industrial-base-policy-shaping-issues. [Accessed: 21- Jul- 2022].

12. A. Little Limbago, "How 2 New Executive Orders May Reshape Cybersecurity & Supply Chains for a Post-Pandemic World", Dark Reading, 2021. [Online]. Available: https://www.darkreading.com/operations/how-2-new-executive-orders-may-reshape-cybersecurity-and-supply-chains-for-a-post-pandemic-world/a/d-id/1340987. [Accessed: 21- Jul- 2022].

13. J. Boyens, A. Smith, N. Bartol, K. Winkler, A. Holbrook and M. Fallon, "SP 800-161 Rev. 1 Cybersecurity Supply Chain Risk Management Practices for Systems and Organizations", 2022. [Online]. Available: https://csrc.nist.gov/publications/detail/sp/800-161/rev-1/final. [Accessed: 21- Jul- 2022].

14. C. Jaikaran, "Cyber Supply Chain Risk Management: An Introduction", Congressional Research Service, 2022. [Online]. Available: https://sgp.fas.org/crs/homesec/IF10920.pdf. [Accessed: 21- Jul- 2022].

15. "Information and Communications Technology Supply Chain Risk Management", Cisa.gov, 2022. [Online]. Available: https://www.cisa.gov/supply-chain. [Accessed: 21- Jul- 2022].

16. "NATIONAL SUPPLY CHAIN INTEGRITY MONTH - CALL TO ACTION BEST PRACTICES", Dni.gov, 2021. [Online]. Available: https://www.dni.gov/files/NCSC/documents/supplychain/SC_Best_Practices_Final_2021.pdf. [Accessed: 21- Jul- 2022].

15 Nuclear Sector

15.0 ABOUT THE NUCLEAR REACTORS, MATERIAL, AND WASTE SECTOR

Drew Spaniel
Lead Researcher, Institute for Critical Infrastructure Technology (ICIT)

The Nuclear Reactors, Materials, and Waste sector is often overlooked in the recounting and consideration of critical infrastructures because its interdependencies with other sectors result in erroneous conflation. As a result, the sector may be underfunded, under-prioritized, and under-secured. Among other interdependencies, the sector produces the chemicals used in some electricity production, generates the radioactive materials used for healthcare procedures, and processes the byproducts of defense research. The sector itself is critically dependent on the transportation sector for secure transit, the Water and Wastewater Management sector for continuous cooling, and the Emergency Services sector for physical incident response. At the time of this writing, annually in the United States:

- Eight active Nuclear Fuel Cycle facilities process natural uranium into 5 percent Uranium-235, which is converted into solid Uranium Dioxide fuel pellets for reactors.
- Ninety-nine active and 18 decommissioning power reactors located in 30 states generate approximately one-fifth of the United States' electricity.
- Thirty-one research and test reactors are operated at universities and national labs to support STEM research and produce the medical and industrial isotopes necessary to treat cancer and perform radiographic services.
- Around 20 million medical procedures depend on these materials.
- Materials are sourced by more than 20,000 licensed users for medical diagnosis and treatment, oil and gas drilling depth measurements, food production sterilization, academic research, import and export monitoring, and other uses.

Despite popular misconceptions conflated by Cold War panic, a fearful conflation of the word "nuclear," false comparisons with Chernobyl and Fukushima, and a media misrepresentation of the events of Three Mile Island, nuclear has proven to be one of the safest and most promising forms of energy. In fact, there have been zero civilian deaths associated with the operation of nuclear power plants in the United States since their introduction over 60 years ago [1]. According to the University of California, living within 50 miles of a nuclear power plant (including right next door) would only impart about 0.09 μSv (microsieverts) on residents. For comparison, an airport security scan imparts about 0.25 μSv and a dental x-ray imparts about 5 μSv. A flight from LA to NY imparts about 40 μSv [2].

The transition to clean and independent energy is imperative for socioeconomic growth, geopolitical resiliency, and national security. Fossil fuels are dwindling, and estimates predict that they will be depleted past the point of economically feasible extraction no later than 2060 [3]. In April 2022, the Biden administration prudently launched a $6 billion initiative to bail out financially distressed nuclear power plants. According to Energy Secretary Jennifer Granholm, "U.S. nuclear power plants contribute more than half of our carbon-free electricity, and President Biden is committed to keeping these plants active to reach our clean energy goals. We're using every tool available to get this country powered by clean energy by 2035, and that includes prioritizing our existing

DOI: 10.1201/9781003243021-15

nuclear fleet to allow for continued emissions-free electricity generation and economic stability for the communities leading this important work" [4]. While this funding is a positive step, it is only a stop-gap and is insufficient to position the United States for future success. Rather than attempting to drag legacy nuclear infrastructure into the modern era, more efforts and resources need to be focused on commissioning efficient and modern nuclear infrastructure that incorporates security-by-design throughout the intended lifecycle of the plant.

If the United States does invest in secure nuclear infrastructure now, we may not have the resources necessary to meet our future energy needs. As global fossil fuel reserves deplete, our continued dependence on foreign energy could result severe challenges to our geopolitical and economic autonomy. The Nuclear Reactors, Material, and Waste sector can draw the United States into a new era; however, its potential value to the nation is proportional to its value as a target for malicious adversaries who are intent on relegating the United States to an economic dependent instead of a global leader. It will be a prime target of threat actors ranging in sophistication from nation-state advanced persistent threat (APTs) groups to ideologically motivated hacktivists. Targeted attacks to disrupt or subvert the operations of nuclear facilities could result in kinetic impacts such as radiation leaks or just do further damage to the public perception of nuclear power and result in a prolonged dependence on foreign resources. To realize the economic and technological growth promised by the nuclear energy, it is imperative that the administration prioritizes security and modernization throughout the nuclear sector.

15.0.1   ABOUT ICIT

The Institute for Critical Infrastructure Technology (ICIT) is a non-profit, non-partisan, and vendor agnostic 501c(3) cybersecurity Think Tank with a mission to cultivate a cybersecurity renaissance that will improve the resiliency of our Nation's critical infrastructure sectors, defend our democratic institutions, and empower generations of cybersecurity leaders.

REFERENCES

1. "Nuclear Reactors, Materials, and Waste Sector | CISA," *Cisa.gov*, 2022. [Online]. Available: https://www.cisa.gov/nuclear-reactors-materials-and-waste-sector. [Accessed: 15 April 2022].
2. "What to Know Before You Go Bananas about Radiation," *University of California*, 2017. [Online]. Available: https://www.universityofcalifornia.edu/news/what-know-you-go-bananas-about-radiation. [Accessed: 15 April 2022].
3. "When Fossil Fuels Run Out, What Then?," *Stanford.edu*, 2019. [Online]. Available: https://mahb.stanford.edu/library-item/fossil-fuels-run/. [Accessed: 15 April 2022].
4. "Biden launches $6B effort to save distressed nuclear plants", *AP News*, 2022. [Online]. Available: https://apnews.com/article/climate-business-environment-nuclear-power-us-department-of-energy-2cf1e633fd4d5b1d5c56bb9ffbb2a50a. [Accessed: 15 April 2022].

15.1 "SECURITY BY ISOLATION" INHIBITS NUCLEAR SECTOR RESILIENCE AND POTENTIAL

Drew Spaniel
Lead Researcher, Institute for Critical Infrastructure Technology (ICIT)

The Nuclear Reactors, Materials, and Waste sector encompasses the Nation's civilian nuclear assets, such as the 96 commercial nuclear power plants that are located at 61 sites, the 31 non-power reactors used for research, training, and radioisotope production, fuel-cycling facilities, and the nuclear materials that are used in healthcare, industrial, and academic settings. The sector also oversees the transportation, storage, and disposal of nuclear materials and radioactive waste. Though the majority of Nuclear sector infrastructure is privately owned, it is considered one of the most highly regulated and secured sectors. The Cybersecurity and Infrastructure Security Agency (CISA) serves as the Nuclear Sector Risk Management Agency (SRMA) and has issued a Sector-Specific Plan (SSP) to guide implementation and define objectives for sector partners' voluntary efforts in the hopes of collectively improving the security and resilience of the sector as a whole. The Nuclear Regulatory Commission (NRC) issues operating licenses in accordance with public health and safety, environmental concerns, and national security. The NRC also regulates the civilian use of nuclear and radiological materials [1]. At the national level, policies and regulations serve as additional tools to bolster against the threat of cyber-attacks. The NRC drafted cyber requirements in the early 2000s and later issued the 10 CFR 73.54 Cyber Security Rule, which requires nuclear plant operators to submit a cybersecurity plan for Commission review and approval. Full implementation of NRC's Cyber Security Rule was completed in 2017. The industry-led Nuclear Energy Institute has also issued industry-standard cybersecurity guidelines for how nuclear plants can meet these NRC requirements [2, 3].

Much fear is associated with the word "nuclear" due to past incidents and the association with nuclear weapons. Nevertheless, nuclear reactors may prove a pivotal alternative to fossil fuels, nuclear materials are essential for healthcare, and even nuclear waste may promise additional energy yields. At a very high level, nuclear reactors work by splitting atoms and using the energy released to heat water and produce steam that is used to rotate a turbine that generates electricity. Commercial nuclear power stations have been in operation in the United States since the Shippingport Atomic Power Station opened in 1958. Further, since 1975, all US submarines and supercarriers built have relied on proprietary naval nuclear reactors. Reportedly, there are no non-nuclear submarines or aircraft carriers operating in the USS Kitty Hawk, which was decommissioned in 2009 [4]. However, it should be noted that the Nuclear Reactors, Materials, and Waste sector does not include the Department of Defense or Department of Energy defense-related nuclear facilities or materials [1].

National nuclear research focuses on the maintenance of naval and commercial reactors, the development of new reactor technology, the refinement of byproducts used in healthcare and other sectors, and the improvement of the sustainability and efficiency of nuclear systems. A process-wise breakdown of the sector would include power generation, material recycling, safe storage, transportation, and disposal. It is at these sector focal points that a remote cyber adversary or insider threat could disrupt operations, achieve a cyber-kinetic outcome, or exfiltrate and later leverage sensitive or proprietary information. Figure 15.1.1 depicts the top security concerns of the sector as identified by CISA and a brief explanation of how each threat could impact the sector. Rather than prognosticate on hypothetical attack scenarios or rehash the extensive recommendations issued by CISA to the sector, this essay will address a few attributes that may inhibit Nuclear sector security in the future [4].

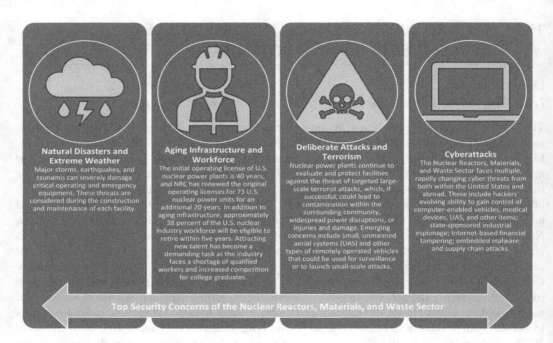

FIGURE 15.1.1 Nuclear sector security considerations.

15.1.1 NO SYSTEM IS AN "ISLAND"

Antiquated cybersecurity strategies were built and dependent upon isolation. Many nuclear plant networks continue to rely on obsolete isolationist network models that leverage hardware and software controls to prevent direct and indirect access to the Internet or that prevent data from migrating across systems. These facilities depend on strict controls centered around portable media, BYOD devices, and IT-OT segregation. Make no mistake; these strategies are cost-effective; however, as malware increases in sophistication, nuclear systems become more attractive targets, and as IT-OT integration promises the temptation of efficiency and profitability, the approach becomes increasingly less viable and realistic. Air-gapped systems feature no outward connectivity, network interfaces, or wired/wireless connections to external networks. They are meant to be segmented from the Internet and all Internet-enabled devices. Malware designed to cross the air gap has propagated since at least the early 2000s, with notable examples ranging from Stuxnet, which proved capable of disrupting operations, to the Ramsay malware toolkit, leveraged for cyberespionage, demonstrating the potential for data theft across air-gapped networks. While the focus of this essay is not on detailing notable airgap malware or incidents, it should not be understated that an isolationist cyber strategy is insufficient in the modern age. Dedicated and resourced adversaries that are sophisticated enough to create custom malware, such as nation-state-sponsored advanced persistent threats (APTs), will be able to bypass an airgap to infect a network. Further, just because a network is strictly isolated now does not mean that it will continue to be so for the duration of the plant's lifecycle. Much like how the Energy sector is struggling to balance security needs with the potentially invaluable improvements in efficiency and profitability derived from IT-OT convergence, there are no guarantees that the Nuclear sector will not pivot in a similar direction at some point in the future. If that reality metastasizes, the rigidly built, perimeter, and control-focused networks might not be compatible with necessary security applications or paradigms.

Even in the absence of malware capable of crossing the air gap or the advent of IT-OT convergence, the sector also faces considerable risk of both malicious and unintentional insider threats. Currently, sector personnel are subject to extensive background screening, evaluation, and training;

however, at the time of this writing, the United States is subject to a cyber talent shortage and a non-cyber talent shortage as a result of COVID-19 losses, an aging workforce, and socioeconomic factors. It is not out of the realm of possibility that as the workforce becomes harder to replace, the rigorous standards of personnel selection may slacken. Perhaps worse, if the workforce is not replenished and instead the duties of unfilled rolls are hoisted onto subordinate positions, the chances of an insider threat may increase. Behavioral analytics and workforce monitoring solutions can aid in insider threat mitigation, but they are not foolproof and should be combined with practices and policies that "keep honest workers honest" [5].

15.1.2   THE SECTOR IS FROZEN IN "COLD WAR" REACTIONISM

Globally, nuclear energy is seen as a promising alternative to fossil fuels, with approximately 10 percent of the world's electricity generated from 440 reactors located in 30 countries, with an additional 50 reactors under construction. Meanwhile, in the United States, many of the 40-year operating licenses for domestic nuclear power plants are reaching term, though NRC has renewed 73 licenses for an additional 20 years. Despite generating approximately a fifth of the Nation's electricity according to CISA, at the time of this writing, the United States has [6, 7]:

- 96 active nuclear power reactors,
- 18 reactors are decommissioning in stages,
- 2 reactors undergoing expansion, and
- 0 reactors under construction.

A balanced assessment of US reluctance to further invest in nuclear facilities may include factors such as the already positive reliability and efficacy of existing reactors, the socioeconomic switching costs associated with the transition away from fossil fuels, and the US historical and popular culture stigmatization of nuclear power. Our use of atomic weapons at the conclusion of World War II; decades of Cold War fear, positioning, and propaganda; popular culture's fetishization of the threat of nuclear war as a lazy, short-hand premise; and serious (though often misrepresented) incidents such as the events of Chornobyl and Three-Mile Island have fused and evolved into a national zeitgeist that fears the word nuclear in any connotation. Consider that there have been no civilian deaths associated with the operation of nuclear power technology in the United States since its introduction over 60 years ago. Based on that metric, it is one of, if not the, safest forms of energy in the country; yet, it is the "boogeyman" of the energy conversation. I propose that an element of this fear contributes to US reluctance to explore and further develop nuclear energy at a greater scale, and more importantly, it contributes to our reluctance to invest in modernized networks and reactors that can be better designed in the digital age with cybersecurity controls built-in throughout the developmental and operational lifecycles of the facilities. However, though it may definitely be a balancing act in terms of positioning and narrative management, this same fear can be leveraged as the impetus for necessary modernization. After all, one of the favorite examples of a cyber-kinetic impact by media personalities includes "a cyber-attack on a nuclear plant" because the public can easily presume that would result in impacts that they have been primed by popular culture to expect. The reality of an attack would be less dramatic but potentially just as impactful, albeit in a different way. Instead of grandiose explosions or containment breaches, a successful cyber-attack would be more likely to disrupt or fatally terminate the operations of expensive and difficult to replace legacy systems. Depending on the system targeted, national power generation may be affected and cause electricity prices to increase, or the materials essential for healthcare and scientific research could be shorted.

The simple truth, though, is that in the sector, the paradigm of "security through isolation" is rapidly transforming into "security through obsolescence." Legacy systems secured through network segmentation and airgaps are not invulnerable to cyber-attacks, and even if they were, the aging systems increasingly lack essential redundancies. Legacy reactors would take years or decades to replace if key elements were rendered inoperable by extreme events, insider threats, or powerful disruptionware.

The United States spent decades propagating that "nuclear" equaled "dangerous," and while that may have been true during the Cold War and may still be true to an extent today, there are differences between nuclear reactors and missiles and differences between safe and unsafe reactor operation that simply were not taught to the public or policymakers. As a result, we designed the systems that now generate one-fifth of our electricity to only be "touched with a ten-foot pole," and while that security paradigm succeeded for decades, it is reaching its inevitable sunset due to diminishing returns. Regulation and strict controls can ensure network isolation and security control implementation for a time, but private companies will not continue to run legacy systems forever. Eventually, either the systems will break down, become inefficient, or be cost-prohibitive to operate. Those firms may try to integrate networked components or may abandon the facilities in favor of more lucrative ventures.

The efforts of Cybersecurity and Infrastructure Security Agency (CISA), Department of Energy (DOE), Nuclear Regulatory Commission (NRC), and many other organizations to secure the Nuclear sector have been admirable and should not be understated. Every civilian nuclear facility's program is inspected regularly by the NRC, and the industry maintains an active partnership with Department of Homeland Security (DHS) and DOE on emerging cyber threats. The success of the sector's security is largely attributable to comprehensive protective measures and the continuous collaboration of private sector stakeholders, public sector regulators and agencies, and plant cybersecurity professionals [5].

However, nuclear reactor technologies were not designed with the digital age in mind. We are continuing to rely on isolationist and reactionary cybersecurity strategies instead of pursuing modernization and proactive cybersecurity design. Increased discourse at the Executive and policymaker levels with nuclear engineers, physicists, and cybersecurity experts should be considered to help craft a national strategy to decouple the fear of the past from the promise of the future. Eventually, the Nuclear sector will have to be either brought into the digital age or entirely decommissioned. Proactive strategic investments in nuclear reactor systems that incorporate security controls throughout their developmental and operational lifecycles could yield significant national benefits, but realizing those returns will require greater focus, investment, and commitment to the Nuclear sector, its modernization, and its cybersecurity.

15.1.3 NEW, SECURE, AND MODERN REACTORS WOULD REVOLUTIONIZE THE COUNTRY

Existing civilian nuclear infrastructure is static against modern, dynamic threats and will prove increasingly more challenging to secure as the needs of operators evolve and the efficacy of their pre-digital design degrades. The application of security by design throughout the development and operational lifecycle in new civilian nuclear systems would provide operators with a robust and resilient security architecture from which proactive, adaptive, and modern security strategies can be based. While it is not a panacea and will not entirely secure systems against evolving persistent adversaries, it would improve the resilience, increase the resource threshold necessary to achieve an impact, and decrease the lifecycle costs associated with trying to secure aging systems against evolving threats [8]. Some of the most significant cyber and cyber-kinetic impacts against civilian nuclear infrastructure include [9]:

- Compromise or sabotage of systems, resulting in radiation release, inaccurate safety readings, etc.
- Temporary or terminal disruption of operations

- Theft/diversion/targeting of separated plutonium (Pu), highly enriched uranium (HEU), or mixed oxide (MOX) fuel
- Reputational harm or mass panic due to a real, potential, or false attack
- The exfiltration of proprietary technical design information and intellectual property
- The theft of transportation plans/routes or plant safety parameters
- The theft of personally identifiable information (PII) from administration networks that could be later leveraged to coerce an insider threat

While they are less bombastic than scenarios depicted on the silver screen and are, for the moment, less frequent than attacks on other sectors' infrastructure, campaigns targeting civilian nuclear infrastructure are not as unheard of as some proponents of "security by isolation" suggest and data indicates that the frequency of attacks is increasing as infrastructure ages and as the technological threshold for attacks decreases. The trend depicted in the Nuclear Threat Initiative (NTI) data set featured in Figure 15.1.2 most likely reflects targeted attacks from sophisticated adversaries, but recent malware resurgences and trend evolutions such as ransomware, disruptionware, and malware-as-a-service will likely make the Nuclear sector a target for "hacktivists" and other cyber-adversaries who are intent on garnering media attention, causing mass panics, coercing a high-likelihood financial return on their attack resources, or making an ideological or geopolitical statement. Figure 15.1.2 visualizes the number of publicly disclosed cyber incidents at nuclear facilities from 1990 to 2016. It is possible that more incidents have occurred that have not been publicly disclosed, discovered, or for which the details are classified or otherwise unavailable [10].

For instance, in September 2019, a cyber-attack breached the administrative network of the Kudankulam Nuclear Power Plant in Tamil Nadu, India. Kudankulam is the biggest nuclear power plant in India, with two 1,000 MW VVER pressurized water reactors at the time of the attack and four more reactors undergoing the design stage. The network leveraged isolation controls, and officials stated that there was no risk of operational, safety, or critical damage. However, this defense solely hinges on their belief that key systems are not themselves networked. Malware could be introduced via a malicious insider threat, infected update media, "poisoned" vendor application or update, rogue device, or via a subcontractor depending on a plethora of procedural factors. Many "isolated" networks now rely on approved access points for necessary third-party updates and monitoring, updates, or bridge solution management between legacy and modern components (such as integrated systems that operate from entirely incongruent code).

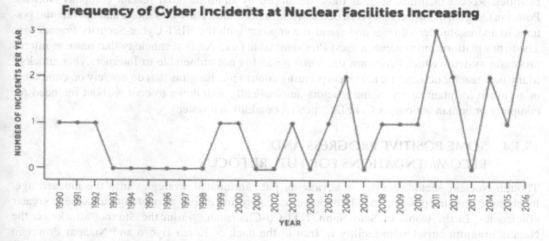

FIGURE 15.1.2   NTI disclosed civilian nuclear cyber incidents (1990–2016).

While an airgap secures devices in theory, in practice, numerous high-profile malware has proven capable of bypassing isolation and segmentation controls. Worse, because the systems are presumed secure, infections tend to go unnoticed for years. A prudent rule of thumb might be that at the time of this writing, an air gap is comparable to a moat; it will prevent unsophisticated, under-resourced, or disinterested attackers from breaching an asset, but it will not stop a targeted attack from a persistent and sophisticated adversary. The disparity between reality and the illusion of theory lies in the confidence that many private sector operators place in the air gap as a failsafe defense. Some fail to invest in cybersecurity solutions past the bare minimum required because they naively trust that the airgap will prevent compromise. The lack of consistent physical or logical connectivity is inadequate security. To abuse the "moat analogy," would medieval castles have been secure if they eschewed portcullises, armed guards, balistraria, and other security controls "because there was a moat?" Even with secure design and a plethora of layered controls, many were breached and overtaken, often due to brute force, novel attack paradigms, or nefarious insiders. In the aforementioned attack against the Kudankulam Nuclear Power Plant, it has been suggested that the North Korean developed Dtrack malware, specifically tailored for the plant, was introduced by a malicious insider [11]. More objectively, prolific cyber-attack campaigns like Stuxnet demonstrated airgap defense strategies were no longer sufficient to secure critical infrastructure, and recent attacks on industrial control systems (ICS) have further confirmed that conclusion. However, the inefficacy of airgap defenses should have been known to the Nuclear sector since at least the 2003 Slammer worm infection of Ohio's Davis–Besse Nuclear Plant. The worm first embedded itself into a contractor's computer and was later passed onto the Davis–Besse corporate network. Once in the corporate network, the worm found its way into the reactor's processing control systems because the processing control system was linked to the public, corporate network. Because of the reactor's lack of separation from a public network, the Slammer worm was able to penetrate and cause harm to the reactor's internal functions. As a result, the worm disabled the Safety Parameter Display System for nearly five hours. This system was responsible for monitoring the most important safety indicators at the plant, such as the core temperature sensors, coolant systems, and external radiation sensors. The incident resulted in more stringent NRC regulations, but it also highlighted the need for enhanced internal network controls [12].

Fortunately, agencies and industries are adapting to better secure Nuclear sector assets. Members of the nuclear power industry participate in frequent briefings and receive quarterly classified briefings on cyber and physical threats from law enforcement to assess threats, develop security strategies, and enhance situational awareness. Hardware-based data diode technologies, developed for high assurance environments, like the DOD, are standardized, and the use of portable media and personal devices is prohibited. The NRC reviews cybersecurity plans for existing and proposed facilities. Recent facilities, such as those developed by small modular reactor company NuScale Power in Oregon, incorporate layered defensive security architecture into safety and operational systems to address modern threats and are also compliant with the NIST Cyber-Security Framework. The firm's platform implements a Field Programmable Gate Array technology that has non-microprocessor systems which "does not use software and is not vulnerable to Internet cyber-attacks." Many new reactor designs are also incorporating control mechanisms that do not rely on computers or software for plant safety. Some reactors automatically shut down to cool without the need for computer or human actions, A.C. or D.C. power, or additional water.

15.1.4 SOME POSITIVE PROGRESS AND RECOMMENDATIONS FOR FUTURE FOCUS

Though Nuclear sector security is advancing past antiquated strategies into the modern age, much more remains possible to help improve resiliency and empower operators to achieve greater efficiencies. In the words of Sam Nunn, NTI Co-Chairman, "From the Stuxnet attacks on the Natanz uranium enrichment facility in Iran to the hack of Korea Hydro and Nuclear Power in South Korea, to disturbing revelations of malware found on systems at a German nuclear power plant—demonstrates that the current approach to cybersecurity at nuclear facilities is not equal to the challenge" [10]. In their 2016 report, *Outpacing Cyber Threats: Priorities for Cybersecurity at Nuclear Facilities*, Nunn realistically explained, "Increased digitalization at nuclear facilities creates critical efficiencies, including for some security practices. At the same time, digitalization creates new and ever-evolving cyber vulnerabilities that require more effective and sustainable response to mitigate risks" [10]. The following recommendations depicted in Figure 15.1.3 are based on the detailed reports issued by the NTI, International Atomic Energy Agency (IAEA), Georgetown University, UC Berkley, George Washington University, Chatham House, and CISA. More information on past incidents, regulatory guidance and mandates, implementation recommendations, and existing sector efforts can be found in the referenced materials [8, 10, 13–16].

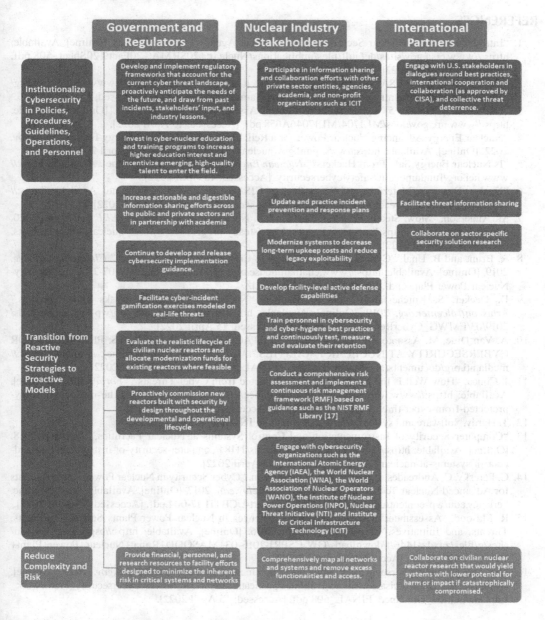

FIGURE 15.1.3   Nuclear Sector stakeholder recommendations.

15.1.4.1 ABOUT THE AUTHOR

As the Lead Researcher at the Institute for Critical Infrastructure Technology, **Drew Spaniel** is an expert in information security and technology across the US critical infrastructure sectors. He serves the Institute as a technical expert in cybersecurity, technology, and data science, as well as emerging adversarial trends, threat actor profiling, and legislation and agency initiatives related to information security and privacy.

Drew earned a Master of Science in Information Security, Policy, and Management from Carnegie Mellon University's Heinz College and a Bachelor of Science in Applied Physics from Allegheny College.

REFERENCES

1. "Introduction to the Nuclear Sector Risk Management Agency," *Cisa.gov*, 2022. [Online]. Available: https://www.cisa.gov/sites/default/files/publications/Nuclear%20SRMA%20Fact%20Sheet_508.pdf. [Accessed: 15 April 2022].
2. "Nuclear Power in the USA," *World-nuclear.org*, 2022. [Online]. Available: https://www.world-nuclear.org/information-library/country-profiles/countries-t-z/usa-nuclear-power.aspx. [Accessed: 15 April 2022].
3. "NEI 13-10 [Revision 5] Cyber Security Control Assessments," *Nrc.gov*, 2017. [Online]. Available: https://www.nrc.gov/docs/ML1704/ML17046A658.pdf. [Accessed: 15 April 2022].
4. "Nuclear Energy Advancing Nuclear Power for a Reliable, Safe, and Secure Energy Future," *Pnnl.gov*, 2022. [Online]. Available: https://www.pnnl.gov/nuclear-energy. [Accessed: 15 April 2022].
5. "Is Nuclear Energy Safe From Hackers?" *Nuclear Energy Institute*, 2022. [Online]. Available: https://www.nei.org/fundamentals/safety/cybersecurity. [Accessed: 15 April 2022].
6. "Nuclear Reactors, Materials, and Waste Sector | CISA," *Cisa.gov*, 2022. [Online]. Available: https://www.cisa.gov/nuclear-reactors-materials-and-waste-sector. [Accessed: 15 April 2022].
7. M. Anderson, "Slow, Steady Progress for Two U.S. Nuclear Power Projects," *IEEE Spectrum*, 2020. [Online]. Available: https://spectrum.ieee.org/slow-steady-progress-for-two-us-nuclear-power-projects. [Accessed: 15 April 2022].
8. R. Brunt and B. Unal, "Cybersecurity by Design in Civil Nuclear Power Plants," *Chathamhouse.org*, 2019. [Online]. Available: https://www.chathamhouse.org/sites/default/files/2019-07-23-Cybersecurity-Nuclear-Power-Plants.pdf. [Accessed: 15 April 2022].
9. D. Decker, S. Kutchesfahani, and K. Rauhut, "Nuclear Cybersecurity Risks and Remedies," *Armscontrolcenter.org*, 2019. [Online]. Available: https://armscontrolcenter.org/wp-content/uploads/2019/03/FMWG_CyberReport_webready.pdf. [Accessed: 15 April 2022].
10. A. Van Dine, M. Assante, and P. Stoutland, "OUTPACING CYBER THREATS: PRIORITIES FOR CYBERSECURITY AT NUCLEAR FACILITIES," *Media.nti.org*, 2016. [Online]. Available: https://media.nti.org/documents/NTI_CyberThreats__FINAL.pdf. [Accessed: 15 April 2022].
11. J. Conca, "How Well Is the Nuclear Industry Protected from Cyber Threats?," *Forbes*, 2019. [Online]. Available: https://www.forbes.com/sites/jamesconca/2019/11/08/how-well-is-the-nuclear-industry-protected-from-cyber-threats/?sh=3e1b9c293497. [Accessed: 15 April 2022].
12. T. Hardy, Software and system safety. Bloomington, IN: AuthorHouse, 2012.
13. "Computer Security of Instrumentation and Control Systems at Nuclear Facilities," *Iaea.org*, 2018. [Online]. Available: https://www.iaea.org/publications/11184/computer-security-of-instrumentation-and-control-systems-at-nuclear-facilities. [Accessed: 15 April 2022].
14. C. Poresky, C. Andreades, J. Kendrick, and P. Peterson, "Cyber Security in Nuclear Power Plants: Insights for Advanced Nuclear Technologies," *Fhr.nuc.berkeley.edu*, 2017. [Online]. Available: https://fhr.nuc.berkeley.edu/wp-content/uploads/2017/09/TH-Report-UCBTH-17-004.pdf. [Accessed: 15 April 2022].
15. R. Masood, "Assessment of Cyber Security Challenges in Nuclear Power Plants Security Incidents, Threats, and Initiatives," *Cspri.seas.gwu.edu*, 2016. [Online]. Available: https://cspri.seas.gwu.edu/sites/g/files/zaxdzs1446/f/downloads/GW-CSPRI-2016-03+MASOOD+Rahat+Nuclear+Power+Plant+Cybersecurity_0.pdf. [Accessed: 15 April 2022].
16. "Nuclear Sector Cybersecurity Framework Implementation Guidance," *Cisa.gov*, 2020. [Online]. Available: https://www.cisa.gov/sites/default/files/publications/Nuclear_Sector_Cybersecurity_Framework_Implementation_Guidance_FINAL_508.pdf. [Accessed: 15 April 2022].

16 Local and State Government

16.0 ABOUT STATE AND LOCAL GOVERNMENT CYBERSECURITY

Rita Reynolds

CIO, National Association of Counties

This next set of essays will focus on the cybersecurity landscape for state and local government. As the CIO for the National Association of Counties (NACo), I have been fortunate to interact with federal, state, and local IT professionals. While I have over 30 years of technology experience working in the non-profit association industry, which supports state and local government, I can comfortably say that the most significant foundational changes have occurred in the past decade. And the more recent challenges have necessitated the need for state and local governments to be creative in these technological times.

Specifically, shoring up security around critical infrastructure, while a priority pre-pandemic, is even more vital post-pandemic. One may ask, why? The pandemic forced everyone to move from in person activities to virtual interaction. For the government this presented some unique challenges as compared to other industries. These challenges include

- Having sufficient financial resources to implement basic cyber security protections
- Having access to experienced technology resources who are willing to work in government positions for compensation that is often well below the private sector, and
- The ability to implement security changes quickly.

Further complicating state and local government cyber efforts are the types of services that they are responsible to provide for the residents of the state and county. Services that include

- **Elections:** Voter registration as well as election management
- **Criminal Justice:** Offender services from court appointment representation to incarceration to adult probation
- **Mental Health:** Evaluation and assessment, access to appropriate resources, and follow-up monitoring
- **Veterans:** Identification and enrollment support for eligible resources
- **Public Assistance:** Eligibility determination and enrollment in financial, food, and medical assistance
- **Homeless:** Development and implementation of programs to provide housing and other needed services for the homeless population
- **Public Nursing Homes:** Support for the elderly who can no longer live alone

While this list is not exhaustive, it should give readers a better understanding of the unique position that state and local governments are in compared to other industries. As one can imagine, protecting residents' data that is housed in all these areas is a huge responsibility and one that states and counties do not take lightly. The infrastructure and security needed to support these services have grown exponentially in recent years. That growth combined with the furious pace of technology innovation, along with the unique pandemic situation, has catapulted government entities toward implementing new technology options, such as moving numerous critical infrastructure components to the cloud. While the move to the cloud is the right direction, this movement, along with the rise in remote work, has given bad actors even more lucrative opportunities for cyberattacks.

DOI: 10.1201/9781003243021-16

In my role as CIO for NACo, I have the privilege to work with CIOs, IT Directors, and CISOs at all levels of government, but especially with counties. We work together to identify the cyber protections that are needed and then how to implement them. To help readers understand the cyber priorities, NACo recently released a publication identifying 11 cybersecurity priorities and best practices. These priorities were developed from input and feedback provided by counties, national associations, and federal agencies focused on cyber. Below is a summary:

- **MFA:** Multi-Factor Authentication for when users access the internet, applications, and servers
- **DMARC:** Domain-based Message Authentication, Reporting and Conformance; and email notification protocol
- **DotGov:** A secure domain option for website and email extension
- **Monitoring Tools:** Aggregation software that monitors, collects and analyzes network, and end user activities (like the dashboard lights in a car)
- **Certified Third-Party Providers:** A process for ensuring that third-party partners and providers are following basic cyber security best practices
- **Regional Expertise and Resources:** Access to local security resources to help implement needed security best practices
- **IT Assessments:** That identify infrastructure weaknesses and areas for improvement
- **End User Education:** Regular training for staff as well as citizens on cyber security awareness and steps to take to protect ones' identity and digital assets
- **End User Protection:** Implementing the next generation of anti-virus software and automatic remote patching will secure endpoints devices including employee mobile devices
- **MS-ISAC:** Joining the Multi-State Information Sharing and Analysis Center to receive access to cyber alerts and other no-cost resources
- **Policies:** Ensuring that security incident policy, forms, and procedures are in place and are tested regularly

While there are many more, these 11 are the focus for the near future. Half the battle is knowing what to focus on. The other half involves communication, education, and problem-solving with elected officials, other government entities, and our much-needed partner community. I would be remiss if I did not mention the importance of corporate partners. They bring great expertise and solutions that all levels of government can rely on to help implement many of these cyber best practices.

In this chapter, you will hear from several cybersecurity experts who will delve further into the challenges, threats, and the importance of cyber security and these best practices. I am looking forward to their thoughts on where technology is leading government, as well as recommendations for the next four years. Beyond that, of course, will depend on the evolution of technology and the threat landscape, as well as how we embrace the subsequent changes needed to continue to protect critical assets and infrastructure!

16.0.1 ABOUT THE AUTHOR

Rita Reynolds serves as NACo's chief information officer. In this capacity, she oversees the internal technology operations of NACo and leads NACo's technology programs and initiatives for counties. She is responsible for the NACo technology blueprint, which includes managing the development and delivering of technology programming on initiatives such as cyber security, technology infrastructure, and cloud computing. Rita brings with her responsibility for serving on multiple boards and workgroups over the years including the PA Digital Advisory Board, the Multi-State Information Sharing & Analysis Center, and the NASCIO Cyber Security Workgroup. Rita also serves as the staff liaison to the NACo Technology Standing Committee and the GIS Subcommittee.

Before joining NACo, Rita served as the CIO for the County Commissioners Association of Pennsylvania, where she spent 20 years mainly focused on similar initiatives for CCAP and with counties in Pennsylvania. Prior to that, Rita was an independent fiscal and computer consultant where she worked with numerous children and youth agencies in Pennsylvania and designed fiscal and data reporting applications, including a statewide AFCARS solution. Rita holds a BA in business administration with a minor in political science from Messiah College in Pennsylvania. Rita has been the recipient of numerous awards over the years, including the Technology Council of Central Pennsylvania's 2019 Moxie Award, Government Technology's 2017 Top 25 Doers, Dreamers and Drivers, and State Tech's "30 State and Local Government IT Influencers" for 2020.

16.0.2 ABOUT CYBER LANTERN

Cyber Lantern is the commercial cybersecurity products and services branch of Digital Lantern. It was founded on the premise that every organization deserves the right to secure its business. Our background is founded in service, with over 20 years of government and military experience among our founders. We believe in promoting a culture that breeds innovation, respect, empathy, compassion, and customer-driven execution.

Cyber Lantern is a first of its kind cyber security Software-as-a-Service Platform that combines getting compliant and staying secure. Cyber Lantern Compliance focuses on providing automated risk assessments and compliance management to identify actions to improve your security posture and get complaint faster. Cyber Lantern Protect then provides scalable and cost-effective security services that integrate into our platform, automatically helping achieve 53% of the compliance requirements for most organizations.

16.1 EMERGING THREATS AND CHALLENGES FACING STATE AND LOCAL GOVERNMENTS AND WHY THEY SHOULD BE CONSIDERED CRITICAL INFRASTRUCTURE

Marcela Denniston
Co-Founder and President
Cyber Lantern

Alycia Farrell
President
Grey Tarian

Peter Liebert
Founder, Liebert Security
CISO, Cerner Government Services
Commander of Cyber Operations, The California State Guard

Jason Smith
Faculty, Coast Guard Chair
National War College

16.1.1 INTRODUCTION

In 2018, the Trump administration signed into law the Cyber Security and Infrastructure Security Agency Act of 2018 (P.L. 115-278). This legislation aimed to better manage public-private sector partnerships for improved cybersecurity and cyber resilience nationwide. It also strengthened and codified efforts previously identified and put into action through Presidential Policy Directive 21 (PPD-21), which established 16 critical infrastructure sectors that would have a devastating effect on national safety, security, and/or economy if they were to be incapacitated. While this legislation and PPD-21 identify the specified sectors that supply critical services and goods to the American people, they neglected to address the challenges, threats, and security needs of a crucial element that ties these services to citizens: State, Local, Tribal, and Territorial (SLTT) governments. These organizations play a key role in the day-to-day management of critical infrastructure yet are largely neglected when it comes to federal support or funding. Without adequate federal support, SLTTs find themselves often forgoing technological advancements that support risk mitigation and security, creating the perfect opportunistic scenario for foreign adversaries to exploit the shortcomings of SLTT's capabilities to manage risk against mass scale disruption of our nation's security. These SLTTs manage the supply chains for many sectors of critical infrastructure and thus face similar cybersecurity threats, yet they lack the resources and adequate funding to ensure risk is managed and security operations are a priority. To ensure risk and security is treated as a priority, it is necessary to treat SLTTs not as an inconsequential manager but as critical infrastructure themselves.

State and local governments are the backbones of the United States. The 331 million citizens that reside in the United States are represented by approximately 88,000 local governments, districts, and commissions. Running this complex network of government institutions are approximately 1.5 million government personnel who oversee over $1 trillion in annual spending [1]. The criticality of these local institutions cannot be overstated as it is where essential services such as public safety, water treatment, schools and libraries, public health services, roads, public transportation, and enforcement are translated from policy to action. While these services are critical to the continuity of every American's daily life and prosperity, they often do not get the support needed to operate safely. Attackers know this, and it is likely the reason why threat actors have dramatically increased the number of attacks against state and local governments over the past five years. A study run by the Public Technology Institute (PTI) indicates that "66% of [County] IT executives feel that their cybersecurity budget is not adequate" [2]. A combination of limited budgets and resources and an expanding attack footprint through digital transformation has proven that it is only a matter of time before a mass cyberattack on SLTT governments will have a more significant and collective impact on US society. Attacks on SLTTs should be considered an attack on critical infrastructure as it is an attack on our nation's citizens and their way of life.

16.1.2 WHAT IS CRITICAL INFRASTRUCTURE?

According to Executive Order 13010 ("Critical Infrastructure Protection") [3], critical infrastructure is defined as follows: "Certain national infrastructures are so vital that their incapacity or destruction would have a debilitating impact on the defense or economic security of the United States. These infrastructures include telecommunications, electrical power systems, gas and oil storage and transportation, banking and finance, transportation, water supply systems, emergency services (including medical, police, fire, and rescue), and continuity of government" [3].

Given that this definition includes many of the infrastructures managed by SLTTs and the debilitating impact that attacks have already had on SLTTs nationwide, it is imperative that SLTTs also be considered a Critical Infrastructure.

16.1.3 THE CONSTRUCT OF STATE AND LOCAL GOVERNMENT IT SECURITY BUDGETS

To better understand the current state of local government IT security, we first need to understand how they operate. SLTTs can vary significantly in size and infrastructure; however, they all deal with similar challenges. Local government budgets, policies, practices, and governance are often executed by part-time local officials who volunteer or get paid very little for their efforts, with little reporting and oversight. This governance structure usually means local governments are disadvantaged when it comes to skilled labor in areas such as budgeting and resources to maintain the security of services they must manage, support, and operate. Also, many SLTT governments utilize legacy IT infrastructure, making them even more susceptible to attacks. A 2020 report by the National Associations of State Chief Information Officers (NASCIO) indicated that cloud migration and renovations of legacy technologies were the top priorities for States, along with improvements to cybersecurity and risk management. While these actions would improve cyber resilience, another top priority was the reduction of costs and budgets, making the goal of IT improvements an increased challenge [4]. In contrast to federal agencies who spend anywhere between 5% and 15% of their IT budgets on security, States often only spend 1–2% on the same efforts [5]. In comparison, commercial businesses who also run essential services, such as financial companies, often spend between 6% and 12% of their budgets on security. Even with higher budgets, many of these organizations, both in the public and private sector, still suffer from significant data breaches and cyberattacks, making it clear that SLTT security budgets are not adequate [6].

When we look further into IT budgets at the local government level, the situation becomes even more critical. The PTI and CompTIA National Survey of Local Government Cybersecurity Programs indicated that 65.52% of local government IT executives from cities and counties of less than 50,000 citizens but upwards of 150,000 citizens felt that their cyber security budgets were inadequate [2]. This lack of budget allocation can be primarily associated with a lack of involvement and understanding by elected officials. The same survey showed IT executives felt only 23% of elected officials were actively engaged in cyber efforts. While some SLTTs have IT executives, many of the small to medium-sized jurisdictions do not have dedicated staff to support regular cyber security operations, leaving the IT Executive and team responsible for managing cyber security efforts. With an increased need for improved IT infrastructure, an already limited budget, and the need to further decrease spending, state and local governments will likely continue to struggle to make significant improvements to the current state of their security needs. Incentives need to be realigned to encourage SLTTs to spend more on cyber security.

16.1.4 IMPLICATIONS OF A CYBER ATTACK ON STATE AND LOCAL GOVERNMENTS

The damage and destruction of a cyberattack on critical infrastructure could quickly escalate to the devastation level equivalent to that of a natural disaster if not properly contained and remediated. In addition to disruption of essential services, these attacks have other detrimental effects: the cost of recovery, loss of critical data, and occasionally, even loss of life. In 2019, the United States began to see the true implications of attacks and their effects on communities, the economy, and their citizens' overall well-being, with 140 ransomware attacks alone against local governments. In August 2019, 22 Texas municipalities were hit with ransomware attacks that crippled their ability to process utility payments, car registrations, and other necessary services crucial to daily operations [7]. The State of Louisiana declared a state of emergency after a ransomware attack on government servers halted its ability to maintain operations for the Department of Motor Vehicles, Department of Transportation, and the Department of Revenue. The City of Baltimore suffered from disruption of services during a 2019 attack and incurred astronomical costs of over $18M to remediate and return regular services to the public. Less than half of SLTTs maintain formal incident response plans, leaving them vulnerable to long remediation times and high recovery costs. These events highlighted the lack of preparedness of SLTTs to respond to such cyber incidents and their essential role in managing the other US designated critical infrastructure [7].

16.1.5 CYBER SECURITY IN 2020 AND THE EFFECTS OF A PANDEMIC ON NECESSARY OPERATIONAL ENVIRONMENTS

The year 2019 only served as a primer for the true implications of cyberattacks for SLTT governments. As the world entered a global shutdown state due to the COVID-19 pandemic, SLTTs had to rapidly adopt new technologies and security measures to support a more digitally connected remote workforce while coping with further decreased budgets resulting from an economic downturn. One study shows that "85% of CISOs surveyed admitted that they had to sacrifice cybersecurity to more quickly enable remote work" [8]. This does not just include budget but also the allocation of IT staff to quickly support the deployment and management of new capabilities to enable remote work. The pandemic is the perfect example of the lack of preparedness of SLTT governments against a national crisis that trickles down to micro-levels of government cyber deficiencies. While SLTTs scrambled to adjust priorities, attackers saw a more significant opportunity to take advantage of an already soft target environment.

This led to increased ransomware attacks that typically target critical operational environments, remote access, and phishing attacks, and delayed response times due to impacted resources from layoffs and other IT projects that took operational priority. The rapid deployment of a remote workforce also created a new landscape of untrained employees now armed with more security freedoms in less monitored environments. This situation is especially a threat when many of those who are not trained to follow standard security policies are often those with executive powers and access to critical government data. Another report indicated that IT executives concerned about VPN (Virtual Private Network) exploitation tripled to 85%; cloud services misconfiguration concerns increased from 48% to 66% [8]. Additionally, the required training and security exceptions provided to elected officials, their staffs, and public safety employees are alarming: "… 15% of IT executives state that their elected officials and their staffs and senior leadership are exempt from their organization's awareness training programs" [2]. Lack of training is already a leading cause of security issues. When key stakeholders are not trained to understand potential security threats or the implication of such threats, it creates a much wider target footprint in the organization. With 95% of security breaches being caused by human error, decreasing training and awareness to accommodate executive privilege poses an added unnecessary challenge to IT and security teams.

The scenarios above have been challenging, to say the least. As attackers become more comfortable understanding the soft targets available to them, it will only increase their ability to cause real harm. Cyberattacks are becoming exponentially more common and more detrimental every year. Nation-state attackers, also known as advanced persistent threats (APTs), become more aware of the soft targets in SLTT governments; catastrophic attacks will quickly become the main source of warfare. The Ukrainian Power Grid attack in 2015 is a notable example of the implication of an attack on Critical Infrastructure. This attack left 225,000 customers without power for several hours and was attributed to Russian cybercriminal groups associated with APT Group 28, known affiliates of Russian government agencies. The groups operated in a joint effort labeled "Russian Hybrid Warfare" and defined as "Sophisticated campaigns that combine low-level conventional and special operations; offensive cyber and space actions; and psychological operations that use social and traditional media to influence popular perception and international opinion" [9].

This attack was not on US soil; however, the ability to prepare and execute this attack is a clear indicator of a foreign adversary's capabilities. This became even more evident in February 2021, when an attacker took remote control over a water treatment plant in the city of Oldsmar near Tampa, Florida, and increased sodium hydroxide levels in the city's drinking water by a factor of 100. Sodium hydroxide is a common chemical used in many soaps and detergents but can be toxic if ingested in high volumes. This attack happened in a city with a relatively low population of 14,000, but which was hosting the Super Bowl only two days later, which more than doubled the population [10]. This attack, which was attempted twice, is considered a felony; and had an operator not been present while the remote takeover occurred, it could have resulted in life-threatening outcomes for local citizens and visitors. The city of Oldsmar runs the water treatment plant, and the investigation was under the local Sheriff's Department jurisdiction. All these services tie back to one common denominator: they are all managed, operated, and maintained by an SLTT. This attempt at bioterrorism carried via cyber means is a national threat, further proving how crucial it is for the SLTTs themselves to be designated as Critical Infrastructures by the US Federal Government, so that federal support and assistance can be immediately available.

16.1.6 SUPPLY CHAIN: PUBLIC-PRIVATE SECTOR RISKS

State, Local, Tribal and Territorial governments rely heavily on commercial products and third-party vendors to manage and support their daily services. These vendors supply critical hardware, software, infrastructure, and services to SLTTs that, if halted or compromised, could have severe effects on their ability to sustain essential services to the community. This threat has been made clear through several supply chain attacks over the past few years against major vendors such as Microsoft, SolarWinds, and Eagle Technologies. These attacks showed both the level of sophistication of foreign adversaries and the complexity of remediating these attacks once they occur.

16.1.6.1 SOLARWINDS ATTACK

In December 2020, cyber researchers discovered that SolarWinds, a provider of a network management system used by SLTTs, the Federal government, and many other large organizations, suffered a breach conducted by nation-state-affiliated hackers from Russia. The hackers were able to embed malware in SolarWinds' Orion software product update that was pushed to every customer. The malware enabled full access to the network management system allowing attackers to set up backdoors into the victim environments giving them full access to their network infrastructure, potentially infecting other machines and covering their tracks in the process. Nearly 18,000 customers were affected. The attack was so severe that the Cybersecurity and Infrastructure Security Agency (CISA) issued an emergency directive urging organizations to check their environments for indicators of compromise and recommended all Orion appliances be taken offline to disrupt potential connections to the hackers [11]. It may take years for government agencies to find all the affected systems, and some will remain undiscovered. SLTTs prominently use the Orion software to manage their network infrastructure. The successful hack gives a powerful nation-state potentially access to local law enforcement's sensitive information and sensitive federal databases.

16.1.6.2 Microsoft Exchange

Microsoft, one of the largest global hardware and software providers, also fell victim to a massive cyberattack that took advantage of unknown email server vulnerabilities known as "zero-day" exploits. The exploit allowed the attackers to access email accounts on the exchange servers and further deploy additional malware granting them long-term access to the environments and the ability to steal data. Again, this breach affects over 100,000 systems and should be especially concerning for SLTTs who still heavily rely on legacy exchange servers for email service. The vulnerability supplies the perfect opportunity for attackers to take advantage of access to further disrupt or deny local operations for political, financial, and warfighting purposes.

16.1.6.3 Current Authorities and Challenges for Federal Support to SLTTs

The SLTT governments need help in securing their respective critical infrastructure, and the Federal Government is aware of this need. Just recognizing that this is important, however, has yet to yield any results. The Department of Homeland Security, through CISA, is the designated Federal entity responsible for collaborating and coordinating with SLTT governments to protect critical infrastructure within their jurisdictions. CISA, however, was only just stood up in 2018 through H.R.3359—Cybersecurity and Infrastructure Security Agency Act of 2018 (P.L.115-278). While CISA reorganizes to better support their mandate, cybercriminals, APTs, and other threats to SLTT networks continue to proliferate. Many of the shortcomings of Federal response and support to SLTTs aren't necessarily tied to a lack of mandates but to a disorganized Federal system, inadequacy of direction and coordination from the Federal level to the local municipalities, and the absence of incentives to encourage SLTT leaders to pursue a greater cybersecurity posture.

While CISA is relatively new, its mandate is not and can be referenced in 6 United States Code (USC) § 652. This Federal statute directs the mission of CISA today. Specifics of CISA's mandate evolved from the original National Infrastructure Protection Plan (NIPP), which sets the stage for collaboration with state, local, territorial and tribal governments. At the time of this writing, the most recent version of this plan was dated 2013 [12]. Even with effective collaboration and communication throughout the many layers of governments involved with the security of critical infrastructure, such an outdated plan cannot meet the security needs in the dynamic environment of cyber and cybersecurity.

Critical Infrastructure, in broad terms, is identified in Federal law as a national goal, so the importance of public-private collaboration is vital because of how much of the infrastructure is owned and operated by private companies. Many of the federal mandates and policies were established in Homeland Security Presidential Directive 7 (HSPD-7) and the NIPP [13].

The HSPD-7 identified lead agencies responsible for coordinating critical infrastructure protection efforts with the public and private stakeholders in their respective sectors. "Government Facilities" encapsulated the SLTT community and continuity of government and was to be overseen by the Department of Homeland Security/CISA.

The recent realignment effort of CISA created the Infrastructure Security Division, which is responsible for directing critical infrastructure security efforts within the Agency. Specifically, this Division is to help critical infrastructure owners, operators, and their partners address risks to their CI, and provide tools and training to help manage risks to these assets, systems, and networks. Perhaps the most direct means of support to the SLTT community will be through the new CISA Central portal, where CI partners and stakeholders can contact CISA directly for assistance. "CISA Central is intended to be a one-stop-shop to request information sharing support or to distribute information to federal, state, local, tribal, and territorial stakeholders across the range of CISA's mission space" [12].

In 2008, there were at least 34 Federal legal requirements within Critical Infrastructure (CI) Sectors for securing privately-owned IT systems and data. There were 18 CI sectors identified at that time, but only eight had any legal mandate or requirement imposed upon them at the Federal level. Those sectors that did report mandates (Food and agriculture, Financial, Chemical, Commercial Facilities, Water Systems, Energy, Nuclear Reactors and Materials, Public Health, and Transportation) all reported some sort of enforcement mechanism that included court injunctions, monetary and criminal penalties, and administrative actions. The other ten, however, did not carry any legal mandate, requirement, or law to validate any sort of cybersecurity or physical security compliance with Federal regulation. One of these such sectors was "Government Facilities."

The issue with CISA and the Federal Government supporting SLTTs isn't due to a lack of authority as much as CISA needs to get clarification and buy-in from Congress and other parts of the Executive Branch. The three-phase reorganization of CISA to better support the evolving NIPP has not been completed yet (the original completion date was December 2020). Some of the critical efforts that remain incomplete are essential for engaging and supporting SLTTs. This includes developing and planning a more robust Federal workforce that can help the Regional Sectors secure critical infrastructure. In report 21-236, the Government Accountability Office (GAO) implied that the Nation would be at a severe disadvantage without completing this task, especially in light of the current cyber events on infrastructure and the Supply Chain.

CISA has three primary mission areas; protection of the critical infrastructure is one of them. Of all the sectors who expressed concerns and areas that need to improve, the critical infrastructure stakeholders (to include government coordinating councils—GCC and sector coordinating councils—SCC) were consistently reporting challenges and concerns [12]. The specific challenges included a lack of timely response to stakeholder requests, inconsistent distribution of information, lack of access to actionable intelligence, and a lack of involvement in developing stakeholder guidance [12]. Because CISA and the Federal Government (and potentially Congress?) did not include the CI stakeholders in helping to shape this new federal touchpoint and its policies, Federally-mandated CISA may already be out of touch with the SLTT community as it finishes up its reorganization. This plan is not in the spirit of the NIPP, which expressed the importance of clear and frequent communications to protect critical infrastructure.

The Federal Government has many other efforts to facilitate collaboration, almost TOO many: CISA established a CI Security and Resilience program, which is grounded in public-private partnerships, coordination, and collaboration; Congress created the Protected Critical Infrastructure Information Program (PCII) through the Critical Infrastructure Act of 2002 to protect private-sector infrastructure information voluntarily shared with the Federal Government for national security purposes; and CISA also has the State, Local, Tribal, and Territorial Government Coordinating Council (SLTTGCC) to pull in these entities for identifying best practices in securing local and state critical infrastructure. It would appear to the average American citizen that the Federal Government is vested and working with SLTT governments and addressing the issue. Therefore, the SLTT entities should have every tool available from the Federal side to meet their mission. Unfortunately, there is no obvious or known program or starting point for SLTT leadership to go to if they need help. The myriad of programs, sharing efforts, regulations (or lack thereof), and ISACs is incredibly overwhelming and confusing.

Operational and budget constraints continue to affect SLTTs significantly; this, in turn, pushes cybersecurity environments into secondary options for those attempting to make corrective actions toward a secure environment. Those attempting to drive for a more secure environment, such as SLTT CISO's and their counterparts, struggle to make the necessary changes due to a lack of authority given to them. Often the person placed in charge of running the SLTT infrastructure lacks the understanding or education of how a cyber environment must be managed. This puts the local CISO in a problematic position, explaining what is necessary to protect the cyber infrastructure without being given the proper authority to affect the changes needed to secure the entirety of the environment.

While the lack of authority negatively impacts the cybersecurity infrastructure, the other element involved is the lack of direction on related resources at their disposal and the initial starting point for SLTTs. The current outlet for resources on cybersecurity management for SLTTs is typically found within CISA and the Multi-State Information Sharing and Analysis Center (MS-ISAC). These outlets house many ways to secure different environments, but there is no real directional guide for SLTT CISO's. Often, SLTT CISO's are not even aware these resources exist, which significantly impacts how they secure their environment and develop an understanding of the assets they manage. By not identifying our SLTTs as critical infrastructure, we continue to fail at the basic security level of securing our root environment from threats.

16.1.7 LESSONS LEARNED FROM A STATE CISO (CHIEF INFORMATION SECURITY OFFICER)

State and local governments are dealing with tight budgets, an ever-increasing threat, and a general lack of skilled labor; thus, it is imperative that they receive greater funding and support from the Federal government. The fact is that many major initiatives supported by the government relies on a State government IT system somewhere. For example, the last major COVID stimulus package from the Federal government provided a large sum of support for efforts such as rent relief and unemployment insurance (both of which States need to implement). None of the money earmarked for these worthy groups had additional carve-outs for local government IT systems to modernize and bolster their security. An easy way to fix this would be to ensure that proper overhead support was allocated for federal programs that are implemented at the State and Local levels as well as provide guidance on what level of security standards that should be met. It is clear that information sharing and general guidance from the Federal government are not enough when tackling the growing cyber threat. Congress should do what it can to ensure that the "last mile" when it comes to critical infrastructure and other critical funding programs is properly secured; otherwise, our nation's way of life will be increasingly at risk.

16.1.8 CONCLUSION

State and local governments can vary significantly in size and scope of operational services; many times, SLTTs can hold and manage more critical services and data than some federal government agencies. These organizations play such a vital role in most Americans' daily lives and currently lack the support and funding required to maintain optimal security standards. This is why the federal government must consider the challenges currently facing SLTTs and the potential effects of these organizations' disruption of services. The lack of an authoritative body to develop and enforce standards, budgets, and incident response support to SLTTs is well-known by adversaries looking to utilize them as soft targets to disrupt or degrade the critical infrastructure and services they provide. This has been demonstrated through the many supply chain attacks and ransomware attacks conducted over the past few years. These attacks have cost SLTTs millions of dollars in lost services, data recovery, and remediations. Many of the supply chain attacks will continue to cause issues for years to come. Without the proper consideration as critical infrastructure, SLTTs will continue to be a known easy target and eventually could even become the genesis of a national-level attack aimed to disrupt the government on a national scale.

16.1.8.1 ABOUT THE AUTHORS

Marcela Denniston is the Co-Founder and President of Cyber Lantern, an evangelist for minorities in cyber, and an advocate for serving the underserved. Marcela Denniston is a security and business professional with a passion for education and publicizing the need for cyber security for all. Her 18 years of international experience across commercial and government sectors has helped Marcela understand the critical gaps in understanding, managing, and implementing security for organizations both large and small. Marcela began her career in the United States Navy, where she worked as a Cyber Analyst for a US Intelligence Agency and quickly demonstrated a natural capacity to become an instructor and leader in the areas of Cyber Intelligence, Network Defense, Intrusion Analysis, and Threat Reporting. Her international consulting experience further expanded on how vast the lack of knowledge in security was globally and highlighted the critical need for diversity and inclusion in the technology/security market.

Alycia Farrell is the President of Grey Tarian. She is the current Government Affairs policy and budget specialist in Aerospace, Defense, and Cybersecurity industries, training for a technical certification in vulnerability assessments and offensive security.

Peter Liebert is the Founder of Liebert Security and is the Chief Information Security Officer for Cerner Government Services and Commander of Cyber Operations for the California State Guard. Throughout Peter's 20+ years of leadership, he has excelled in roles such as CISO for the State of California and was selected by his peers in 2019 as the Chief Security Officer of the year for SC Magazine. A security technology guru and information security policy wizard, he is practiced in implementing and operating industry-leading technologies (such as SecDevOps teams, Security Operations Centers, and advanced Artificial Intelligence-driven solutions) and is a recognized subject matter expert, cybersecurity speaker, and investor in the security community.

Jason Smith is Faculty, Coast Guard Chair at National War College. He is a combat-wounded veteran of the Army and has led soldiers during three combat deployments, to include Iraq and Afghanistan, as an AH-64A Attack Helicopter Pilot and Commander. Jason has experience working with national-level leaders in the Executive Branch and in the US Senate and as part of several foreign delegations in support of National Defense, including cyber security of critical infrastructures. Jason has a BS from Sam Houston State University, a Master of International Relations from St Mary's University, and a Master of Public Administration from Harvard University.

REFERENCES

1. S. Faulkner, "Counties: Backbone of Local Government, Core of Our Civic Culture – Constituting America", *Constitutingamerica.org*, 2019. [Online]. Available: https://constitutingamerica.org/county-leadership-guest-essayist-scot-faulkner/. [Accessed: 21- Jul- 2022].
2. "PTI/CompTIA 2020 National Survey of Local Government Cybersecurity Programs", *Public Technology Institute*, 2020. [Online]. Available: https://comptiacdn.azureedge.net/webcontent/docs/default-source/advocacy-documents/2020-pti-cybersecurity-national-survey.pdf?sfvrsn=b0488502_2. [Accessed: 21- Jul- 2022].
3. "Executive Order 13010—Critical Infrastructure Protection", *Federal Register*, 1996. [Online]. Available: https://www. hsdl.org/?view&did=1613. [Accessed: 21- Jul- 2022].
4. "State CIO Top 10 Priorities: 2021 Strategies, Policy Issues and Management Processes", *NASCIO*, 2021. [Online]. Available: https://www.nascio.org/wp-content/uploads/2020/12/NASCIO_CIOTopTenPriorities.pdf. [Accessed: 21- Jul- 2022].
5. J. Bergal, "State Cybersecurity Offices Need More Money and Staff, Report Finds", *Pewtrusts.org*, 2018. [Online]. Available: https://www.pewtrusts.org/en/research-and-analysis/blogs/stateline/2018/10/23/state-cybersecurity-offices-need-more-money-and-staff-report-finds. [Accessed: 21- Jul- 2022].

6. J. Comtios, "Financial services firms spend 6% to 14% of IT budget on cybersecurity – survey", *Pensions & Investments*, 2019. [Online]. Available: https://www.pionline.com/article/20190501/ONLINE/190509988/financial-services-firms-spend-6-to- 14-of-it-budget-on-cybersecurity-survey. [Accessed: 21- Jul- 2022].

7. B. Allyn, "22 Texas Towns Hit With Ransomware Attack In 'New Front' Of Cyberassault", *Npr.org*, 2019. [Online]. Available: https://www.npr.org/2019/08/20/752695554/23-texas-towns-hit-with-ransomware-attack-in-new-frontof- cyberassault. [Accessed: 21- Jul- 2022].

8. "2020 Cyber Threat Report", *Netwrix.com*, 2020. [Online]. Available: https://www.netwrix.com/download/collaterals/2020_Cyber_Threats_Report.pdf. [Accessed: 21- Jul- 2022].

9. "Chapter Five: Russia and Eurasia", *The Military Balance*, vol. 117, no. 1, pp. 183-236, 2017. Available: https://www.tandfonline.com/doi/abs/10.1080/04597222.2017.1271211. [Accessed 21 July 2022].

10. B. Chappell, "FBI Called In After Hacker Tries To Poison Tampa-Area City's Water With Lye", *Npr.org*, 2021. [Online]. Available: https://www.npr.org/2021/02/09/965791252/fbi-called-in-after-hacker-tries-to-poison-tampa-area-citywater- with-lye. [Accessed: 21- Jul- 2022].

11. S. Coble, "SolarWinds Hackers "Impacting" State and Local Governments", *Info Security Group*, 2020. [Online]. Available: https://www.infosecurity-magazine.com/news/solarwinds-hackers-impacting/. [Accessed: 21- Jul- 2022].

12. "CYBERSECURITY AND INFRASTRUCTURE SECURITY AGENCY Actions Needed to Ensure Organizational Changes Result in More Effective Cybersecurity for Our Nation", *Gao.gov*, 2021. [Online]. Available: https://www.gao.gov/assets/gao-21-236.pdf. [Accessed: 21- Jul- 2022].

13. J. Langevin and S. Jackson-Lee, "Information Technology: Federal Laws, Regulations, and Mandatory Standards for Securing Private Sector Information Technology Systems and Data in Critical Infrastructure Sector", *Gao.gov*, 2008. [Online]. Available: https://www.gao.gov/assets/gao-08-1075r.pdf. [Accessed: 21- Jul- 2022].

16.2 INNOVATIONS FOR STATE AND LOCAL GOVERNMENTS

Marcela Denniston, Alycia Farrell, Peter Liebert, and Jason Smith
Digital Lantern

16.2.1 INTRODUCTION

The COVID-19 pandemic forced many organizations to rapidly adopt a digital transformation strategy in support of a safer, more socially distanced, and internet-connected commercial market space. With the expansion of remote work, e-commerce, and virtual services came a massive opportunity for cybercriminals looking for soft targets. State and local governments were required to adopt remote work capabilities on legacy technologies without the resources and expertise to secure their new digital environment. While some organizations such as the Cybersecurity and Infrastructure Security Agency (CISA), provided a way to help advise and coordinate State, Local, Tribal, and Territorial (SLTT) on mitigating their digital risk, the Federal Government still lacked a sense of urgency or a means to provide direct funding to SLTT organizations. CISA has advocated and supported the Multi-State Information Sharing and Analysis Center (MS-ISAC) to engage and mitigate SLTT risk, but the MS-ISAC is also not properly equipped to fully assist in the management of risk, information sharing, and continuous cyber support through resource allocations to SLTTs. With limited resources and nation-state and cybercriminal threats, SLTTs need to turn to more innovative approaches for cyber security that focus on the mitigation of risk through managed services by nationally trained cyber security professionals, with the support of automation and orchestration tools to improve the speed of adoption. Additionally, SLTTs should leverage the power of information sharing and big data technologies from various collected data sets across several systems to establish risk visibility, behavioral analysis through system baselining, and anomaly detection for identification of potential supply chain attacks and advanced persistent threats.

Given budgetary and resource constraints imposed on state and local governments, the primary focus for improving cyber resilience should be centered around methods that incentivize risk reduction through a holistic operational approach. Such an effort requires a thorough mapping of current IT environments and their business functions and understanding, which are the essential components to sustaining critical services and institutions to state and local governments. It also requires a clear understanding of cost efficiencies associated with people, processes, and technologies within the organization. Removal of old technologies and outdated, resource-intensive systems that the service providers no longer support is imperative to simplifying user workflows and reducing vulnerabilities and costs to an SLTT.

State and local governments should also consider maximizing centralized technology approaches that focus on data standardization, automation, and orchestration tools to make daily operational management and system integration and updates more manageable and less manual. This approach could include adopting advanced platforms that support the concept of a cyber security single source of truth providing asset and network visibility, ingestion of security log data, continuous risk modeling, and advanced machine learning and analytics modeling. This innovation to security helps provide a centralized source of management, ensuring less time spent learning how to manage and maintain disparate product sets while improving operational insights, which would generally require a team of subject matter experts in many different security arenas. Additionally, resource constraints among SLTTs mean a more concerted effort in information sharing across the industry would support their cyber resilience. While automation and orchestration can be extremely useful for daily operations, human subject matter expertise is still essential. The utilization of outsourced subject matter experts and Cyber Security Operations Centers that support private-public sector partnerships could speed up State and local governments' ability to detect and respond to threats and vulnerabilities faster while providing reliable industry-based risk analysis.

16.2.2 MODERNIZE LEGACY IT

A key component to improving security is removing outdated technologies, known as legacy systems, that do not fit current technological requirements. Legacy systems that are kept operational beyond their functional or intended need can pose a significant threat from a cyber security perspective. The return on investment of managing and supporting these systems also decreases significantly as the technology becomes obsolete. A study conducted by the Center for Digital Government (CDG) in 2018, which provided feedback from 190 State and local government technology professionals, indicated that over 42% of respondents claimed to spend at least a quarter of their budget on maintaining legacy systems [1]. SLTTs already operate with limited staff and budget, making a 25% budget allocation impactful. Streamlining and consolidating technologies focused on secure and easy-to-manage systems should be a priority for SLTTs. This will remove unnecessary costs and simplify network infrastructure that already deals with a lack of funding and resources. The COVID-19 pandemic has become a catalyst for modernization efforts as states and municipalities scrambled to rapidly adopt remote work systems that were both efficient and secure. These modernizations will reduce cost, improve security by removing non-supported systems, and increase the confidentiality, integrity, and availability of critical services to community citizens.

16.2.3 IMPROVING SUPPLY CHAIN SECURITY

Supply chain risks remain one of the biggest threats to State and local governments. SLTTs rely heavily on third-party technologies to provide continuous services within the community. Each supplier comes with additional connectivity to the government IT networks that create potential risks. Recent events, such as the SolarWinds attacks and the Microsoft Exchange Server compromise, are examples of the significant impact a supply chain breach can have globally. Since SLTTs do not have direct control over their 3rd party suppliers, they must look to innovative approaches to ensure they are protected from supply chain risks. The Department of Defense is adopting the Cybersecurity Maturity Model Certification (CMMC), which helps standardized risk assessments across DoD supply chain vendors. This model requires a 3rd party accreditation process that ensures supply chain providers maintain specific security standards and practices if they desire to continue working with the Department of Defense. A similar approach could be adopted for SLTT and critical infrastructures. This would ensure that supply chain providers address security issues and inject accountability into the system to ensure continuous improvements and measures are put into place to include secure coding, system hardening, and identification of critical data and systems associated with the providers. Adopting such a process should consist of a predefined accreditation construct that includes: Secure Software Lifecycle Development; mandatory security training and awareness for supply chain developers; and cyclical and automated penetration testing to ensure hardware and software providers are maintaining best practices in security.

As these efforts can be a costly detractor for organizations looking to work with critical infrastructure sectors, the government should look to provide incentive programs to supply chain providers who are willing to go the extra mile to work with them. An example of a great public-private collaboration is the National Institute of Standards and Technology's (NIST) National Network Manufacturing Extension Partnership (MEP). All 50 States and Puerto Rico have an MEP Center that offers programs to support DoD contractors through non-profit organization partnerships [2]. They provide resources and funding for Small to Medium size manufacturers who wish to bid on the Department of Defense and require DFARS/CMMC compliance. Programs such as MEP allow the smaller organization to remain competitive in government bids while also promoting improved overall cyber security posture by supply chain providers.

Adopting a centralized data platform that helps standardize and manage supply chain partner data is also essential. Before working with a provider, organizations should understand what technologies and critical data will be procured and shared through their services. By identifying the risk through a standardized assessment process, organizations can then ingest data from the supply chain provider to correlate risk and threat susceptibility to real-time data.

16.2.4 THE ZERO TRUST MODEL AND SUPPLY CHAIN SECURITY

Another approach that is becoming popular in supply chain risk management is the adoption of Zero Trust Models. As cloud integrations, virtual services, and Software-as-a-Service (SaaS) applications become more prevalent, security controls are shifting to adopt to the new IT landscape. With the adoption of new technologies, organizations are beginning to apply a perimeter-less security model that does not rely on inherent trust but instead creates micro segmentations within the environment that only grants access to specific users, systems, and/or applications. This idea implies that to get into any particular area of an IT environment, one must have granted access to it to avoid lateral movement within an IT infrastructure's critical areas. Instead of focusing on blocking specific types of access at entry points into the network, Zero Trust requires organizations to identify where users require access and provide the most limited access possible to prevent unprivileged access to sensitive or critical data sources. This suggested practice is highly beneficial for supply chain risk management; it allows organizations to focus on creating limited access points from 3rd party users, systems, and applications to their network's critical components. This helps ensure that if there were to be a supply chain breach or risk, organizations could quickly isolate the affected third-party asset, system, user, or application without risk of further infiltration into critical data or systems providing essential services to the community. Zero trust models require the utilization of several technologies, including Identity and Access Management (IAM), next-generation firewalls, data encryption, analytics, secure backups, and advanced user/system segmentation. While this approach may require the adoption of several security products and measures, many products on the market offer a centralized Zero Trust modeling approach focused on virtual network segmentation, application-based access control, and data modeling alerting of anomalies. If a Zero Trust model is applied correctly and continuously monitored for behavioral anomalies, organizations can significantly decrease supply chain risks.

16.2.5 CYCLICAL RISK MANAGEMENT

Risk Management has become an increasingly vital component of cyber resilience. It enables identifying, evaluating, and then prioritizing an organization's cyber risk to create actionable measures in reducing the likelihood of cyberattacks. By understanding the environment, naming critical systems and assets, and understanding the susceptibility and impact of particular threats, organizations can prioritize the most critical security tasks first to avoid worst-case scenarios. Once there is a clear understanding of risk, it is easier to prepare for scenarios with a high likelihood of causing denial or disruption of services. An important risk mitigation measure for an SLTT government is ensuring the regular creation of critical data back-ups to minimize the risk of disruption in essential services in a ransomware attack. Another example is conducting routine patch management of IT system vulnerabilities to avoid exploiting systems that lead to more significant breaches. Risk management alone is not an innovation; however, the methods used to improve the efficiency and effectiveness of risk management through automation, orchestration, and use of contextual information provide many opportunities to apply innovative technologies to streamline operations and reduce resources and costs.

One of the most significant issues with risk management today is the lack of standardization and solid methodologies for automated quantitative and qualitative assessments. The concept of the CMMC has provided an innovative opportunity for standardized risk modeling based on Department of Defense (DoD) standards. The model requires organizations that provide goods and services to the DoD to conduct a 3rd party assessment of their risk posture before securing a contract to minimize supply chain risks from public-private sector business engagements. Other partner organizations such as the Department of Homeland Security (DHS) and General Services Administration (GSA), are also beginning to adopt CMMC standards. Utilizing this consistent model across all other government organizations would help improve uniformity and increase the chances of developing automated capabilities to support the assessment and certification process.

16.2.6 QUANTITATIVE RISK INNOVATIONS

Quantitative assessments, which include identifying assets or systems operating in the environment and what they are vulnerable to, and how accessible they are to external and internal systems and users, have been common approaches used to define risk. However, this standard method doesn't account for the human ability hackers have to bypass basic controls. Innovation in this area includes considering the technology and how the human attacker maneuvers through the environment with specific tactics and techniques to evade security measures in place by an organization. Running regular penetration tests helps solve this; however, they often do not fit into the budgetary constraints of SLTTs due to the need for highly expert personnel and the considerable time allocations to conduct the tests. This scenario is where recent technologies that run auto simulations of attacks that follow the tactics, techniques, and procedures of human hackers become valuable. Simulation tools allow organizations to run detailed tests on their networks to understand human tactics that reach beyond system vulnerabilities. Simulations can range from simple end-user awareness through the deployment of spear phishing emails to understand a user's susceptibility to an attack to more advanced tools which allow for end-to-end attack simulations, capturing an attacker's tactics and techniques in different environments. This will enable organizations to run automated penetration testing methods while utilizing human-driven tactics without the high cost and resource-intensive requirements of human penetration testing projects.

16.2.7 QUALITATIVE RISK INNOVATIONS

Understanding risks based on what your organization is susceptible to from an asset perspective can be easy to quantify. On the other hand, evaluating qualitative risk is more complex. It requires discussions with various stakeholders and understanding scenario-based risks associated with policy, practice, and technology. These assessments are often conducted by costly third-party representatives and require several weeks of interactions with various stakeholders to understand how the organization's policies, practices, and technologies are identified, protected, and monitored. This also includes a review of what reporting and response mechanisms are in place to manage risks when they arise. State and local governments manage and operate a wide array of services that all require different risk analysis approaches. This is why risk management efficiency is so imperative. Qualitative questions with both binary yes or no responses and responses that range in likelihood often require a third-party assessor to remove bias.

Additionally, the process needed to review and quantify qualitative risk can be lengthy and tedious. Efficiencies in this process require innovation in automating the qualitative process and assigning quantitative values that can be further used on a sliding scale to define risk and susceptibility levels. The latest innovations centered around simplifying the qualitative analysis will help improve the likelihood that SLTTs will adopt a continuous risk management approach. By automating and assigning specific stakeholders to the policy, practice, and technology questionnaire associated with every risk assessment, organizations can simplify and standardize the process so that risk assessments can happen more frequently. Continuous automated risk assessment is best for supporting security in an evolving dynamic threat environment without relying on human resource-intense capital.

16.2.8 UTILIZING AUTOMATION AND ORCHESTRATION TO CONTINUOUSLY MONITOR AND IMPROVE RISK

With automated quantitative and qualitative processes aligned to national compliance standards, organizations can now begin to apply cyclical assessments to ensure their security posture's continuous improvement. This approach is critical to the ongoing security of critical infrastructures. As digital transformation progresses with the adoption of new technologies, remote connectivity, and more reliance on third-party software and services, it is imperative to have an ongoing ability to reassess and evaluate security measures regularly. It supplies an opportunity for organizations to understand their current risk posture, identify areas of improvement, and provide consistent and standardized reporting methods back to government organizations such as CISA and the MS-ISAC to ensure all SLTTs meet compliance standards. The data derived from the automated assessments also play a key role in the continuous detection and monitoring of real threats. By using the collected risk assessment data to understand the organization's actual susceptibility to specific attacks, SLTTs can utilize less time and resources to address alerts and events that are not relevant to their current environment. However, this is not attainable without the ability to automate the risk assessment processes and collect the valuable data points that will help contextualize and correlate significant events that require prioritized attention by SLTTs to improve security. Additionally, aggregation of risk assessment data obtained through automated assessments and stored on bug data platforms could be further utilized by CISA and the MS-ISAC to drive valid situational awareness and national-level risk postures of SLTTs and other critical infrastructures. It could also aid in developing new policies and directives relevant to the active threats that affect critical infrastructures across the nation.

16.2.9 CENTRALIZED SECURITY DATA MANAGEMENT

One of the biggest challenges state and local governments face is the sheer volume of technologies required to provide the critical services expected by local citizens. Technology brings forth a significant amount of data, and additional security measures to maintain the confidentiality, availability, and integrity of those systems can be complex. Security products can help identify suspicious activities; however, security data, without context, correlation, and analysis, does not provide a holistic view of an organization's actual security posture. This is why aggregating security data, system data, and shared intelligence is imperative to improve critical infrastructures' cyber resilience.

As organizations (including state and local governments) migrate toward cloud adoption, data centralization becomes more straightforward, cost-effective, and efficient. SLTTS can then begin to avoid data silos with multifunctional platforms that support security operations, provide efficiency, and create a single truth source for security needs. This decreases the monitoring complexity faced by SLTTs, who typically have limited staff to monitor all data continuously. This concept also avoids undermining technology implementations by using one centralized platform to manage security operations and cuts down on the training required to make user adoption a success. Centralized data management also helps improve return on investment on security products purchased for the environment. By using a centralized data platform, organizations can take advantage of context and correlation across disparate data sources, ensuring that the use of products deployed in the environment is being maximized.

16.2.10 DATA STANDARDIZATION, MODELING, AND ANALYTIC SHARING

With a centralized data model, state and local governments can also utilize data standardization, modeling, and analytics. Machine learning has enabled many big data platforms to perform advanced analytics that allows organizations to look for anomalies across various data sets and identify behaviors that do not follow the expected operations of said environments' technology and communications. When appropriately applied, data standardization and analytics can be very powerful. Centralized Big Data Platforms (BDPs) provide the ability to visualize, organize and correlate data from various levels of operational environments. Cyberattacks are multi-faceted and often require attackers to access several technology components to carry out a full-scope attack. With a centralized data platform, security analysts and engineers can utilize a single truth source to track attack behaviors. This helps decrease the time to detect cyberattacks and reduces the time to identify the attack's root cause, leading to improved attack visibility and remediation times.

Additionally, centralized data platforms enable users to access a holistic operational picture beyond just security alerts. True cyber resilience requires more than just identifying security alerts. It requires organizations to identify and understand the environment through asset identification and management, classifications of the assets to understand what components of the infrastructure are truly most critical to operations, and then the protection of said assets through standardized controls. After the initial breakdown of this risk management cycle, organizations can begin to truly monitor the environment with a clear understanding of what is genuinely malicious and how remediation actions should be prioritized based on the contextual risk data. All of this information can be stored, standardized, and analyzed using advanced analytic methods by using a centralized big data platform. This means increased cost efficiencies by removing siloed data environments, simplified operations through machine learning and behavioral analysis, and reduced resource allocations by decreasing the number of hours operators spend learning, managing, and maintaining technologies and security products.

16.2.11   INFORMATION SHARING ACROSS PRIVATE-PUBLIC SECTORS

Centralized platforms also allow for more fluid data sharing mechanisms across similar sectors and communities. Today, Informational Sharing and Analysis Centers (ISACs) exist to help protect critical infrastructures from physical and cyber threats. Most ISACs provide a wide range of services; however, some have adopted more advanced capabilities that would be beneficial across all Critical Infrastructure ISACs. The Multi-State Information Sharing and Analysis Center (MS-ISAC), which was developed in partnership with the Department of Homeland Security (DHS), helps support private-public information sharing and security posture guidance for SLTTs. [3] The MS-ISAC provides a platform for collaboration amongst SLTTs but is limited in its ability to provide support for the response and remediation of attacks. It also does not give state-level chief information security officers (CISOs) enough information due to "need to know" standards. While State CISOs do have access to information sharing from DHS-level reporting, the information often lacks the detail required to create actionable threat intelligence plans that effectively thwart cyberattacks.

However, the Financial Sector ISAC (FS-ISAC) has implemented improved methods of information sharing that could be utilized as the standard sharing model across all ISACs. The model provides the ability to share information about breaches while victim organizations maintain anonymity from other ISAC members. Anonymization of breached data for information sharing encourages ISAC members to provide essential details to prevent other organizations from suffering similar attacks. The FS-ISAC's adoption of this model has made it an exemplary standard among the ISAC community. It encourages private-public sector collaboration without the added risk of impacting brand reputation, a significant disincentive to most information-sharing efforts.

Beyond basic sharing of technical indicators of compromise and non-technical contextual data, centralized environments can add new value propositions to data sharing. Using a centralized data collection approach, private-public sector information sharing communities can also begin to share advanced analytics and threat modeling approaches without the added costs of new products and data feeds. As SLTTs operate on limited resources and budgets, this anonymized and centralized approach supported by community sharing provides a low-cost and efficient method of getting high-quality threat information.

16.2.12 PRIVATE-PUBLIC PARTNERSHIPS FOR TRAINING AND OPERATIONS

For State and local governments, cybersecurity has become a mainstream issue that affects the trust and operational stability of critical services provided to its citizens. While technology innovations help improve SLTTs cyber resilience, it does not address the added cost and resource burdens associated with their adoption. Since the state of cyber security for SLTTs is a community issue, it would only make sense to adopt a private-public partnership eco-system that improves State and local government security postures while also developing an entire ecosystem of training, jobs, and economic growth within the community. These partnerships, which are already being adopted in many states and localities, offer centralized security operations and information sharing with cross-collaborative initiatives that utilize educational institutions, city, state, and federal organizational resources.

Many states are deploying these partnerships in some capacity. Michigan is leading state security efforts by supporting small to medium-sized businesses with free cyber assessment tools. The State is also improving overall training and cyber awareness through the Michigan Cyber Range, which "provides secure cybersecurity training, research and exercise environment for IT security professionals in educational institutions, private businesses and the public sector — including local governments" [4]. These initiatives allow for the development of "fusion centers" where educational institutions can create a centralized security operations center. This would create local job opportunities in Science, Technology, Engineering, and Math (STEM) and support research and innovation in the field of cybersecurity while also providing security services to local communities at lower costs than most commercial cybersecurity providers. With federal, state, and local government support, these fusion centers can operate as regional technology hubs for advanced data analytics and information sharing across private-public sector organizations who wish to participate. An example of such a partnership would be developing a cybersecurity curriculum at a local community college or state university, which provides consolidated Managed Security Services to local companies and state and local government organizations. The centralized hub provides local tech jobs to boost the economy and GDP and provides on-the-job training and internships so students can graduate with experience, which is often a basic requirement for cybersecurity work. Finally, it offers local centralized situational awareness for cross-sector collaboration with other fusion centers. This helps reduce costs imposed directly on state and local governments while incentivizing shared responsibility and establishing a community-driven approach to cybersecurity, focused on improving security rather than reactively responding to incidents.

16.2.13 OUTSOURCING

When organizations operate with limited budgets and resources, it is not uncommon for them to consider outsourcing services to providers. This practice is often frowned upon in government due to its lack of regulation and supply chain risk. Regardless, outsourcing to Managed Security Services Providers (MSSP) could be a cost-efficient way to provide after-hour security services to every SLTT and incentivize centralized information sharing and situational awareness. At the state level, governments could identify a "gold standard" list of security providers who meet the pricing, subject matter expertise, and minimum security requirements in their area. The state can then encourage local governments to work with pre-approved vendors at discounted rates, ensuring the MSSPs are cross-collaborating to ensure optimal information sharing across the state level. States can then utilize information aggregated across these providers to share critical threat and risk information across local and state organizations. Today, many ex-federal employees have crossed into the private sector to provide national-level subject matter expertise in commercial technologies development. State and local governments can leverage these companies' expertise by building partnerships that help boost the economy while also benefiting from previous federal government expertise at reduced costs.

16.2.14 CONCLUSION

For SLTTs, innovation means more than just improved technologies; it must also consider deficiencies in current processes intended to support the overall advancement of cyber resilience nationwide. A centralized effort to consolidate and simplify IT systems management and data aggregation help to improve technology adoption. However, without the proper cross-collaboration with other private-public sector industry professionals, information-sharing organizations, and the continued support of research and development, security and IT teams at the state and local government level will continue to operate in silos and fail to treat security as an ongoing cyclical process focused on continuous improvements to people, processes, and technologies.

REFERENCES

1. "Keeping Pace with Modernization in the Age of Rapid Obsolescence", *Media.erepublic.com*, 2018. [Online]. Available: https://media.erepublic.com/document/CDG19_REPORT_OutSystems_V.pdf. [Accessed: 21- Jul- 2022].
2. "Manufacturing Extension Partnership (MEP) | NIST", *NIST*, 2014. [Online]. Available: https://www. nist.gov/mep. [Accessed: 21- Jul- 2022].
3. "MS-ISAC® Charter", *CIS*, 2021. [Online]. Available: https://www.cisecurity.org/ms-isac/ms-isac-charter/. [Accessed: 21- Jul- 2022].
4. C. McFarland, B. Rivett, K. Funk, R. Kim and S. Wagner, "State and Local Partnerships for Cybersecurity: A STATE-BY-STATE ANALYSIS", *Nlc.org*, 2020. [Online]. Available: https://www. nlc.org/wp-content/uploads/2020/04/SML_2020Report_web-1.pdf. [Accessed: 21- Jul- 2022].

16.3 RECOMMENDATIONS TO IMPROVE THE CYBER RESILIENCE OF STATE AND LOCAL GOVERNMENTS

Marcela Denniston, Alycia Farrell, Peter Liebert, and Jason Smith
Digital Lantern

16.3.1 INTRODUCTION

As we enter a new era of the Information Age, the methods in which wars are wagered are drastically changing. Physical attacks are becoming less prevalent, while cyberattacks increase exponentially. While the earlier Presidential administration has taken some level of action in supporting the development of the necessary resources to recognize and support state and local governments as a crucial part of critical infrastructure, there is still a significant amount of effort needed to execute these ideas effectively. This includes the consideration of state and local government as one of the sectors of Critical Infrastructure. Such a determination will elevate State, Local, Tribal, and Territorial (SLTT) governments to a level where they may qualify and receive the same funding and resource considerations as its critical infrastructure counterparts. This, in turn, aids in the increase of cyber resilience to SLTT's internal IT environments that operate as supply chains to other critical infrastructures. The administration should also consider giving more authority to Cybersecurity and Infrastructure Security Agency (CISA) beyond advising and aiding. CISA should have the ability to supply grants and other necessary incentives and resources; specifically, aid in the cyber resilience of said critical infrastructures to support enforcement of standards and policies, as well as the implementation of modern technologies to support iterative risk management, removal of outdated/legacy technologies, and adoption of improved systems that support more secure environments, and implementation of information sharing across all sectors. Reassessing and adjusting resources to address the current threat from near-peer competitors will better align national effort with the daily gray zone operations conducted against the United States.

The character of war is changing, and to maintain its position as the top world power, the United States needs to adjust how it looks at war and position resources to the decisive points on the battlefield. Many advanced foreign adversaries such as Russia, Iran, North Korea, and China have pivoted their efforts to fight wars in a "gray zone" operational environment. Gray zone operations are less physically invasive and often incorporate the use of non-military criminal involvement to impact the spread of misinformation through information warfare, economic coercion, and the use of ambiguous non-military force [1]. Gray operations are more difficult to counter as attribution is harder when a nation-state utilizes criminal organizations, digital currencies, and virtual activities to weaken the US global position as an economic and political leader.

State and local governments and their infrastructures are primary targets for gray zone attacks. State and local governments provide control, oversight, security, and management of much of what is considered critical infrastructure. US adversaries are aware that these targets lack the federal support in funding and resources to properly harden local infrastructures against gray zone attacks. The Department of Defense has high-end capabilities, and these capabilities are necessary to defend the United States and its allies from direct attack. However, if the same standards and support are not pushed down into states and local communities, the United States is likely to lose the battle before any actual shots are fired. In this new gray zone battlespace, the United States is already at war today, and state and local governments are on the battlefield. Protecting state and local governments are essential if the United States is going to win the left of "boom" on the competition continuum.

16.3.1.1 RECOMMENDATION 1: RESTRUCTURING OF CYBER AUTHORITIES

In assessing the current structure for national support to SLTT governments, it is clear that there is both a lack of standards and a lack of resources provided to ensure their cyber resilience. Gray zone operations aimed at disrupting national security through local attacks should be a primary factor in creating the proper authorities to help support these efforts. Many organizations exist today that provide guidance and assistance in supporting the development of policy, workforce training, and the securing of critical infrastructures. At the state level, the National Governor's Association has a dedicated resource center focused on providing tools and recommendations to governors on improving cyber response and resilience. The development of the National Council of Information Sharing and Analysis Centers (ISACs) was also a driver in supporting the betterment of situational awareness and information sharing across critical infrastructure sectors and sub-sectors. These efforts are beneficial to SLTTs; however, they do not impose specified standards or guidelines that would help provide a long-term structure around risk management, incident response, and minimum requirements for operational security.

The CISA, established by the Department of Homeland Security, provides good initial steps to help protect critical infrastructures through private-public sector collaboration. With many incidents, such as the SolarWinds breach utilizing US IT infrastructures, private-public sector collaboration and information sharing, and security standardizations are critical to protecting the national security of our nation. Unfortunately, organizations such as CISA do not have the authority to enforce security standards on critical infrastructures or their private supply chain counterparts. The same problem was identified in the Department of Defense supply chain structure, leading to the development of the Cybersecurity Maturity Model Certification (CMMC), which sets 3rd party accreditation standards based on already existing frameworks provided by the National Institute of Standards and Technology. CISA can address the threat to SLTTs in similar ways that provide incentives for stronger cyber security and resilience.

16.3.1.1.1 Increase CISA Authority

It is not enough to develop a National Director of Cyber to lead engagement with private sectors; there needs to be a clear plan of action beyond strategy that focuses on the private-public sector intersections as they pertain to state and local governments. To achieve this, CISA must be empowered (financially and legally) to act in developing strategic and operational guidelines, enforcing cyber mandates, and including local/state governments as a separate sector of critical infrastructure. This includes setting a standard for cyber security policies, compliance, risk management, and incident response preparedness.

16.3.1.1.2 Institute Improved Funding and Collaboration

As the primary integration center for private-public sector security collaboration on the security of critical infrastructures, CISA should also be provided with improved tools and resources that aid in the development, implementation, and collaboration of information sharing efforts. This requires improved buy-in from federal agencies who can directly provide resources with the required subject matter expertise to help propel CISA's authority and capabilities to more mature levels. The 2020 joint DHS, DOE, and DOD Pathfinder Initiative was a step in the right direction encouraging cooperation by federal agencies [2]. By developing a Cyber Fusion Center consisting of federal, state, and critical infrastructure stakeholders, CISA can build on these types of initiatives and provide improved proactive risk management and incident response. This effort should include not only the development of a de facto Fusion Center but also a centralized platform that allows for broad spectrum situational awareness of critical infrastructure threats by sector and region. The centralized platform can also provide an avenue for enhanced information sharing to state and local government stakeholders, as well as providing the ability to share advanced analytics and data modeling. By providing a centralized approach through a Fusion Center, state and local governments can have a trusted and cost-effective method of managing real-time risks as they arise from sanitized and reputable data sources curated by federal, private, and state-level stakeholders.

16.3.1.2 RECOMMENDATION 2: DEVELOP STANDARDS AND INCENTIVES FOR MEETING SECURITY MATURITY LEVELS

Having additional authority will also require a standardization of efforts across SLTTs and their supply chains. Many models for compliance that are effective already exist, however, none are set as the overall standard for SLTTs and their supply chains. This should include requirements for periodic assessments, incorporating legacy technology risk, supply chain risk, and sector-specific assessments depending on the specific critical infrastructures managed by SLTT governments. Assessments should also be conducted by third-party government operators to avoid additional costs and self-assessment bias. Assessment results should also be further documented and ingested into a centralized database to help support Fusion Center's awareness of the current threat levels of SLTTs nationwide.

16.3.1.2.1 Standardize State and Local Government Compliance

Since many standards already exist, CISA should utilize current methods, such as the CMMC compliance standard, as a baseline to incentivize security best practices within the SLTT governments. Since states and local governments vary greatly in size, business functions, and technology, the maturity level for each SLTT should be derived by first assessing at the state level the scope of cyber resilience required to safeguard the state from a cyber emergency, and then push down to counties and local governments. SLTTs who are responsible for a higher number of critical infrastructures and services should be held to higher security practices and thus provided greater incentives for maintaining cyber security compliance requirements. For example, states should work with local governments to identify the most critical components of their businesses and infrastructures. Once they are identified, the local governments should align their responsibilities for safeguarding these assets with other critical infrastructure sectors aligned to those services. Once identified, CISA should have the authority to set the standards of compliance for the state and local governments and directly provide federal funding and resources toward conducting risk assessments, purchasing protection hardware/software, and establishing incident response and readiness plans and exercises. CISA should also have oversight on SLTT compliance to better understand the actual threat level and risk each SLTT poses at the national level.

16.3.1.2.2 Supply Chain Standardization and Incentives

CISA needs to have the authority to enforce security standards over private supply chains that affect the security of the critical infrastructure. Many private sector organizations are hesitant to share information on breaches due to legal and branding repercussions, making it more difficult for critical SLTT infrastructure providers to obtain the information needed to protect their supply chain connections. This can be remediated by implementing a set standard, such as the CMMC, to critical infrastructure supply chain providers, as well as federal incentives in maintaining certain security standards. Non-cyber programs that have successfully achieved this include Leadership in Energy and Environmental Design (LEED) established by the US Green Building Council (USGBC). This program established certification standards for new building designs focused on energy efficiency and waste reduction. The program provides various certification levels that can be achieved through third-party assessments, which often later pay off in the form of local and state tax breaks. A similar program could be instituted at the national level among private-public sector collaborations, giving private organizations tax incentives or federal grants to support improved cyber compliance standards, which help secure critical infrastructure supply chains, promote information sharing, and support rapid incident response. Private sector organizations willing to work within the CISA standards can then be ranked by compliance level and added to a "preferred partner" list or grouping that gives privileged access to government information sharing and cyber resources. This same methodology can easily be applied to supply chain vendors to promote and incentivize commercial businesses who are willing to abide by CISA standards to provide goods and services to the public sector.

16.3.1.3   RECOMMENDATION 3: IMPROVE CYBER READINESS AND INCIDENT RESPONSE

The US experiences tens of thousands of cyberattacks every day, making it impossible to defend against every attack [3]. Therefore, incident preparedness and response should be a top priority for every state and local government. Many states, such as Wisconsin, have employed National Guard Cyber Units known as "Cyber Protection Teams" to provide cyber security support through data analytics and incident preparedness. Utilizing National Guard resources has helped improve cost efficiencies. DHS also has Cyber Security Incident and Response Teams and access to the Coast Guard's Cyber Protection Teams. Incentivizing and standardizing information sharing through above-mentioned fusion centers allows quick dissemination of information to other possible targets and hastens response times. It is essential to better integrate agencies that respond to cyber incidents. The exchange of responders from the different levels of government and coordinated exercises will make prevention, response, and recovery more efficient.

16.3.1.3.1   Outsourcing to Subject Matter Experts

In addition to utilizing available resources from federal and local governments through partnerships with National Guard, federal agencies, and local universities, special consideration should be placed on outsourcing services that are not feasible to accomplish on the limited budgets and resources available to SLTTs. Since outsourcing adds additional risks to government agencies through the supply chain, service providers should be closely vetted to meet minimum standards of subject matter expertise and security. This capability can be created by sourcing Managed Security Service Providers who have a proven record of national-level security expertise. Providers can be held accountable for similar security standards as those set in the CMMC to ensure they meet the national level of requirements for security, as well as having minimum requirements associated with their level of knowledge regarding the specific threats, intelligence, and information sharing methodologies known at federal agency levels. Outsourcing these services could be beneficial for many reasons: they would provide improved situational awareness through 24/7 continuous detection and monitoring currently not available to most SLTTs, a centralized hub for information sharing, and reduced costs for security operations while still maintaining national security level standards of cyber resilience. The government could set a minimum standard for providing these services and further incentivize local government subscriptions by subsidizing the cost to state and local governments.

16.3.2   CONCLUSION

The cyber threats affecting state and local governments have a significant impact on the state of national security. If a coordinated attack against several critical infrastructures operated by SLTTs was to occur, the results could lead to disruptions of many services that support and sustain daily life for American citizens. These attacks can even become life threatening in some cases, further making the case that state and local governments are, in fact, a key component of critical infrastructures. To ensure that our state and local governments are prepared for a mass cyberattack, it is crucial for the federal government to acknowledge the critical role SLTTs play in managing and maintaining necessary services to citizens. This includes expansion of budget and resources from federal agencies and cross-collaboration with other available resources such as state colleges and universities and National Guard support.

The federal government should also enact a centralized authority through CISA developing national standards that funnel into state and local government levels and providing incentives to organizations willing to meet or supersede said standards as both private and public sector supply chain providers to national government initiatives. The federal government should also support enhanced data sharing capabilities that provide the most up-to-date threat information and analytic methods to prevent the propagation of attacks beyond their initial access. A centralized concerted effort with standards for risk management, continuous monitoring, and incident response could help improve the overall cyber resilience of state and local governments. Cyber security must become an accepted necessity, supported and backed by national-level awareness, resources and budget in order to ensure the long-term protection of American society and life.

16.3.2.1 ABOUT THE AUTHORS

Marcela Denniston is the Co-Founder and President of Cyber Lantern, an evangelist for minorities in cyber, and an advocate for serving the underserved. Marcela Denniston is a security and business professional with a passion for education and publicizing the need for cyber security for all. Her 18 years of international experience across commercial and government sectors has helped Marcela understand the critical gaps in understanding, managing, and implementing security for organizations both large and small. Marcela began her career in the United States Navy, where she worked as a Cyber Analyst for a US Intelligence Agency and quickly demonstrated a natural capacity to become an instructor and leader in the areas of Cyber Intelligence, Network Defense, Intrusion Analysis, and Threat Reporting. Her international consulting experience further expanded on how vast the lack of knowledge in security was globally and highlighted the critical need for diversity and inclusion in the technology/security market.

Alycia Farrell is the President of Grey Tarian. She is the current Government Affairs policy and budget specialist in Aerospace, Defense, and Cybersecurity industries, training for a technical certification in vulnerability assessments and offensive security.

Peter Liebert is the Founder of Liebert Security and is the Chief Information Security Officer for Cerner Government Services and Commander of Cyber Operations for the California State Guard. Throughout Peter's 20+ years of leadership, he has excelled in roles such as CISO for the State of California and was selected by his peers in 2019 as the Chief Security Officer of the year for SC Magazine. A security technology guru and information security policy wizard, he is practiced in implementing and operating industry-leading technologies (such as SecDevOps teams, Security Operations Centers, and advanced Artificial Intelligence-driven solutions) and is a recognized subject matter expert, cybersecurity speaker, and investor in the security community.

Jason Smith is Faculty, Coast Guard Chair at National War College. He is a combat-wounded veteran of the Army and has led soldiers during three combat deployments, to include Iraq and Afghanistan, as an AH-64A Attack Helicopter Pilot and Commander. Jason has experience working with national-level leaders in the Executive Branch and in the US Senate and as part of several foreign delegations in support of National Defense, including cyber security of critical infrastructures. Jason has a BS from Sam Houston State University, a Master of International Relations from St Mary's University, and a Master of Public Administration from Harvard University.

REFERENCES

1. "Competing in the Gray Zone: Countering Competition in the Space between War and Peace", *Csis.org*, 2020. [Online]. Available: https://www.csis.org/features/competing-gray-zone. [Accessed: 21- Jul- 2022].
2. "U.S. Department of Energy, U.S. Department of Homeland Security, and U.S. Department of Defense Announce Pathfinder Initiative to Protect U.S. Energy Critical Infrastructure", *Energy.gov*, 2020. [Online]. Available: https://www.energy.gov/articles/us-department-energy-us-department-homeland-security-and-us-department-defense-announce. [Accessed: 21- Jul- 2022].
3. M. Cukier, "Study: Hackers Attack Every 39 Seconds", *Eng.umd.edu*, 2007. [Online]. Available: https://eng.umd.edu/news/story/study-hackers-attack-every-39-seconds. [Accessed: 21- Jul- 2022].

17 Transportation

17.0 ABOUT THE TRANSPORTATION SECTOR

Jerry L. Davis
Founder, Gryphon X, LLC
Vice President, Chief Security Officer at Pacific Gas and Electric Company

Within the US critical infrastructure sectors, the Transportation System Sector can be thought of as a complex "system of systems" at work within the United States to support the mobility of goods, services, and people that are moved intern and external to, and throughout the country. The current system of systems has two primary components; a system of modes (airways to include space, seaways, highways, and railways) and a system of means (aircraft and spacecraft, maritime vessels, motorcars/freight vehicles, and trains).

In addition to maintaining the safety, reliability, and resiliency of the labyrinth of airways, seaways, highways, and railways, federal agencies and local municipalities responsible for the management of these pathways of mobility also have significant responsibility for instituting governance to ensure the safe, reliable and resilient function of the means by which mobility takes place.

Ensuring the safety, reliability, and resiliency of both the modes and means that make up the Transportations System are challenging objectives as our country is faced with the digitization of the entire Transportation System. Achieving safety, reliability, and resiliency of a digitized system is a daunting and challenging one for three underlying reasons.

1. Adequately securing any standalone digital system is difficult enough, but now the overseers are saddled with establishing a low friction, highly effective governance framework to secure the means of a digitized transportation system. This is compounded by the fact that each digitized means of transportation, largely defined by software, hardware, and network persistence, are designed and operated using a cohort of a different and diffused set of standards, protocols, and proprietary frameworks. The absence of cybersecurity consideration in the design and operation of these means is an unfortunate and forgone conclusion that can lead to a profound and deleterious effect on the systems' core attributes of safety, reliability, and resiliency.

2. The pace at which the means of digitized transportation are being developed and operated far outpace national governance. In the highly competitive world of transportation means development of the winning strategy is speed to market. Whether they are tried, and true legacy companies or newly formed agile startups, companies that are in competition for market share or market domination in their respective industries are pushing their solutions into the market at a pace that is well beyond the pace of our lumbering government's ability to define, develop, and implement effective governance to ensure safety, reliability, and resiliency objectives.

3. Nationally, our systems of modes are operating in an analog fashion, while the system of means is transitioning into one that is digitized. This has the potential for catastrophic economical and physical outcomes. Those states, cities, towns, and localities that are unable to support a digitized transportation system will certainly miss out on the access to derived economic benefits that are available and are to become "forgotten" and "lost in time."

DOI: 10.1201/9781003243021-17

Physically, the inability to support a digitized Transportation System but allowing volumi-
nous, high-speed, fully autonomous transportation means of transportation into an unsupported environment can have serious and unintended consequences on safety, reliability,
and resiliency of the entire Transportation System.

To this end, as a nation, we must carefully and thoughtfully imagine and embrace a safe, reliable,
and digitized Transportation System. We must develop a consistent framework of cybersecurity
standards and guidance concepts in a public-private partnership that lays the foundation for digitized modes and means of transportation. This is our opportunity to lead the world into and beyond
the Fourth Industrial Revolution, create new industries and take advantage of the available and
tremendous economic benefits.

17.0.1   ABOUT GRYPHON X, LLC

Gryphon X, or simply "GX," is a transformative cyber and risk management firm. GX focuses on
mitigating the inherent security risks that often accompany technology products or services within
any industry or domain. GX has provided risk mitigation services nationally and internationally for
public and private sector entities. GX consultants have quietly and discreetly performed risk mitigation engagements in aerospace/astronautics, not-for-profit, financial, waste and sanitary management, legal, high-net-worth family foundations, and high-tech industries.

17.1 FROM THE GROUND, THROUGH THE AIR, AND BEYOND OUT THERE: OVER THE HORIZON OPPORTUNITIES, RISKS, AND CHALLENGES IN THE TRANSPORTATION SYSTEM SECTOR

Jerry L. Davis
Founder, Gryphon X, LLC
Vice President, Chief Security Officer at Pacific Gas and Electric Company

17.1.1 INTRODUCTION

Generally, when one thinks of the word "transportation," pictures that might illuminate within the mind are images of colossal maritime cargo ships trimming from bow to stern and listing from port to starboard in a seemingly rudderless fashion in the vast and darkened emptiness of Neptune's seas. The senses can instantly reconstruct the distinct whistle, and adjoining vibration of a behemoth diesel-engine powered locomotive passing by; a majestic sight to behold, akin to witnessing a modern-day General Hannibal Barca riding his regally adorned elephants across the Alps on a mission to war. Perhaps others conjure up visions of airplane travel, passengers robotically lined up like ducks in a row, waiting to board, each evaluating the dimensions of every other person's carry-on luggage, making wagers in their own minds against the bags least likely to fit in the overhead storage bin.

The current day transportation ecosystem is transforming, literally. An entirely new digital global transportation ecosystem is emerging, driven by advances in artificial intelligence and machine learning (AI/ML), exotic semiconductor technology, robotics, sensing/autonomy technologies, and data analytics, to name but a handful. This digital transportation ecosystem will enhance commerce in ways that one would never have thought possible a mere decade ago. For those nations that can purposefully capitalize on the realities of this emerging ecosystem, they will become the co-recipients of the single greatest transfer of wealth that this century, and perhaps the next, has to offer.

The fourth iteration of the industrial revolution (Industry 4.0 or I4) is the core thesis and purveyor of this new transportation ecosystem. In his book *The Fourth Industrial Revolution*,[1] world-renowned professor, founder, and Executive Chairman of the World Economic Forum, Dr. Klaus Schwab, states:

> Digital Technologies that have computer hardware, software and networks at their core are not new, but in a break with the third industrial revolution, they are becoming more sophisticated and integrated and are, as a result, transforming societies and the global economy.

This emerging transportation ecosystem is as vast as the means and modes that are designed to enable it. However, there are three very distinct and ubiquitous means and modes that standout and are already beginning to set the stage for an economic transfer of wealth:

- Autonomous and e-enabled ground transportation
- Advanced Air Mobility (AAM) & Urban Air Mobility (UAM) services
- Commercial space tourism and space launch/transport services

These three means and modes are no longer spoken in terms of the "potential future," "cautious optimism," or "the art of the possible"; rather, they are in the present, having quickly surpassed "the art of the probable" and into the realm of "with great certainty," "disruptive," and "strategic necessity."

This new system will deliver unbridled and endless opportunities to those nations that have national strategies and plans in place to appropriate the needed skills and technologies and continuously incubate and champion innovation. Likewise, with such extravagant opportunities presented by I4 come significant challenges in the form of cyberthreats and ensuring the cyber resiliency of the modern-day digital transportation system architectures.

These means and modes share common functionality attributes: the consummation of sophisticated software, hardware, and persistent digital connectedness, attributes that are exposed and prone to manipulation by bad actors who have nothing more than malevolent and insidious intentions. We must take note that these bad actors exist, will attack with great certainty, will be highly disruptive, and, for the nation state, operate out of strategic necessity.

To this end, we must, as a sovereign nation, embrace the lead role in the new digital transportation ecosystem and make certain that we have a national strategy and plans in place to apprehend the needed skills and technologies and continuously incubate and champion innovation in support of institutionalizing a cyber resilient transportation architecture—from the ground, through the air and beyond out there.

17.1.2   A SLUGGISHLY TRANSPOSITIONING TRANSPORTATION SYSTEM

The majority of our nation's transportation foundational model operates in the analog realm, while the modes and means of transportation that the foundational model is designed to support have transitioned into a highly integrated digital model. Whether they be cars, airplanes, or space vehicles, they all share common features in that their operation are heavily reliant upon the integration of software and hardware and are connected to a digital grid and, by default, converge security, safety, and privacy into a single digital domain. These modes and means of transportation often consume the same digital spectrum of resources and services such as the Global Positioning System (GPS). Once reserved strictly for the global militaries for the precise position, navigation, and timing (PNT), GPS is now a commodity and abundant publicly available resource. Since 1990 nearly every new vehicle built, starting with the Japanese manufactured *Eunos Cosmo*, likely has GPS available as a standard feature or at least as an option. Coincidently, the year 1990 is the same year that the World Wide Web became a global commercial network and subsequently commoditized for public access in 1993.[2]

As with all innovation, the digitization of powered mobility has far outstripped the ability of the underlying transportation foundational model to keep pace. One of the complicit indicators is the lack of information and communication technology (ICT) complements (i.e., governance in the form of policies and standards) specific to cybersecurity which should serve as key drivers in the development of a cyber reliant transportation ecosystem. While there have been some decades-long fractured and stovepiped discussions expended in both the executive and legislative branches of the federal government, the United States still lacks a cohesive and unified approach codified in law; one that presumes a path forward for ensuring the cyber resiliency of critical infrastructure to include the transportation ecosystem that supports the increasingly digitization of our powered mobility systems. With respect to fractured and stovepiped focus on cybersecurity, the Congressional Research Service (CRS), in its opening statement within the March 1, 2017 summary report *In Focus*,[3] presents the following facts:

> The legislative framework for cybersecurity is complex, with more than 50 federal laws affecting various aspects of it. Nevertheless, since the 111th Congress, more than *300 bills* [emphasis added] have been introduced that would address a range of cybersecurity issues …

The lack of a unified approach perpetuates the cyber insecurities found in the design, development, and operation of a cyber reliant transportation ecosystem and places at risk the ability of the United States to consistently derive the economic benefits that newly digitized modes and means of powered mobility are anticipated to deliver. The transportation system within the US critical infrastructure sector must make it a strategic imperative to take part in and perhaps serve as a key stakeholder in seeking to unify cybersecurity and cyber resiliency as a whole-of-government approach. This whole-of-government approach will certainly preempt the disruption caused by cyber insecurity to the evolving digitized transportation ecosystem.

17.1.3 FROM THE GROUND: AUTONOMOUS AND E-ENABLED GROUND TRANSPORTATION

17.1.3.1 OPPORTUNITIES

If Schwab's definition of what constitutes I4 is sufficient, then the autonomous and e-enabled road transportation vehicle (e.g., an e-enabled car and/or multi-axel vehicles) is the widely adopted and physical manifestation of his definition. Clearly, the e-enabled road vehicle is the de facto example of sophisticated integration of hardware, software, and networks and is unapologetically pervasive on a global scale. Autonomous operation is an underpinning feature for e-cars. The underlying technologies such as AI/ML, computer vision, and dozens of exotic semiconductors that provide and manage safety countenances such as "sense and avoid," facilitate vehicle-to-vehicle (V2V), and transportation infrastructure communications (such as those found in "smart cities") are bonded together by nearly 200 *million* lines of software code. Today's modern e-enabled vehicle does, in fact, "run on code," as articulated in the 2009 IEEE Spectrum article,[4] and, as forecasted, has grown in complexity. The intricacy of these multi-tonnage mobile computer systems empowers a host of applications and opportunities in the age of digitization. Authors with the McKinsey Center for Future Mobility produced an article entitled *Rethinking Car Software and Electronics Architecture*[5] and highlighted the benefits of innovation in e-enabled vehicles. One such category of benefit is what McKinsey calls "diverse mobility," where users can use shared mobility and robo-taxis via an app, and another allows for the driver to have a completely customizable driver experience. The introduction of autonomous and e-enabled ground transportation represents all the markers of generating significant contributions to the enhancement of commerce and accumulation of wealth to those entities, big or small, who can ingest, extrapolate and make use of the underlying technologies in a manner that provide *economic nutritional value* to the majority of the consumer populous.

17.1.3.2 RISKS AND CHALLENGES

However, in the Government Accountability Office (GAO) December 2020 Report *Automated Technologies—DOT should Take Steps to Ensure its Workforce has Skills Needed to Oversee Safety*,[6] GAO auditors identified gaps in DOT's assessment and tracking of workforce skills related to cybersecurity of automated technologies. As the pervasive use of automated technologies such as e-enable ground transportation grows, so will the potential economic opportunities, and unfortunately, so will grow the appetite for hostile adversaries to disrupt, degrade, and confound these capabilities with the direct or indirect effect of dislocating and delaying economic advantages.

In the e-enabled car engineering discipline, safety is perhaps the core characteristic. There is little doubt that in light of the underlying digital foundations of e-enabled ground transportation that cybersecurity has a profound impact on safety. The International Standards Organization (ISO) is the globally adopted body for the creation of and maintenance of standards and, as such, publication *ISO 26262—1:2018 Road Vehicles—Functional Safety*,[7] which supersedes ISO 26262—1:2011 enhances functional safety with the addition of many critical elements to further pursue the safety of road vehicles. One such addition is the inclusion of references to cybersecurity. In their wisdom to bring to light the importance of cybersecurity to safety, ISO is currently developing a companion document to 26262, *ISO 21434 Road Vehicles—Cybersecurity Engineering*.[8] The impact that cyber-insecurity has on safety cannot be overstated. Likewise, the impact that the lack of critical cybersecurity engineering skills required to oversee safety in automated vehicles will potentially result in precipitously driving the e-enabled ground transportation vehicle into very unsafe and precarious situations.

This is not a narrative about the lack of cybersecurity edicts, laws, executive orders, standards, or guidance frameworks. There are plenty being considered in legislation and public/private partnerships such as Information Sharing and Analysis Centers (ISACs). Along with this, the National Institute of Standards and Technology (NIST) has done a remarkable job serving as the heavy lifters in the development and integration of nearly 200 Special Publications. These publications are recognized and adopted worldwide by every industry imaginable, providing turnkey and tailorable guidance to building cyber resilient systems through cybersecurity engineering practices and disciplines. This narrative does, however, contest that the United States lacks a unified and integrated set of coordinated and purposeful complements to ensure that transportation safety in e-enabled ground transportation is not impacted by gaps in security. Furthermore, the United States lacks sufficient skills in the cybersecurity engineering workforce who can expertly implement, maintain or oversee the integration of system security engineering into the e-enabled infrastructure. The lack of associated complements, combined with the lack of workforce skills, place at risk the potential economic advantages derived from e-enabled ground transportation by undermining the confidence in the security of the hardware, software, and persistent digital connectedness and implicating the compromise of safety, security, and privacy of the individual consumer.

17.1.4 THROUGH THE AIR: ADVANCED AIR MOBILITY AND URBAN AIR MOBILITY SERVICES

17.1.4.1 Opportunities

6:30 AM: Get up, clean up, get dressed, grab your percolating coffee and head out the door.

7:15 AM: Hop in the driverless, autonomous e-enabled, ground transportation vehicle waiting outside your home.

7:38 AM: Arrive at the Vertical Lift Air Mobility Park and hop into the autonomous electric-vertical takeoff and landing (e-VTOL) vehicle along with Drew, Joyce, and Parham, who have been waiting patiently for your arrival.

7:45 AM: The carbon fiber quadrotors cycle up to lifting power, you slowly ascend vertically and transition to horizontal flight into the National Airspace (NAS). Your flight path takes you promptly northbound above the densely traffic packed highway 101 freeway toward San Francisco International Airport. Inflight, you take notice of several "air taxis" some flying in the opposite direction at slightly different altitudes, others are flying perpendicular to your line of travel, seamlessly merging into their assigned flight paths. What you don't see is the V2V communications taking place, which allows for that seamless orchestration of autonomous air traffic management.

8:07 AM: The eVTOL vehicle slows, transitions from horizontal to vertical flight, and begins a slow and controlled hovering descent, landing on tarmac space 16. The rotors spin down completely, the cabin doors unlock, and the four of you hop out and walk past a group of passengers waiting to board the same eVTOL vehicle that you just disembarked. You then board the awaiting autonomous ground shuttle (which has been in constant communication with the eVTOL vehicle since 7:45 AM). You sit down, and the shuttle quietly but swiftly navigates the parking lot and heads to the main terminal.

8:15 AM: The autonomous shuttle pulls up to the terminal, everyone disembarks, and you are on your way.

This is happening. It may seem farfetched, but this is happening today. Led by NASA's Aeronautics Research Mission Directorate, with some of the implementation living under the auspices of the

NASA Aeronautics Institute (NARI)[9] and supported by a large international community of interest, Advanced Air Mobility (AAM) is here; it is growing, and it is bringing tremendous opportunities to nations around the world, including the United States. NASA describes the AAM vision as:

> NASA's vision for Advanced Air Mobility (AAM) Mission is to help emerging aviation markets to safely develop an air transportation system that moves people and cargo between places previously not served or underserved by aviation—local, regional, intraregional, urban—using revolutionary new aircraft that are only just now becoming possible. AAM includes NASA's work on Urban Air Mobility and will provide substantial benefit to U.S. industry and the public.[10]

Take in the scenario provided above. Imagine the time saved in transition from home to the airport in rush hour traffic. Now imagine this same infrastructure being used to transport cargo to remote or urban sites. Scale the eVTOL aircraft from passenger size to a size just big enough to carry a 15 kg package, and you have a small unmanned aerial system (sUAS) delivery system. AAM is going to significantly change the global economy. We have already witnessed the delivery of goods using sUASes. Major companies such as Amazon have been testing the use of sUASes for a number of years under their Amazon Prime Air[11] line of business, intent on delivering packages to their customers in 30 minutes from the time of ordering. The logistical science of moving a vast and mind-boggling number of people and things to places through the NAS safely is a complex science that must be integrated and choreographed across a number of industries. AAM and UAM have already begun to start the economic boost. Establishing the necessary ecosystem means creating new services and enhancing legacy services in a trickle down fashion. The AAM and UAM ecosystem, according to NARI, include components such as aircraft, airspace, community integration, and cross-cutting (initiatives).[12] This means that careers in aircraft manufacturing, airframe, propulsion, flight operations, integrated automation, and many, many others are being created and thus will contribute to the national economy through the broadening of goods and services and the development and employment of a skilled workforce. The contribution to the national economy can also be said of each of the three remaining components of the ecosystem. Purposeful investment in the AAM and UAM mode and means of transportation is a considerable investment in the nation's economy with the upside of a very positive return on investment. This return on investment is not completely and directly monetary. The AAM and UAM mode and means of transportation provide tangible returns in the form of innovation, the creation of new markets, sustainment, and reduction in emissions.

17.1.4.2 RISKS AND CHALLENGES

In 2016, the author of this chapter had the distinct pleasure of delivering one of two commencement addresses at Cal Poly Pomona's Cyber Corps graduating class. The other commencement address would be delivered by Mr. Roger Schell,[13] President of ÆSec[14] and the founding Deputy Director of what is now known as the National Computer Security Center (NCSC) under the National Security Agency (NSA). During an exchange of dialog over dinner the evening prior to the graduation ceremony, the author opined that the Internet was troublesome technology because of its security fragility and that it exposed systems to considerable risks. Mr. Schell responded immediately and very authoritatively with the following comment:

> The Internet was not designed to ensure security. Its purpose was communications resiliency. It was always assumed that the end node attached to the Internet was secure.

This was certainly a teachable moment, and the author positively acknowledged Mr. Schell's comment and continues to do so to this day.

The AAM and UAM transportation ecosystem is highly reliant on the same common transportation foundational ecosystem as e-enabled ground transportation vehicles: tight integration of sophisticated software and hardware that is persistently connected to a digital network. In order for the United States to take economic advantage of the capabilities and services that are offered through AAM and UAM, the end nodes must adopt security assurance and resiliency as core characteristics. The end nodes in this architecture not only include the vehicle themselves but the entire ecosystem. The ecosystem architecture includes the vehicle manufacturing supply chain, the Unmanned Aerial System Traffic Management (UTM) services, satellite communications systems, and radio communications systems. Furthermore, assurances must be made to guarantee protection against attacks such as GPS spoofing, malware-laced critical software, critical hardware tampering, and ensure cellular communications services such as 5G are designed in a highly resilient form factor. Cyber insecurity is the new and genuine antagonist to safety in the cyber-physical world and, more aptly put, airworthiness in the world of things that fly. It is incumbent upon those that have a role in the governance of the US transportation system to take notice that securing this incredibly complex system of systems is not trivial and demands a coordinated cybersecurity strategy, investments, and skilled workforce. Failure to adequately address the risk of cyber insecurity within the entire ecosystem can lead to extremely dire and punitive consequences of the severest kind.

17.1.5 AND BEYOND OUT THERE: SPACE TOURISM AND SPACE LAUNCH/TRANSPORT SERVICES

17.1.5.1 Opportunities

In fact, one of the things I'm working on now is the 100-year plan for the company. We're really focused on this trillion-dollar economy that is largely focused on improving life on Earth from space, not going off Earth and settling on other planets.

Chris Kemp, CEO and Co-Founder Astra Space, Inc.[15]

No matter where one goes in the world, no matter whom one is speaking to, there is a tremendous amount of organic romanticism that swells when the topic of rocketry and space commences. Perhaps this is because most are enamored with human ingenuity and our ability to do complex things and solve intractable problems. Perhaps it is also the wanderlust that many share beyond the gravitational forces that keep us pinned to Earth. Make no mistake about it, rocketry is hard, dangerous, and unequivocally risky, and more often times than not, failure is actually a calculated option. But with great risk come great rewards. The commercial space business is booming. Launching rockets into space by an entity other than a government was a foreign concept barely 15 years ago. Expensive and risky, the appetite to take on this venture was not palatable to investors or entrepreneurs alike, the barriers to entry were simply too high. With the recent rise in I4 driven technological advances and with the adoption and fostering of commercial entrepreneurship from agencies like NASA, commercial space tourism and space launch and transport services are here for the foreseeable future, and the United States is well-positioned to take advantage of this trillion-dollar plus industry.

In the Space Capital *Q4 2020 edition of the Space Investment Quarterly Report*,[16] it is noted that there has been $177.7B of cumulative investments in commercial space initiatives since 2011. These investments represent approximately 61% of NASA's aggregated budget during this same time period. This $177.7B in investments has been distributed across a staggering 1,343 companies in the commercial space race, and in Q4 of 2020 alone, some $5.7B was invested in 80 space-based commercial entities. The distribution of investments categories included PNT satellites, Earth Observing Remote Sensing, satellite communications, manufacturing and components, small, medium, and heavy launch services, and many more. This is indeed a thriving industry steeped in innovation and bringing new economic and sustainability opportunities not only to the United States but the entire world.

Another indication of growth within the space tourism and space launch services is the number of active (12) spaceport licenses granted by the Federal Aviation Administration (FAA), Office of Commercial Space Transportation. The mere fact that a commercial space transportation office exists is evidence that commercial space transportation is a high-growth and important industry. Perhaps the most noteworthy metric that correlates best to commercial space tourism and space launch services growth is the number of licensed launches granted by the FAA. According to the Office of Commercial Space Transportation website, some 387 licensed commercial launches have taken place between 1989 and present day,[17] with ten different commercial space launch and transport providers currently holding 23 active launch licenses.

The reality of one day "ordinary" everyday citizens being able to travel into space with regularity is here. While still in the embryonic stages with regard to regular flights to space, civilians are, in fact traveling to space. Space Exploration Technologies Corporation (Space X), Blue Origin, and Virgin Galactic all promise civilian crew launches and regular "space taxi" services in the near future.

Finally, there is increasing growth in space launch/transport services (transport such as cargo or payloads, non-human flights), demonstrated by newer rocket companies such as Rocket Lab and Astra. As access to space becomes cheaper and therefore more ubiquitous, companies that provide remote sensing or Earth-observing technology in the form of Smallsats, Nanosats, and CubeSats can get their technology onto a commercially available launch manifest in minutes and actually have that technology flown in days to weeks vice waiting years to generate enough capital to afford a flight, and years to get on payload manifest for a flight that may be years away. In a 2021 interview with SpaceNews, Astra CEO and co-founder Chris Kemp stated that his company has already sold 50 Low Earth Orbit (LEO) launches. This is significant because Astra only recently, in December 2020, had a successful launch of its space vehicle. As Kemp put it, *"There's so much demand and opportunities …."* Evidence shows that there are tremendous demands and opportunities to apprehend in what is arguably the most intriguing, economically advantages mode and means of transportation in the US transportation ecosystem.

17.1.5.2 RISKS AND CHALLENGES

With launch after successful launch, space pioneers such as NASA, Space X, Rocket Lab, and, recently, Astra can make space operations look trivial. However, space operations are a very risky and unforgiving proposition should something go wrong. The US military and cybersecurity professionals focused on the space community characterized space as a contested environment, or the fifth warfighting domain. The space system architecture is a complex system-of-systems, highly redundant architecture that encompassed six primary segments. In today's contested domain of space operations, the cyber resiliency of each segment is an essential design requirement. The segments representing the space system architecture are as follows:

- Spacecraft | design and engineering
- Launch | ascent to orbital insertion
- Space operations | in orbit
- Ground | including command, control, and mission operations
- Network | commodity terrestrial layers both physical and logical
- Consumer | user of space asset provided services

The individual segments that comprise a space system architecture are vulnerable to cyber-based threats. Such vulnerabilities are present throughout the space system lifecycle, from its conception to decommissioning, and if not addressed, can provide a vector to disrupt, degrade, and/or destroy a space system along any segments within the architecture. Disruption, degradation, or destruction of any segment of the space architecture, promulgated by intentional or unintentional occurrences can result in grave consequences and can turn the US space tourism and space launch/transport services industry back decades. There is little room for error in space, particularly where human-rated flight is concerned.

In the design of a space system architecture, cybersecurity system engineering remains a fringe requirement because of several factors. First, cyber threats are not well understood by traditional space system engineers/architects. Second, cyber vulnerabilities are not understood or articulated to the space system engineers/architects. Third, traditional cybersecurity professionals have limited, or no knowledge of complex space system engineering beyond commodity networking protocols used to connect ground stations. Space vehicles are portioned into subsystems (e.g. power, propulsion, radiation protection, thermo protection, etc.) where tradeoffs are made in order to adequately meet capability requirements. Because of the three aforementioned examples, cybersecurity is denied consideration as a necessary subsystem. The fundamental core of the space system architecture, especially those developed within the past decade, share the same I4 characteristics as the first two transportation sector modes and means discussed earlier in this chapter: sophisticated hardware, software, and persistent digital connectedness. Because of this, the overseers of the transportation ecosystem must aggressively seek to ensure that cybersecurity system engineering is designed into the core cyber components, seek to develop a skilled cyber security engineering workforce, and invest in the development of a cyber resilient digital transportation ecosystem.

17.1.5.3 RECOMMENDATIONS

There are several common themes and repetitive dialogs that emerged in the course of this chapter. Most recognizable are the technologies that define I4: the consummation of sophisticated hardware, software, and persistent digital connectedness; the lack of a unified set of governance complements to provide guide rails in the use of I4 technologies in digital, powered modes and means that are driving tremendous economic opportunities; the lack of a skilled cybersecurity system engineering workforce; shortsightedness in investments to transition the US analog transportation ecosystem into a digital ecosystem; and the pervasive threat and highly impactful consequences to safety, security and privacy that cyber insecurity can have on powered modes and means.

While there are many recommendations of consideration, presented here are but a few that can serve as a starting point with the objective of preserving and further gaining an economic advantage through the delivery of a cyber resilient transportation ecosystem.

1. Develop a unified and integrated national strategy for cyber resiliency for the transportation ecosystem. Use a whole-of-government approach, bringing together all stakeholders who have cognizant authority in the operation, health, and maintenance of the transportation system ecosystem.
2. Develop a cybersecurity system engineering caucus with membership from aviation, aerospace, and ground transportation agencies. While the maritime sector was not discussed in this chapter, it should have cognizant representation within the caucus. The purpose of the caucus will be to identify common cyber issues and develop resolutions relative to I4 technologies (e.g., supply chain issues in software, hardware, and downstream suppliers, and cyber impacts to safety, security, and privacy).
3. Seek to develop a transportation sector cybersecurity system engineering workforce. This workforce would serve as embedded practitioners within the transportation ecosystem and oversee the collaboration and implementation of cyber resilient processes and procedures into the system engineering processes.
4. Invest additional resources into the conversation of the transportation ecosystem from an analog system to a digital, cyber resilient system.
5. Develop a construct to ensure that access to digitally based, sophisticated transportation modes and means is equitably proportional across the nation.

17.1.6 CONCLUSION

The US transportation sector bears co-responsibility in shaping the country's economic opportunity and global sustainability by transitioning the underlying analog transportation ecosystem into one that fully adopts, embraces, and confidently supports new forms of digitally powered modes and means of mobility. Highly sophisticated integration of hardware, software, and persistent connectivity in mobility is changing lives and will continue to do so, but not without risk and consequences organic to any technology.

As our way of life becomes increasingly digitized, more that cyber insecurity becomes the antagonist to economic opportunity and global sustainability. Cyber insecurity undermines public confidence and will delay and decay the public's ability to embrace and adopt digitally powered mobility modes and means of transportation, and with that, the delay and decay of economic benefit will undoubtedly follow. Stakeholders within the US transportation sector stakeholders must address cybersecurity as a natural and required feature for ensuring the safety, security, and privacy of its citizenry, whether on the ground, in the air, or beyond out there.

17.1.6.1 ABOUT THE AUTHORS

A technophile since he was a young kid, Jerry L. Davis is the Founder of Gryphon X, LLC, a transformative cyber and risk management firm. Jerry focuses on "over-the-horizon" security strategies for reducing risk in emerging technology. Prior to forming Gryphon X, LLC, Jerry had a long and distinguished career as the top senior security executive for multiple agencies within the United States federal government to include NASA, the US Department of Veterans Affairs, and the US Department of Education. Jerry has also spent time as a counterintelligence officer with the Central Intelligence Agency (CIA) and as a United States Marine and was key in the identification, apprehension, and subsequent conviction of some of the most notorious spies in US history.

REFERENCES

1. K. Schwab, *The Fourth Industrial Revolution*. New York: Crown Business, 2017.
2. D. Grossman, "On This Day 25 Years Ago, the Web Became Public Domain", *Popular Mechanics*, 2018. [Online]. Available: https://www.popularmechanics.com/culture/web/a20104417/www-public-domain/#:~:text=Twenty% 2Dfive%20years%20ago%20today,altered%20the%20past%20quarter%2Dcentury. [Accessed: 21- Jul- 2022].
3. E. Fischer, "Cybersecurity Legislation in the 113th and 114th Congresses", *Congressional Research Service*, 2017. [Online]. Available: https://crsreports.congress.gov/product/pdf/IF/IF10610. [Accessed: 21- Jul- 2022].
4. R. Charette, "This Car Runs on Code", *IEEE Spectrum*, 2009. [Online]. Available: https://spectrum.ieee.org/transportation/systems/this-car-runs-on-code. [Accessed: 21- Jul- 2022].
5. O. Burkacky, J. Deichmann, G. Doll and C. Knochenhauer, "Rethinking car software and electronics architecture", *Mckinsey & Company*, 2018. [Online]. Available: https://www.mckinsey.com/industries/automotive-and-assembly/our-insights/rethinking-car-software-and-electronics-architecture. [Accessed: 21- Jul- 2022].
6. "Automated Technologies: DOT Should Take Steps to Ensure Its Workforce Has Skills Needed to Oversee Safety", *Gao.gov*, 2020. [Online]. Available: https://www.gao.gov/products/gao-21-197. [Accessed: 21- Jul- 2022].
7. "ISO 26262-1:2018 Road vehicles — Functional safety — Part 1: Vocabulary", *ISO*, 2018. [Online]. Available: https://www.iso.org/standard/68383.html. [Accessed: 21- Jul- 2022].
8. "ISO/SAE 21434:2021 Road vehicles — Cybersecurity engineering", *ISO*, 2021. [Online]. Available: https://www.iso.org/standard/70918.html. [Accessed: 21- Jul- 2022].
9. "NASA Aeronautics Research Institute", *Nari.arc.nasa.gov*, 2022. [Online]. Available: https://nari.arc.nasa.gov/. [Accessed: 21- Jul- 2022].
10. L. Gipson, "Advanced Air Mobility Mission Overview", *NASA*, 2021. [Online]. Available: https://www.nasa.gov/aam/overview/. [Accessed: 21- Jul- 2022].

11. D. Stuckenberg and S. Maddox, "Drones in the U.S. National Airspace System", *International Journal of Aviation Systems, Operations and Training*, vol. 1, no. 2, pp. 1–22, 2014. Available: 10.4018/ijasot. 2014070101.

12. "NASA Advanced Air Mobility Ecosystem Working Groups", *aam-portal*, 2022. [Online]. Available: https://nari.arc.nasa.gov/aam-portal/. [Accessed: 21- Jul- 2022].

13. "Roger R. Schell | Academic Influence", *Academicinfluence.com*, 2022. [Online]. Available: https://academicinfluence.com/people/roger-r-schell. [Accessed: 21- Jul- 2022].

14. "Aesec", *Aesec.com*, 2022. [Online]. Available: http://www.aesec.com/. [Accessed: 21- Jul- 2022].

15. J. Foust, "Astra's 100-year plan: Q&A with CEO Chris Kemp - SpaceNews", *SpaceNews*, 2021. [Online]. Available: https://spacenews.com/astras-100-year-plan-qa-with-ceo-chris-kemp/. [Accessed: 21- Jul- 2022].

16. "Space Investment Quarterly Reports | Space Capital", *Spacecapital.com*, 2021. [Online]. Available: https://www.spacecapital.com/quarterly#:~:text=With%2520another%2520%25245.7B%2520invested, %252425.6B%2520invested%2520in%25202020. [Accessed: 21- Jul- 2022].

17. "Spaceport License", 2022. [Online]. Available: https://www.faa.gov/space/licenses/spaceport_license/. [Accessed: 21- Jul- 2022].

18 Water and Wastewater Management

18.0 ABOUT THE WATER AND WASTEWATER SYSTEMS SECTOR

Dr. Bradford Sims
President, Capitol Technology University

The Water and Wastewater Systems Sector is one of the identified 16 critical infrastructures that need to be protected. Safe drinking water is vital to public health as it has been a factor throughout all known history. Several historical events had opposing forces contaminating the drinking water in order to prevail without a physical battle. What was true then is true today in modern society. The facilities of today that are constructed to treat and distribute safe drinking water to all cities are built with concrete, pipes, pumps, values, and control rooms to control all the processes electronically. The Cybersecurity and Infrastructure Security Agency website notes, "there are approximately 153,000 public drinking water systems and more than 16,000 publicly owned wastewater treatment systems in the United States. More than 80 percent of the US population receives their potable water from these drinking water systems, and about 75 percent of the US population has its sanitary sewerage treated by these wastewater systems."

Safe drinking water, also called potable water, is used in every imaginable way such as in cooking, showers, drinking fountains, flushing toilets, washing hands in a sink, etc. While there are thousands of miles of pipes distributing water that has been treated to be potable water and thousands of miles of pipes returning water to be treated in cities across the world, the facilities that collect and treat water are central to ensuring water is safe. In the United States, the Environmental Protection Agency provides testable water standards to ensure that the water being distributed is safe for everyone.

These facilities are commonly called wastewater treatment plants and have controlled access to the facilities, usually by fencing, as a physical attack is a possibility. Historically physical attacks are what was prepared for when facilities were constructed in the past. Now with all processes in a wastewater treatment plant being connected via the industrial Internet of things (IIOT), a foreign entity can attack the supervisory control and data acquisition (SCADA), the industrial control systems (ICSs), and especially the operational technology (OT) that operates all the devices. This includes turning on and off valves and pumps that control the water treatment process. While information technology directs the operational technology, a danger lies within what each is designed to due in its operation. Information technology provides instruction and collects data and will shut down to protect its data, while operational technology is designed to keep the mechanical process functioning as long as possible to make sure an important process keeps going even at a loss of its data. Therefore, if a cybersecurity attack can take control of the information technology, it can control the operational technology and cause catastrophic system damage. This could result in having a mechanical device failure and shutting down an entire facility for a long time.

The inability of a city to have a continuous flow of potable water for an extended period of time could see detrimental effects. It could shut down food production, stop hospitals from functioning, prevent firefighters from stopping fires, create sewage problems, and force the general population to seek out alternative water sources creating major health and economic challenges.

DOI: 10.1201/9781003243021-18

18.0.1 ABOUT THE AUTHOR

Dr. Bradford Sims is the current President of Capitol Technology University, where he added degrees in critical infrastructure to complement the university's already strong degrees in cyber-security. He worked around the United States in the project management of building industrial facilities before moving into higher education, where he founded several programs in construction management. His background includes computer information skills, and as he gained the knowledge of the systems operations of industrial facilities, he became aware and concerned about how the modernization of industrial control systems being connected to the internet could be a future concern for all facilities.

18.0.2 ABOUT CAPITOL TECHNOLOGY UNIVERSITY

Since its start in 1927, Capitol Technology University has remained true to its mission—preparing students for careers in a quickly changing world. With a tradition of academic excellence and practical learning, Capitol Tech has equipped its alumni with the knowledge and skills to evolve with the advanced sophistication of technology. While innovations spur new developments and industries, the foundations taught at Capitol Tech– thinking critically, actively, and creatively—remain. Capitol Tech is committed to providing students with a quality education and the relevant experience to excel in a rapidly changing world filled with new technology and global commerce both now and in the future.

18.1 FLORIDA WATER TREATMENT ATTACK AND THE IMPLICATIONS FOR CRITICAL INFRASTRUCTURE AND CYBERSECURITY—AN EXEGESIS

Dr. Ian McAndrew
Dean of Doctoral Programs, Capitol Technology University

18.1.1 INTRODUCTION

Americans and any visitors visiting the State of Florida seldom think that drinking water, having ice in their drinks, or cooking with water will cause any health issues. For those that prefer drinking bottled mineral water as they like the taste in preference to tap water is a lifestyle choice; and not one to keep you safe, unlike many places where water is to be avoided unless in a sealed bottle. They would be outside the risk of these attacks if we adopt this approach to safety we have lost before we start. In this essay, the implications of what could have happened indirectly and directly from the attack on the Florida Water treatment plant are presented and discussed. Its focus is not repeating that is already covered but the wider issues both relating to and resulting from this occurrence.

A brief historical timeline is needed in this example to show how not to ignore potential risks but how ignoring trends and possibilities has just made the risk unacceptable to most people wherever situated in the world. Cybersecurity can protect, to a level, the support infrastructure must be there to support those protecting. This essay covers the basic facts that have been reported extensively, its focus is on the deeper and wider complications and concerns for those charged with protecting critical infrastructures.

Hindsight and the reasons why it could happen easily were identified and a dedicated worker recognized the problem or it could have been serious. Cybersecurity issues, the cost, and effectiveness need to be included as utilities cannot charge as they like and cover costs. Likewise, adding security patches are no real long-term solution. What is more of an unrecognized consequence is the possibility of triggering ideas for others to copy, this was not the first and unlikely to be the last. The interrelationship of these issues is presented and options of how it can be prevented formulated to address this and wider issues of critical infrastructure both in the United States and abroad.

A summer's night in England, just north of London, and several unknown men in a small truck drove to the local reservoir, which at the time in the 1960s was unguarded. They parked and removed a large chemical drum from the back and discharged the contents into the water. As fast as they had appeared, they were finished and drove away. The parallels, in this case, are there and it was a concern, it was also not a problem in many peoples' views. The reason is why was many in England had been admiring the success of the American's adding fluoride to the water supply to reduce tooth decay and improve the quality of life. The men, in this case, were not nefarious, they were academics and scientists trying to force the issue. Subsequently, the addition of fluoride to their water supplies for the benefit of the people, albeit their actions were illegal even if the best intentions were meant. If nowadays, they would have physical barriers preventing access of the reservoir and CCTV to identify the predators. That is not to say that the mechanical security is beyond the approach to the most dedicated attacker.

It is clear where the Florida Water Treatment problem started, and it has been extensively reported that the Microsoft Windows system was version 7, passwords were all the same, and not difficult to hack with rudimentary equipment. What followed as more information shared was that this may be correct, it was a software that was obsolete and should not have been on the system where the detailed hacker focused. Even the most modestly aware computer user will know this operating system is dated and released when cybersecurity issues were not even addressed. Furthermore, if a system is not used it needs removing fully, not easy for basic level IT, Jaafar et al. (2019). These are facts and recognized by most, and all reading this story was probably horrified at this laconic

TABLE 18.1.1
Top 20 German Passwords Used

123456	123456789	12345678	Hallo123
Hallo	12345	Passwort	Lol123
1234	123	Qwerty	Ficken
1234567	Arscholoch	1234567890	1q2w3e4r
Killer	Sommer	Schalke04	Dennis

Source: www.safetydectivies.com.

approach to a critical infrastructure. Yet ask yourself, how many of us have unique passwords for every system, shopping account, communication device? The simple errors can start with decisions and procedures, as when an employee leaves, especially if a disgruntled employee, and removing access if fully managed is an added risk.

As users, too many of us have become lazy and complacent with passwords now and a search of the top passwords used in America and 123456 is used by more than 2 million and 123456789 account for approximately 4 million (www.nordpass.com). It is not just in America, a survey in Germany showed a similar problem. The results captured in Table 18.1.1 suggest the same approach to passwords, a global problem? In Russia, it has been qwerty since studies started. The average smartphone user typically have 30 passwords at a minimum stored and some many more; and fingerprint identification makes people less likely to remember (Chanda, 2016).

In an organization with multiusers unique identification is not difficult for each employee to set up, but here it seems that was a demand too far for their IT department. Human nature tends to lead to lapses and omissions, a specialized subject of Human Factors was developed for the Aviation Industry, and maybe a subset of this discipline is needed in Cybersecurity (Habibu & Sam, 2018). In the past decade, Cybersecurity Psychology has started to be recognized as a discipline in its own right, and likely this will influence more and more.

Firewall walls are needed for systems to be at a safer level, it does not mean safe but safer, all need to know it does not stop internal threats and only removes the basic risks that are most common. Have organizations planned for the threat of a security guard on a late shift or cleaners been assessed if they are going to access a system and load, even accidentally, malware or any other system problem? This may read as if going back to the Cold War spies, but this time it is not for global domination, it is money and that drives people more in many ways. Threats from everywhere exist when computers are linked. It is ironic that if you study to be an aircraft maintainer, the exam questions have to be stored on a computer with no internet access and a separate locked room. If this would be utilized in more situations, imagine the success it would have stopping threats.

18.1.2 WATER TREATMENT IMPLICATIONS FOR THE FLORIDA BREACH

In the Florida Water Treatment, the attacker increased the level of sodium hydroxide by 100 times normal level. This unique chemical is added to water as it raises the pH level and makes the water less corrosive to pipes and faucets plus it reduces the amount of lead, copper, and toxic metals that can be dissolved into water. Its common name is caustic soda, and can be very harmful to the skin and eyes, if swallowed, the effects can be fatal. It is not known if the attacker knew this or was just trying to change any levels of additions. If the operator had not been as observant, then the deaths, long-term injuries, and short-term skin rashes would be the focus point. It was a near-miss of epic proportions. An operating system that allows significant changes in settings without an authority agreement also must be questioned. Many of our accounts we use in everyday life have double verifications or approval, clearly were not in the system and need adding urgently.

18.1.3 CURRENT METHOD/INVESTIGATIVE APPROACH

A review of contaminations to water supplies will stretch back in history to the beginning of records. During Operation Barbarossa, the Soviet Army poisoned all the possible sources for the advancing Army. This tactic was to load the supply lines and slow the advancement of the German army. In the summer of 2020, there were two cyber-attacks in Israel on water plants, where they tried to increase the Chlorine levels, another fatal health risk. The prescient was already established, and this advance warning was not, but should have been, noted, and the company in Florida complete a risk assessment. It asks the question of what other water treatment plants in America and the world plans to limit future attacks. There is a history of snowballing with high-profile events. It could be argued that the worst response is to share these events to avoid copycat attacks. Likewise, to shame executives to prepare for attacks might be a better way to reduce them in the future.

18.1.4 CURRENT STANDARDS

Water treatment plants in America are under Federal and regional standards for the quality of the water, procedures, and documentations. The safe water drinking Act by Congress in 1974 and updated in 1986 and 1996 addressed the quality of water and effluent (coc.gov). What they are not able to do is ensure cyber-attacks are impossible and when these Acts were verified cyber-attacks were not even on a level of interest. The US Department of Defence, DoD, is implementing a Cyber Maturity Model Certification, CMMC, for all contractors that work for the DoD. Their philosophy is that cyber-attacks are easier at vendors and suppliers than the DoD directly. There are levels of risk depending on what work undertaken. It does ensure, via training and audits, these companies are prepared for attacks with known risks evaluated and planned to be accommodated. This is no small task as the defense of the DoD is critical and is that of all critical infrastructures. If the defense of the nation is to be protected in all aspects at appropriate levels, then water treatment must be too. Changes that require investment without the threat of legal action tend not to happen. Legislation is never to be used unnecessarily, in this case, it shows it cannot be left to those who expect profits.

18.1.5 CURRENT BARRIERS

As within the DoD, there is a shortage of cyber experts, this might result from the lack of STEM students wanting to study at university. The supply is limited before STEM graduates can start to specialize; there is little to suggest the future is going to see a drastic change. Almost two-thirds of companies are reporting current shortages, of those that report they are satisfied, it would be interesting to know if this water treatment facility in Florida would have described themselves this way? What is clear and support is that there will be a *500,000 shortage* soon in the United States to address these issues and that cannot be plugged by overseas recruitment and this was the expectation before the pandemic.

18.1.6 COSTS TO PROTECT

The average price of water per household in the United States is somewhere between *$80 and $100 per month*; assuming average consumption usage. If needing to upgrade any system for cyber protection needs to stop all but the highest levels of risk, add 10% to the cost on average; that would be approximately $13 billion extra per year. Compound this with electricity and other critical infrastructures, and the cost per household will become a major issue and burden for many. Yet the undesired cost and lack of skills to enable protection will only grow and the risks and incidents will likely increase. We maybe at the start of cyber-attacks that spread from classic attacks to personal ones as IoT is becoming used more and more (Lykou et al., 2018). Prevention is always better than a cure, and this example personifies more than many, deaths were prevented this time, next time maybe not (Tolubko et al., 2018).

18.1.7 EDUCATION

Customers are unlikely to pay for something they do not understand or comprehend. A lack of awareness globally about the risks is a problem for consumers. As discussed earlier, the neglect of robust passwords is a seminal problem that has not to be reduced regardless of the advice from banks and governments to be careful. Without educating customers about the risks from an early stage and reinforcing then this argument would not be won and resentment. Of course, legal threats shareholders will consider seriously.

Additionally, incentives to encourage more to be cyber experts cannot hurt and certainly assist organizations attempting to stop attacks from being successful. In a world where more and more things are dependent the technology, it is critical that it is used to solve problems, not generate new ones.

18.1.8 CONCLUSION

It can be argued that this attack was a surprise and also not. First, poisoning water supplies has been used since classic times up to nowadays. Second, this is not the first water treatment cyber-attack, it is just the first publicized in America, and given that many critical infrastructures are attacked daily, it was only a matter of time for this event. Anyone following current news events now, and it's clear an epoch of cyber-attacks being regular occurrences by nations, individuals, and criminals. What can be highlighted is that many are where companies and industries have not taken the basic level of protection to protect systems. The balance now is to ensure an economically acceptable level of protection without making products and services significantly expensive. Defining what a critical infrastructure is now more significant than ever. No longer can this protection be left to chance, and it must be a legal directive of those that lead, as with safety laws. Until the law dictates, these incidents are likely to increase, and one day a disaster will happen; however, it is important to support the industry achieve the skill sets needed both for the short term and longer term.

18.1.8.1 ABOUT THE AUTHOR

Dr. Ian McAndrew is an internationally recognized leader in research and expert on the low-speed flight, Dr. McAndrew has five degrees: a PhD, two master's degrees and two bachelor's degrees. He is a Fellow of the Royal Aeronautical Society. Dr. McAndrew chairs several international conferences and journals and is invited to give keynote speeches all over the world. He started his career in the automotive industry as an engine designer and has worked at several universities across the globe. Dr. McAndrew is the Dean of doctoral programs at Capitol Technology University. An external examiner on the worldwide stage (United Kingdom, United States, Germany, Italy, Jordan, Japan, Australia, Greece, and Kenya), his experience includes over 127 successful Doctorate successes.

REFERENCES

Chanda, K. (2016). Password security: An analysis of password strengths and vulnerabilities. International Journal of Computer Network and Information Security, 8(7), 23–30. https://doi.org/10.5815/ijcnis.2016.07.04

Habibu, T., & Sam, A. E. (2018). Assessment of vulnerabilities of the biometric template protection mechanism. International Journal of Advanced Technology and Engineering Exploration, 5(45), 243–254.

Jaafar, G. A., Abdullah, S. M., & Ismail, S. (2019). Review of recent detection methods for HTTP DDoS attack. Journal of Computer Networks and Communications, 2019, 1–10. https://doi.org/10.1155/2019/1283472

Lykou, G., Anagnostopoulou, A., & Gritzalis, D. (2018). Smart Airport Cybersecurity: Threat Mitigation and Cyber Resilience Controls. Proceedings of the 2018 IEEE Global IoT Summit (GIoTS), Spain, 4–7.

Tolubko, V., Vyshnivskyi, V., Mukhin, V., Haidur, H., Dovzhenko, N., Ilin, O., & Vasylenko, V. (2018). Method for determination of cyber threats based on machine learning for real-time information system. International Journal of Intelligent Systems and Applications, 10(8), 11–18. http://franklin.captechu.edu:2123/10.5815/ijisa.2018.08.02

18.2 ADHERING TO 12-STAGE PROCESS FOR ACHIEVING CYBER SECURED WATER AND SEWAGE OPERATIONS

Daniel Ehrenreich
Consultant and Lecturer, SCCE

18.2.1 INTRODUCTION

During the past decade, cyber security experts worldwide started seeing a growing number of severe cyber-attacks aimed to harm industrial facilities, manufacturing processes, utility operations, and water facilities. These physical operations are supervised by computer and communication-based control systems called operation technology (OT), also known as industrial control systems (ICS). Water- and sewage-related ICS/OT are required to cover wide geographical area installations and utilize wireless communications. In most cases, they use Supervisory Control and Data Acquisition (SCADA) systems which are like the ICS-OT but have a different system architecture.

While for protecting IT organizations, we use the term "Confidentiality-Integrity-Availability (CIA)," for protecting the ICS/OT, we rather use the term SRP for "Safety-Reliability-Productivity (SRP)." Achieving the SRP goals, industry experts must combine multiple capabilities in the field of ICS-OT processes, cyber-secured data communication, IT networks' technologies, and physical security. Cyber security experts know well that physical/perimeter security is a critical and mandatory precondition to cyber security and cyber security is a critical and mandatory precondition for achieving operating safety.

Furthermore, cyber security experts know well that there is no single factor (often we say "no silver bullet") that may absolutely achieve cyber security, operation, and safety goals. According to the traditionally used PPT (People-Policies-Technologies) Triad, adherence to all PPT factors is mandatory. It is critical to state here that water and sewage organizations must also be prepared for incident response (IR).

To achieve the SRP goals set by regulators worldwide, ICS-OT and SCADA experts must follow cyber security guidelines as outlined in the ISA-IEC 62443 or the NIST 800-82 [1]. Furthermore, the International Safety Standard IEC 61508 is specifically referring to the safety instrumented systems (SIS), and the AWWA guidelines are specifically referring to protecting water and sewage systems.

This essay is aimed to outline the practical guidelines for the deployment of cyber defense for water and sewage operations and listing of best practices to assure their operation safety and reliability.

18.2.2 UNDERSTANDING THE WATER AND SEWAGE RISKS

Water and sewage system are considered critical infrastructures worldwide, as they are directly affecting the well-being of the population across the country, in cities, villages, buildings, hospitals, campuses, etc. Supply of water at lower-than-normal pressure cause wasting of water and inconvenience. Higher than normal water pressure or pressure fluctuation might create a "hammer effect" or pressure shockwaves. These shockwaves propagating through the piping system might rupture the pipes and cause a lengthy supply outage. Furthermore, important mentioning that manipulation of the setting might confuse the operator and lead to incorrect action.

Malfunction of sewage lift stations might cause severe spillage and environment contamination. Such incidents might lead to the instant evacuation of people from homes, office buildings, and schools and disrupt their normal life.

18.2.2.1 Poorly Secured System Architectures

The ICS-OT computer and communications-based architecture for controlling the water and sewage operations are spread over a broad geographical area and require consistent data exchange between the control center and remote sites where pumping stations, water reservoirs, water wells, sewage treatment plants, and sewage lift stations are installed. The communication media in these physical installations is usually wireless, and due to the use of legacy type equipment, the ICS-OT data channels cannot be protected by encryption. Upgrading of water system is a critical problem, as water utilities are usually working on very low profitability as dictated by authorities in a country. Unaccounted for water (UFW) in many countries is not a concern, and this is another reason for water infrastructure remaining not maintained properly.

Consequently, the connection of maintenance devices and service computers (highly important action during the COVID-19 period) cannot be authenticated. Such "self-created" vulnerability might allow unauthorized access to the control system, manipulating sensors, and unauthorized intervention for the purpose of interfering with the control process and for creating confusion in the control room [2].

18.2.2.2 ADHERENCE TO THE PPT TRIAD

Both IT and ICS-OT systems must be secured by adherence to the PPT Triad because it is the firm umbrella for all cyber security actions and initiatives. The "P" on top of the Triad stands for People, and they must be trained related to cyber risks and defense solutions. Consequently, organizations must enforce the 2nd "P" for policies related to the use of passwords, remote access for service, change authorization, reporting on incidents, etc.

Finally, an important saying related to the PPT Triad that all organizations must have a long-term technology "T" related plans for upgrades, retrofits, new installations, adding of cyber defense technologies, etc. The management must be aware of existing risks to the operation and assure that their ICS-OT is properly and accurately documented as related to products, hardware and software, data protocols, wiring, maintenance processes, etc. [3–5].

18.2.2.3 CORRECTLY DESIGNED ICS ARCHITECTURE

Water and sewage systems are controlled by SCADA architecture, considered as a subset of ICS-OT. They shall utilize encrypted wireless communication and perform authentication of connecting devices, service computers, and people. The remote access process must be always supervised by authorized and experienced engineers.

The endpoint devices in these systems often utilize remote terminal units (RTU), programmable logic controllers (PLC), and advanced sensors known as intelligent electronic devices (IED). These devices must be properly configured, capable of detecting changes in the operation process, and generate alerts to the control center if an unusual/anomaly condition is detected or in case of unauthorized physical access.

Furthermore, those control devices which handle critical processes must be capable of turning to safe operation (called "fail-safe") in case the communication with the control center or any operation failure [2, 6].

18.2.2.4 EFFECTIVE CYBER DEFENSE

SCADA systems are built to control remote sites spread over a wide geographical area. The control devices at the remote sites (RTUs, PLCs, etc.) must be protected with a strong password. They are reporting to the control center according to the polling cycle or report by exception, which requires two-way data exchange. The unmanned remote sites where field machinery is installed must be physically protected for preventing unauthorized access. Cyber defense turned into a major problem during the COVID-19 period, as technical experts could not travel to remote sites and utilities had no choice but allowing the remote connection. Attacker detecting this situation and connected to the system by spoofed identity [7, 8–10].

The physical access to field installed sensors (often called "Purdue level 0") must be constantly monitored, and any manipulation such as connection, disconnection, rewiring of field devices, sensors, and control devices must be instantly detected and reported to the control center. Interruption of the communication must be automatically detected and reported as an alarm to the control room. To prevent unauthorized access, the secured connection of service computers to the network must be authenticated prior data exchange. According to what we learned for the cyberattack on the water system in the city of Oldsmar (FL) occurred on February 5, 2021, this incident happened due to allowing the negligent remote connection [6–8, 10].

18.2.2.5 COMPLIANCE WITH THE SRP TRIAD

ICS-OT operation must also adhere to the Safety, Reliability and Productivity (SRP) Triad. The "S" for safety is located on the top of the Triad, and it means that the operating machinery controlled by PLCs, RTUs, and IEDs must be protected from getting damaged due to control malfunction or an unintentional or mistaken action be an authorized person. In case of malfunction, the design must prevent hurting people, and therefore the field-side machinery must have built-in measures and mechanisms to assure safe shut-down ("fail-safe") [3, 6].

The system must operate reliably (R) and accurately, and the entire operation must be designed for consistent and high productivity (P) and business operation continuity. In case of a failure or unexpected outage, the system architecture must be ready for activating secondary/redundant production and control means [1–3].

18.2.2.6 ICS-OT CROSS TEAMS' COLLABORATIONS

Nowadays, modern control technologies use a similar computer and communications-related components and network solutions such as are used in IT systems. Among these are TCP-type communication protocols, computer networks, switches, routers, intrusion detection systems (IDS), and more. In most organizations that operate control systems, such knowledge does not exist among the industrial experts, and often we see situations that technology upgrades are delayed or incorrectly performed.

Collaboration among ICS-OT and IT teams may lead to the deployment of effective and cost-effective cyber defense solutions, integration to the Security Information and Event Management (SIEM) system, connection to the Security Operation Center (SOC) and SOAR (Security Orchestration, Automation and Response) systems [2, 3].

18.2.2.7 CYBER SECURITY AND SAFETY ASSESSMENTS

Operation Safety is highly critical for water and sewage systems, as a malfunction in these operations might lead to environmental contamination and risk lives of people. As already mentioned, physical/perimeter security is a strong precondition to cyber security and cyber security is a mandatory precondition to operating safety.

Confirming compliance with these requirements must be done through periodic assessments including asset inventory inspection, periodic updates according to Common Vulnerabilities and Exposures (CVE) publications for products and software, detection of unauthorized connections to the public Internet, detection of backdoor-related vulnerabilities created by an authorized person, an inspection of the SIS where applicable and more [1, 11].

18.2.2.8 APPLICABLE CYBER DEFENSE STANDARDS

The American Water and Wastewater Association (AWWA) issued cybersecurity guidance in alignment with the NIST Cybersecurity Framework [6]. Collectively these resources provide a sector-specific approach for implementing cybersecurity controls and recommendations, which were particularly created for the water and sewage sectors. Important saying that these documents are regulations and frameworks rather than standards.

On the other hand, the ISA-IEC 62443 documents created mainly by the ISA99 Working Group is an international standard applicable for a broad range of industry segments, including water and sewage sectors. It deals with network segregation among zones, matching the predefined Security Level (SL), Foundational Requirements (FR), risk assessment, commitment among vendors of products, integrators, and the system owner [1, 3, 11].

18.2.2.9 WATER AND SEWAGE INCIDENTS IN PAST DECADE

Until now, there were not too many cyber security incidents that were specifically targeted for harming water and sewage infrastructures. However, none can take this information as a reliable prediction for the future, and therefore organization must be prepared for "the unexpected." Among the known incidents are: the Maroochy Shire event in Australia (1998) cyber-attack against a water utility in Springfield, IL (2011), Key largo Wastewater plant (2012), Undisclosed utility (2016) in the United States (known as "Kemuri water company"), Onslow Water and Sewage utility (2018), Fort Collins Loveland utility (2019), which destroyed a pump, and the recent attack against Israeli water utility (2020) aimed to poison the potable water. Fortunately, this incident was detected and blocked [7, 9, 10, 12].

We are aware of many other incidents related to Ransomware-type attacking and Denial of Service (DoS/DDoS), which are affecting the IT operations of industrial facilities. Obviously, some of these attacks might harm the water utility operation, but they are considered as direct risks related to cyber physical operations [4, 5].

18.2.2.10 DEPLOYMENT OF IN-HOUSE CYBER RANGE

Organization operating large-scale control facilities may have a need to deploy an "ICS-OT replica" system which is built with identical components and software as their real system, however, it is not wired to the real water control network. That replica receives actual operation data from the real system (through a unidirectional diode), and its Human Machine Interface (HMI) computer looks identical to the real HMI.

This system is also called as "cyber range" as it may serve as a training facility for new operators, for inspection of the expected impact caused by recently discovered vulnerability (published as a CVE), serve for inspecting new application programs prior to being installed into the real system, an inspection of antivirus and operating system upgrades, testing of new components prior the installation of any new program, etc. [2, 3].

18.2.2.11 RISK MITIGATION THROUGH BCP, DRP AND IR

ICS experts responsible for managing critical infrastructure know that effective cyber defense for water and sewage systems is mandatory for achieving the SRP goals of the organization. Therefore, their cyber defense methods must be selected according to the potential impact (I) factor and the factor expressing the probability of occurrence (P). The overall risk factor (R), as defined by the ISA 62443 standard, is calculated according to the formula $R = P*I$ [2, 3, 5].

Furthermore, to achieve their business goals, organizations are obliged conducting Business Continuity Preparedness (BCP) process aimed to prevent lengthy operation outage, conduct Disaster Recovery Planning (DRP) aimed to returning quickly to normal operation, and Incident Response (IR) process for being ready to properly handle unexpected incidents. The IR team must include representatives from all management sections including legal, HR, etc. Consequently, for assurance of consistent water and sewage service operations, management shall take proactive steps and invest in technologies, training, and development of enforceable policies [2, 3, 5].

18.2.3 SUMMARY AND CONCLUSIONS

Water and sewage utilities operating worldwide are critical infrastructures, as they directly affect the well-being and the health of citizens living in their countries. With the rapid growth of sophisticated cyber capabilities by attackers who are financed and directed by enemy countries and hostile organizations, the challenges of protecting SCADA, ICS, and OT systems (using legacy hardware, software, and communication), have become a complex task.

Consequently, the technical and cyber security management in organizations must deploy a modern and incrementally improving approach combining a range of technical solutions and accurately adapted policies. Furthermore, the training and drills for each team must be defined according to their roles and the specific technologies they operate. Employees must be trained related cyber security risks and defense solutions. This defense measure has the highest Return on Investment (RoI) among all other ICS cyber defense measures, and it is worth the investment [1, 2, 5].

Financial investment and allocation of resources for technologies and training of the personnel shall match the level of the calculated risk (R). Deployment of consistently improving methods and enforcement of effective policies will support your efforts targeted to keeping your cyber defense posture at least one big step ahead of hostile attackers.

18.2.3.1 ABOUT THE AUTHOR

Daniel Ehrenreich, BSc. is a consultant and lecturer acting at Secure Communications and Control Experts, periodically teaches in colleges and present at industry conferences topics on integration of cyber defense with ICS; Daniel has over 30 years of engineering experience with ICS and SCADA for Electricity, water, gas, and power plants as part of his activities at Tadiran Electronics, Motorola Solutions, Siemens and Waterfall Security. He was selected as the Chairman for the 5th ICS Cybersec 2021 virtual international conference.

REFERENCES

1. Incident Action Checklist EPA, https://www.epa.gov/sites/production/files/2017-11/documents/171013-incidentactionchecklist-cybersecurity_form_508c.pdf
2. Cyber Defense for Regional Water & Sewage Utilities, Daniel Ehrenreich, https://cyberstartupobservatory.com/cyber-defense-for-regional-water-sewage-utilities/
3. Selection among ICS Cyber Defense Methods, Daniel Ehrenreich, https://cyberstartupobservatory.com/selection-among-ics-cyber-defense-methods/
4. Evolution of ICS Attacks and the Prospects for Future Disruptive Events, https://www.dragos.com/wp-content/uploads/Evolution-of-ICS-Attacks-and-the-Prospects-for-Future-Disruptive-Events-Joseph-Slowik-1.pdf
5. Defending ICS and SCADA Systems from Cyber Attacks, https://iiot-world.com/ics-security/cybersecurity/defending-ics-and-scada-systems-from-cyber-attacks/
6. AWWA Publication Water Loss Control Terms Defined, https://www.awwa.org/Portals/0/AWWA/ETS/Resources/WLCwater-loss-control-terms-defined-awwa-updated.pdf?ver=2014-12-30-084848-790#:~:text=%22unaccounted%20for%22%20water%20volumes.&text=The%20term%20%22Non%2Drevenue%22%20Water%20is%20defined%20to%20reflect,firefighting%2C%20flushing%2C%20etc
7. A Review of Cybersecurity Incidents in the Water Sector, https://www.scribd.com/document/431343714/A-Review-of-Cybersecurity-Incidents-in-the-Water-Sector
8. Top 20 Cyber-Attacks on ICS, Andrew Ginter, https://www.fireeye.com/content/dam/fireeye-www/products/pdfs/wp-top-20-cyberattacks.pdf
9. Review of Cyber Incidents in the Water Sector, Journal of Environmental Engineering 146 (2020) https://arxiv.org/pdf/2001.11144.pdf
10. New York Times Publication "Dangerous Stuff": Hackers Tried to Poison Water Supply of Florida Town, https://www.nytimes.com/2021/02/08/us/oldsmar-florida-water-supply-hack.html
11. Water Sector Cyber Security Brief of States, https://www.epa.gov/sites/production/files/2018-06/documents/cybersecurity_guide_for_states_final_0.pdf
12. Security Week 04-2020, Eduard Kovacs, https://www.securityweek.com/hackers-knew-how-target-plcs-israel-water-facility-attacks-sources

Closing

CONCLUSION

Joyce Hunter
Executive Director, ICIT

As the nation's leading cybersecurity think tank, we believe cybersecurity should be objective, and nonpartisan, providing research, advisory, and education to legislative, commercial, and public-sector cybersecurity stakeholders.

Despite the financial damage caused by cybercrime, many organizations remain underprepared. The mission of the Institute for Critical Infrastructure Technology (ICIT) is to "improve the resiliency of our Nation's 16 critical infrastructure sectors, defend our democratic institutions, and empower generations of cybersecurity leaders" by way of webinars, executive roundtables, Fall and Spring Briefings, monthly Legislative updates and Fellows publications.

Cybersecurity Ventures estimated cybercrime cost the world in excess of $6 trillion in 2021, up from $3 trillion in 2015. The report further adds that this represents the greatest transfer of economic wealth in history; cybercrime risks the incentives for innovation and investment and will be more profitable than the global trade of all major illegal drugs combined.

The essays that you have read are the experiential thoughts and ideas on the problem of cybersecurity and its dynamic implementation. Acquiring the subject matter experts for each of the 17 critical infrastructures (we added election security) was no small task, and in some cases, we had to do the in-depth research and writing ourselves. As we did the research and peer reviewed the essays, we learned a lot about the strengths, weaknesses, opportunities, and threats in each sector, which sometimes made us think and ask more questions. For example, some of these fundamental or critical infrastructures include integrated systems/features like the transportation system, electricity, and other energy requirements, as well as the health and agriculture systems. It also included the financial framework, telecommunication, and the supply of water. So, while these may seem like standalone entities, they must be considered as part of the whole, or we end up with gaping holes in our desire for a unified approach.

As the coronavirus pandemic continues to disrupt global health, economic, political, and social systems, there's another unseen threat rising in the digital space: the risk of cyberattacks that prey on our increased reliance on digital tools and the uncertainty of the crisis.

I believe one of the lingering issues is the workforce, as was severely tested during the height of the COVID-19 pandemic. Promoting the ability of such workers to continue to work during periods of community restriction, access management, social distancing, or closure orders/directives is crucial to community resilience and continuity of essential functions. The term "workers" as used in this guidance is intended to apply to both employees and contractors performing the described functions. The Internet has almost instantly become the channel for effective human interaction and the primary way we work, contact, and support one another.

Modernization, information sharing, and cyber-hygiene are shared problems across all sectors and the Cybersecurity Information Sharing Act of 2015 is supposed to be the designated hub for the sharing of cyber threat indicators and defensive measures between the federal government and private sector. This law grants liability protection, privacy protections, and other protections to organizations that share cyber threat indicators and defensive measures in accordance with the Act's requirements. Is it being used? You tell me.

DOI: 10.1201/9781003243021-19

Meanwhile, threats are continuing to evolve

- Many critical infrastructures still depend on legacy systems or are decades behind modernization
- Low-level attacks are becoming easier, more successful, and more impactful – ex. ransomware and malware-as-a-service (MaaS)
- Advanced persistent threats (APTs) are constantly evolving and are engaged in asymmetric conflict with critical infrastructure systems

Walt Disney said, "The way to get started is to quit talking and begin doing." I refer to myself as a "strategic doer," which means not only having your eye on where the puck is going but putting a road map in place and asking the important questions:

What are we trying to accomplish, *How* are we going to accomplish it, *Who* are the resources to get it done, *Where* are we getting the resources (money, people, etc.), *When* are we getting started, and *where* do we start (which department/organization). The most difficult part of any strategy is to put down the pen and DO. Here are some Do's for consideration and implementation. Please feel free to add your own, replacing the words we will consider, we are thinking about and the (dreaded) committee will take it under advisement. Action words only:

- All organizations should implement their business continuity and pandemic plans or put plans in place if they do not exist. Delaying implementation is not advised and puts at risk the viability of the business and the health and safety of the workers.
- Whenever possible, local governments should consider adopting specific state guidance on essential workers to reduce potential complications of workers crossing jurisdictional boundaries. When this is not possible, local jurisdictions should consider aligning access and movement control policies with neighboring jurisdictions to reduce the burden of cross-jurisdictional movement of essential critical infrastructure workers.
- Workers will be needed to preempt and respond to cyber incidents involving critical infrastructure, including medical facilities; state, local, tribal, and territorial (SLTT) governments and federal facilities; energy and utilities; banks and financial institutions; securities and other exchanges; other entities that support the functioning of capital markets, public works, critical manufacturing, food, and agricultural production; transportation; and other critical infrastructure categories and personnel, in addition to all cyber defense workers who can't perform their duties remotely.

The sectors are governed by the executive branch and the administration can lead in efforts to better deter emerging threats. Government agencies such as the US NSA or the UK's GCHQ have shared widely their cybersecurity expertise through forums such as the National Institute of Standards and Technology (NIST). But the connection of sensitive to untrusted systems typically referred to as "cross domain solutions" – remains a poorly trodden frontier where knowledge is not widely shared, even among government services. Indeed, until recently, in most countries, much of the information was classified and export controlled. But with increasing political realization that protecting often commercially held critical infrastructure and services is today just as important as protecting military and diplomatic secrets, many governments are, in principle, now open to sharing their knowledge.

Few commercial cybersecurity professionals, however, know that this body of knowledge exists. Since it sits at the heart of how spies protect themselves from other spies, perhaps this is not surprising. Perhaps it is equally unsurprising that when the topic is communicated, incomprehension is perpetuated by language that can be prohibitive. Just as commercial security services are unfamiliar with government experience, so government services are frequently unfamiliar with the realities of today's enterprise environment. Such differing starting points between the two communities means that communication is a barrier even when it is attempted.

Ten years ago, awareness of cyber risk was low: public-private partnership for threat intelligence sharing has dramatically changed that and brought cyber risk to the top of corporate and government agendas. With a new public-private partnership focused on the strong cybersecurity measures that can effectively mitigate the risk of cyberattacks, over the coming decade, we can start to drive that risk back down.

The 44th Administration created the Center for Strategic and International Studies (CSIS) Commission on Cybersecurity to advise the 45th Administration. The CSIS Strategic Technologies Program provided pragmatic, data-driven analysis and recommendations on cybersecurity, privacy and surveillance, technology and innovation, and internet governance, written for a global audience. Their projects explore the challenges of digital technologies and how these technologies are reshaping the global economy and society. They bring together technologists, policymakers, civil society, and business leaders from around the world to identify global policy solutions to the social, economic, and security challenges created by disruptive technologies. We hope that they leverage this "Guide," its contributors and the ICIT Fellows to create a new CSIS to provide central direction and leadership from the White House to create and implement a comprehensive and coordinated approach since cybersecurity cuts across the mission of many different agencies and corporate entities.

ABOUT THE AUTHOR

Joyce Hunter is the Executive Director of the ICIT. Previously, she served as both the Interim CIO and Deputy CIO of the US Department of Agriculture and held other senior leadership roles within the federal government, Lotus Development Corp, Lawson Software, and Computer Sciences Corporation (CSC). She's managed multi-billion dollar IT budgets and established or led several data governance and PMO initiatives. She understands how to communicate with and across diverse communities and how to forge relationships that enable those stakeholders to succeed. She regularly uses these skills in both her TEDx talks and publications.

Joyce has a BA from Villanova University and an MBA in Marketing from the University of Pennsylvania, Wharton School of Business. She holds certificates in Emotional Intelligence, Design Thinking, Technology Business Management (TBM), and Scaled Agile Framework (SAFe). She sits on multiple industry boards and is active in several philanthropies focused on advancing STEM and Data Science education for underserved and underrepresented youth.

AFTERWORD: SOME THINGS CHANGE, SOME THINGS STAY THE SAME

Suzette Kent
Former US Federal Chief Information Officer

The technology tools and approaches of "the day" will change, but the enormous risks posed to our nation's critical infrastructure are ever-present. Over the last decade, we have seen a digital move to the prominent mode of commerce, business management, operations, manufacturing, and even areas of human connection. Over the course of 2020 and early 2021, the pandemic has driven digital interactions to be not only a dominant mode of business interactions but the prevalent mode of human communications as well. We are at a remarkable turning point in our nation and world where societies are questioning the existing model of work, the importance of connectivity,[1] and the boundaries of individual privacy. Like other significant turning points in history, we are at a precipice of technological, socioeconomic, and cultural transition driven by the extraordinary evolution of scientific and technical capabilities.

When I started the role of Federal CIO, I was somewhat surprised to learn that the formal directives for information security (FISMA), agency responsibilities for information security, and the role of the CIO had only been formalized in 2002 under the E-government Act.[1] That Act was the national recognition of the importance of government-wide enterprise architecture, system interoperability, information sharing, and effective information security and privacy controls across the federal government. Having spent my 30-year career developing and deploying transformational technology in the private sector (online banking, image capability, advanced workflow tools, digital services, cloud-based technologies), I had a deep history of working with CIOs to achieve the mission of a company while protecting the assets of the company and data of its customers. It struck me then, as it does now – *We have to move faster.*

Moving faster requires experiential information for decision-making. Moving faster requires the public and private sectors to collaborate, share information, and partner to defeat adversaries. *Securing the Nation's Critical Infrastructure: A Guide for the 2021–2025 Administration* captures that experiential learning across sectors points out opportunities for collaboration and shares clear directives about information sharing.

Regardless of industry or area, technology is constantly changing and accelerating at an incredible pace. The challenges to operate any entity, government agency, or private sector business safely and securely while constantly improving and updating products and capabilities require expert thinking on balancing risk and innovation. I remember reading an article that shaped my own thinking about the impact of the increasing pace of technological change. The article was written by the founder and then executive chairman of the World Economic Forum, Klaus Schwab. The article contained this statement:

> There are three reasons why today's transformations represent not merely a prolongation of the Third Industrial Revolution but rather the arrival of a Fourth and distinct one: velocity, scope, and systems impact. The speed of current breakthroughs has no historical precedent. When compared with previous industrial revolutions, the Fourth is evolving at an exponential rather than a linear pace. Moreover, it is disrupting almost every industry in every country. And the breadth and depth of these changes herald the transformation of entire systems of production, management, and governance.[2]

This statement also influenced my own way of delivering large-scale, transformational change in that it crystallized the point that the incredible speed and complexity of change required more sophisticated, comprehensive approaches to delivering results. I use the terms "comprehensive" and "sophisticated" to imply that that successful technical change cannot be delivered in an isolated silo.

The business processes, people impact, governance requirements, and advanced perspectives on risk management had to evolve alongside technology capabilities in order to achieve secure, sustainable outcomes.

As businesses and governments expanded the interconnectivity of enterprise systems and the use of data, the risk profile subtly began to expand. Higher achievements in enterprise connectivity and data-driven processes likewise exponentially increased the risk profile of unauthorized and inappropriate access, misuse of data, and nefarious intent. As data collection devices proliferate and dependence on digital tools expands, a vulnerability can appear anywhere, making the threat surface akin to a fictional shapeshifter.

There is a wealth of information in this publication, but from the big picture, there are two significant values to the reader. This accelerates the reader's pace of learning, and the various points of view presented extend appreciation for the complexity of the operating environments. Through capturing perspectives from the many angles of each critical infrastructure sector, one gains a working snapshot of tactics and challenges. The value of the writers' views on emerging and potential future state issues will also support a reader's formation of a more comprehensive point of view on the risk environment. In reading this publication, you appreciate the macro demands of the cybersecurity world in an environment of continuous technological and operational change. The need for modernization is constant, as is the need for diligence in addressing the threats of the moment and the emerging threats. As leaders make strategic and day-to-day decisions about priorities and funding for cyber defense, there are many factors that can influence the results of a course of action. For example, although there has been widespread adoption of the importance of sharing threat intelligence data and concepts like zero trust architecture, the pathways and tools available to turn concepts into operational protocols are widely varied. In one situation, I was discussing the strategic plan for zero trust implementation with a specific agency, and the conversation was focused on "how." There was not a question about strategic direction, but there was much discussion and consideration about the sequence of activities, dependencies between activities, and the combination of actions that best addressed visible risks. This publication also includes reflections on decision criteria that are valuable to those who are responsible for today's decision-making.

When I was a newcomer to government, I experienced the intense demands of absorbing the details of the many sector-specific technical and operational environments, then applying those learnings and observations to the assessment of risk against the current-state threat environment. As a leader charged with responsibilities of prioritization and resource allocation, the more facts and informed perspectives that I could compile, the better the outcome achieved.

By consolidating this expanse of information in a single volume, *Securing the Nation's Critical Infrastructure: A Guide for the 2021–2025 Administration,* ICIT has created an important tool supporting the success of executives, leaders, and influencers in government leadership.

This is not just a "technical" publication. The essays and comments relay the critical interlock of human behavior, policy, regulation, and technical capabilities. In some areas, like the Food and Agriculture chapter, the relationships are more nuanced. Whereas, in heavily regulated industries, such as Transportation, the demands for alignment of policy and technology are more pronounced and urgent. Those new to or re-entering government spaces can augment their own base of knowledge with the perspectives from these many experts.

Although the essays are specific to topical areas, there are overarching themes that cross all sectors. To achieve targeted citizen services, multiple contributors – federal, state, and private sector – must be integrated technically and aligned operationally to safeguard the fidelity of the end-to-end process. As our nation and world become more connected and automated, the responsible management of data and identity and access credentials creates more complex considerations for leaders and new challenges for securing our critical infrastructure.

There are important details to understand in each critical infrastructure sector, and there are common best practices that apply to all sectors. Many thanks to ICIT for their vision and work in the construction of this collection to balance both the sector details and the common security themes. To the readers, it is hoped that these insights support your individual contributions to securing our nation's critical infrastructure.

I'll close by reiterating one of Glen Gerstell's statements in the opening, *"we have in hand solutions to managing the chronic condition of cyber insecurity"…* but I'll add to his statement my own reminder that we must move with urgency and an obsession to keep cybersecurity at the forefront of the technology innovation journey.

ABOUT THE AUTHOR

Suzette Kent is a global business transformation executive and, most recently, served as the Federal Chief Information Officer for the United States. Appointed by President Donald Trump in January 2018, Kent served until July 2020. Kent's career has included leadership roles ranging from partner at Accenture and EY to president of consulting at Carreker Corporation (FiServ), to managing director at JP Morgan. She currently leads her own advisory business continuing strategic transformation work with clients around the world, across industries, and in the public and private sectors. Throughout her career, her focus has always centered on technology modernization, cybersecurity, digital enablement, and ways that technology can be leveraged to solve business challenges. Suzette is a strategic advisor to multiple organizations, is on the board of Directors of Hancock Whitney Bank, a National Board member of the LSU Foundation, and works with many technology company Advisory Boards. She is a frequent public speaker at Industry Forums, a publisher of thought leadership holds patents in banking processes.

REFERENCES

1. *E-Government Act of 2002, including* The Federal Information Security Management Act of 2002 as Title III of the E-Government Act of 2002. https://www.congress.gov/bill/107th-congress/house-bill/2458
2. *The Fourth Industrial Revolution: What it means, How to respond. Foreign Affairs* December 12, 2015, Schwab, Klaus.

Index

TECHNOLOGIES